The SPARC Architecture Manual

Version 9

SPARC International, Inc.

Menlo Park, California

David L. Weaver / Tom Germond

Editors

SAV09R1429309

PTR Prentice Hall, Englewood Cliffs, New Jersey 07632

Published by PTR Prentice Hall
Prentice-Hall, Inc.
A Paramount Communications Company
Englewood Cliffs, New Jersey 07632

The publisher offers discounts on this book when ordered in bulk quantities. For more information, contact:

Corporate Sales Department
PTR Prentice Hall
113 Sylvan Avenue
Englewood Cliffs, NJ 07632

Phone: (201) 592-2863
Fax: (201) 592-2249

Printed in the United States of America

10   9   8   7   6   5

ISBN   0-13-099227-5

PRENTICE-HALL INTERNATIONAL (UK) LIMITED, *London*
PRENTICE-HALL OF AUSTRALIA PTY. LIMITED, *Sydney*
PRENTICE-HALL CANADA INC., *Toronto*
PRENTICE-HALL HISPANOAMERICANA, S.A., *Mexico*
PRENTICE-HALL OF INDIA PRIVATE LIMITED, *New Delhi*
PRENTICE-HALL OF JAPAN, INC., *Tokyo*
SIMON & SCHUSTER ASIA PTE. LTD., *Singapore*
EDITORA PRENTICE-HALL DO BRASIL, LTDA., *Rio de Janeiro*

Contents

Introduction

Welcome to SPARC-V9, the most significant change to the SPARC architecture since it was announced in 1987. SPARC-V9 extends the addresses of SPARC to 64 bits and adds a number of new instructions and other enhancements to the architecture.[1]

SPARC-V9, like its predecessor SPARC-V8, is a microprocessor specification created by the SPARC Architecture Committee of SPARC International. SPARC-V9 is not a specific chip; it is an architectural specification that can be implemented as a microprocessor by anyone securing a license from SPARC International.

SPARC International is a consortium of computer makers, with membership open to any company in the world. Executive member companies each designate one voting member to participate on the SPARC Architecture Committee. Over the past several years, the architecture committee has been hard at work designing the next generation of the SPARC architecture.

Typically, microprocessors are designed and implemented in secret by a single company. Then the company spends succeeding years defending its proprietary rights in court against its competitors. With SPARC, it is our intention to make it easy for anyone to design and implement to this architectural specification. Several SPARC-V9 implementations are already underway, and we expect many more companies to design systems around this microprocessor standard in the coming years.

0.1 SPARC

SPARC stands for a **S**calable **P**rocessor **ARC**hitecture. SPARC has been implemented in processors used in a range of computers from laptops to supercomputers. SPARC International member companies have implemented over a dozen different compatible microprocessors since SPARC was first announced—more than any other microprocessor family with this level of binary compatibility. As a result, SPARC today boasts over 8000 compatible software application programs. SPARC-V9 maintains upwards binary compatibility for application software, which is a very important feature.

Throughout the past six years, the SPARC architecture has served our needs well. But at the same time, VLSI technology, compiler techniques and users' needs have changed. The time is right to upgrade SPARC for the coming decade.

---

1. For a complete list of changes between SPARC-V8 and SPARC-V9, see Appendix K.

0.2 Processor Needs for the 90s and Beyond

The design of Reduced Instruction Set Processors (RISC) began in earnest in the early 1980s. Early RISC processors typically were characterized by a load-store architecture, single instruction-per-cycle execution, and 32-bit addressing. The instruction set architecture of these early RISC chips was well matched to the level of computer optimization available in the early 1980s, and provided a minimal interface for the UNIX™ operating system.

The computer industry has grown significantly in the last decade. Computer users need more for the 1990s than these early RISCs provided; they demand more powerful systems today, and yet they continue to want their systems to have good performance growth and compatibility into the future.The applications of the future—highly interactive and distributed across multiple platforms—will require larger address spaces and more sophisticated operating system interfaces. Tomorrow's architectures must provide better support for multiprocessors, lightweight threads, and object oriented programming. Modern computer systems must also perform more reliably than in the past.

It is interesting to observe the evolution of RISC architectures. Without sufficient instruction encoding, some microprocessors have been unable to provide for either larger address spaces or new instruction functionality. Others have provided 64-bit addressing, but still have not changed much from the RISCs of the 1980s. Fortunately, SPARC's designers had sufficient foresight to allow for all of the changes we felt were needed to keep SPARC a viable architecture for the long term.

0.3 SPARC-V9: A Robust RISC for the Next Century

SPARC-V9 is a robust RISC architecture that will remain competitive well into the next century. The SPARC-V9 architecture delivers on this promise by enhancing SPARC-V8 to provide explicit support for:

— 64-bit virtual addresses and 64-bit integer data

— Improved system performance

— Advanced optimizing compilers

— Superscalar implementations

— Advanced operating systems

— Fault tolerance

— Extremely fast trap handling and context switching

— Big- and little-endian byte orders

0.3.1 64-bit Data and Addresses

SPARC-V9 directly supports 64-bit virtual addresses and integer data sizes up to 64 bits. All SPARC-V8 integer registers have been extended from 32 to 64 bits. There are also several new instructions that explicitly manipulate 64-bit values. For example, 64-bit integer values can be loaded and stored directly with the LDX and STX instructions.

Despite these changes, 64-bit SPARC-V9 microprocessors will be able to execute programs compiled for 32-bit SPARC-V8 processors. The principles of two's complement arithmetic made upward compatibility straightforward to accomplish. Arithmetic operations, for example, specified arithmetic on registers, independent of the length of the register. The low order 32-bits of arithmetic operations will continue to generate the same values they did on SPARC-V8 processors. Since SPARC-V8 programs paid attention to only the low order 32-bits, these programs will execute compatibly. Compatibility for SPARC-V9 was accomplished by making sure that all previously existing instructions continued to generate exactly the same result in the low order 32-bits of registers. In some cases this meant adding new instructions to operate on 64-bit values. For example, shift instructions now have an additional 64-bit form.

In order to take advantage of SPARC-V9's extended addressing and advanced capabilities, SPARC-V8 programs must be recompiled. SPARC-V9 compilers will take full advantage of the new features of the architecture, extending the addressing range and providing access to all of the added functionality.

0.3.2 Improved System Performance

Performance is one of the biggest concerns for both computer users and manufacturers. We've changed some basic things in the architecture to allow SPARC-V9 systems to achieve higher performance. The new architecture contains 16 additional double-precision floating-point registers, bringing the total to 32. These additional registers reduce memory traffic, allowing programs to run faster. The new floating-point registers are also addressable as eight quad-precision registers. SPARC-V9's support for a 128-bit quad floating-point format is unique for microprocessors.

SPARC-V9 supports four floating-point condition code registers, where SPARC-V8 supported only one. SPARC-V9 processors can provide more parallelism for a Superscalar machine by launching several instructions at a time. With only one condition code register, instructions would have a serial dependence waiting for the single condition code register to be updated. The new floating-point condition code registers allow SPARC-V9 processors to initiate up to four floating-point compares simultaneously.

We've also extended the instruction set to increase performance by adding:

— 64-bit integer multiply and divide instructions.

— Load and store floating-point quadword instructions.

— Software settable branch prediction, which gives the hardware a greater probability of keeping the processor pipeline full.

— Branches on register value, which eliminate the need to execute a compare instruction. This provides the appearance of multiple integer condition codes, eliminating a potential bottleneck and creating similar possibilities for parallelism in integer calculations that we obtained from multiple floating-point condition codes.

— Conditional move instructions, which allow many branches to be eliminated.

0.3.3 Advanced Optimizing Compilers

We expect to see many new optimizing compilers in the coming decade, and we have included features in SPARC-V9 that these compilers will be able to use to provide higher performance. SPARC-V9 software can explicitly prefetch data and instructions, thus reducing the memory latency, so a program need not wait as long for its code or data. If compilers generate code to prefetch code and data far enough in advance, the data can be available as soon as the program needs to use it, reducing cache miss penalties and pipeline stalls.

SPARC-V9 has support for loading data not aligned on "natural" boundaries. Because of the way the FORTRAN language is specified, compilers often cannot determine whether double-precision floating-point data is aligned on doubleword boundaries in memory. In many RISC architectures, FORTRAN compilers generate two single-precision loads instead of one double-precision load. This can be a severe performance bottleneck. SPARC-V9 allows the compiler to always use the most efficient load and store instructions. On those rare occasions when the data is not aligned, the underlying architecture provides for a fast trap to return the requested data, without the encumbrances of providing unaligned accesses directly in the memory system hardware. This net effect is higher performance on many FORTRAN programs.

SPARC-V9 also supports non-faulting loads, which allow compilers to move load instructions ahead of conditional control structures that guard their use. The semantics of non-faulting loads are the same as for other loads, except when a nonrecoverable fault such as an address-out-of-range error occurs. These faults are ignored, and hardware and system software cooperate to make the load appear to complete normally, returning a zero result. This optimization is particularly useful when optimizing for superscalar processors. Consider this C program fragment:

```
if (p != NULL) x  = *p + y;
```

With non-faulting loads, the load of *p can be moved up by the compiler to before the check for p != NULL, allowing overlapped execution. A normal load on many processors would cause the program to be aborted if this optimization was performed and p was NULL. The effect is equivalent to this transformation:

```
temp_register  = *p;

if ( p != NULL ) x  = temp_register + y;
```

Imagine a superscalar processor that could execute four instructions per cycle, but only one of which could be a load or store. In a loop of eight instructions containing two loads, it might turn out that without this transformation it would not be possible to schedule either of the loads in the first group of four instructions. In this case a third or possibly fourth clock cycle might be necessary for each loop iteration instead of the minimal two cycles. Improving opportunities for better instruction scheduling could have made a factor of two difference in performance for this example. Good instruction scheduling is critical.

Alias detection is a particularly difficult problem for compilers. If a compiler cannot tell whether two pointers might point to the same value in memory, then it is not at liberty to move loads up past previous store instructions. This can create a difficult instruction scheduling bottleneck. SPARC-V9 contains specific instructions to enable the hardware to detect pointer aliases, and offers the compiler a simple solution to this difficult problem. Two pointers can be compared and the results of this comparison stored in an integer register. The FMOVRZ instruction, for example, will conditionally move a floating-point register based on the result of this prior test. This instruction can be used to correct aliasing problems and allow load instructions to be moved up past stores. As with the previous example, this can make a significant difference in overall program performance.

Finally, we've added a TICK register, which is incremented once per machine cycle. This register can be read by a user program to make simple and accurate measurements of program performance.

0.3.4 Advanced Superscalar Processors

SPARC-V9 includes support for advanced Superscalar processor designs. CPU designers are learning to execute more instructions per cycle every year with new pipelines. Two to three instructions at a time is becoming commonplace. We eventually expect to be able to execute eight to sixteen instructions at a time with the SPARC architecture. To accomplish this, we've made enhancements to provide better support for Superscalar execution.

Many of these changes were driven by the experience gained from implementing Texas Instruments' SuperSPARC and Ross Technologies' HyperSPARC, both Superscalar chips. SPARC's simple-to-decode, fixed-length instructions, and separate integer and floating-point units lend themselves to Superscalar technology.

In addition, SPARC-V9 provides more floating-point registers, support for non-faulting loads, multiple condition codes, branch prediction, and branches on integer register contents. All of these features allow for more parallelism within the processor. For the memory system, we've added a sophisticated memory barrier instruction, which allows system programmers to specify the minimum synchronization needed to ensure correct operation.

0.3.5 Advanced Operating Systems

The operating system interface has been completely redesigned in SPARC-V9 to better support operating systems of the 1990s. There are new privileged registers and a new structure to those registers, which makes it much simpler to access important control information in the machine. Remember, the change in the operating system interface has no effect on application software; user-level programs do not see these changes, and thus, are binary compatible without recompilation.

Several changes were made to support the new microkernel style of operating system design. Nested trap levels allow more modular structuring of code, and are more efficient as well. SPARC-V9 provides improved support for lightweight threads and faster context switching than was possible in previous SPARC architectures. We've accomplished this by making register windows more flexible than they were in earlier SPARC processors, allowing the kernel to provide a separate register bank to each running process. Thus, the processor can perform a context switch with essentially no overhead. The new register window implementation also provides better support for object-oriented operating systems by speeding up interprocess communication across different domains. There is a mechanism to provide efficient server access to client address spaces using user address space identifiers. The definition of a nucleus address space allows the operating system to exist in a different address space than that of the user program.

Earlier SPARC implementations supported multiprocessors; now we've added support for very large-scale multiprocessors, including a memory barrier instruction and a new memory model we call relaxed memory order (RMO). These features allow SPARC-V9 CPUs to schedule memory operations to achieve high performance, while still doing the synchronization and locking operations needed for shared-memory multiprocessing.

Finally we've added architectural support that helps the operating system provide "clean" register windows to its processes. A clean window is guaranteed to contain zeroes initially, and only data or addresses generated by the process during its lifetime. This makes it easier to implement a secure operating system, which must provide absolute isolation between its processes.

0.3.6 Fault Tolerance

Most existing microprocessor architectures do not provide explicit support for reliability and fault-tolerance. You might build a reliable and fault-tolerant machine without explicit support, but providing it saves a lot of work, and the machine will cost less in the long run.

We've incorporated a number of features in SPARC-V9 to address these shortcomings. First, we've added a compare-and-swap instruction. This instruction has well-known fault-tolerant features and is also an efficient way to do multiprocessor synchronization.

We've also added support for multiple levels of nested traps, which allow systems to recover gracefully from various kinds of faults, and to contain more efficient trap handlers. Nested traps are described in the next section.

Finally, we've added a special new processor state called RED_state, short for **R**eset, **E**rror and **D**ebug state. It fully defines the expected behavior when the system is faced with catastrophic errors, and during reset processing when it is returning to service. This level of robustness is required to build fault-tolerant systems.

0.3.7 Fast Traps and Context Switching

We have also worked hard to provide very fast traps and context switching in SPARC-V9. We have re-architected the trap entry mechanism to transfer control into the trap handlers very quickly. We've also added eight new registers called "alternate globals," so the trap handler has a fresh register set to use immediately upon entry; the software need not store registers before it can begin to do its work. This allows very fast instruction emulation and very short interrupt response times.

We have also added support for multiple levels of nested traps. It is very useful for the machine to allow a trap handler to generate a trap. SPARC-V8 trap handlers were not allowed to cause another trap. With support for nested traps, we have seen some trap handlers reduced from one hundred instructions to less than twenty. Obviously, this creates a big performance improvement, but it also allows a much simpler operating system design.

We've also found a way to reduce the number of registers saved and restored between process executions, which provides faster context switching. The architecture provides separate dirty bits for the original (lower) and the new (upper) floating-point registers. If a program has not modified any register in one of the sets, there is no need to save that set during a context switch.

0.3.8 Big- and Little-Endian Byte Orders

Finally, we have provided support for data created on little-endian processors such as the 80x86 family. The architecture allows both user and supervisor code to explicitly access data in little-endian byte order. It is also possible to change the default byte order to little-endian in user mode only, in supervisor mode only, or in both. This allows SPARC-V9 to support mixed byte order systems.

0.4 Summary

As you can see, SPARC-V9 is a significant advance over its predecessors. We have provided 64-bit data and addressing, support for fault tolerance, fast context switching, support for advanced compiler optimizations, efficient design for Superscalar processors, and a clean structure for modern operating systems. And we've done it all with 100% upwards binary compatibility for application programs. We believe that this is a significant achievement.

In the future, we envision superior SPARC-V9 implementations providing high performance, stellar reliability, and excellent cost efficiency—just what computer users are asking for. SPARC has been the RISC leader for the last five years. With the changes we have made in SPARC-V9, we expect it to remain the RISC leader well into the next century.

Speaking for the Committee members, we sincerely hope that you profit from our work.

— David R. Ditzel
   Chairman, SPARC Architecture Committee

Editors' Notes

Acknowledgments

The members of SPARC International's Architecture Committee devoted a great deal of time over a period of three years designing the SPARC-V9 architecture. As of Summer 1993, the committee membership was: Dennis Allison, Hisashige Ando, Jack Benkual, Joel Boney (vice-chair), David Ditzel (chair), Hisakazu Edamatsu, Kees Mage, Steve Krueger, Craig Nelson, Chris Thomson, David Weaver, and Winfried Wilcke.

Joel Boney wrote the original "V9 Delta Documents" that supplied much of the new material for this specification.

Others who have made significant contributions to SPARC-V9 include Greg Blanck, Jeff Broughton (former vice-chair), David Chase, Steve Chessin, Bob Cmelik, David Dill, Kourosh Gharachorloo, David Hough, Bill Joy, Ed Kelly, Steve Kleiman, Jaspal Kohli, Shing Kong, Paul Loewenstein, Guillermo "Matute" Maturana, Mike McCammon, Bob Montoye, Chuck Narad, Andreas Nowatzyk, Seungjoon Park, David Patterson, Mike Powell, John Platko, Steve Richardson, Robert Setzer, Pradeep Sindhu, George Taylor, Marc Tremblay, Rudolf Usselmann, J. J. Whelan, Malcolm Wing, and Robert Yung.

Joel Boney, Dennis Allison, Steve Chessin, and Steve Muchnick deserve distinction as "Ace" reviewers. They performed meticulous reviews, eliminating countless bugs in the specification.

Our thanks to all of the above people for their support, critiques, and contributions to this book over the last three years!

Personal Notes

Three years — that's a long time to be in labor! It is with a great deal of pride (and frankly, relief!) that I see this book go to print.

The SPARC Architecture Committee comprised roughly a dozen people, all top computer architects in the industry, from diverse companies. Yet — and this was the most incredible part of the whole process — this group was able to set aside personal egos and individual company interests, and work not just as a committee, but as a real **Team**. This kind of cooperation and synergy doesn't happen every day. Years from now, I'll look back at this work and still be proud to have been a part of this group, and of what we created. . . . "Way to go, gang — we done good!"

Special kudos are due Tom Germond, whose expertise and sharp eye for detail were instrumental in preparing this book. He fearlessly performed a complex but accurate conversion of this specification from one document-preparation system to a wildly different one. Tom made countless improvements to the specification's substance and style, and tenaciously followed numerous open technical issues through to resolution. This book would simply not have been the same without him. Thanks for being there, Tom.

— David Weaver, Editor

Well, it's three o'clock in the morning and I'm in the middle of yet another SPARC-V9 all-nighter. I haven't lost this much sleep since my firstborn was first born. But I must say, it's been great fun bringing this baby to life.

My deepest gratitude to every member of our team, and a tiny extra measure of thanks to a special few. To Joel Boney for his generous and unwavering support. To Dennis Allison for his constant striving for excellence and clarity. To Steve Muchnick for his astonishing mastery of the details. To Steve Chessin for always going to the heart of the issues. And to Jane Bonnell, our editor at Prentice-Hall, for helping us turn a technical specification into a real book.

And finally, warm thanks to Dave Weaver, a good friend and an easy person to work for. You created the opportunity for me to join the team, and you got me through the rough times with all those great movie-and-hot-tub parties. Until next time....

— Tom Germond, Co-editor

1 Overview

This specification defines a 64-bit architecture called SPARC-V9, which is upward-compatible with the existing 32-bit SPARC-V8 microprocessor architecture. This specification includes, but is not limited to, the definition of the instruction set, register model, data types, instruction opcodes, trap model, and memory model.

1.1 Notes About this Book

1.1.1 Audience

Audiences for this specification include implementors of the architecture, students of computer architecture, and developers of SPARC-V9 system software (simulators, compilers, debuggers, and operating systems, for example). Software developers who need to write SPARC-V9 software in assembly language will also find this information useful.

1.1.2 Where to Start

If you are new to the SPARC architecture, read Chapter 2 and Chapter 3 for an overview, then look into the subsequent chapters and appendixes for more details in areas of interest to you.

If you are already familiar with SPARC-V8, you will want to review the list of changes in Appendix K, "Changes From SPARC-V8 to SPARC-V9." For additional detail, review the following chapters:

— Chapter 5, "Registers," for a description of the register set.

— Chapter 6, "Instructions," for a description of the new instructions.

— Chapter 7, "Traps," for a description of the trap model.

— Chapter 8, "Memory Models," for a description of the memory models.

— Appendix A, "Instruction Definitions," for descriptions of new or changed instructions.

1.1.3 Contents

The manual contains these chapters:

— Chapter 1, "Overview," describes the background, design philosophy, and high-level features of the architecture.

— Chapter 2, "Definitions," defines some of the terms used in the specification.

— Chapter 3, "Architectural Overview," is an overview of the architecture: its organization, instruction set, and trap model.

— Chapter 4, "Data Formats," describes the supported data types.

— Chapter 5, "Registers," describes the register set.

— Chapter 6, "Instructions," describes the instruction set.

— Chapter 7, "Traps," describes the trap model.

— Chapter 8, "Memory Models," describes the memory models.

These appendixes follow the chapters:

— Appendix A, "Instruction Definitions," contains definitions of all SPARC-V9 instructions, including tables showing the recommended assembly language syntax for each instruction.

— Appendix B, "IEEE Std 754-1985 Requirements for SPARC-V9," contains information about the SPARC-V9 implementation of the IEEE 754 floating-point standard.

— Appendix C, "SPARC-V9 Implementation Dependencies," contains information about features that may differ among conforming implementations.

— Appendix D, "Formal Specification of the Memory Models," contains a formal description of the memory models.

— Appendix E, "Opcode Maps," contains tables detailing the encoding of all opcodes.

— Appendix F, "SPARC-V9 MMU Requirements," describes the requirements that SPARC-V9 imposes on Memory Management Units.

— Appendix G, "Suggested Assembly Language Syntax," defines the syntactic conventions used in the appendixes for the suggested SPARC-V9 assembly language. It also lists synthetic instructions that may be supported by SPARC-V9 assemblers for the convenience of assembly language programmers.

— Appendix H, "Software Considerations," contains general SPARC-V9 software considerations.

— Appendix I, "Extending the SPARC-V9 Architecture," contains information on how an implementation can extend the instruction set or register set.

— Appendix J, "Programming With the Memory Models," contains information on programming with the SPARC-V9 memory models.

— Appendix K, "Changes From SPARC-V8 to SPARC-V9," describes the differences between SPARC-V8 and SPARC-V9.

A bibliography and an index complete the book.

1.1.4 Editorial Conventions

1.1.4.1 Fonts and Notational Conventions

Fonts are used as follows:

— *Italic* font is used for register names, instruction fields, and read-only register fields. For example: "The *rs1* field contains...."

— `Typewriter` font is used for literals and for software examples.

— **Bold** font is used for emphasis and the first time a word is defined. For example: "A **precise trap** is induced...."

— UPPER CASE items are acronyms, instruction names, or writable register fields. Some common acronyms appear in the glossary in Chapter 2. Note that names of some instructions contain both upper- and lower-case letters.

— *Italic sans serif* font is used for exception and trap names. For example, "The *privileged_action* exception...."

— Underbar characters join words in register, register field, exception, and trap names. Note that such words can be split across lines at the underbar without an intervening hyphen. For example: "This is true whenever the integer_condition_ code field...."

— Reduced-size font is used in informational notes. See 1.1.4.4, "Informational Notes."

The following notational conventions are used:

— Square brackets '[ ]' indicate a numbered register in a register file. For example: "r[0] contains...."

— Angle brackets '< >' indicate a bit number or colon-separated range of bit numbers within a field. For example: "Bits FSR<29:28> and FSR<12> are...."

— Curly braces '{ }' are used to indicate textual substitution. For example, the string "ASI_PRIMARY{_LITTLE}" expands to "ASI_PRIMARY" and "ASI_PRIMARY_LITTLE".

— The ⬚ symbol designates concatenation of bit vectors. A comma ',' on the left side of an assignment separates quantities that are concatenated for the purpose of assignment. For example, if X, Y, and Z are 1-bit vectors, and the 2-bit vector T equals 11_2, then

$$(X, Y, Z) \leftarrow 0 \ \Box \ T$$

results in X = 0, Y = 1, and Z = 1.

1.1.4.2 Implementation Dependencies

Definitions of SPARC-V9 architecture implementation dependencies are indicated by the notation "**IMPL. DEP. #*nn***: Some descriptive text." The number ***nn*** is used to enumerate the dependencies in Appendix C, "SPARC-V9 Implementation Dependencies." References to

SPARC-V9 implementation dependencies are indicated by the notation "(impl. dep. #*nn*)." Appendix C lists the page number on which each definition and reference occurs.

1.1.4.3 Notation for Numbers

Numbers throughout this specification are decimal (base-10) unless otherwise indicated. Numbers in other bases are followed by a numeric subscript indicating their base (for example, 1001_2, FFFF 0000_{16}). Long binary and hex numbers within the text have spaces inserted every four characters to improve readability. Within C or assembly language examples, numbers may be preceded by "0x" to indicate base-16 (hexadecimal) notation (for example, `0xffff0000`).

1.1.4.4 Informational Notes

This manual provides several different types of information in notes; the information appears in a reduced-size font. The following are illustrations of the various note types:

Programming Note:
> These contain incidental information about programming using the SPARC-V9 architecture.

Implementation Note:
> These contain information that may be specific to an implementation or may differ in different implementations.

Compatibility Note:
> These contain information about features of SPARC-V9 that may not be compatible with SPARC-V8 implementations.

1.2 The SPARC-V9 Architecture

1.2.1 Features

SPARC-V9 includes the following principal features:

— A linear address space with 64-bit addressing.

— Few and simple instruction formats: All instructions are 32 bits wide, and are aligned on 32-bit boundaries in memory. Only load and store instructions access memory and perform I/O.

— Few addressing modes: A memory address is given as either "register + register" or "register + immediate."

— Triadic register addresses: Most computational instructions operate on two register operands or one register and a constant, and place the result in a third register.

— A large windowed register file: At any one instant, a program sees 8 global integer registers plus a 24-register window of a larger register file. The windowed registers can be used as a cache of procedure arguments, local values, and return addresses.

— Floating-point: The architecture provides an IEEE 754-compatible floating-point instruction set, operating on a separate register file that provides 32 single-precision (32-bit), 32 double-precision (64-bit), 16 quad-precision (128-bit) registers, or a mixture thereof.

— Fast trap handlers: Traps are vectored through a table.

— Multiprocessor synchronization instructions: One instruction performs an atomic read-then-set-memory operation; another performs an atomic exchange-register-with-memory operation; another compares the contents of a register with a value in memory and exchanges memory with the contents of another register if the comparison was equal; two others are used to synchronize the order of shared memory operations as observed by processors.

— Predicted branches: The branch with prediction instructions allow the compiler or assembly language programmer to give the hardware a hint about whether a branch will be taken.

— Branch elimination instructions: Several instructions can be used to eliminate branches altogether (e.g., move on condition). Eliminating branches increases performance in superscalar and superpipelined implementations.

— Hardware trap stack: A hardware trap stack is provided to allow nested traps. It contains all of the machine state necessary to return to the previous trap level. The trap stack makes the handling of faults and error conditions simpler, faster, and safer.

— Relaxed memory order (RMO) model: This weak memory model allows the hardware to schedule memory accesses in almost any order, as long as the program computes the correct result.

1.2.2 Attributes

SPARC-V9 is a CPU **instruction set architecture** (ISA) derived from SPARC-V8; both architectures come from a reduced instruction set computer (RISC) lineage. As architectures, SPARC-V9 and SPARC-V8 allow for a spectrum of chip and system **implementations** at a variety of price/performance points for a range of applications, including scientific/engineering, programming, real-time, and commercial.

1.2.2.1 Design Goals

SPARC-V9 is designed to be a target for optimizing compilers and high-performance hardware implementations. SPARC-V9 implementations provide exceptionally high execution rates and short time-to-market development schedules.

1.2.2.2 Register Windows

SPARC-V9 is derived from SPARC, which was formulated at Sun Microsystems in 1985. SPARC is based on the RISC I and II designs engineered at the University of California at Berkeley from 1980 through 1982. SPARC's "register window" architecture, pioneered in the UC Berkeley designs, allows for straightforward, high-performance compilers and a significant reduction in memory load/store instructions over other RISCs, particularly for large application programs. For languages such as C++, where object-oriented programming is dominant, register windows result in an even greater reduction in instructions executed.

Note that supervisor software, not user programs, manages the register windows. The supervisor can save a minimum number of registers (approximately 24) during a context switch, thereby optimizing context-switch latency.

One major difference between SPARC-V9 and the Berkeley RISC I and II is that SPARC-V9 provides greater flexibility to a compiler in its assignment of registers to program variables. SPARC-V9 is more flexible because register window management is not tied to procedure call and return instructions, as it is on the Berkeley machines. Instead, separate instructions (SAVE and RESTORE) provide register window management. The management of register windows by privileged software is very different too, as discussed in Appendix H, "Software Considerations."

1.2.3 System Components

The architecture allows for a spectrum of input/output (I/O), memory-management unit (MMU), and cache system subarchitectures. SPARC-V9 assumes that these elements are best defined by the specific requirements of particular systems. Note that they are invisible to nearly all user programs, and the interfaces to them can be limited to localized modules in an associated operating system.

1.2.3.1 Reference MMU

The SPARC-V9 ISA does not mandate a single MMU design for all system implementations. Rather, designers are free to use the MMU that is most appropriate for their application, or no MMU at all, if they wish. Appendix F, "SPARC-V9 MMU Requirements," discusses the boundary conditions that a SPARC-V9 MMU is expected to satisfy.

1.2.3.2 Privileged Software

SPARC-V9 does not assume that all implementations must execute identical privileged software. Thus, certain traits of an implementation that are visible to privileged software can be tailored to the requirements of the system. For example, SPARC-V9 allows for implementations with different instruction concurrency and different trap hardware.

1.2.4 Binary Compatibility

The most important SPARC-V9 architectural mandate is binary compatibility of nonprivileged programs across implementations. Binaries executed in nonprivileged mode should behave identically on all SPARC-V9 systems when those systems are running an operating system known to provide a standard execution environment. One example of such a standard environment is the SPARC-V9 Application Binary Interface (ABI).

Although different SPARC-V9 systems may execute nonprivileged programs at different rates, they will generate the same results, as long as they are run under the same memory model. See Chapter 8, "Memory Models," for more information.

Additionally, SPARC-V9 is designed to be binary upward-compatible from SPARC-V8 for applications running in nonprivileged mode that conform to the SPARC-V8 ABI.

1.2.5 Architectural Definition

The SPARC Version 9 Architecture is defined by the chapters and normative appendixes of this document. A correct implementation of the architecture interprets a program strictly according to the rules and algorithms specified in the chapters and normative appendixes. Only two classes of deviations are permitted:

(1) Certain elements of the architecture are defined to be implementation-dependent. These elements include registers and operations that may vary from implementation to implementation, and are explicitly identified in this document using the notation "**IMPL. DEP. #NN:** Some descriptive text." Appendix C, "SPARC-V9 Implementation Dependencies," describes each of these references.

(2) Functional extensions are permitted, insofar as they do not change the behavior of any defined operation or register. Such extensions are discouraged, since they limit the portability of applications from one implementation to another. Appendix I, "Extending the SPARC-V9 Architecture," provides guidelines for incorporating enhancements in an implementation.

This document defines a nonprivileged subset, designated SPARC-V9-NP. This includes only those elements that may be executed or accessed while the processor is executing in nonprivileged mode.

The informative appendixes provide supplementary information such as programming tips, expected usage, and assembly language syntax. These appendixes are not binding on an implementation or user of a SPARC-V9 system.

The Architecture Committee of SPARC International has sole responsibility for clarification of the definitions in this document.

1.2.6 SPARC-V9 Compliance

SPARC International is responsible for certifying that implementations comply with the SPARC-V9 Architecture. Two levels of compliance are distinguished; an implementation may be certified at either level.

Level 1:

The implementation correctly interprets all of the nonprivileged instructions by any method, including direct execution, simulation, or emulation. This level supports user applications and is the architecture component of the SPARC-V9 ABI.

Level 2:

> The implementation correctly interprets both nonprivileged and privileged instructions by any method, including direct execution, simulation, or emulation. A Level 2 implementation includes all hardware, supporting software, and firmware necessary to provide a complete and correct implementation.

Note that a Level-2-compliant implementation is also Level-1-compliant.

IMPL. DEP. #1: Whether an instruction is implemented directly by hardware, simulated by software, or emulated by firmware is implementation-dependent.

SPARC International publishes a document, *Implementation Characteristics of Current SPARC-V9-based Products, Revision 9.x*, listing which instructions are simulated or emulated in existing SPARC-V9 implementations.

Compliant implementations shall not add to or deviate from this standard except in aspects described as implementation-dependent. See Appendix C, "SPARC-V9 Implementation Dependencies."

An implementation may be claimed to be compliant only if it has been

(1) Submitted to SPARC International for testing, and

(2) Issued a Certificate of Compliance by S. I.

A system incorporating a certified implementation may also claim compliance. A claim of compliance must designate the level of compliance.

Prior to testing, a statement must be submitted for each implementation; this statement must:

— Resolve the implementation dependencies listed in Appendix C

— Identify the presence (but not necessarily the function) of any extensions

— Designate any instructions that require emulation

These statements become the property of SPARC International, and may be released publicly.

2 Definitions

The following subsections define some of the most important words and acronyms used in this manual

2.1   **address space identifier**: An eight-bit value that identifies an address space. For each instruction or data access, the **integer unit** appends an ASI to the address. *See also*: **implicit ASI**.

2.2   **ASI**: Abbreviation for **address space identifier**.

2.3   **application program**: A program executed with the processor in **nonprivileged mode**. Note that statements made in this document regarding application programs may not be applicable to programs (for example, debuggers) that have access to **privileged** processor state (for example, as stored in a memory-image dump).

2.4   **big-endian**: An addressing convention. Within a multiple-byte integer, the byte with the smallest address is the most significant; a byte's significance decreases as its address increases.

2.5   **byte**: Eight consecutive bits of data.

2.6   **clean window**: A register window in which all of the registers contain either zero, a valid address from the current address space, or valid data from the current address space.

2.7   **completed**: A memory transaction is said to be completed when an idealized memory has executed the transaction with respect to all processors. A load is considered completed when no subsequent memory transaction can affect the value returned by the load. A store is considered completed when no subsequent load can return the value that was overwritten by the store.

2.8   **current window**: The block of 24 *r* **registers** that is currently in use. The Current Window Pointer (CWP) register points to the current window.

2.9   **dispatch**: Issue a fetched instruction to one or more functional units for execution.

2.10   **doublet**: Two bytes (16 bits) of data.

2.11   **doubleword**: An aligned **octlet**. Note that the definition of this term is architecture-dependent and may differ from that used in other processor architectures.

2.12   **exception**: A condition that makes it impossible for the processor to continue executing the current instruction stream without software intervention.

2.13   **extended word**: An aligned octlet, nominally containing integer data. Note that the definition of this term is architecture-dependent and may differ from that used in other processor architectures.

2.14   *f* **register**: A floating-point register. SPARC-V9 includes single- double- and quad-precision *f* registers.

2.15   *fccn*: One of the floating-point condition code fields: *fcc0*, *fcc1*, *fcc2*, or *fcc3*.

2.16   **floating-point exception**: An exception that occurs during the execution of a floating-point operate (FPop) instruction. The exceptions are: *unfinished_FPop*, *unimplemented_FPop*, *sequence_error*, *hardware_error*, *invalid_fp_register*, and *IEEE_754_exception*.

2.17   **floating-point IEEE-754 exception**: A floating-point exception, as specified by IEEE Std 754-1985. Listed within this manual as *IEEE_754_exception*.

2.18   **floating-point trap type**: The specific type of floating-point exception, encoded in the FSR.*ftt* field.

2.19   **floating-point operate (FPop) instructions**: Instructions that perform floating-point calculations, as defined by the FPop1 and FPop2 opcodes. FPop instructions do not include FBfcc instructions, or loads and stores between memory and the **floating-point unit**.

2.20   **floating-point unit**: A processing unit that contains the floating-point registers and performs floating-point operations, as defined by this specification.

2.21   **FPU**: Abbreviation for **floating-point unit**.

2.22   **halfword**: An aligned **doublet**. Note that the definition of this term is architecture-dependent and may differ from that used in other processor architectures.

2.23   **hexlet**: Sixteen bytes (128 bits) of data.

2.24   **implementation**: Hardware and/or software that conforms to all of the specifications of an ISA.

2.25   **implementation-dependent**: An aspect of the architecture that may legitimately vary among implementations. In many cases, the permitted range of variation is specified in the standard. When a range is specified, compliant implementations shall not deviate from that range.

2.26   **implicit ASI**: The **address space identifier** that is supplied by the hardware on all instruction accesses, and on data accesses that do not contain an explicit ASI or a reference to the contents of the ASI register.

2.27   **informative appendix**: An appendix containing information that is useful but not required to create an implementation that conforms to the SPARC-V9 specification. *See also*: **normative appendix**.

2.28   **initiated**. *See* **issued**.

2.29   **instruction field**: A bit field within an instruction word.

2.30   **instruction set architecture (ISA)**: An ISA defines instructions, registers, instruction and data memory, the effect of executed instructions on the registers and memory, and an algorithm for controlling instruction execution. An ISA does not define clock cycle times, cycles per instruction, data paths, etc. This specification defines an ISA.

2.31   **integer unit**: A processing unit that performs integer and control-flow operations and contains general-purpose integer registers and processor state registers, as defined by this specification.

2.32   **interrupt request**: A request for service presented to the processor by an external device.

2.33   **IU**: Abbreviation for **integer unit**.

2.34   **ISA**: Abbreviation for **instruction set architecture**.

2.35   **issued**: In reference to memory transaction, a load, store, or atomic load-store is said to be issued when a processor has sent the transaction to the memory subsystem and the completion of the request is out of the processor's control. *Synonym*: **initiated**.

2.36   **leaf procedure**: A procedure that is a leaf in the program's call graph; that is, one that does not call (using CALL or JMPL) any other procedures.

2.37   **little-endian**: An addressing convention. Within a multiple-byte integer, the byte with the smallest address is the least significant; a byte's significance increases as its address increases.

2.38   **may**: A key word indicating flexibility of choice with no implied preference. Note: "may" indicates that an action or operation is allowed, "can" indicates that it is possible.

2.39   **must**: *Synonym*: **shall**.

2.40   **next program counter (nPC)**: A register that contains the address of the instruction to be executed next, if a trap does not occur.

2.41   **non-faulting load**: A load operation that will either complete correctly (in the absence of any faults) or will return a value (nominally zero) if a fault occurs. *See* **speculative load**.

2.42   **nonprivileged**: An adjective that describes (1) the state of the processor when PSTATE.PRIV = 0, that is, **nonprivileged mode**; (2) processor state information that is accessible to software while the processor is in either **privileged mode** or nonprivileged mode, for example, nonprivileged registers, nonprivileged ASRs, or, in general, nonprivileged state; (3) an instruction that can be executed when the processor is in either privileged mode or nonprivileged mode.

2.43   **nonprivileged mode**: The processor mode when PSTATE.PRIV = 0. *See also*: **nonprivileged**.

2.44   **normative appendix**: An appendix containing specifications that must be met by an implementation conforming to the SPARC-V9 specification. *See also*: **informative appendix**.

2.45   **NWINDOWS**: The number of register windows present in an implementation.

2.46   **octlet**: Eight bytes (64 bits) of data. Not to be confused with an "octet," which has been commonly used to describe eight bits of data. In this document, the term **byte**, rather than octet, is used to describe eight bits of data.

2.47   **opcode**: A bit pattern that identifies a particular instruction.

2.48   **prefetchable**: An attribute of a memory location which indicates to an MMU that PREFETCH operations to that location may be applied. Normal memory is prefetchable. Nonprefetchable locations include those that, when read, change state or cause external events to occur. *See also*: **side effect**.

2.49   **privileged**: An adjective that describes (1) the state of the processor when PSTATE.PRIV = 1, that is , **privileged mode**; (2) processor state information that is accessible to software only while the processor is in privileged mode, for example, privileged registers, privileged ASRs, or, in general, privileged state; (3) an instruction that can be executed only when the processor is in privileged mode.

2.50   **privileged mode**: The processor mode when PSTATE.PRIV = 1. *See also*: **nonprivileged**.

2.51   **processor**: The combination of the **integer unit** and the **floating-point unit**.

2.52   **program counter (PC)**: A register that contains the address of the instruction currently being executed by the **IU**.

2.53   **quadlet**: Four bytes (32 bits) of data.

2.54   **quadword**: An aligned **hexlet**. Note that the definition of this term is architecture-dependent and may be different from that used in other processor architectures.

2.55   ***r* register**: An integer register. Also called a general purpose register or working register.

2.56   **RED_state**: **R**eset, **E**rror, and **D**ebug state. The processor state when PSTATE.RED = 1. A restricted execution environment used to process resets and traps that occur when TL = MAXTL − 1.

2.57   **reserved**: Used to describe an instruction field, certain bit combinations within an instruction field, or a register field that is reserved for definition by future versions of the architecture. **Reserved instruction fields** shall read as zero, unless the implementation supports extended instructions within the field. The behavior of SPARC-V9-compliant processors when they encounter non-zero values in reserved instruction fields is undefined. **Reserved bit combinations within instruction fields** are defined in Appendix A; in all cases, SPARC-V9-compliant processors shall decode and trap on these reserved combinations. **Reserved register fields** should only be written to zero by software; they should read as zero in hardware. Software intended to run on future version of SPARC-V9 should not assume that these field will read as zero or any other particular value. Throughout this manual, figures and tables illustrating registers and instruction encodings indicate reserved fields and combinations with an em dash '—'.

2.58   **reset trap**: A vectored transfer of control to privileged software through a fixed-address reset trap table. Reset traps cause entry into **RED_state**.

2.59   **restricted**: An adjective used to describe an **address space identifier** (ASI) that may be accessed only while the processor is operating in **privileged mode**.

2.60   *rs1, rs2, rd*: The integer register operands of an instruction, where *rs1* and *rs2* are the source registers and *rd* is the destination register.

2.61   **shall**: A key word indicating a mandatory requirement. Designers shall implement all such mandatory requirements to ensure interoperability with other SPARC-V9-conformant products. *Synonym*: **must**.

2.62   **should**: A key word indicating flexibility of choice with a strongly preferred implementation. *Synonym*: it is recommended.

2.63   **side effect**: An operation has a side effect if it induces a secondary effect as well as its primary effect. For example, access to an I/O location may cause a register value in an I/O device to change state or initiate an I/O operation. A memory location is deemed to have side effects if additional actions beyond the reading or writing of data may occur when a memory operation on that location is allowed to succeed. *See also*: **prefetchable**.

2.64   **speculative load**: A load operation that is issued by the processor speculatively, that is, before it is known whether the load will be executed in the flow of the program. Speculative accesses are used by hardware to speed program execution and are transparent to code. Contrast with **non-faulting load**, which is an explict load that always completes, even in the presence of faults. *Warning*: some authors confuse speculative loads with non-faulting loads.

2.65   **supervisor software**: Software that executes when the processor is in **privileged mode**.

2.66   **trap**: The action taken by the processor when it changes the instruction flow in response to the presence of an **exception**, a Tcc instruction, or an interrupt. The action is a vectored transfer of control to **supervisor software** through a table, the address of which is specified by the privileged Trap Base Address (TBA) register.

2.67   **unassigned**: A value (for example, an **address space identifier**), the semantics of which are not architecturally mandated and may be determined independently by each implementation within any guidelines given.

2.68   **undefined**: An aspect of the architecture that has deliberately been left unspecified. Software should have no expectation of, nor make any assumptions about, an undefined feature or behavior. Use of such a feature may deliver random results, may or may not cause a trap, may vary among implementations, and may vary with time on a given implementation. Notwithstanding any of the above, undefined aspects of the architecture shall not cause security holes such as allowing user software to access privileged state, put the processor into supervisor mode, or put the processor into an unrecoverable state.

2.69   **unrestricted**: An adjective used to describe an **address space identifier** that may be used regardless of the processor mode, that is, regardless of the value of PSTATE.PRIV.

2.70   **user application program**: *Synonym*: **application program**.

2.71   **word**: An aligned **quadlet**. Note that the definition of this term is architecture-dependent and may differ from that used in other processor architectures.

3 Architectural Overview

SPARC-V9 is an instruction set architecture (ISA) with 32- and 64-bit integer and 32-, 64- and 128-bit floating-point as its principal data types. The 32- and 64- bit floating point types conforms to IEEE Std 754-1985. The 128-bit floating-point type conforms to IEEE Std 1596.5-1992. SPARC-V9 defines general-purpose integer, floating-point, and special state/status register instructions, all encoded in 32-bit-wide instruction formats. The load/store instructions address a linear, 2^{64}-byte address space.

3.1 SPARC-V9 Processor

A SPARC-V9 processor logically consists of an integer unit (**IU**) and a floating-point unit (**FPU**), each with its own registers. This organization allows for implementations with concurrency between integer and floating-point instruction execution. Integer registers are 64 bits wide; floating-point registers are 32, 64, or 128 bits wide. Instruction operands are single registers, register pairs, register quadruples, or immediate constants.

The processor can be in either of two modes: **privileged** or **nonprivileged**. In privileged mode, the processor can execute any instruction, including privileged instructions. In non-privileged mode, an attempt to execute a privileged instruction causes a trap to privileged software.

3.1.1 Integer Unit (IU)

The integer unit contains the general-purpose registers and controls the overall operation of the processor. The IU executes the integer arithmetic instructions and computes memory addresses for loads and stores. It also maintains the program counters and controls instruction execution for the FPU.

IMPL. DEP. #2: An implementation of the IU may contain from 64 to 528 general-purpose 64-bit r registers. this corresponds to a grouping of the registers into 8 global r registers, 8 alternate global r registers, plus a circular stack of from 3 to 32 sets of 16 registers each, known as register windows. Since the number of register windows present (NWINDOWS) is implementation-dependent, the total number of registers is implementation-dependent.

At a given time, an instruction can access the 8 *global*s (or the 8 *alternate globals*) and a register window into the r registers. The 24-register window consists of a 16-register set — divided into 8 *in* and 8 *local* registers — together with the 8 *in* registers of an adjacent register set, addressable from the current window as its *out* registers. See figure 2 on page 32.

The current window is specified by the current window pointer (CWP) register. The processor detects window spill and fill exceptions via the CANSAVE and CANRESTORE registers, respectively, which are controlled by hardware and supervisor software. The actual number of windows in a SPARC-V9 implementation is invisible to a user application program.

Whenever the IU accesses an instruction or datum in memory, it appends an **address space identifier (ASI)**, to the address. All instruction accesses and most data accesses append an **implict ASI**, but some instructions allow the inclusion of an explict ASI, either as an immediate field within the instruction, or from the ASI register. The ASI determines the byte order of the access. All instructions are accessed in big-endian byte order; data can be referenced in either big- or little-endian order. See 5.2.1, "Processor State Register (PSTATE)," for information about changing the default byte order.

3.1.2 Floating-Point Unit (FPU)

The FPU has 32 32-bit (single-precision) floating-point registers, 32 64-bit (double-precision) floating-point registers, and 16 128-bit (quad-precision) floating-point registers, some of which overlap. Double-precision values occupy an even-odd pair of single-precision registers, and quad-precision values occupy a quad-aligned group of four single-precision registers. The 32 single-precision registers, the lower half of the double-precision registers, and the lower half of the quad-precision registers overlay each other. The upper half of the double-precision registers and the upper half of the quad-precision registers overlay each other, but do not overlay any of the single-precision registers. Thus, the floating-point registers can hold a maximum of 32 single-precision, 32 double-precision, or 16 quad-precision values. This is described in more detail in 5.1.4, "Floating-Point Registers."

Floating-point load/store instructions are used to move data between the FPU and memory. The memory address is calculated by the IU. Floating-Point **operate** (FPop) instructions perform the floating-point arithmetic operations and comparisons.

The floating-point instruction set and 32- and 64-bit data formats conform to the IEEE Standard for Binary Floating-Point Arithmetic, IEEE Std 754-1985. The 128-bit floating-point data type conforms to the IEEE Standard for Shared Data Formats, IEEE Std 1596.5-1992.

If an FPU is not present or is not enabled, an attempt to execute a floating-point instruction generates an *fp_disabled* trap. In either case, privileged-mode software must:

— Enable the FPU and reexecute the trapping instruction, or

— Emulate the trapping instruction.

3.2 Instructions

Instructions fall into the following basic categories:

— Memory access

— Integer operate

— Control transfer

— State register access

— Floating-point operate

— Conditional move

— Register window management

These classes are discussed in the following subsections.

3.2.1 Memory Access

Load and store instructions and the atomic operations, CASX, SWAP, and LDSTUB, are the only instructions that access memory. They use two *r* registers or an *r* register and a signed 13-bit immediate value to calculate a 64-bit, byte-aligned memory address. The IU appends an ASI to this address.

The destination field of the load/store instruction specifies either one or two *r* registers, or one, two, or four *f* registers, that supply the data for a store or receive the data from a load.

Integer load and store instructions support byte, halfword (16-bit), word (32-bit), and doubleword (64-bit) accesses. Some versions of integer load instructions perform sign extension on 8-, 16-, and 32-bit values as they are loaded into a 64-bit destination register. Floating-point load and store instructions support word, doubleword, and quadword memory accesses.

CAS, SWAP, and LDSTUB are special atomic memory access instructions that are used for synchonization and memory updates by concurrent processes.

3.2.1.1 Memory Alignment Restrictions

Halfword accesses shall be **aligned** on 2-byte boundaries; word accesses (which include instruction fetches) shall be aligned on 4-byte boundaries; extended-word and doubleword accesses shall be aligned on 8-byte boundaries; and quadword quantities shall be aligned on 16-byte boundaries. An improperly aligned address in a load, store, or load-store instruction causes a trap to occur, with the possible exception of cases described in 6.3.1.1, "Memory Alignment Restrictions."

3.2.1.2 Addressing Conventions

SPARC-V9 uses big-endian byte order by default: the address of a quadword, doubleword, word, or halfword is the address of its most significant byte. Increasing the address means decreasing the significance of the unit being accessed. All instruction accesses are performed using big-endian byte order. SPARC-V9 also can support little-endian byte order for data accesses only: the address of a quadword, doubleword, word, or halfword is the address of its least significant byte. Increasing the address means increasing the significance of the unit being accessed. See 5.2.1, Processor State Register (PSTATE), for information about changing the implicit byte order to little-endian.

Addressing conventions are illustrated in figure 35 on page 69 and figure 36 on page 70.

3.2.1.3 Load/Store Alternate

Versions of load/store instructions, the **load/store alternate** instructions, can specify an arbitrary 8-bit address space identifier for the load/store data access. Access to alternate spaces $00_{16}..7F_{16}$ is restricted, and access to alternate spaces $80_{16}..FF_{16}$ is unrestricted. Some of the ASIs are available for implementation-dependent uses (impl. dep. #29). Supervisor software can use the implementation-dependent ASIs to access special protected registers, such as MMU, cache control, and processor state registers, and other processor- or system-dependent values. See 6.3.1.3, "Address Space Identifiers (ASIs)," for more information.

Alternate space addressing is also provided for the atomic memory access instructions, LDSTUB, SWAP, and CASX.

3.2.1.4 Separate I and D Memories

Most of the specifications in this manual ignore the issues of memory mapping and caching. The interpretation of addresses can be unified, in which case the same translations and caching are applied to both instructions and data, or they can be split, in which case instruction references use one translation mechanism and cache and data references another, although the same main memory is shared. In such split-memory systems, the coherency mechanism may be unified and include both instructions and data, or it may be split. For this reason, programs that modify their own code (self-modifying code) must issue FLUSH instructions, or a system call with a similar effect, to bring the instruction and data memories into a consistent state.

3.2.1.5 Input/Output

SPARC-V9 assumes that input/output registers are accessed via load/store alternate instructions, normal load/store instructions, or read/write Ancillary State Register instructions (RDASR, WRASR).

IMPL. DEP. #123: The semantic effect of accessing input/output (I/O) locations is implementation-dependent.

IMPL. DEP. #6: Whether the I/O registers can be accessed by nonproviileged code is implementation-dependent.

IMPL. DEP. #7: The addresses and contents of I/O registers are implementation-dependent.

3.2.1.6 Memory Synchronization

Two instructions are used for synchronization of memory operations: FLUSH and MEMBAR. Their operation is explained in A.20, "Flush Instruction Memory," and A.31, "Memory Barrier," respectively.

3.2.2 Arithmetic/Logical/Shift Instructions

The arithmetic/logical/shift instructions perform arithmetic, tagged arithmetic, logical, and shift operations. With one exception, these instructions compute a result that is a function of two source operands; the result is either written into a destination register or discarded. The exception, SETHI, may be used in combination with another arithmentic or logical instruction to create a 32-bit constant in an r register.

Shift instructions are used to shift the contents of an r register left or right by a given count. The shift distance is specified by a constant in the instruction or by the contents of an r register.

The integer multiply instruction performs a $64 \times 64 \rightarrow 64$-bit operation. The integer division instructions perform $64 \div 64 \rightarrow 64$-bit operations. In addition, for compatibility with SPARC-V8, $32 \times 32 \rightarrow 64$-bit multiply, $64 \div 32 \rightarrow 32$-bit divide, and multiply step instructions are included. Division by zero causes a trap. Some versions of the 32-bit multiply and divide instructions set the condition codes.

The tagged arithmetic instructions assume that the least-significant two bits of each operand are a data-type tag. The nontrapping versions of these instructions set the integer condition code (icc) and extended integer condition code (xcc) overflow bits on 32-bit (icc) or 64-bit (xcc) arithmetic overflow. In addition, if any of the operands' tag bits are nonzero, icc is set. The xcc overflow bit is not affected by the tag bits.

3.2.3 Control Transfer

Control-transfer instructions (**CTI**s) include PC-relative branches and calls, register-indirect jumps, and conditional traps. Most of the control-transfer instructions are delayed; that is, the instruction immediately following a control-transfer instruction in logical sequence is dispatched before the control transfer to the target address is completed. Note that the next instruction in logical sequence may not be the instruction following the control-transfer instruction in memory.

The instruction following a delayed control-transfer instruction is called a **delay** instruction. A bit in a delayed control-transfer instruction (the **annul bit**) can cause the delay instruction to be annulled (that is, to have no effect) if the branch is not taken (or in the "branch always" case, if the branch is taken).

Compatibility Note:
   SPARC-V8 specified that the delay instruction was always fetched, even if annulled, and that an annulled instruction could not cause any traps. SPARC-V9 does not require the delay instruction to be fetched if it is annulled.

Branch and CALL instructions use PC-relative displacements. The jump and link (JMPL) and return (RETURN) instructions use a register-indirect target address. They compute their target addresses as either the sum of two r registers, or the sum of an r register and a 13-bit signed immediate value. The branch on condition codes without prediction instruction provides a displacement of ±8 Mbytes; the branch on condition codes with prediction instruction provides a displacement of ±1 Mbyte; the branch on register contents instruction provides a displacement of ±128 Kbytes, and the CALL instruction's 30-bit word displacement allows a control transfer to any address within ±2 gigabytes (±2^{31} bytes). Note that when 32-bit address masking is enabled (see 5.2.1.6, "PSTATE_address_mask (AM)"), the CALL instruction may transfer control to an arbitrary 32-bit address. The return from privileged trap instructions (DONE and RETRY) get their target address from the appropriate TPC or TNPC register.

3.2.4 State Register Access

The read and write state register instructions read and write the contents of state registers visible to nonprivileged software (Y, CCR, ASI, PC, TICK, and FPRS). The read and write privileged register instructions read and write the contents of state registers visible only to privileged software (TPC, TNPC, TSTATE, TT, TICK, TBA, PSTATE, TL, PIL, CWP, CANSAVE, CANRESTORE, CLEANWIN, OTHERWIN, WSTATE, FPQ, and VER).

IMPL. DEP. #8: Software can use read/write ancillary state register instructions to read/write implementation-dependent processor registers (ASRs 16..31).

IMPL. DEP. #9: Which if any of the implementation-dependent read/write ancillary state register instructions (for ASRS 16..31) is privileged is implementation-dependent.

3.2.5 Floating-Point Operate

Floating-point operate (FPop) instructions perform all floating-point calculations; they are register-to-register instructions that operate on the floating-point registers. Like arithmetic/logical/shift instructions, FPops compute a result that is a function of one or two source operands. Specific floating-point operations are selected by a subfield of the FPop1/FPop2 instruction formats.

3.2.6 Conditional Move

Conditional move instructions conditionally copy a value from a source register to a destination register, depending on an integer or floating-point condition code or upon the contents of an integer register. These instructions increase performance by reducing the number of branches.

3.2.7 Register Window Management

These instructions are used to manage the register windows. SAVE and RESTORE are nonprivileged and cause a register window to be pushed or popped. FLUSHW is nonprivileged and causes all of the windows except the current one to be flushed to memory. SAVED and RESTORED are used by privileged software to end a window spill or fill trap handler.

3.3 Traps

A **trap** is a vectored transfer of control to privileged software through a trap table that may contain the first eight instructions (thirty-two for fill/spill traps) of each trap handler. The base address of the table is established by software in a state register (the Trap Base Address register, TBA). The displacement within the table is encoded in the type number of each trap and the level of the trap. One half of the table is reserved for hardware traps; one quarter is reserved for software traps generated by trap (Tcc) instructions; the final quarter is reserved for future expansion of the architecture.

A trap causes the current PC and nPC to be saved in the TPC and TNPC registers. It also causes the CCR, ASI, PSTATE, and CWP registers to be saved in TSTATE. TPC, TNPC, and TSTATE are entries in a hardware trap stack, where the number of entries in the trap stack is equal to the number of trap levels supported (impl. dep. #101). A trap also sets bits in the PSTATE register, one of which can enable an alternate set of global registers for use by the trap handler. Normally, the CWP is not changed by a trap; on a window spill or fill trap, however, the CWP is changed to point to the register window to be saved or restored.

A trap may be caused by a Tcc instruction, an asynchronous exception, an instruction-induced exception, or an **interrupt request** not directly related to a particular instruction. Before executing each instruction, the processor behaves as though it determines if there are any pending exceptions or interrupt requests. If any are pending, the processor selects the highest-priority exception or interrupt request and causes a trap.

See Chapter 7, "Traps," for a complete description of traps.

4 Data Formats

The SPARC-V9 architecture recognizes these fundamental data types:

— Signed Integer: 8, 16, 32, and 64 bits

— Unsigned Integer: 8, 16, 32, and 64 bits

— Floating Point: 32, 64, and 128 bits

The widths of the data types are:

— Byte: 8 bits

— Halfword: 16 bits

— Word: 32 bits

— Extended Word: 64 bits

— Tagged Word: 32 bits (30-bit value plus 2-bit tag)

— Doubleword: 64 bits

— Quadword: 128 bits

The signed integer values are stored as two's-complement numbers with a width commensurate with their range. Unsigned integer values, bit strings, boolean values, strings, and other values representable in binary form are stored as unsigned integers with a width commensurate with their range. The floating-point formats conform to the IEEE Standard for Binary Floating-Point Arithmetic, IEEE Std 754-1985. In tagged words, the least significant two bits are treated as a tag; the remaining 30 bits are treated as a signed integer.

Subsections 4.1 through 4.11 illustrate the signed integer, unsigned integer, and tagged formats. Subsections 4.12 through 4.14 illustrate the floating-point formats. In 4.4, 4.9, 4.13, and 4.14, the individual subwords of the multiword data formats are assigned names. The arrangement of the subformats in memory and processor registers based on these names is shown in table 1. Tables 2 through 5 define the integer and floating-point formats.

4.1 Signed Integer Byte

4.2 Signed Integer Halfword

15 14   0

4.3 Signed Integer Word

31 30   0

4.4 Signed Integer Double

SD–0

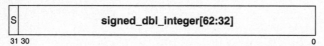

signed_dbl_integer[62:32]

31 30   0

SD–1

signed_dbl_integer[31:0]

31   0

4.5 Signed Extended Integer

SX

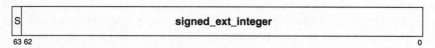

signed_ext_integer

63 62   0

4.6 Unsigned Integer Byte

7   0

4.7 Unsigned Integer Halfword

15   0

4.8   Unsigned Integer Word

31   0

4.9   Unsigned Integer Double

UD–0

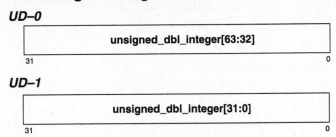

4.10   Unsigned Extended Integer

UX

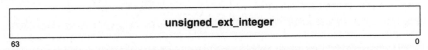

63   0

4.11   Tagged Word

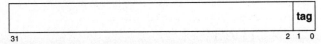

31   2 1 0

4.12   Floating-Point Single Precision

S	exp[7:0]	fraction[22:0]

31 30   23 22   0

4.13 Floating-Point Double Precision

FD–0

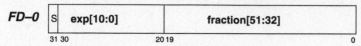

31 30   20 19   0

FD–1

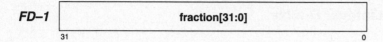

31   0

4.14 Floating-Point Quad Precision

FQ–0

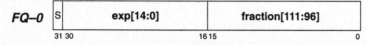

31 30   16 15   0

FQ–1

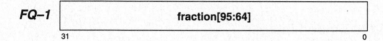

31   0

FQ–2

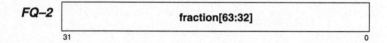

31   0

FQ–3

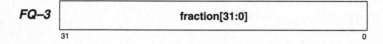

31   0

Table 1—Double- and Quadwords in Memory & Registers

Subformat Name	Subformat Field	Required Address Alignment	Memory Address	Register Number Alignment	Register Number
SD-0	signed_dbl_integer[63:32]	0 mod 8	n	0 mod 2	r
SD-1	signed_dbl_integer[31:0]	4 mod 8	$n + 4$	1 mod 2	$r + 1$
SX	signed_ext_integer[63:0]	0 mod 8	n	—	r
UD-0	unsigned_dbl_integer[63:32]	0 mod 8	n	0 mod 2	r
UD-1	unsigned_dbl_integer[31:0]	4 mod 8	$n + 4$	1 mod 2	$r + 1$
UX	unsigned_ext_integer[63:0]	0 mod 8	n	—	r
FD-0	s:exp[10:0]:fraction[51:32]	0 mod 4 [†]	n	0 mod 2	f
FD-1	fraction[31:0]	0 mod 4 [†]	$n + 4$	1 mod 2	$f + 1$
FQ-0	s:exp[14:0]:fraction[111:96]	0 mod 4 [‡]	n	0 mod 4	f
FQ-1	fraction[95:64]	0 mod 4 [‡]	$n + 4$	1 mod 4	$f + 1$
FQ-2	fraction[63:32]	0 mod 4 [‡]	$n + 8$	2 mod 4	$f + 2$
FQ-3	fraction[31:0]	0 mod 4 [‡]	$n + 12$	3 mod 4	$f + 3$

[†] Although a floating-point doubleword is only required to be word-aligned in memory, it is recommended that it be doubleword-aligned (i.e., the address of its FD-0 word should be 0 **mod** 8).

[‡] Although a floating-point quadword is only required to be word-aligned in memory, it is recommended that it be quadword-aligned (i.e., the address of its FQ-0 word should be 0 **mod** 16).

Table 2—Signed Integer, Unsigned Integer, and Tagged Format Ranges

Data type	Width (bits)	Range
Signed integer byte	8	-2^7 to $2^7 - 1$
Signed integer halfword	16	-2^{15} to $2^{15} - 1$
Signed integer word	32	-2^{31} to $2^{31} - 1$
Signed integer tagged word	32	-2^{29} to $2^{29} - 1$
Signed integer double	64	-2^{63} to $2^{63} - 1$
Signed extended integer	64	-2^{63} to $2^{63} - 1$
Unsigned integer byte	8	0 to $2^8 - 1$
Unsigned integer halfword	16	0 to $2^{16} - 1$
Unsigned integer word	32	0 to $2^{32} - 1$
Unsigned integer tagged word	32	0 to $2^{30} - 1$
Unsigned integer double	64	0 to $2^{64} - 1$
Unsigned extended integer	64	0 to $2^{64} - 1$

Table 3—Floating-Point Single-Precision Format Definition

s = sign (1 bit) e = biased exponent (8 bits) f = fraction (23 bits) u = undefined	
Normalized value (0 < e < 255):	$(-1)^s \times 2^{e-127} \times 1.f$
Subnormal value (e = 0):	$(-1)^s \times 2^{-126} \times 0.f$
Zero (e = 0)	$(-1)^s \times 0$
Signalling NaN	s = u; e = 255 (max); f = $.0uu$ - uu (At least one bit of the fraction must be nonzero)
Quiet NaN	s = u; e = 255 (max); f = $.1uu$ - uu
$-\infty$ (negative infinity)	s = 1; e = 255 (max); f = .000 - 00
$+\infty$ (positive infinity)	s = 0; e = 255 (max); f = .000 - 00

Table 4—Floating-Point Double-Precision Format Definition

s = sign (1 bit) e = biased exponent (11 bits) f = fraction (52 bits) u = undefined	
Normalized value (0 < e < 2047):	$(-1)^s \times 2^{e-1023} \times 1.f$
Subnormal value (e = 0):	$(-1)^s \times 2^{-1022} \times 0.f$
Zero (e = 0)	$(-1)^s \times 0$
Signalling NaN	s = u; e = 2047 (max); f = $.0uu$ - uu (At least one bit of the fraction must be nonzero)
Quiet NaN	s = u; e = 2047 (max); f = $.1uu$ - uu
$-\infty$ (negative infinity)	s = 1; e = 2047 (max); f = .000 - 00
$+\infty$ (positive infinity)	s = 0; e = 2047 (max); f = .000 - 00

Table 5—Floating-Point Quad-Precision Format Definition

s = sign (1 bit) e = biased exponent (15 bits) f = fraction (112 bits) u = undefined	
Normalized value (0 < e < 32767):	$(-1)^s \times 2^{e-16383} \times 1.f$
Subnormal value (e = 0):	$(-1)^s \times 2^{-16382} \times 0.f$
Zero (e = 0)	$(-1)^s \times 0$
Signalling NaN	s = u; e = 32767 (max); f = $.0uu - uu$ (At least one bit of the fraction must be nonzero)
Quiet NaN	s = u; e = 32767 (max); f = $.1uu - uu$
$-\infty$ (negative infinity)	s = 1; e = 32767 (max); f = $.000 - 00$
$+\infty$ (positive infinity)	s = 0; e = 32767 (max); f = $.000 - 00$

5 Registers

A SPARC-V9 processor includes two types of registers: general-purpose, or working data registers, and control/status registers.

Working registers include:

— Integer working registers (*r* registers)

— Floating-point working registers (*f* registers)

Control/status registers include:

— Program Counter register (PC)

— Next Program Counter register (nPC)

— Processor State register (PSTATE)

— Trap Base Address register (TBA)

— Y register (Y)

— Processor Interrupt Level register (PIL)

— Current Window Pointer register (CWP)

— Trap Type register (TT)

— Condition Codes Register (CCR)

— Address Space Identifier register (ASI)

— Trap Level register (TL)

— Trap Program Counter register (TPC)

— Trap Next Program Counter register (TNPC)

— Trap State register (TSTATE)

— Hardware clock-tick counter register (TICK)

— Savable windows register (CANSAVE)

— Restorable windows register (CANRESTORE)

— Other windows register (OTHERWIN)

— Clean windows register (CLEANWIN)

— Window State register (WSTATE)

— Version register (VER)

— Implementation-dependent Ancillary State Registers (ASRs) (impl. dep. #8)

— Implementation-dependent IU Deferred-Trap Queue (impl. dep. #16)

— Floating-Point State Register (FSR)

— Floating-Point Registers State register (FPRS)

— Implementation-dependent Floating-Point Deferred-Trap Queue (FQ) (impl. dep. #24)

For convenience, some registers in this chapter are illustrated as fewer than 64 bits wide. Any bits not shown are reserved for future extensions to the architecture. Such reserved bits read as zeroes and, when written by software, should always be written as zeroes.

5.1 Nonprivileged Registers

The registers described in this subsection are visible to nonprivileged (application, or "user-mode") software.

5.1.1 General Purpose *r* Registers

At any moment, general-purpose registers appear to nonprivileged software as shown in figure 1.

An implementation of the IU may contain from 64 to 528 general-purpose 64-bit *r* registers. They are partitioned into 8 *global* registers, 8 *alternate global* registers, plus an implementation-dependent number of 16-register sets (impl. dep. #2). A register window consists of the current 8 *in* registers, 8 *local* registers, and 8 *out* registers. See table 6.

5.1.1.1 Global *r* Registers

Registers $r[0]..r[7]$ refer to a set of eight registers called the global registers ($g0..g7$). At any time, one of two sets of eight registers is enabled and can be accessed as the global registers. Which set of globals is currently enabled is selected by the AG (alternate global) field in the PSTATE register. See 5.2.1, "Processor State Register (PSTATE)," for a description of the AG field.

Global register zero (g0) always reads as zero; writes to it have no program-visible effect.

Compatibility Note:

> Since the PSTATE register is only writable by privileged software, existing nonprivileged SPARC-V8 software will operate correctly on a SPARC-V9 implementation if supervisor software ensures that nonprivileged software sees a consistent set of global registers.

i7	r[31]
i6	r[30]
i5	r[29]
i4	r[28]
i3	r[27]
i2	r[26]
i1	r[25]
i0	r[24]
l7	r[23]
l6	r[22]
l5	r[21]
l4	r[20]
l3	r[19]
l2	r[18]
l1	r[17]
l0	r[16]
o7	r[15]
o6	r[14]
o5	r[13]
o4	r[12]
o3	r[11]
o2	r[10]
o1	r[9]
o0	r[8]
g7	r[7]
g6	r[6]
g5	r[5]
g4	r[4]
g3	r[3]
g2	r[2]
g1	r[1]
g0	r[0]

Figure 1—General-Purpose Registers (Nonprivileged View)

Programming Note:

> The alternate global registers are present to give trap handlers a set of scratch registers that are independent of nonprivileged software's registers. The AG bit in PSTATE allows supervisor software to access the normal global registers if required (for example, during instruction emulation).

5.1.1.2 Windowed *r* Registers

At any time, an instruction can access the 8 *globals* and a 24-register **window** into the *r* registers. A register window comprises the 8 *in* and 8 *local* registers of a particular register set, together with the 8 *in* registers of an adjacent register set, which are addressable from the current window as *out* registers. See figure 2 and table 6.

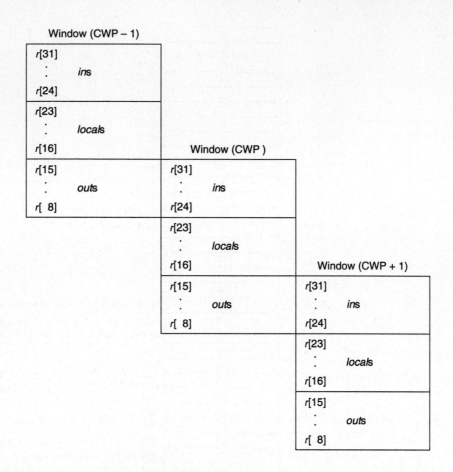

Figure 2—Three Overlapping Windows and the Eight Global Registers

The number of windows or register sets, NWINDOWS, is implementation-dependent and ranges from 3 to 32 (impl. dep. #2). The total number of *r* registers in a given implementation is 8 (for the *globals*), plus 8 (for the alternate *globals*), plus the number of sets times 16 registers/set. Thus, the minimum number of *r* registers is 64 (3 sets plus the 16 *globals* and alternate *globals*) and the maximum number is 528 (32 sets plus the 16 *globals* and alternate *globals*).

Table 6—Window Addressing

Windowed Register Address	*r* Register Address
in[0] – *in*[7]	*r*[24] – *r*[31]
local[0] – *local*[7]	*r*[16] – *r*[23]
out[0] – *out*[7]	*r*[8] – *r*[15]
global[0] – *global*[7]	*r*[0] – *r*[7]

The current window into the *r* registers is given by the current window pointer (CWP) register. The CWP is decremented by the RESTORE instruction and incremented by the SAVE instruction. Window overflow is detected via the CANSAVE register and window underflow is detected via the CANRESTORE register, both of which are controlled by privileged software. A window overflow (underflow) condition causes a window spill (fill) trap.

5.1.1.3 Overlapping Windows

Each window shares its *in*s with one adjacent window and its *out*s with another. The *out*s of the CWP−1 (modulo NWINDOWS) window are addressable as the *in*s of the current window, and the *out*s in the current window are the *in*s of the CWP+1 (modulo NWINDOWS) window. The *local*s are unique to each window.

An *r* register with address *o*, where $8 \leq o \leq 15$, refers to exactly the same register as $(o+16)$ does after the CWP is incremented by 1 (modulo NWINDOWS). Likewise, a register with address *i*, where $24 \leq i \leq 31$, refers to exactly the same register as address $(i-16)$ does after the CWP is decremented by 1 (modulo NWINDOWS). See figures 2 and 3.

Since CWP arithmetic is performed modulo NWINDOWS, the highest numbered implemented window overlaps with window 0. The *out*s of window NWINDOWS−1 are the *in*s of window 0. Implemented windows must be numbered contiguously from 0 through NWINDOWS−1.

Programming Note:

Since the procedure call instructions (CALL and JMPL) do not change the CWP, a procedure can be called without changing the window. See H.1.2, "Leaf-Procedure Optimization."

Because the windows overlap, the number of windows available to software is one less than the number of implemented windows, or NWINDOWS−1. When the register file is full, the *out*s of the newest window are the *in*s of the oldest window, which still contains valid data.

The *local* and *out* registers of a register window are guaranteed to contain either zeroes or an old value that belongs to the current context upon reentering the window through a SAVE instruction. If a program executes a RESTORE followed by a SAVE, the resulting window's *local*s and *out*s may not be valid after the SAVE, since a trap may have occurred between the RESTORE and the SAVE. However, if the *clean_window* protocol is being used, system software must guarantee that registers in the current window after a SAVE will always contain only zeroes or valid data from that context. See 5.2.10.6, "Clean Windows (CLEANWIN) Register."

Subsection 6.4, "Register Window Management," describes how the windowed integer registers are managed.

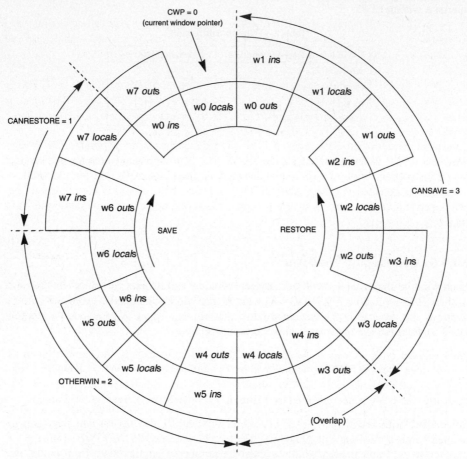

$$CANSAVE + CANRESTORE + OTHERWIN = NWINDOWS - 2$$

The current window (window 0) and the overlap window (window 4) account for the two windows in the right-hand side of the equation. The "overlap window" is the window that must remain unused because its ins and outs overlap two other valid windows. In SPARC-V8 this is called the "trap window."

Figure 3—The Windowed *r* Registers for NWINDOWS = 8

5.1.2 Special *r* Registers

The usage of two of the *r* registers is fixed, in whole or in part, by the architecture:

— The value of *r*[0] is always zero; writes to it have no program-visible effect.

— The CALL instruction writes its own address into register *r*[15] (*out* register 7).

5.1.2.1 Register-Pair Operands

LDD, LDDA, STD, and STDA instructions access a pair of words in adjacent *r* registers and require even-odd register alignment. The least-significant bit of an *r* register number in these instructions is reserved, and should be supplied as zero by software.

When the *r*[0] – *r*[1] register pair is used as a destination in LDD or LDDA, only *r*[1] is modified. When the *r*[0] – *r*[1] register pair is used as a source in STD or STDA, a zero is written to the 32-bit word at the lowest address and the least significant 32 bits of *r*[1] are written to the 32-bit word at the highest address (in big-endian mode).

An attempt to execute an LDD, LDDA, STD, or STDA instruction that refers to a mis-aligned (odd) destination register number causes an *illegal_instruction* trap.

5.1.2.2 Register Usage

See H.1.1, "Registers," for information about the conventional usage of the *r* registers.

In figure 3, NWINDOWS = 8. The 8 *global*s are not illustrated. CWP = 0, CANSAVE = 3, OTHERWIN = 2, and CANRESTORE = 1. If the procedure using window *w0* executes a RESTORE, window *w7* becomes the current window. If the procedure using window *w0* executes a SAVE, window *w1* becomes the current window.

5.1.3 IU Control/Status Registers

The nonprivileged IU control/status registers include the program counters (PC and nPC), the 32-bit multiply/divide (Y) register (and possibly optional) implementation-dependent Ancillary State Registers (ASRs) (impl. dep. #8).

5.1.3.1 Program Counters (PC, nPC)

The PC contains the address of the instruction currently being executed by the IU. The nPC holds the address of the next instruction to be executed, if a trap does not occur. The low-order two bits of PC and nPC always contain zero.

For a delayed control transfer, the instruction that immediately follows the transfer instruction is known as the delay instruction. This delay instruction is executed (unless the control transfer instruction annuls it) before control is transferred to the target. During execution of the delay instruction, the nPC points to the target of the control transfer instruction, while the PC points to the delay instruction. See Chapter 6, "Instructions."

The PC is used implicitly as a destination register by CALL, Bicc, BPcc, BPr, FBfcc, FBPfcc, JMPL, and RETURN instructions. It can be read directly by an RDPC instruction.

5.1.3.2 32-Bit Multiply/Divide Register (Y)

> The Y register is deprecated; it is provided only for compatibility with previous versions of the architecture. It should not be used in new SPARC-V9 software. It is recommended that all instructions that reference the Y register (i.e., SMUL, SMULcc, UMUL, UMULcc, MULScc, SDIV, SDIVcc, UDIV, UDIVcc, RDY, and WRY) be avoided. See the appropriate pages in Appendix A, "Instruction Definitions," for suitable substitute instructions.

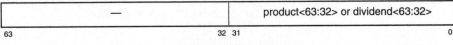

—	product<63:32> or dividend<63:32>
63 32 31	0

Figure 4—Y Register

The low-order 32 bits of the Y register, illustrated in figure 4, contain the more significant word of the 64-bit product of an integer multiplication, as a result of either a 32-bit integer multiply (SMUL, SMULcc, UMUL, UMULcc) instruction or an integer multiply step (MULScc) instruction. The Y register also holds the more significant word of the 64-bit dividend for a 32-bit integer divide (SDIV, SDIVcc, UDIV, UDIVcc) instruction.

Although Y is a 64-bit register, its high-order 32 bits are reserved and always read as 0.

The Y register is read and written with the RDY and WRY instructions, respectively.

5.1.3.3 Ancillary State Registers (ASRs)

SPARC-V9 provides for optional ancillary state registers (ASRs). Access to a particular ASR may be privileged or nonprivileged (impl. dep. #9); see 5.2.11, "Ancillary State Registers (ASRs)," for a more complete description of ASRs.

5.1.4 Floating-Point Registers

The FPU contains:

— 32 single-precision (32-bit) floating-point registers, numbered $f[0], f[1], .. f[31]$.

— 32 double-precision (64-bit) floating-point registers, numbered $f[0], f[2], .. f[62]$.

— 16 quad-precision (128-bit) floating-point registers, numbered $f[0], f[4], .. f[60]$.

The floating-point registers are arranged so that some of them overlap, that is, are aliased. The layout and numbering of the floating-point registers are shown in figures 5, 6, and 7. Unlike the windowed r registers, all of the floating-point registers are accessible at any time. The floating-point registers can be read and written by FPop (FPop1/FPop2 format) instructions, and by load/store single/double/quad floating-point instructions.

Figure 5—Single-Precision Floating-Point Registers, with Aliasing

Operand register ID	Operand from
f31	f31<31:0>
f30	f30<31:0>
f29	f29<31:0>
f28	f28<31:0>
f27	f27<31:0>
f26	f26<31:0>
f25	f25<31:0>
f24	f24<31:0>
f23	f23<31:0>
f22	f22<31:0>
f21	f21<31:0>
f20	f20<31:0>
f19	f19<31:0>
f18	f18<31:0>
f17	f17<31:0>
f16	f16<31:0>
f15	f15<31:0>
f14	f14<31:0>
f13	f13<31:0>
f12	f12<31:0>
f11	f11<31:0>
f10	f10<31:0>
f9	f9<31:0>
f8	f8<31:0>
f7	f7<31:0>
f6	f6<31:0>
f5	f5<31:0>
f4	f4<31:0>
f3	f3<31:0>
f2	f2<31:0>
f1	f1<31:0>
f0	f0<31:0>

Figure 6—Double-Precision Floating-Point Registers, with Aliasing

Operand register ID	Operand field	From register
f62	<63:0>	f62<63:0>
f60	<63:0>	f60<63:0>
f58	<63:0>	f58<63:0>
f56	<63:0>	f56<63:0>
f54	<63:0>	f54<63:0>
f52	<63:0>	f52<63:0>
f50	<63:0>	f50<63:0>
f48	<63:0>	f48<63:0>
f46	<63:0>	f46<63:0>
f44	<63:0>	f44<63:0>
f42	<63:0>	f42<63:0>
f40	<63:0>	f40<63:0>
f38	<63:0>	f38<63:0>
f36	<63:0>	f36<63:0>
f34	<63:0>	f34<63:0>
f32	<63:0>	f32<63:0>
f30	<31:0>	f31<31:0>
	<63:32>	f30<31:0>
f28	<31:0>	f29<31:0>
	<63:32>	f28<31:0>
f26	<31:0>	f27<31:0>
	<63:32>	f26<31:0>
f24	<31:0>	f25<31:0>
	<63:32>	f24<31:0>
f22	<31:0>	f23<31:0>
	<63:32>	f22<31:0>
f20	<31:0>	f21<31:0>
	<63:32>	f20<31:0>
f18	<31:0>	f19<31:0>
	<63:32>	f18<31:0>
f16	<31:0>	f17<31:0>
	<63:32>	f16<31:0>
f14	<31:0>	f15<31:0>
	<63:32>	f14<31:0>
f12	<31:0>	f13<31:0>
	<63:32>	f12<31:0>
f10	<31:0>	f11<31:0>
	<63:32>	f10<31:0>
f8	<31:0>	f9<31:0>
	<63:32>	f8<31:0>
f6	<31:0>	f7<31:0>
	<63:32>	f6<31:0>
f4	<31:0>	f5<31:0>
	<63:32>	f4<31:0>
f2	<31:0>	f3<31:0>
	<63:32>	f2<31:0>
f0	<31:0>	f1<31:0>
	<63:32>	f0<31:0>

Figure 7—Quad-Precision Floating-Point Registers, with Aliasing

Operand register ID	Operand field	From register
f60	<63:0>	f62<63:0>
	<127:64>	f60<63:0>
f56	<63:0>	f58<63:0>
	<127:64>	f56<63:0>
f52	<63:0>	f54<63:0>
	<127:64>	f52<63:0>
f48	<63:0>	f50<63:0>
	<127:64>	f48<63:0>
f44	<63:0>	f46<63:0>
	<127:64>	f44<63:0>
f40	<63:0>	f42<63:0>
	<127:64>	f40<63:0>
f36	<63:0>	f38<63:0>
	<127:64>	f36<63:0>
f32	<63:0>	f34<63:0>
	<127:64>	f32<63:0>
f28	<31:0>	f31<31:0>
	<63:32>	f30<31:0>
	<95:64>	f29<31:0>
	<127:96>	f28<31:0>
f24	<31:0>	f27<31:0>
	<63:32>	f26<31:0>
	<95:64>	f25<31:0>
	<127:96>	f24<31:0>
f20	<31:0>	f23<31:0>
	<63:32>	f22<31:0>
	<95:64>	f21<31:0>
	<127:96>	f20<31:0>
f16	<31:0>	f19<31:0>
	<63:32>	f18<31:0>
	<95:64>	f17<31:0>
	<127:96>	f16<31:0>
f12	<31:0>	f15<31:0>
	<63:32>	f14<31:0>
	<95:64>	f13<31:0>
	<127:96>	f12<31:0>
f8	<31:0>	f11<31:0>
	<63:32>	f10<31:0>
	<95:64>	f9<31:0>
	<127:96>	f8<31:0>
f4	<31:0>	f7<31:0>
	<63:32>	f6<31:0>
	<95:64>	f5<31:0>
	<127:96>	f4<31:0>
f0	<31:0>	f3<31:0>
	<63:32>	f2<31:0>
	<95:64>	f1<31:0>
	<127:96>	f0<31:0>

5.1.4.1 Floating-Point Register Number Encoding

Register numbers for single, double, and quad registers are encoded differently in the 5-bit register number field in a floating-point instruction. If the bits in a register number field are labeled: b<4>..b<0> (where b<4> is the most-significant bit of the register number), the encoding of floating-point register numbers into 5-bit instruction fields is as given in table 7.

Table 7—Floating-Point Register Number Encoding

Register operand type	6-bit register number						Encoding in a 5-bit register field in an instruction				
Single	0	b<4>	b<3>	b<2>	b<1>	b<0>	b<4>	b<3>	b<2>	b<1>	b<0>
Double	b<5>	b<4>	b<3>	b<2>	b<1>	0	b<4>	b<3>	b<2>	b<1>	b<5>
Quad	b<5>	b<4>	b<3>	b<2>	0	0	b<4>	b<3>	b<2>	0	b<5>

Compatibility Note:
> In SPARC-V8, bit 0 of double and quad register numbers encoded in instruction fields was required to be zero. Therefore, all SPARC-V8 floating-point instructions can run unchanged on a SPARC-V9 implementation using the encoding in table 7.

5.1.4.2 Double and Quad Floating-Point Operands

A single f register can hold one single-precision operand, a double-precision operand requires an aligned pair of f registers, and a quad-precision operand requires an aligned quadruple of f registers. At a given time, the floating-point registers can hold a maximum of 32 single-precision, 16 double-precision, or 8 quad-precision values in the lower half of the floating-point register file, plus an additional 16 double-precision or 8 quad-precision values in the upper half, or mixtures of the three sizes.

Programming Note:
> Data to be loaded into a floating-point double or quad register that is not doubleword-aligned in memory must be loaded into the lower 16 double registers (8 quad registers) using single-precision LDF instructions. If desired, it can then be copied into the upper 16 double registers (8 quad registers).

An attempt to execute an instruction that refers to a misaligned floating-point register operand (that is, a quad-precision operand in a register whose 6-bit register number is not 0 **mod** 4) shall cause an *fp_exception_other* trap, with FSR.*ftt* = 6 (*invalid_fp_register*).

Programming Note:
> Given the encoding in table 7, it is impossible to specify a misaligned double-precision register.

5.1.5 Condition Codes Register (CCR)

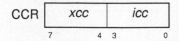

Figure 8—Condition Codes Register

The Condition Codes Register (CCR) holds the integer condition codes.

5.1.5.1 CCR Condition Code Fields (*xcc* and *icc*)

All instructions that set integer condition codes set both the *xcc* and *icc* fields. The *xcc* condition codes indicate the result of an operation when viewed as a 64-bit operation. The *icc* condition codes indicate the result of an operation when viewed as a 32-bit operation. For example, if an operation results in the 64-bit value 0000 0000 FFFF FFFF$_{16}$, the 32-bit result is negative (*icc*.N is set to 1) but the 64-bit result is nonnegative (*xcc*.N is set to 0).

Each of the 4-bit condition-code fields is composed of four 1-bit subfields, as shown in figure 9.

xcc: 7   6   5   4
icc: 3   2   1   0

Figure 9—Integer Condition Codes (CCR_icc and CCR_xcc)

The *n* bits indicate whether the 2's-complement ALU result was negative for the last instruction that modified the integer condition codes. 1 = negative, 0 = not negative.

The *z* bits indicate whether the ALU result was zero for the last instruction that modified the integer condition codes. 1 = zero, 0 = nonzero.

The *v* bits indicate whether the ALU result was within the range of (was representable in) 64-bit (*xcc*) or 32-bit (*icc*) 2's complement notation for the last instruction that modified the integer condition codes. 1 = overflow, 0 = no overflow.

The *c* bits indicate whether a 2's complement carry (or borrow) occurred during the last instruction that modified the integer condition codes. Carry is set on addition if there is a carry out of bit 63 (*xcc*) or bit 31 (*icc*). Carry is set on subtraction if there is a borrow into bit 63 (*xcc*) or bit 31 (*icc*). 1 = carry, 0 = no carry.

5.1.5.1.1 CCR_extended_integer_cond_codes (*xcc*)

Bits 7 through 4 are the IU condition codes that indicate the results of an integer operation with both of the operands considered to be 64 bits long. These bits are modified by the arithmetic and logical instructions the names of which end with the letters "cc" (e.g., ANDcc) and by the WRCCR instruction. They can be modified by a DONE or RETRY instruction, which replaces these bits with the CCR field of the TSTATE register. The BPcc and Tcc instructions may cause a transfer of control based on the values of these bits. The MOVcc instruction can conditionally move the contents of an integer register based on the state of these bits. The FMOVcc instruction can conditionally move the contents of a floating-point register based on the state of these bits.

5.1.5.1.2 CCR_integer_cond_codes (*icc*)

Bits 3 through 0 are the IU condition codes, which indicate the results of an integer operation with both of the operands considered to be 32 bits. These bits are modified by the arithmetic and logical instructions the names of which end with the letters "cc" (e.g., ANDcc) and by the WRCCR instruction. They can be modified by a DONE or RETRY instruction, which replaces these bits with the CCR field of the TSTATE register. The BPcc, Bicc, and Tcc instructions may cause a transfer of control based on the values of these bits. The MOVcc instruction can conditionally move the contents of an integer register based on the state of these bits. The FMOVcc instruction can conditionally move the contents of a floating-point register based on the state of these bits.

5.1.6 Floating-Point Registers State (FPRS) Register

Figure 10—Floating-Point Registers State Register

The Floating-Point Registers State (FPRS) register holds control information for the floating-point register file; this information is readable and writable by nonprivileged software.

5.1.6.1 FPRS_enable_fp (FEF)

Bit 2, FEF, determines whether the FPU is enabled. If it is disabled, executing a floating-point instruction causes an *fp_disabled* trap. If this bit is set but the PSTATE.PEF bit is not set, then executing a floating-point instruction causes an *fp_disabled* trap; that is, both FPRS.FEF and PSTATE.PEF must be set to enable floating-point operations.

5.1.6.2 FPRS_dirty_upper (DU)

Bit 1 is the "dirty" bit for the upper half of the floating-point registers; that is, f32..f62. It is set whenever any of the upper floating-point registers is modified. Its setting may be pessimistic; that is, it may be set in some cases even though no register was actually modified. It is cleared only by software.

5.1.6.3 FPRS_dirty_lower (DL)

Bit 0 is the "dirty" bit for the lower 32 floating-point registers; that is, f0..f31. It is set whenever any of the lower floating-point registers is modified. Its setting may be pessimistic; that is, it may be set in some cases even though no register was actually modified. It is cleared only by software.

Implementation Note:
> The pessimistic setting of FPRS.DL and FPRS.DU allows hardware to set these bits even though the modification of a floating-point register might be cancelled before data is written.

5.1.7 Floating-Point State Register (FSR)

The FSR register fields, illustrated in figure 11, contain FPU mode and status information. The lower 32 bits of the FSR are read and written by the STFSR and LDFSR instructions; all 64 bits of the FSR are read and written by the STXFSR and LDXFSR instructions, respectively. The *ver*, *ftt*, and *reserved* fields are not modified by LDFSR or LDXFSR.

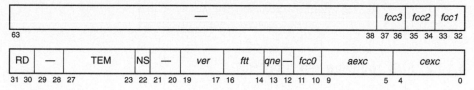

Figure 11—FSR Fields

Bits 63..38, 29..28, 21..20, and 12 are reserved. When read by an STXFSR instruction, these bits shall read as zero. Software should only issue LDXFSR instructions with zero values in these bits, unless the values of these bits are exactly those derived from a previous STFSR.

Subsections 5.1.7.1 through 5.1.7.10.5 describe the remaining fields in the FSR.

5.1.7.1 FSR_fp_condition_codes (*fcc0*, *fcc1*, *fcc2*, *fcc3*)

There are four sets of floating-point condition code fields, labeled *fcc0*, *fcc1*, *fcc2*, and *fcc3*.

Compatibility Note:

   SPARC-V9's *fcc0* is the same as SPARC-V8's *fcc*.

The *fcc0* field consists of bits 11 and 10 of the FSR, *fcc1* consists of bits 33 and 32, *fcc2* consists of bits 35 and 34, and *fcc3* consists of bits 37 and 36. Execution of a floating-point compare instruction (FCMP or FCMPE) updates one of the *fccn* fields in the FSR, as selected by the instruction. The *fccn* fields are read and written by STXFSR and LDXFSR instructions, respectively. The *fcc0* field may also be read and written by STFSR and LDFSR, respectively. FBfcc and FBPfcc instructions base their control transfers on these fields. The MOVcc and FMOVcc instructions can conditionally copy a register based on the state of these fields.

In table 8, f_{rs1} and f_{rs2} correspond to the single, double, or quad values in the floating-point registers specified by a floating-point compare instruction's *rs1* and *rs2* fields. The question mark ('?') indicates an unordered relation, which is true if either f_{rs1} or f_{rs2} is a signalling NaN or quiet NaN. If FCMP or FCMPE generates an *fp_exception_ieee_754* exception, then *fccn* is unchanged.

Table 8—Floating-Point Condition Codes (*fccn*) Fields of FSR

Content of *fccn*	Indicated relation
0	$f_{rs1} = f_{rs2}$
1	$f_{rs1} < f_{rs2}$
2	$f_{rs1} > f_{rs2}$
3	$f_{rs1} ? f_{rs2}$ (*unordered*)

5.1.7.2 FSR_rounding_direction (RD)

Bits 31 and 30 select the rounding direction for floating-point results according to IEEE Std 754-1985. Table 9 shows the encodings.

Table 9—Rounding Direction (RD) Field of FSR

RD	Round toward
0	Nearest (even if tie)
1	0
2	$+\infty$
3	$-\infty$

5.1.7.3 FSR_trap_enable_mask (TEM)

Bits 27 through 23 are enable bits for each of the five IEEE-754 floating-point exceptions that can be indicated in the current_exception field (*cexc*). See figure 12 on page 48. If a floating-point operate instruction generates one or more exceptions and the TEM bit corresponding to any of the exceptions is 1, an *fp_exception_ieee_754* trap is caused. A TEM bit value of 0 prevents the corresponding exception type from generating a trap.

5.1.7.4 FSR_nonstandard_fp (NS)

IMPL. DEP. #18: When set to 1, bit 22 causes the FPU to produce implementation-defined results that may not correspond to IEEE Std 754-1985.

For instance, to obtain higher performance, implementations may convert a subnormal floating-point operand or result to zero when FSR.NS is set. SPARC-V9 implementations are permitted but not encouraged to deviate from IEEE 754 requirements when the nonstandard mode bit of the FSR is 1. For implementations in which no nonstandard floating-point mode exists, the NS bit of the FSR should always read as 0, and writes to it should be ignored.

See *Implementation Characteristics of Current SPARC-V9-based Products, Revision 9.x*, a document available from SPARC International, for a description of how this field is used in existing implementations.

5.1.7.5 FSR_version (*ver*)

IMPL. DEP. #19: Bits 19 through 17 identify one or more particular implementations of the FPU architecture.

For each SPARC-V9 IU implementation (as identified by its VER.*impl* field), there may be one or more FPU implementations, or none. This field identifies the particular FPU implementation present. Version number 7 is reserved to indicate that no hardware floating-point controller is present. See *Implementation Characteristics of Current SPARC-V9-based Products, Revision 9.x*, a document available from SPARC International, for a description of the values of this field in existing implementations.

The *ver* field is read-only; it cannot be modified by the LDFSR and LDXFSR instructions.

5.1.7.6 FSR_floating-point_trap_type (*ftt*)

Several conditions can cause a floating-point exception trap. When a floating-point exception trap occurs, *ftt* (bits 16 through 14 of the FSR) identifies the cause of the exception, the "floating-point trap type." After a floating-point exception occurs, the *ftt* field encodes the type of the floating-point exception until an STFSR or an FPop is executed.

The *ftt* field can be read by the STFSR and STXFSR instructions. The LDFSR and LDXFSR instructions do not affect *ftt*.

Privileged software that handles floating-point traps must execute an STFSR (or STXFSR) to determine the floating-point trap type. STFSR and STXFSR shall zero *ftt* after the store completes without error. If the store generates an error and does not complete, *ftt* shall remain unchanged.

Programming Note:
> Neither LDFSR nor LDXFSR can be used for this purpose, since both leave *ftt* unchanged. However, executing a nontrapping FPop such as "fmovs %f0,%f0" prior to returning to nonprivileged mode will zero *ftt*. The *ftt* remains valid until the next FPop instruction completes execution.

The *ftt* field encodes the floating-point trap type according to table 10. Note that the value "7" is reserved for future expansion.

Table 10—Floating-Point Trap Type (*ftt*) Field of FSR

ftt	Trap type
0	None
1	*IEEE_754_exception*
2	*unfinished_FPop*
3	*unimplemented_FPop*
4	*sequence_error*
5	*hardware_error*
6	*invalid_fp_register*
7	—

The *sequence_error* and *hardware_error* trap types are unlikely to arise in the normal course of computation. They are essentially unrecoverable from the point of view of user applications. In contrast, *IEEE_754_exception*, *unfinished_FPop*, and *unimplemented_FPop* will likely arise occasionally in the normal course of computation and must be recoverable by system software.

When a floating-point trap occurs, the following results are observed by user software:

(1) The value of *aexc* is unchanged.

(2) The value of *cexc* is unchanged, except that for an *IEEE_754_exception* a bit corresponding to the trapping exception is set. The *unfinished_FPop*, *unimplemented_FPop*, *sequence_error*, and *invalid_fp_register* floating-point exceptions do not affect *cexc*.

(3) The source registers are unchanged (usually implemented by leaving the destination registers unchanged).

(4) The value of *fccn* is unchanged.

The foregoing describes the result seen by a user trap handler if an IEEE exception is signalled, either immediately from an *IEEE_754_exception* or after recovery from an *unfinished_FPop* or *unimplemented_FPop*. In either case, *cexc* as seen by the trap handler reflects the exception causing the trap.

In the cases of *unfinished_FPop* and *unimplemented_FPop* exceptions that do not subsequently generate IEEE traps, the recovery software should define *cexc*, *aexc*, and the destination registers or *fccs*, as appropriate.

5.1.7.6.1 *ftt* = IEEE_754_exception

The *IEEE_754_exception* floating-point trap type indicates that a floating-point exception conforming to IEEE Std 754-1985 has occurred. The exception type is encoded in the *cexc* field. Note that *aexc*, the *fccs*, and the destination *f* register are not affected by an *IEEE_754_exception* trap.

5.1.7.6.2 *ftt* = unfinished_FPop

The *unfinished_FPop* floating-point trap type indicates that an implementation's FPU was unable to generate correct results, or that exceptions as defined by IEEE Std 754-1985 have occurred. In the latter case, the *cexc* field is unchanged.

5.1.7.6.3 *ftt* = unimplemented_FPop

The *unimplemented_FPop* floating-point trap type indicates that an implementation's FPU decoded an FPop that it does not implement. In this case, the *cexc* field is unchanged.

Programming Note:

> For the *unfinished_FPop* and *unimplemented_FPop* floating-point traps, software should emulate or reexecute the exception-causing instruction and update the FSR, destination *f* register(s), and *fccs*.

5.1.7.6.4 *ftt* = sequence_error

The *sequence_error* floating-point trap type indicates one of three abnormal error conditions in the FPU, all caused by erroneous supervisor software:

— An attempt was made to read the floating-point deferred-trap queue (FQ) on an implementation without an FQ.

Implementation Note:
> **IMPL. DEP #25:** On implementations without a floating-point queue, an attempt to read the fq with an RDPR instruction shall cause either an *illegal_instruction* exception or an *fp_exception_other* exception with FSR.*ftt* set to 4 (*sequence_error*).

— An attempt was made to execute a floating-point instruction when the FPU was unable to accept one. This type of *sequence_error* arises from a logic error in supervisor software that has caused a previous floating-point trap to be incompletely serviced (for example, the floating-point queue was not emptied after a previous floating-point exception).

— An attempt was made to read the floating-point deferred-trap queue (FQ) with a RDPR instruction when the FQ was empty; that is, when FSR.*qne* = 0. Note that generation of *sequence_error* is recommended but not required in this case.

Programming Note:
> If a *sequence_error* floating-point exception occurs while executing user code due to any of the above conditions, it may not be possible to recover sufficient state to continue execution of the user application.

5.1.7.6.5 *ftt* = hardware_error

The *hardware_error* floating-point trap type indicates that the FPU detected a catastrophic internal error, such as an illegal state or a parity error on an *f* register access.

Programming Note:
> If a *hardware_error* occurs while executing user code, it may not be possible to recover sufficient state to continue execution of the user application.

5.1.7.6.6 *ftt* = invalid_fp_register

The *invalid_fp_register* trap indicates that one (or more) operands of an FPop are misaligned; that is, a quad-precision register number is not 0 **mod** 4. An implementation shall generate an *fp_exception_other* trap with FSR.*ftt* = *invalid_fp_register* in this case.

5.1.7.7 FSR_FQ_not_empty (*qne*)

Bit 13 indicates whether the optional floating-point deferred-trap queue (FQ) is empty after a deferred floating-point exception trap or after a read privileged register (RDPR) instruction that reads the queue has been executed. If *qne* = 0, the queue is empty; if *qne* = 1, the queue is not empty.

The *qne* bit can be read by the STFSR and STXFSR instructions. The LDFSR and LDXFSR instructions do not affect *qne*. However, executing successive "RDPR %fpq" instructions will (eventually) cause the FQ to become empty (*qne* = 0). If an implementation does not provide an FQ, this bit shall read as zero. Supervisor software must arrange for this bit to always read as zero to user-mode software.

5.1.7.8 FSR_accrued_exception (*aexc*)

Bits 9 through 5 accumulate IEEE_754 floating-point exceptions while floating-point exception traps are disabled using the TEM field. See figure 13 on page 49. After an FPop completes, the TEM and *cexc* fields are logically ANDed together. If the result is nonzero, *aexc* is left unchanged and an *fp_exception_ieee_754* trap is generated; otherwise, the new *cexc* field is ORed into the *aexc* field and no trap is generated. Thus, while (and only while) traps are masked, exceptions are accumulated in the *aexc* field.

5.1.7.9 FSR_current_exception (*cexc*)

Bits 4 through 0 indicate that one or more IEEE_754 floating-point exceptions were generated by the most recently executed FPop instruction. The absence of an exception causes the corresponding bit to be cleared. See figure 14 on page 49.

The *cexc* bits are set as described in 5.1.7.10, "Floating-Point Exception Fields," by the execution of an FPop that either does not cause a trap or causes an *fp_exception_ieee_754* trap with FSR.*ftt* = *IEEE_754_exception*. An *IEEE_754_exception* that traps shall cause exactly one bit in FSR.*cexc* to be set, corresponding to the detected IEEE Std 754-1985 exception.

In the case of an overflow (underflow) *IEEE_754_exception* that does **not** trap (because neither OFM (UFM) nor NXM is set), more than one bit in *cexc* is set: such an overflow (underflow) sets both *ofc* (*ufc*) and *nxc*. An overflow (underflow) *IEEE_754_exception* that **does** trap (because OFM (UFM) or NXM or both are set) shall set *ofc* (*ufc*), but not *nxc*.

If the execution of an FPop causes a trap other than an *fp_exception_ieee_754* due to an IEEE Std 754-1985 exception, FSR.*cexc* is left unchanged.

5.1.7.10 Floating-Point Exception Fields

The current and accrued exception fields and the trap enable mask assume the following definitions of the floating-point exception conditions (per IEEE Std 754-1985):

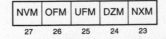

Figure 12—Trap Enable Mask (TEM) Fields of FSR

Figure 13—Accrued Exception Bits (*aexc*) Fields of FSR

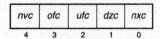

Figure 14—Current Exception Bits (*cexc*) Fields of FSR

5.1.7.10.1 FSR_invalid (*nvc, nva*)

An operand is improper for the operation to be performed. For example, $0.0 \div 0.0$ and $\infty - \infty$ are invalid. 1 = invalid operand(s), 0 = valid operand(s).

5.1.7.10.2 FSR_overflow (*ofc, ofa*)

The result, rounded as if the exponent range were unbounded, would be larger in magnitude than the destination format's largest finite number. 1 = overflow, 0 = no overflow.

5.1.7.10.3 FSR_underflow (*ufc, ufa*)

The rounded result is inexact and would be smaller in magnitude than the smallest normalized number in the indicated format. 1 = underflow, 0 = no underflow.

Underflow is never indicated when the correct unrounded result is zero. Otherwise:

If UFM = 0:   Underflow occurs if a nonzero result is tiny and a loss of accuracy occurs. Tininess may be detected before or after rounding (impl. dep. #55). Loss of accuracy may be either a denormalization loss or an inexact result.

If UFM = 1:   Underflow occurs if a nonzero result is tiny. Tininess may be detected before or after rounding (impl. dep. #55).

5.1.7.10.4 FSR_division-by-zero (*dzc, dza*)

$X \div 0.0$, where X is subnormal or normalized. Note that $0.0 \div 0.0$ does **not** set the *dzc* or *dza* bits. 1 = division by zero, 0 = no division by zero.

5.1.7.10.5 FSR_inexact (*nxc, nxa*)

The rounded result of an operation differs from the infinitely precise unrounded result. 1 = inexact result, 0 = exact result.

5.1.7.11 FSR Conformance

IMPL. DEP. #22: An implementation may choose to implement the TEM, *cexc*, and *aexc* fields in hardware in either of two ways (both of which comply with IEEE Std 754-1985):

(1) Implement all three fields conformant to IEEE Std 754-1985.

(2) Implement the NXM, *nxa*, and *nxc* bits of these fields conformant to IEEE Std 754-1985. Implement each of the remaining bits in the three fields either

   (a) Conformant to IEEE Std 754-1985, or

   (b) As a state bit that may be set by software that calculates the IEEE Std 754-1985 value of the bit. For any bit implemented as a state bit:

      [1] The IEEE exception corresponding to the state bit must **always** cause an exception (specifically, an *unfinished_FPop* exception). During exception processing in the trap handler, the bit in the state field can be written to the appropriate value by an LDFSR or LDXFSR instruction.

      [2] The state bit must be implemented in such a way that if it is written to a particular value by an LDFSR or LDXFSR instruction, it will be read back as the same value by a subsequent STFSR or STXFSR.

Programming Note:
> Software must be capable of simulating the operation of the FPU in order to handle the *unimplemented_FPop*, *unfinished_FPop*, and *IEEE_754_exception* floating-point trap types properly. Thus, a user application program always sees an FSR that is fully compliant with IEEE Std 754-1985.

5.1.8 Address Space Identifier Register (ASI)

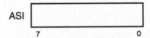

Figure 15—ASI Register

The ASI register specifies the address space identifier to be used for load and store alternate instructions that use the "*rs1 + simm13*" addressing form. Nonprivileged (user-mode) software may write any value into the ASI register; however, values with bit 7 = 0 indicate restricted ASIs. When a nonprivileged instruction makes an access that uses an ASI with bit 7 = 0, a *privileged_action* exception is generated. See 6.3.1.3, "Address Space Identifiers (ASIs)," for details.

5.1.9 TICK Register (TICK)

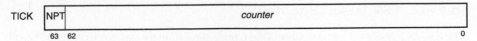

Figure 16—TICK Register

The *counter* field of the TICK register is a 63-bit counter that counts CPU clock cycles. Bit 63 of the TICK register is the Nonprivileged Trap (NPT) bit, which controls access to the TICK register by nonprivileged software. Privileged software can always read the TICK register with either the RDPR or RDTICK instruction. Privileged software can always write the TICK register with the WRPR instruction; there is no WRTICK instruction.

Nonprivileged software can read the TICK register using the RDTICK instruction; TICK.-NPT must be 0. When TICK.NPT = 1, an attempt by nonprivileged software to read the TICK register causes a *privileged_action* exception. Nonprivileged software cannot write the TICK register.

TICK.NPT is set to 1 by a power-on reset trap. The value of TICK.*counter* is undefined after a power-on reset trap.

After the TICK register is written, reading the TICK register returns a value incremented (by one or more) from the last value written, rather than from some previous value of the counter. The number of counts between a write and a subsequent read need not accurately reflect the number of processor cycles between the write and the read. Software may only rely on read-to-read counts of the TICK register for accurate timing, not on write-to-read counts.

IMPL. DEP. #105: The difference between the values read from the TICK register on two reads should reflect the number of processor cycles executed between the reads. If an accurate count cannot always be returned, any inaccuracy should be small, bounded, and documented. An implementation may implement fewer than 63 bits in TICK.*counter*; however, the counter as implemented must be able to count for at least 10 years without overflowing. Any upper bits not implemented must read as zero.

Programming Note:
> TICK.NPT may be used by a secure operating system to control access by user software to high-accuracy timing information. The operation of the timer might be emulated by the trap handler, which could read TICK.*counter* and "fuzz" the value to lower accuracy.

5.2 Privileged Registers

The registers described in this subsection are visible only to software running in privileged mode; that is, when PSTATE.PRIV = 1. Privileged registers are written using the WRPR instruction and read using the RDPR instruction.

5.2.1 Processor State Register (PSTATE)

Figure 17—PSTATE Fields

The PSTATE register holds the current state of the processor. There is only one instance of the PSTATE register. See Chapter 7, "Traps," for more details.

Writing PSTATE is nondelayed; that is, new machine state written to PSTATE is visible to the next instruction executed. The privileged RDPR and WRPR instructions are used to read and write PSTATE, respectively.

Implementation Note:

> To ensure the nondelayed semantics, a write to PSTATE may take multiple cycles to complete on some implementations.

5.2.1.1 through 5.2.1.9 describe the fields contained in the PSTATE register.

5.2.1.1 PSTATE_current_little_endian (CLE)

When PSTATE.CLE = 1, all data reads and writes using an implicit ASI are performed in little-endian byte order with an ASI of ASI_PRIMARY_LITTLE. When PSTATE.CLE = 0, all data reads and writes using an implicit ASI are performed in big-endian byte order with an ASI of ASI_PRIMARY. Instruction accesses are always big-endian.

5.2.1.2 PSTATE_trap_little_endian (TLE)

When a trap is taken, the current PSTATE register is pushed onto the trap stack and the PSTATE.TLE bit is copied into PSTATE.CLE in the new PSTATE register. This allows system software to have a different implicit byte ordering than the current process. Thus, if PSTATE.TLE is set to 1, data accesses using an implicit ASI in the trap handler are little-endian. The original state of PSTATE.CLE is restored when the original PSTATE register is restored from the trap stack.

5.2.1.3 PSTATE_mem_model (MM)

This 2-bit field determines the memory model in use by the processor. Its values are:

Value	Memory model
00	Total Store Order (TSO)
01	Partial Store Order (PSO)
10	Relaxed Memory Order (RMO)
11	—

An implementation must provide a memory model that allows programs conforming to the TSO model to run correctly; that is, TSO or a stronger model. Whether the Partial Store Order (PSO) model or the Relaxed Memory Ordering (RMO) model is supported is implementation-dependent (impl. dep. #113).

The current memory model is determined by the value of PSTATE.MM. The effect of setting PSTATE.MM to an unsupported value is implementation-dependent (impl. dep. #119).

5.2.1.4 PSTATE_RED_state (RED)

When PSTATE.RED is set to 1, the processor is operating in RED (Reset, Error, and Debug) state. See 7.2.1, "RED_state." The IU sets PSTATE.RED when any hardware reset occurs. It also sets PSTATE.RED when a trap is taken while TL = (MAXTL − 1). Software can exit RED_state by one of two methods:

(1) Execute a DONE or RETRY instruction, which restores the stacked copy of PSTATE and clears PSTATE.RED if it was 0 in the stacked copy.

(2) Write a 0 to PSTATE.RED with a WRPR instruction.

Programming Note:

> Changing PSTATE.RED may cause a change in address mapping on some systems. It is recommended that writes of PSTATE.RED be placed in the delay slot of a JMPL; the target of this JMPL should be in the new address mapping. The JMPL sets the nPC, which becomes the PC for the instruction that folows the WPR in its delay slot. The effect of the WPR instruction is immediate.

5.2.1.5 PSTATE_enable_floating-point (PEF)

When set to 1, this bit enables the floating-point unit, which allows privileged software to manage the FPU. For the floating-point unit to be usable, both PSTATE.PEF and FPRS.-FEF must be set. Otherwise, a floating-point instruction that tries to reference the FPU will cause an *fp_disabled* trap.

5.2.1.6 PSTATE_address_mask (AM)

When PSTATE.AM = 1, both instruction and data addresses are interpreted as if the high-order 32 bits were masked to zero before being presented to the MMU or memory system. Thirty-two-bit application software must run with this bit set.

Branch target addresses (sent to the nPC) and addresses sent to registers by CALL, JMPL, and RDPC instructions are always 64-bit values, but the value of the high-order 32-bits are implementation-dependent. Similarly, the value of the high-order 32-bits of TPC and TNPC after a trap taken while PSTATE.AM = 1 is implementation-dependent.

IMPL. DEP. #125: When PSTATE.AM = 1, the value of the high-order 32-bits of the PC transmitted to the specified destination register(s) by CALL, JMLP, RDPC, and on a trap is implementation-dependent.

5.2.1.7 PSTATE_privileged_mode (PRIV)

When PSTATE.PRIV = 1, the processor is in privileged mode.

5.2.1.8 PSTATE_interrupt_enable (IE)

When PSTATE.IE = 1, the processor can accept interrupts.

5.2.1.9 PSTATE_alternate_globals (AG)

When PSTATE.AG = 0, the processor interprets integer register numbers in the range 0..7 as referring to the normal global register set. When PSTATE.AG = 1, the processor interprets integer register numbers in the range 0..7 as referring to the alternate global register set.

5.2.2 Trap Level Register (TL)

Figure 18—Trap Level Register

The trap level register specifies the current trap level. TL = 0 is the normal (nontrap) level of operation. TL > 0 implies that one or more traps are being processed. The maximum valid value that the TL register may contain is "MAXTL." This is always equal to the number of supported trap levels beyond level 0. See Chapter 7, "Traps," for more details about the TL register. An implementation shall support at least four levels of traps beyond level 0; that is, MAXTL shall be ≥ 4.

IMPL. DEP. #101: How many additional trap levels, if any, past level 4 are supported is implementation-dependent.

The remainder of this subsection assumes that there are four trap levels beyond level 0.

Programming Note:

> Writing the TL register with a `wrpr %tl` instruction does not alter any other machine state; that is, it is not equivalent to taking or returning from a trap.

5.2.3 Processor Interrupt Level (PIL)

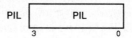

Figure 19—Processor Interrupt Level Register

The processor interrupt level (PIL) is the interrupt level above which the processor will accept an interrupt. Interrupt priorities are mapped such that interrupt level 2 has greater priority than interrupt level 1, and so on. See table 15 on page 101 for a list of exception and interrupt priorities.

Compatibility Note:

> On SPARC-V8 processors, the level 15 interrupt is considered to be nonmaskable, so it has different semantics from other interrupt levels. SPARC-V9 processors do not treat level 15 interrupts differently from other interrupt levels. See 7.6.2.4, "Externally Initiated Reset (XIR) Traps," for a facility in SPARC-V9 that is similar to a nonmaskable interrupt.

5.2.4 Trap Program Counter (TPC)

TPC$_1$	PC from trap while TL = 0	00
TPC$_2$	PC from trap while TL = 1	00
TPC$_3$	PC from trap while TL = 2	00
TPC$_4$	PC from trap while TL = 3	00

63   2 1 0

Figure 20—Trap Program Counter Register

The TPC register contains the program counter (PC) from the previous trap level. There are MAXTL instances of the TPC (impl. dep. #101), but only one is accessible at any time. The current value in the TL register determines which instance of the TPC register is accessible. An attempt to read or write the TPC register when TL = 0 shall cause an *illegal_ instruction* exception.

5.2.5 Trap Next Program Counter (TNPC)

TNPC$_1$	nPC from trap while TL = 0	00
TNPC$_2$	nPC from trap while TL = 1	00
TNPC$_3$	nPC from trap while TL = 2	00
TNPC$_4$	nPC from trap while TL = 3	00

63   2 1 0

Figure 21—Trap Next Program Counter Register

The TNPC register is the next program counter (nPC) from the previous trap level. There are MAXTL instances of the TNPC (impl. dep. #101), but only one is accessible at any time. The current value in the TL register determines which instance of the TNPC register is accessible. An attempt to read or write the TNPC register when TL = 0 shall cause an *illegal_instruction* exception.

5.2.6 Trap State (TSTATE)

	CCR	ASI		PSTATE		CWP
TSTATE$_1$	CCR from TL = 0	ASI from TL = 0	—	PSTATE from TL = 0	—	CWP from TL = 0
TSTATE$_2$	CCR from TL = 1	ASI from TL = 1	—	PSTATE from TL = 1	—	CWP from TL = 1
TSTATE$_3$	CCR from TL = 2	ASI from TL = 2	—	PSTATE from TL = 2	—	CWP from TL = 2
TSTATE$_4$	CCR from TL = 3	ASI from TL = 3	—	PSTATE from TL = 3	—	CWP from TL = 3

39   32 31   24 23   18 17   8 7   5 4   0

Figure 22—Trap State Register

TSTATE contains the state from the previous trap level, comprising the contents of the CCR, ASI, CWP, and PSTATE registers from the previous trap level. There are MAXTL instances of the TSTATE register, but only one is accessible at a time. The current value in the TL register determines which instance of TSTATE is accessible. An attempt to read or write the TSTATE register when TL = 0 causes an *illegal_instruction* exception.

5.2.7 Trap Type Register (TT)

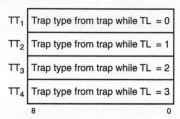

Figure 23—Trap Type Register

The TT register normally contains the trap type of the trap that caused entry to the current trap level. On a reset trap the TT field contains the trap type of the reset (see 7.2.1.1, "RED_state Trap Table"), except when a watchdog (WDR) or externally initiated (XIR) reset occurs while the processor is in error_state. When this occurs, the TT register will contain the trap type of the exception that caused entry into error_state.

There are MAXTL instances of the TT register (impl. dep. #101), but only one is accessible at a time. The current value in the TL register determines which instance of the TT register is accessible. An attempt to read or write the TT register when TL = 0 shall cause an *illegal_instruction* exception.

5.2.8 Trap Base Address (TBA)

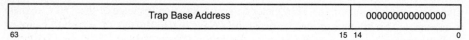

Figure 24—Trap Base Address Register

The TBA register provides the upper 49 bits of the address used to select the trap vector for a trap. The lower 15 bits of the TBA always read as zero, and writes to them are ignored.

The full address for a trap vector is specified by the TBA, TL, TT[TL], and five zeroes:

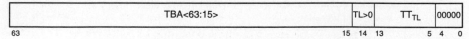

Figure 25—Trap Vector Address

Note that the "(TL>0)" bit is 0 if TL = 0 when the trap was taken, and 1 if TL > 0 when the trap was taken. This implies that there are two trap tables: one for traps from TL = 0 and one for traps from TL > 0. See Chapter 7, "Traps," for more details on trap vectors.

5.2.9 Version Register (VER)

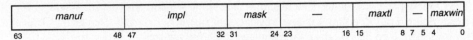

manuf	impl	mask	—	maxtl	—	maxwin

63   48 47   32 31   24 23   16 15   8 7 5 4   0

Figure 26—Version Register

The version register specifies the fixed parameters pertaining to a particular CPU implementation and mask set. The VER register is read-only.

IMPL. DEP. #104: VER.*manuf* contains a 16-bit manufacturer code. This field is optional and, if not present, shall read as 0. VER.manuf may indicate the original supplier of a second-sourced chip. It is intended that the contents of VER.*manuf* track the JEDEC semiconductor manufacturer code as closely as possible. If the manufacturer does not have a JEDEC semiconductor manufacturer code, SPARC International will assign a value for VER.*manuf*.

IMPL. DEP. #13: VER.*impl* uniquely identifies an implementation or class of software-compatible implementations of the architecture. Values $FFF0_{16}..FFFF_{16}$ are reserved and are not available for assignment.

The value of VER.*impl* is assigned as described in C.3, "Implementation Dependency Categories."

VER.*mask* specifies the current mask set revision, and is chosen by the implementor. It generally increases numerically with successive releases of the processor, but does not necessarily increase by one for consecutive releases.

VER.*maxtl* contains the maximum number of trap levels supported by an implementation (impl. dep. #101), that is, MAXTL, the maximum value of the contents of the TL register.

VER.*maxwin* contains the maximum index number available for use as a valid CWP value in an implementation; that is, VER.*maxwin* contains the value "NWINDOWS – 1" (impl. dep. #2).

5.2.10 Register-Window State Registers

The state of the register windows is determined by a set of privileged registers. They can be read/written by privileged software using the RDPR/WRPR instructions. In addition, these registers are modified by instructions related to register windows and are used to generate traps that allow supervisor software to spill, fill, and clean register windows.

The details of how the window-management registers are used by hardware are presented in 6.3.6, "Register Window Management Instructions."

5.2.10.1 Current Window Pointer (CWP)

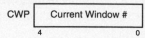

Figure 27—Current Window Pointer Register

The CWP register is a counter that identifies the current window into the set of integer registers. See 6.3.6, "Register Window Management Instructions," and Chapter 7, "Traps," for information on how hardware manipulates the CWP register.

Compatibility Note:

> The following differences between SPARC-V8 and SPARC-V9 are not visible to nonprivileged software:
>
> 1) In SPARC-V9, SAVE increments CWP and RESTORE decrements CWP. In SPARC-V8, the opposite is true: SAVE decrements PSR.CWP and RESTORE increments PSR.CWP.
>
> 2) PSR.CWP in SPARC-V8 is changed on each trap. In SPARC-V9, CWP is affected only by a trap caused by a window fill or spill exception.
>
> 3) In SPARC-V8, writing a value into PSR.CWP that is greater than the number of implemented windows causes an *illegal_instruction* exception. This is not true for CWP in SPARC-V9.

5.2.10.2 Savable Windows (CANSAVE) Register

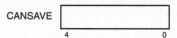

Figure 28—CANSAVE Register

The CANSAVE register contains the number of register windows following CWP that are not in use and are, hence, available to be allocated by a SAVE instruction without generating a window spill exception.

5.2.10.3 Restorable Windows (CANRESTORE) Register

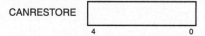

Figure 29—CANRESTORE Register

The CANRESTORE register contains the number of register windows preceding CWP that are in use by the current program and can be restored (via the RESTORE instruction) without generating a window fill exception.

5.2.10.4 Other Windows (OTHERWIN) Register

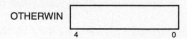

Figure 30—OTHERWIN Register

The OTHERWIN register contains the count of register windows that will be spilled/filled using a separate set of trap vectors based on the contents of WSTATE_OTHER. If OTHERWIN is zero, register windows are spilled/filled using trap vectors based on the contents of WSTATE_NORMAL.

The OTHERWIN register can be used to split the register windows among different address spaces and handle spill/fill traps efficiently by using separate spill/fill vectors.

5.2.10.5 Window State (WSTATE) Register

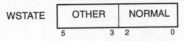

Figure 31—WSTATE Register

The WSTATE register specifies bits that are inserted into $TT_{TL}<4:2>$ on traps caused by window spill and fill exceptions. These bits are used to select one of eight different window spill and fill handlers. If OTHERWIN = 0 at the time a trap is taken due to a window spill or window fill exception, then the WSTATE.NORMAL bits are inserted into TT[TL]. Otherwise, the WSTATE.OTHER bits are inserted into TT[TL]. See 6.4, "Register Window Management," for details of the semantics of OTHERWIN.

5.2.10.6 Clean Windows (CLEANWIN) Register

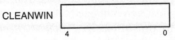

Figure 32—CLEANWIN Register

The CLEANWIN register contains the number of windows that can be used by the SAVE instruction without causing a *clean_window* exception.

The CLEANWIN register counts the number of register windows that are "clean" with respect to the current program; that is, register windows that contain only zeros, valid addresses, or valid data from that program. Registers in these windows need not be cleaned before they can be used. The count includes the register windows that can be restored (the value in the CANRESTORE register) and the register windows following CWP that can be used without cleaning. When a clean window is requested (via a SAVE instruction) and none is available, a *clean_window* exception occurs to cause the next window to be cleaned.

5.2.11 Ancillary State Registers (ASRs)

SPARC-V9 provides for up to 25 ancillary state registers (ASRs), numbered from 7 through 31.

ASRs numbered 7..15 are reserved for future use by the architecture and should not be referenced by software.

ASRs numbered 16..31 are available for implementation-dependent uses (impl. dep. #8), such as timers, counters, diagnostic registers, self-test registers, and trap-control registers. An IU may choose to implement from zero to sixteen of these ASRs. The semantics of accessing any of these ASRs is implementation-dependent. Whether access to a particular ancillary state register is privileged is implementation-dependent (impl. dep. #9).

An ASR is read and written with the RDASR and WRASR instructions, respectively. An RDASR or WRASR instruction is privileged if the accessed register is privileged.

5.2.12   Floating-Point Deferred-Trap Queue (FQ)

If present in an implementation, the FQ contains sufficient state information to implement resumable, deferred floating-point traps.

IMPL. DEP. #23: Floating-point traps may be precise or deferred. If deferred, a floating-point deferred-trap queue (FQ) shall be present.

The FQ can be read with the read privileged register (RDPR) floating-point queue instruction. In a given implementation, it may also be readable or writable via privileged load/store double alternate instructions (LDDA, STDA), or by read/write ancillary state register instructions (RDASR, WRASR).

IMPL. DEP. #24: The presence, contents of, and operations upon the FQ are implementation-dependent.

If an FQ is present, however, supervisor software must be able to deduce the exception-causing instruction's opcode (*opf*), operands, and address from its FQ entry. This also must be true of any other pending floating-point operations in the queue. See *Implementation Characteristics of Current SPARC-V9-based Products, Revision 9.x*, a document available from SPARC International, for a discussion of the formats and operation of implemented floating-point queues in existing SPARC-V9 implementations.

In implementations with a floating-point queue, an attempt to read the FQ with a RDPR instruction when the FQ is empty (FSR.*qne* = 0) shall cause an *fp_exception_other* trap with FSR.*ftt* set to 4 (*sequence_error*).In implementations without an FQ, the *qne* bit in the FSR is always 0.

IMPL. DEP. #25: In implementations without a floating-point queue, an attempt to read the FQ with an RDPR instruction shall cause either an *illegal_instruction* trap or an *fp_exception_other* trap with FSR.*ftt* SET TO 4 (*sequence_error*).

5.2.13   IU Deferred-Trap Queue

An implementation may contain zero or more IU deferred-trap queues. Such a queue contains sufficient state to implement resumable deferred traps caused by the IU. See 7.3.2, "Deferred Traps," for more information. Note that deferred floating-point traps are handled by the floating-point deferred-trap queue. See *Implementation Characteristics of Current SPARC-V9-based Products, Revision 9.x*, a document available from SPARC International, for a discussion of such queues in existing implementations.

IMPL. DEP. #16: The existence, contents, and operation of an IU deferred-trap queue are implementation-dependent; it is not visible to user application programs under normal conditions.

6   Instructions

Instructions are accessed by the processor from memory and are executed, annulled, or trapped. Instructions are encoded in four major formats and partitioned into eleven general categories.

6.1   Instruction Execution

The instruction at the memory location specified by the program counter is fetched and then executed. Instruction execution may change program-visible processor and/or memory state. As a side-effect of its execution, new values are assigned to the program counter (PC) and the next program counter (nPC).

An instruction may generate an exception if it encounters some condition that makes it impossible to complete normal execution. Such an exception may in turn generate a precise trap. Other events may also cause traps: an exception caused by a previous instruction (a deferred trap), an interrupt or asynchronous error (a disrupting trap), or a reset request (a reset trap). If a trap occurs, control is vectored into a trap table. See Chapter 7, "Traps," for a detailed description of exception and trap processing.

If a trap does not occur and the instruction is not a control transfer, the next program counter (nPC) is copied into the PC and the nPC is incremented by 4 (ignoring overflow, if any). If the instruction is a control-transfer instruction, the next program counter (nPC) is copied into the PC and the target address is written to nPC. Thus, the two program counters provide for a delayed-branch execution model.

For each instruction access and each normal data access, the IU appends an 8-bit address space identifier, or ASI, to the 64-bit memory address. Load/store alternate instructions (see 6.3.1.3, "Address Space Identifiers (ASIs),") can provide an arbitrary ASI with their data addresses, or use the ASI value currently contained in the ASI register.

Implementation Note:

> The time required to execute an instruction is implementation-dependent, as is the degree of execution concurrency. In the absence of traps, an implementation should cause the same program-visible register and memory state changes as if a program had executed according to the sequential model implied in this document. See Chapter 7, "Traps," for a definition of architectural compliance in the presence of traps.

6.2   Instruction Formats

Instructions are encoded in four major 32-bit formats and several minor formats, as shown in figures 33 and 34.

Format 1 (*op* = 1): CALL

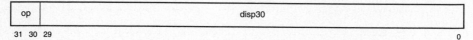

Format 2 (*op* = 0): SETHI & Branches (Bicc, BPcc, BPr, FBfcc, FBPfcc)

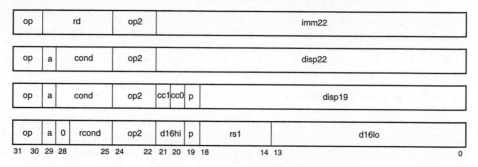

Format 3 (*op* = 2 or 3): Arithmetic, Logical, MOVr, MEMBAR, Load, and Store

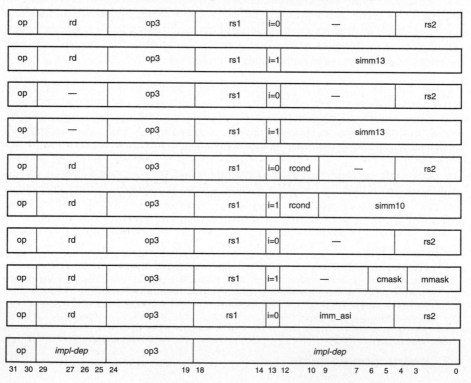

Figure 33—Summary of Instruction Formats: Formats 1, 2, and 3

Format 3 (op = 2 or 3): *Continued*

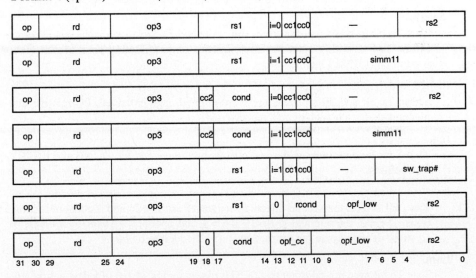

Format 4 (op = 2): MOVcc, FMOVr, FMOVcc, and Tcc

Figure 34—Summary of Instruction Formats: Formats 3 and 4

6.2.1 Instruction Fields

The instruction fields are interpreted as follows:

a:

> The *a* bit annuls the execution of the following instruction if the branch is conditional and untaken, or if it is unconditional and taken.

cc0, cc1, and cc2:

> *cc2*:*cc1*:*cc0* specify the condition codes (*icc*, *xcc*, *fcc0*, *fcc1*, *fcc2*, *fcc3*) to be used in the instruction. Individual bits of the same logical field are present in several other instructions: Branch on Floating-Point Condition Codes with Prediction Instructions (FBPfcc), Branch on Integer Condition Codes with Prediction (BPcc), Floating-Point Compare Instructions, Move Integer Register if Condition is Satisfied (MOVcc), Move Floating-Point Register if Condition is Satisfied (FMOVcc), and Trap on Integer Condition Codes (Tcc). In instructions such as Tcc that do not contain the *cc2* bit, the missing *cc2* bit takes on a default value. See table 38 on page 273 for a description of these fields' values.

cmask:

> This 3-bit field specifies sequencing constraints on the order of memory references and the processing of instructions before and after a MEMBAR instruction.

cond:

> This 4-bit field selects the condition tested by a branch instruction. See Appendix E, "Opcode Maps," for descriptions of its values.

d16hi and d16lo:

> These 2-bit and 14-bit fields together comprise a word-aligned, sign-extended, PC-relative displacement for a branch-on-register-contents with prediction (BPr) instruction.

disp19:

> This 19-bit field is a word-aligned, sign-extended, PC-relative displacement for an integer branch-with-prediction (BPcc) instruction or a floating-point branch-with-prediction (FBPfcc) instruction.

disp22 and disp30:

> These 22-bit and 30-bit fields are word-aligned, sign-extended, PC-relative displacements for a branch or call, respectively.

fcn:

> This 5-bit field provides additional opcode bits to encode the DONE and RETRY instructions.

i:

> The *i* bit selects the second operand for integer arithmetic and load/store instructions. If $i = 0$, the operand is r[rs2]. If $i = 1$, the operand is *simm10*, *simm11*, or *simm13*, depending on the instruction, sign-extended to 64 bits.

imm22:

> This 22-bit field is a constant that SETHI places in bits 31..10 of a destination register.

imm_asi:
This 8-bit field is the address space identifier in instructions that access alternate space.

impl-dep:
The meaning of these fields is completely implementation-dependent for IMP-DEP1 and IMPDEP2 instructions.

mmask:
This 4-bit field imposes order constraints on memory references appearing before and after a MEMBAR instruction.

op and op2:
These 2- and 3-bit fields encode the three major formats and the Format 2 instructions. See Appendix E, "Opcode Maps," for descriptions of their values.

op3:
This 6-bit field (together with one bit from *op*) encodes the Format 3 instructions. See Appendix E, "Opcode Maps," for descriptions of its values.

opf:
This 9-bit field encodes the operation for a floating-point operate (FPop) instruction. See Appendix E, "Opcode Maps," for possible values and their meanings.

opf_cc:
Specifies the condition codes to be used in FMOVcc instructions. See **cc0, cc1, and cc2** above for details.

opf_low:
This 6-bit field encodes the specific operation for a Move Floating-Point Register if Condition is satisfied (FMOVcc) or Move Floating-Point register if contents of integer register match condition (FMOVr) instruction.

p:
This 1-bit field encodes static prediction for BPcc and FBPfcc instructions, as follows:

p	Branch prediction
0	Predict branch will not be taken
1	Predict branch will be taken

rcond:
This 3-bit field selects the register-contents condition to test for a move based on register contents (MOVr or FMOVr) instruction or a branch on register contents with prediction (BPr) instruction. See Appendix E, "Opcode Maps," for descriptions of its values.

rd:
This 5-bit field is the address of the destination (or source) *r* or *f* register(s) for a load, arithmetic, or store instruction.

rs1:
This 5-bit field is the address of the first *r* or *f* register(s) source operand.

rs2:
> This 5-bit field is the address of the second *r* or *f* register(s) source operand with $i = 0$.

shcnt32:
> This 5-bit field provides the shift count for 32-bit shift instructions.

shcnt64:
> This 6-bit field provides the shift count for 64-bit shift instructions.

simm10:
> This 10-bit field is an immediate value that is sign-extended to 64 bits and used as the second ALU operand for a MOVr instruction when $i = 1$.

simm11:
> This 11-bit field is an immediate value that is sign-extended to 64 bits and used as the second ALU operand for a MOVcc instruction when $i = 1$.

simm13:
> This 13-bit field is an immediate value that is sign-extended to 64 bits and used as the second ALU operand for an integer arithmetic instruction or for a load/store instruction when $i = 1$.

sw_trap#:
> This 7-bit field is an immediate value that is used as the second ALU operand for a Trap on Condition Code instruction.

x:
> The *x* bit selects whether a 32- or 64-bit shift will be performed..

6.3 Instruction Categories

SPARC-V9 instructions can be grouped into the following categories:

— Memory access

— Memory synchronization

— Integer arithmetic

— Control transfer (CTI)

— Conditional moves

— Register window management

— State register access

— Privileged register access

— Floating-point operate

— Implementation-dependent

— Reserved

Each of these categories is further described in the following subsections.

6.3.1 Memory Access Instructions

Load, Store, Prefetch, Load Store Unsigned Byte, Swap, and Compare and Swap are the only instructions that access memory. All of the instructions except Compare and Swap use either two *r* registers or an *r* register and *simm13* to calculate a 64-bit byte memory address. Compare and Swap uses a single *r* register to specify a 64-bit byte memory address. To this 64-bit address, the IU appends an ASI that encodes address space information.

The destination field of a memory reference instruction specifies the *r* or *f* register(s) that supply the data for a store or receive the data from a load or LDSTUB. For SWAP, the destination register identifies the *r* register to be exchanged atomically with the calculated memory location. For Compare and Swap, an *r* register is specified whose value is compared with the value in memory at the computed address. If the values are equal, the destination field specifies the *r* register that is to be exchanged atomically with the addressed memory location. If the values are unequal, the destination field specifies the *r* register that is to receive the value at the addressed memory location; in this case, the addressed memory location remains unchanged.

The destination field of a PREFETCH instruction is used to encode the type of the prefetch.

Integer load and store instructions support byte (8-bit), halfword (16-bit), word (32-bit), and doubleword (64-bit) accesses. Floating-point load and store instructions support word, doubleword, and quadword memory accesses. LDSTUB accesses bytes, SWAP accesses words, and CAS accesses words or doublewords. PREFETCH accesses at least 64 bytes.

Programming Note:
> By setting $i = 1$ and *rs1* $= 0$, any location in the lowest or highest 4K bytes of an address space can be accessed without using a register to hold part of the address.

6.3.1.1 Memory Alignment Restrictions

Halfword accesses shall be **aligned** on 2-byte boundaries, word accesses (which include instruction fetches) shall be aligned on 4-byte boundaries, extended word and doubleword accesses shall be aligned on 8-byte boundaries, and quadword accesses shall be aligned on 16-byte boundaries, with the following exceptions.

An improperly aligned address in a load, store, or load-store instruction causes a *mem_ address_not_aligned* exception to occur, except:

— An LDDF or LDDFA instruction accessing an address that is word-aligned but not doubleword-aligned may cause an *LDDF_mem_address_not_aligned* exception, or may complete the operation in hardware (impl. dep. #109).

— An STDF or STDFA instruction accessing an address that is word-aligned but not doubleword-aligned may cause an *STDF_mem_address_not_aligned* exception or may complete the operation in hardware (impl. dep. #110).

— An LDQF or LDQFA instruction accessing an address that is word-aligned but not quadword-aligned may cause an *LDQF_mem_address_not_aligned* exception or may complete the operation in hardware (impl. dep. #111).

— An STQF or STQFA instruction accessing an address that is word-aligned but not quadword aligned may cause an *STQF_mem_address_not_aligned* exception or may complete the operation in hardware (impl. dep. #112).

6.3.1.2 Addressing Conventions

SPARC-V9 uses big-endian byte order for all instruction accesses and, by default, for data accesses. It is possible to access data in little-endian format by using selected ASIs. It is also possible to change the default byte order for implicit data accesses. See 5.2.1, "Processor State Register (PSTATE)," for more information.[1]

6.3.1.2.1 Big-Endian Addressing Convention

Within a multiple-byte integer, the byte with the smallest address is the most significant; a byte's significance decreases as its address increases. The big-endian addressing conventions are illustrated in figure 35 and defined as follows:

byte:
> A load/store byte instruction accesses the addressed byte in both big- and little-endian modes.

halfword:
> For a load/store halfword instruction, two bytes are accessed. The most significant byte (bits 15..8) is accessed at the address specified in the instruction; the least significant byte (bits 7..0) is accessed at the address + 1.

word:
> For a load/store word instruction, four bytes are accessed. The most significant byte (bits 31..24) is accessed at the address specified in the instruction; the least significant byte (bits 7..0) is accessed at the address + 3.

doubleword or extended word:
> For a load/store extended or floating-point load/store double instruction, eight bytes are accessed. The most significant byte (bits 63..56) is accessed at the address specified in the instruction; the least significant byte (bits 7..0) is accessed at the address + 7.
>
> For the deprecated integer load/store double instructions (LDD/STD), two big-endian words are accessed. The word at the address specified in the instruction corresponds to the even register specified in the instruction; the word at address + 4 corresponds to the following odd-numbered register.

---

1. See Cohen, D., "On Holy Wars and a Plea for Peace," *Computer* 14:10 (October 1981), pp. 48-54.

quadword:

For a load/store quadword instruction, sixteen bytes are accessed. The most significant byte (bits 127..120) is accessed at the address specified in the instruction; the least significant byte (bits 7..0) is accessed at the address + 15.

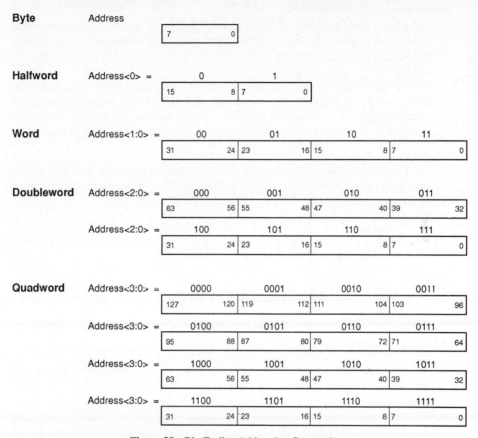

Figure 35—Big-Endian Addressing Conventions

6.3.1.2.2 Little-Endian Addressing Convention

Within a multiple-byte integer, the byte with the smallest address is the least significant; a byte's significance increases as its address increases. The little-endian addressing conventions are illustrated in figure 36 and defined as follows:

byte:

A load/store byte instruction accesses the addressed byte in both big- and little-endian modes.

halfword:

For a load/store halfword instruction, two bytes are accessed. The least significant byte (bits 7..0) is accessed at the address specified in the instruction; the most significant byte (bits 15..8) is accessed at the address + 1.

word:

For a load/store word instruction, four bytes are accessed. The least significant byte (bits 7..0) is accessed at the address specified in the instruction; the most significant byte (bits 31..24) is accessed at the address + 3.

doubleword or extended word:

For a load/store extended or floating-point load/store double instruction, eight bytes are accessed. The least significant byte (bits 7..0) is accessed at the address specified in the instruction; the most significant byte (bits 63..56) is accessed at the address + 7.

For the deprecated integer load/store double instructions (LDD/STD), two little-endian words are accessed. The word at the address specified in the instruction + 4 corresponds to the even register specified in the instruction; the word at the address specified in the instruction corresponds to the following odd-numbered register.

quadword:

For a load/store quadword instruction, sixteen bytes are accessed. The least significant byte (bits 7..0) is accessed at the address specified in the instruction; the most significant byte (bits 127..120) is accessed at the address + 15

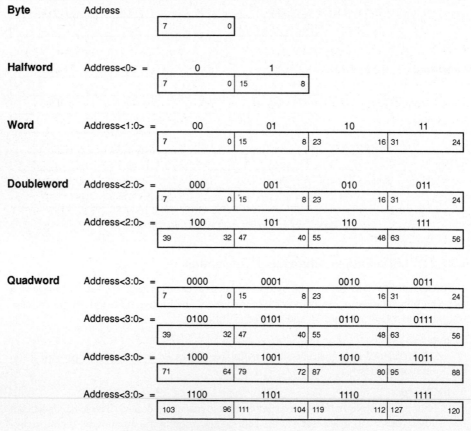

Figure 36—Little-Endian Addressing Conventions

6.3.1.3 Address Space Identifiers (ASIs)

Load and store instructions provide an implicit ASI value of ASI_PRIMARY or ASI_PRIMARY_LITTLE. Load and store alternate instructions provide an explicit ASI, specified by the *imm_asi* instruction field when $i = 0$, or the contents of the ASI register when $i = 1$.

ASIs 00_{16} through $7F_{16}$ are restricted; only privileged software is allowed to access them. An attempt to access a restricted ASI by nonprivileged software results in a *privileged_action* exception. ASIs 80_{16} through FF_{16} are unrestricted; software is allowed to access them whether the processor is operating in privileged or nonprivileged mode. This is illustrated in table 11.

Table 11—Allowed Accesses to ASIs

Value	Access Type	Processor state (PSTATE.PRIV)	Result of ASI access
$00_{16}..7F_{16}$	Restricted	Nonprivileged (0)	*privileged_action* exception
		Privileged (1)	Valid access
$80_{16}..FF_{16}$	Unrestricted	Nonprivileged (0)	Valid access
		Privileged (1)	Valid access

The required ASI assignments are shown in table 12. In the table, "R" indicates a restricted ASI, and "U" indicates an unrestricted ASI.

IMPL. DEP. #29: These ASI assignments are implementation-dependent: restricted ASIs $00_{16}..03_{16}$, $05_{16}..0B_{16}$, $0D_{16}..0F_{16}$, $12_{16}..17_{16}$, AND $1A_{16}..7F_{16}$; and unrestricted ASIs $C0_{16}..FF_{16}$.

IMPL. DEP. #30: An implementation may choose to decode only a subset of the 8-bit ASI specifier; however, it shall decode at least enough of the ASI to distinguish ASI_PRIMARY, ASI_PRIMARY_LITTLE, ASI_AS_IF_USER_PRIMARY, ASI_AS_IF_USER_PRIMARY_LITTLE, ASI_PRIMARY_NOFAULT, ASI_PRIMARY_NOFAULT_LITTLE, ASI_SECONDARY, ASI_SECONDARY_LITTLE, ASI_AS_IF_USER_SECONDARY, ASI_AS_IF_USER_SECONDARY_LITTLE, ASI_SECONDARY_NOFAULT, and ASI_SECONDARY_NOFAULT_LITTLE. If the nucleus context is supported, then ASI_NUCLEUS and ASI_NUCLEUS_LITTLE must also be decoded (impl. dep. #124). Finally, an implementation must always decode ASI bit<7> while PSTATE.PRIV = 0, so that an attempt by nonprivileged software to access a restricted ASI will always cause a *privileged_action* exception.

Table 12—Address Space Identifiers (ASIs)

Value	Name	Access	Address space
$00_{16}..03_{16}$	—	R	*Implementation-dependent*[1]
04_{16}	ASI_NUCLEUS	R	*Implementation-dependent*[2]
$05_{16}..0B_{16}$	—	R	*Implementation-dependent*[1]
$0C_{16}$	ASI_NUCLEUS_LITTLE	R	*Implementation-dependent*[2]
$0D_{16}..0F_{16}$	—	R	*Implementation-dependent*[1]
10_{16}	ASI_AS_IF_USER_PRIMARY	R	Primary address space, user privilege[3]
11_{16}	ASI_AS_IF_USER_SECONDARY	R	Secondary address space, user privilege[3]
$12_{16}..17_{16}$	—	R	*Implementation-dependent*[1]
18_{16}	ASI_AS_IF_USER_PRIMARY_LITTLE	R	Primary address space, user privilege, little-endian[3]
19_{16}	ASI_AS_IF_USER_SECONDARY_LITTLE	R	Secondary address space, user priv., little-endian[3]
$1A_{16}..7F_{16}$	—	R	*Implementation-dependent*[1]
80_{16}	ASI_PRIMARY	U	Primary address space
81_{16}	ASI_SECONDARY	U	Secondary address space
82_{16}	ASI_PRIMARY_NOFAULT	U	Primary address space, no fault[4]
83_{16}	ASI_SECONDARY_NOFAULT	U	Secondary address space, no fault[4]
$84_{16}..87_{16}$	—	U	*Reserved*
88_{16}	ASI_PRIMARY_LITTLE	U	Primary address space, little-endian
89_{16}	ASI_SECONDARY_LITTLE	U	Secondary address space, little-endian
$8A_{16}$	ASI_PRIMARY_NOFAULT_LITTLE	U	Primary address space, no fault, little-endian[4]
$8B_{16}$	ASI_SECONDARY_NOFAULT_LITTLE	U	Secondary address space, no fault, little-endian[4]
$8C_{16}..BF_{16}$	—	U	*Reserved*
$C0_{16}..FF_{16}$	—	U	*Implementation-dependent*[1]

[1] These ASI assignments are implementation-dependent (impl. dep. #29) and available for use by implementors. Code that references any of these ASIs may not be portable.

[2] ASI_NUCLEUS{_LITTLE} are implementation-dependent (impl. dep. #124); they may not be supported in all implementations. See F.4.4, "Contexts," for more information.

[3] Use of these ASIs causes access checks to be performed as if the memory access instruction were issued while PSTATE.PRIV = 0 (that is, in nonprivileged mode) and directed towards the corresponding address space.

[4] ASI_PRIMARY_NOFAULT{_LITTLE} and ASI_SECONDARY_NOFAULT{_LITTLE} refer to the same address spaces as ASI_PRIMARY{_LITTLE} and ASI_SECONDARY{_LITTLE}, respectively, with additional semantics as described in 8.3, "Addressing and Alternate Address Spaces."

6.3.1.4 Separate Instruction Memory

A SPARC-V9 implementation may choose to place instruction and data in the same shared address space and use hardware to keep the data and instruction memory consistent at all times. It may also choose to overload independent address spaces for data and instructions and allow them to become inconsistent when data writes are made to addresses shared with the instruction space. A program containing such self-modifying code must issue a FLUSH instruction or appropriate calls to system software to bring the address spaces to a consistent state. See H.1.6, "Self-Modifying Code," for more information.

6.3.2 Memory Synchronization Instructions

Two forms of memory barrier (MEMBAR) instructions allow programs to manage the order and completion of memory references. Ordering MEMBARs induce a partial ordering between sets of loads and stores and future loads and stores. Sequencing MEMBARs exert explicit control over completion of loads and stores. Both barrier forms are encoded in a single instruction, with sub-functions bit-encoded in an immediate field.

Compatibility Note:
> The deprecated STBAR instruction is a subcase of the MEMBAR instruction; it is identical in operation to the STBAR instruction of SPARC-V8, and is included only for compatibility.

6.3.3 Integer Arithmetic Instructions

The integer arithmetic instructions are generally triadic-register-address instructions that compute a result which is a function of two source operands. They either write the result into the destination register $r[rd]$ or discard it. One of the source operands is always r[$rs1$]. The other source operand depends on the i bit in the instruction; if $i = 0$, the operand is $r[rs2]$; if $i = 1$, the operand is the constant $simm10$, $simm11$, or $simm13$ sign-extended to 64 bits.

Note that the value of $r[0]$ always reads as zero, and writes to it are ignored.

6.3.3.1 Setting Condition Codes

Most integer arithmetic instructions have two versions; one sets the integer condition codes (icc and xcc) as a side effect; the other does not affect the condition codes. A special comparison instruction for integer values is not needed, since it is easily synthesized using the "subtract and set condition codes" (SUBcc) instruction. See G.3, "Synthetic Instructions," for details.

6.3.3.2 Shift Instructions

Shift instructions shift an r register left or right by a constant or variable amount. None of the shift instructions changes the condition codes.

6.3.3.3 Set High 22 Bits of Low Word

The "set high 22 bits of low word of an r register" instruction (SETHI) writes a 22-bit constant from the instruction into bits 31 through 10 of the destination register. It clears the low-order 10 bits and high-order 32 bits, and does not affect the condition codes. Its primary use is to construct constants in registers.

6.3.3.4 Integer Multiply/Divide

The integer multiply instruction performs a $64 \times 64 \rightarrow 64$-bit operation; the integer divide instructions perform $64 \div 64 \rightarrow 64$-bit operations. For compatibility with SPARC-V8,

$32 \times 32 \rightarrow$ 64-bit multiply instructions, $64 \div 32 \rightarrow$ 32-bit divide instructions, and the multiply step instruction are provided. Division by zero causes a *division_by_zero* exception.

6.3.3.5 Tagged Add/Subtract

The tagged add/subtract instructions assume tagged-format data, in which the tag is the two low-order bits of each operand. If either of the two operands has a nonzero tag, or if 32-bit arithmetic overflow occurs, tag overflow is detected. TADDcc and TSUBcc set the CCR.*icc*.V bit if tag overflow occurs; they set the CCR.*xcc*.V bit if 64-bit arithmetic overflow occurs. The trapping versions (TADDccTV, TSUBccTV) of these instructions cause a *tag_overflow* trap if tag overflow occurs. If 64-bit arithmetic overflow occurs but tag overflow does not, TADDccTV and TSUBccTV set the CCR.*xcc*.V bit but do not trap.

6.3.4 Control-Transfer Instructions (CTIs)

These are the basic control-transfer instruction types:

— Conditional branch (Bicc, BPcc, BPr, FBfcc, FBPfcc)

— Unconditional Branch

— Call and Link (CALL)

— Jump and Link (JMPL, RETURN)

— Return from trap (DONE, RETRY)

— Trap (Tcc)

A control-transfer instruction functions by changing the value of the next program counter (nPC) or by changing the value of both the program counter (PC) and the next program counter (nPC). When only the next program counter, nPC, is changed, the effect of the transfer of control is delayed by one instruction. Most control transfers in SPARC-V9 are of the delayed variety. The instruction following a delayed control transfer instruction is said to be in the **delay slot** of the control transfer instruction. Some control transfer instructions (branches) can optionally annul, that is, not execute, the instruction in the delay slot, depending upon whether the transfer is taken or not-taken. Annulled instructions have no effect upon the program-visible state nor can they cause a trap.

Programming Note:

> The annul bit increases the likelihood that a compiler can find a useful instruction to fill the delay slot after a branch, thereby reducing the number of instructions executed by a program. For example, the annul bit can be used to move an instruction from within a loop to fill the delay slot of the branch that closes the loop. Likewise, the annul bit can be used to move an instruction from either the "else" or "then" branch of an "if-then-else" program block to the delay slot of the branch that selects between them. Since a full set of conditions are provided, a compiler can arrange the code (possibly reversing the sense of the condition) so that an instruction from either the "else" branch or the "then" branch can be moved to the delay slot.

Table 13 below defines the value of the program counter and the value of the next program counter after execution of each instruction. Conditional branches have two forms: branches that test a condition, represented in the table by "Bcc," and branches that are unconditional, that is, always or never taken, represented in the table by "B." The effect of an annulled branch is shown in the table through explicit transfers of control, rather than by fetching and annulling the instruction.

The effective address, EA in table 13, specifies the target of the control transfer instruction. The effective address is computed in different ways, depending on the particular instruction:

PC-relative Effective Address:
> A PC-relative effective address is computed by sign extending the instruction's immediate field to 64-bits, left-shifting the word displacement by two bits to create a byte displacement, and adding the result to the contents of the PC.

Register-Indirect Effective Address:
> A register-indirect effective address computes its target address as either $r[rs1]+r[rs2]$ if $i = 0$, or $r[rs1]+sign\_ext(simm13)$ if $i = 1$.

Trap Vector Effective Address:
> A trap vector effective address first computes the software trap number as the least significant seven bits of $r[rs1]+r[rs2]$ if $i = 0$, or as the least significant seven bits of $r[rs1]+sw\_trap\#$ if $i = 1$. The trap level, TL, is incremented. The hardware trap type is computed as $256 + sw\_trap\#$ and stored in TT[TL]. The effective address is generated by concatenating the contents of the TBA register, the "TL>0" bit, and the contents of TT[TL]. See 5.2.8, "Trap Base Address (TBA)," for details.

Trap State Effective Address:
> A trap state effective address is not computed, but is taken directly from either TPC[TL] or TNPC[TL].

Compatibility Note:
> SPARC-V8 specified that the delay instruction was always fetched, even if annulled, and that an annulled instruction could not cause any traps. SPARC-V9 does not require the delay instruction to be fetched if it is annulled.

Compatibility Note:
> SPARC-V8 left as undefined the result of executing a delayed conditional branch that had a delayed control transfer in its delay slot. For this reason, programmers should avoid such constructs when backwards compatibility is an issue.

Table 13—Control Transfer Characteristics

Instruction group	Address form	Delayed	Taken	Annul bit	New PC	New nPC
Non-CTIs	—	—	—	—	nPC	nPC + 4
Bcc	PC-relative	Yes	Yes	0	nPC	EA
Bcc	PC-relative	Yes	No	0	nPC	nPC + 4
Bcc	PC-relative	Yes	Yes	1	nPC	EA
Bcc	PC-relative	Yes	No	1	nPC + 4	nPC + 8
B	PC-relative	Yes	Yes	0	nPC	EA
B	PC-relative	Yes	No	0	nPC	nPC + 4
B	PC-relative	Yes	Yes	1	EA	EA + 4
B	PC-relative	Yes	No	1	nPC + 4	nPC + 8
CALL	PC-relative	Yes	—	—	nPC	EA
JMPL, RETURN	Register-ind.	Yes	—	—	nPC	EA
DONE	Trap state	No	—	—	TNPC[TL]	TNPC[TL] + 4
RETRY	Trap state	No	—	—	TPC[TL]	TNPC[TL]
Tcc	Trap vector	No	Yes	—	EA	EA + 4
Tcc	Trap vector	No	No	—	nPC	nPC + 4

6.3.4.1 Conditional Branches

A conditional branch transfers control if the specified condition is true. If the annul bit is 0, the instruction in the delay slot is always executed. If the annul bit is 1, the instruction in the delay slot is **not** executed **unless** the conditional branch is taken. Note that the annul behavior is the reverse of that for unconditional branches.

6.3.4.2 Unconditional Branches

An unconditional branch transfers control unconditionally if its specified condition is "always"; it never transfers control if its specified condition is "never." If the annul bit is 0, the instruction in the delay slot is always executed. If the annul bit is 1, the instruction in the delay slot is **never** executed. Note that the annul behavior is the reverse of that for conditional branches.

6.3.4.3 CALL and JMPL instructions

The CALL instruction writes the contents of the PC, which points to the CALL instruction itself, into $r[15]$ (*out* register 7) and then causes a delayed transfer of control to a PC-relative effective address. The value written into $r[15]$ is visible to the instruction in the delay slot.

The JMPL instruction writes the contents of the PC, which points to the JMPL instruction itself, into $r[rd]$ and then causes a delayed transfer of control to a PC-relative effective address. The value written into $r[rd]$ is visible to the instruction in the delay slot.

When PSTATE.AM = 1, the value of the high order 32-bits transmitted to $r[15]$ by the CALL instruction or to $r[rd]$ by the JMPL instruction is implementation-dependent. (impl. dep #125).

6.3.4.4 RETURN Instruction

The RETURN instruction is used to return from a trap handler executing in nonpriviliged mode. RETURN combines the control-transfer characteristics of a JMPL instruction with $r[0]$ specified as the destination register and the register-window semantics of a RESTORE instruction.

6.3.4.5 DONE and RETRY Instructions

The DONE and RETRY instructions are used by privileged software to return from a trap. These instructions restore the machine state to values saved in the TSTATE register.

RETRY returns to the instruction that caused the trap in order to reexecute it. DONE returns to the instruction pointed to by the value of nPC associated with the instruction that caused the trap, that is, the next logical instruction in the program. DONE presumes that the trap handler did whatever was requested by the program and that execution should continue.

6.3.4.6 Trap Instruction (Tcc)

The Tcc instruction initiates a trap if the condition specified by its *cond* field matches the current state of the condition code register specified by its *cc* field, otherwise it executes as a NOP. If the trap is taken, it increments the TL register, computes a trap type which is stored in TT[TL], and transfers to a computed address in the trap table pointed to by TBA. See 5.2.8, "Trap Base Address (TBA)."

A Tcc instruction can specify one of 128 software trap types. When a Tcc is taken, 256 plus the seven least significant bits of the sum of the Tcc's source operands is written to TT[TL]. The only visible difference between a software trap generated by a Tcc instruction and a hardware trap is the trap number in the TT register. See Chapter 7, "Traps," for more information.

Programming Note:
> Tcc can be used to implement breakpointing, tracing, and calls to supervisor software. Tcc can also be used for run-time checks, such as out-of-range array index checks or integer overflow checks.

6.3.5 Conditional Move Instructions

6.3.5.1 MOVcc and FMOVcc Instructions

The MOVcc and FMOVcc instructions copy the contents of any integer or floating-point register to a destination integer or floating-point register if a condition is satisfied. The condition to test is specified in the instruction and may be any of the conditions allowed in conditional delayed control-transfer instructions. This condition is tested against one of the six condition codes (*icc*, *xcc*, *fcc0*, *fcc1*, *fcc2*, and *fcc3*) as specified by the instruction. For example:

```
fmovdg     %fcc2, %f20, %f22
```

moves the contents of the double-precision floating-point register %f20 to register %f22 if floating-point condition code number 2 (*fcc2*) indicates a greater-than relation (FSR.*fcc2* = 2). If *fcc2* does not indicate a greater-than relation (FSR.*fcc2* ≠ 2), then the move is not performed.

The MOVcc and FMOVcc instructions can be used to eliminate some branches in programs. In most implementations, branches will be more expensive than the MOVcc or FMOVcc instructions. For example, the following C statement:

```
if (A > B) X  = 1; else X  = 0;
```

can be coded as:

```
cmp     %i0, %i2          ! (A > B)
or      %g0, 0, %i3       ! set X  = 0
movg    %xcc, %g0,1, %i3  ! overwrite X with 1 if A > B
```

which eliminates the need for a branch.

6.3.5.2 MOVr and FMOVr Instructions

The MOVr and FMOVr instructions allow the contents of any integer or floating-point register to be moved to a destination integer or floating-point register if a condition specified by the instruction is satisfied. The condition to test may be any of the following:

Condition	Description
NZ	Nonzero
Z	Zero
GEZ	Greater than or equal to zero
LZ	Less than zero
LEZ	Less than or equal to zero
GZ	Greater than zero

Any of the integer registers may be tested for one of the conditions, and the result used to control the move. For example,

```
movrnz     %i2, %l4, %l6
```

moves integer register %l4 to integer register %l6 if integer register %i2 contains a non-zero value.

MOVr and FMOVr can be used to eliminate some branches in programs, or to emulate multiple unsigned condition codes by using an integer register to hold the result of a comparison.

6.3.6 Register Window Management Instructions

This subsection describes the instructions used to manage register windows in SPARC-V9. The privileged registers affected by these instructions are described in 5.2.10, "Register-Window State Registers."

6.3.6.1 SAVE Instruction

The SAVE instruction allocates a new register window and saves the caller's register window by incrementing the CWP register.

If CANSAVE = 0, execution of a SAVE instruction causes a *window_spill* exception.

If CANSAVE ≠ 0, but the number of clean windows is zero, that is:

$$(CLEANWIN - CANRESTORE) = 0$$

then SAVE causes a *clean_window* exception.

If SAVE does not cause an exception, it performs an ADD operation, decrements CANSAVE, and increments CANRESTORE. The source registers for the ADD are from the old window (the one to which CWP pointed before the SAVE), while the result is written into a register in the new window (the one to which the incremented CWP points).

6.3.6.2 RESTORE Instruction

The RESTORE instruction restores the previous register window by decrementing the CWP register.

If CANRESTORE = 0, execution of a RESTORE instruction causes a *window_fill* exception.

If RESTORE does not cause an exception, it performs an ADD operation, decrements CANRESTORE, and increments CANSAVE. The source registers for the ADD are from the "old" window (the one to which CWP pointed before the RESTORE), while the result is written into a register in the "new" window (the one to which the decremented CWP points).

Programming Note:

> The following describes a common convention for use of register windows, SAVE, RESTORE, CALL, and JMPL instructions.
>
> A procedure is invoked by executing a CALL (or a JMPL) instruction. If the procedure requires a register window, it executes a SAVE instruction. A routine that does not allocate a register window of its own (possibly a leaf procedure) should not modify any windowed registers except *out* registers 0 through 6. See H.1.2, "Leaf-Procedure Optimization."
>
> A procedure that uses a register window returns by executing both a RESTORE and a JMPL instruction. A procedure that has not allocated a register window returns by executing a JMPL only. The target address for the JMPL instruction is normally eight plus the address saved by the calling instruction, that is, to the instruction after the instruction in the delay slot of the calling instruction.

The SAVE and RESTORE instructions can be used to atomically establish a new memory stack pointer in an *r* register and switch to a new or previous register window. See H.1.4, "Register Allocation within a Window."

6.3.6.3 SAVED Instruction

The SAVED instruction should be used by a spill trap handler to indicate that a window spill has completed successfully. It increments CANSAVE:

$$\text{CANSAVE} \leftarrow (\text{CANSAVE} + 1)$$

If the saved window belongs to a different address space (OTHERWIN $\neq$ 0), it decrements OTHERWIN:

$$\text{OTHERWIN} \leftarrow (\text{OTHERWIN} - 1)$$

Otherwise, the saved window belongs to the current address space (OTHERWIN = 0), so SAVED decrements CANRESTORE:

$$\text{CANRESTORE} \leftarrow (\text{CANRESTORE} - 1)$$

6.3.6.4 RESTORED Instruction

The RESTORED instruction should be used by a fill trap handler to indicate that a window has been filled successfully. It increments CANRESTORE:

$$\text{CANRESTORE} \leftarrow (\text{CANRESTORE} + 1)$$

If the restored window replaces a window that belongs to a different address space (OTHERWIN $\neq$ 0), it decrements OTHERWIN:

$$\text{OTHERWIN} \leftarrow (\text{OTHERWIN} - 1)$$

Otherwise, the restored window belongs to the current address space (OTHERWIN = 0), so RESTORED decrements CANSAVE:

$$\text{CANSAVE} \leftarrow (\text{CANSAVE} - 1)$$

If CLEANWIN is not equal to NWINDOWS, the RESTORED instruction increments CLEANWIN:

$$\textbf{if } (\text{CLEANWIN} < \text{NWINDOWS}) \textbf{ then } \text{CLEANWIN} \leftarrow (\text{CLEANWIN} + 1)$$

6.3.6.5 Flush Windows Instruction

The FLUSHW instruction flushes all of the register windows except the current window, by performing repetitive spill traps. The FLUSHW instruction is implemented by causing a spill trap if any register window (other than the current window) has valid contents. The number of windows with valid contents is computed as

$$\text{NWINDOWS} - 2 - \text{CANSAVE}$$

If this number is nonzero, the FLUSHW instruction causes a spill trap. Otherwise, FLUSHW has no effect. If the spill trap handler exits with a RETRY instruction, the FLUSHW instruction will continue causing spill traps until all the register windows except the current window have been flushed.

6.3.7 State Register Access

The read/write state register instructions access program-visible state and status registers. These instructions read/write the state registers into/from *r* registers. A read/write Ancillary State Register instruction is privileged only if the accessed register is privileged.

6.3.8 Privileged Register Access

The read/write privileged register instructions access state and status registers that are visible only to privileged software. These instructions read/write privileged registers into/from *r* registers. The read/write privileged register instructions are privileged.

6.3.9 Floating-Point Operate (FPop) Instructions

Floating-point operate instructions (FPops) are generally triadic-register-address instructions. They compute a result that is a function of one or two source operands and place the result in one or more destination *f* registers. The exceptions are:

— Floating-point convert operations, which use one source and one destination operand

— Floating-point compare operations, which do not write to an *f* register, but update one of the *fccn* fields of the FSR instead

The term "FPop" refers to those instructions encoded by the FPop1 and FPop2 opcodes and does **not** include branches based on the floating-point condition codes (FBfcc and FBPfcc) or the load/store floating-point instructions.

The FMOVcc instructions function for the floating-point registers as the MOVcc instructions do for the integer registers. See 6.3.5.1, "MOVcc and FMOVcc Instructions."

The FMOVr instructions function for the floating-point registers as the MOVr instructions do for the integer registers. Scc 6.3.5.2, "MOVr and FMOVr Instructions."

If there is no floating-point unit present or if PSTATE.PEF = 0 or FPRS.FEF = 0, any instruction that attempts to access an FPU register, including an FPop instruction, generates an *fp_disabled* exception.

All FPop instructions clear the *ftt* field and set the *cexc* field, unless they generate an exception. Floating-point compare instructions also write one of the *fccn* fields. All FPop instructions that can generate IEEE exceptions set the *cexc* and *aexc* fields, unless they generate an exception. FABS(s,d,q), FMOV(s,d,q), FMOVcc(s,d,q), FMOVc(s,d,q), and FNEG(s,d,q) cannot generate IEEE exceptions, so they clear *cexc* and leave *aexc* unchanged.

IMPL. DEP. #3: An implementation may indicate that a floating-point instruction did not produce a correct IEEE STD 754-1985 result by generating a special *unfinished_FPop* or *unimplemented_ FPop* exception. Privileged-mode software must emulate any functionality not present in the hardware.

6.3.10 Implementation-Dependent Instructions

SPARC-V9 provides two instructions that are entirely implementation-dependent, IMP-DEP1 and IMPDEP2 (impl. dep. #106).

Compatibility Note:
> The IMPDEP*n* instructions replace the CPop*n* instructions in SPARC-V8.

See A.23, "Implementation-Dependent Instructions," for more information.

6.3.11 Reserved Opcodes and Instruction Fields

An attempt to execute an opcode to which no instruction is assigned shall cause a trap. Specifically, attempting to execute a reserved FPop causes an *fp_exception_other* trap (with FSR.*ftt* = *unimplemented_FPop*); attempting to execute any other reserved opcode shall cause an *illegal_instruction* trap. See Appendix E, "Opcode Maps," for a complete enumeration of the reserved opcodes.

6.4 Register Window Management

The state of the register windows is determined by the contents of the set of privileged registers described in 5.2.10, "Register-Window State Registers." Those registers are affected by the instructions described in 6.3.6, "Register Window Management Instructions." Privileged software can read/write these state registers directly by using RDPR/ WRPR instructions.

6.4.1 Register Window State Definition

In order for the state of the register windows to be consistent, the following must always be true:

$$\text{CANSAVE} + \text{CANRESTORE} + \text{OTHERWIN} = \text{NWINDOWS} - 2$$

Figure 3 on page 34 shows how the register windows are partitioned to obtain the above equation. In figure 3, the partitions are as follows:

— The current window and the window that overlaps two other valid windows and so must not be used (in the figure, windows 0 and 4, respectively) are always present and account for the 2 subtracted from NWINDOWS in the right-hand side of the equation.

— Windows that do not have valid contents and can be used (via a SAVE instruction) without causing a spill trap. These windows (windows 1, 2 and 3 in the figure) are counted in CANSAVE.

— Windows that have valid contents for the current address space and can be used (via the RESTORE instruction) without causing a fill trap. These windows (window 7 in the figure) are counted in CANRESTORE.

— Windows that have valid contents for an address space other than the current address space. An attempt to use these windows via a SAVE (RESTORE) instruction results in a spill (fill) trap to a separate set of trap vectors, as discussed in the following subsection. These windows (windows 5 and 6 in the figure) are counted in OTHERWIN.

In addition,

$$\text{CLEANWIN} \geq \text{CANRESTORE}$$

since CLEANWIN is the sum of CANRESTORE and the number of clean windows following CWP.

In order to use the window-management features of the architecture as described here, the state of the register windows must be kept consistent at all times, except in trap handlers for window spilling, filling, and cleaning. While handling window traps the state may be inconsistent. Window spill/fill strap handlers should be written such that a nested trap can be taken without destroying state.

6.4.2 Register Window Traps

Window traps are used to manage overflow and underflow conditions in the register windows, to support clean windows, and to implement the FLUSHW instruction.

6.4.2.1 Window Spill and Fill Traps

A window overflow occurs when a SAVE instruction is executed and the next register window is occupied (CANSAVE = 0). An overflow causes a spill trap that allows privileged software to save the occupied register window in memory, thereby making it available for use.

A window underflow occurs when a RESTORE instruction is executed and the previous register window is not valid (CANRESTORE = 0). An underflow causes a fill trap that allows privileged software to load the registers from memory.

6.4.2.2 Clean-Window Trap

SPARC-V9 provides the *clean_window* trap so that software can create a secure environment in which it is guaranteed that register windows contain only data from the same address space.

A clean register window is one in which all of the registers, including uninitialized registers, contain either zero or data assigned by software executing in the address space to which the window belongs. A clean window cannot contain register values from another process, that is, software operating in a different address space.

Supervisor software specifies the number of windows that are clean with respect to the current address space in the CLEANWIN register. This includes register windows that can be restored (the value in the CANRESTORE register) and the register windows following CWP that can be used without cleaning. Therefore, the number of clean windows that are available to be used by the SAVE instruction is

$$\text{CLEANWIN} - \text{CANRESTORE}$$

The SAVE instruction causes a *clean_window* trap if this value is zero. This allows supervisor software to clean a register window before it is accessed by a user.

6.4.2.3   Vectoring of Fill/Spill Traps

In order to make handling of fill and spill traps efficient, SPARC-V9 provides multiple trap vectors for the fill and spill traps. These trap vectors are determined as follows:

— Supervisor software can mark a set of contiguous register windows as belonging to an address space different from the current one. The count of these register windows is kept in the OTHERWIN register. A separate set of trap vectors (*fill_n_other* and *spill_n_other*) is provided for spill and fill traps for these register windows (as opposed to register windows that belong to the current address space).

— Supervisor software can specify the trap vectors for fill and spill traps by presetting the fields in the WSTATE register. This register contains two subfields, each three bits wide. The WSTATE.NORMAL field is used to determine one of eight spill (fill) vectors to be used when the register window to be spilled (filled) belongs to the current address space (OTHERWIN = 0). If the OTHERWIN register is non-zero, the WSTATE.OTHER field selects one of eight *fill_n_other* (*spill_n_other*) trap vectors.

See Chapter 7, "Traps," for more details on how the trap address is determined.

6.4.2.4   CWP on Window Traps

On a window trap the CWP is set to point to the window that must be accessed by the trap handler, as follows (note that all arithmetic on CWP is done modulo NWINDOWS):

— If the spill trap occurs due to a SAVE instruction (when CANSAVE = 0), there is an overlap window between the CWP and the next register window to be spilled

$$\text{CWP} \leftarrow (\text{CWP} + 2) \bmod \text{NWINDOWS}$$

If the spill trap occurs due to a FLUSHW instruction, there can be unused windows (CANSAVE) in addition to the overlap window, between the CWP and the window to be spilled

$$\text{CWP} \leftarrow (\text{CWP} + \text{CANSAVE} + 2) \bmod \text{NWINDOWS}$$

Implementation Note:
    All spill traps can use:

$$\text{CWP} \leftarrow (\text{CWP} + \text{CANSAVE} + 2) \bmod \text{NWINDOWS}$$

since CANSAVE is zero whenever a trap occurs due to a SAVE instruction.

— On a fill trap, the window preceding CWP must be filled

$$\text{CWP} \leftarrow (\text{CWP} - 1) \textbf{ mod } \text{NWINDOWS}$$

— On a clean_window trap, the window following CWP must be cleaned. Then

$$\text{CWP} \leftarrow (\text{CWP} + 1) \textbf{ mod } \text{NWINDOWS}$$

6.4.2.5 Window Trap Handlers

The trap handlers for fill, spill and *clean_window* traps must handle the trap appropriately and return using the RETRY instruction, to reexecute the trapped instruction. The state of the register windows must be updated by the trap handler, and the relationship among CLEANWIN, CANSAVE, CANRESTORE, and OTHERWIN must remain consistent. The following recommendations should be followed:

— A spill trap handler should execute the SAVED instruction for each window that it spills.

— A fill trap handler should execute the RESTORED instruction for each window that it fills.

— A *clean_window* trap handler should increment CLEANWIN for each window that it cleans:

$$\text{CLEANWIN} \leftarrow (\text{CLEANWIN} + 1)$$

Window trap handlers in SPARC-V9 can be very efficient. See H.2.2, "Example Code for Spill Handler," for details and sample code.

7 Traps

7.1 Overview

A trap is a vectored transfer of control to supervisor software through a trap table that contains the first eight (thirty-two for fill/spill traps) instructions of each trap handler. The base address of the table is established by supervisor software, by writing the Trap Base Address (TBA) register. The displacement within the table is determined by the trap type and the current trap level (TL). One-half of the table is reserved for hardware traps; one-quarter is reserved for software traps generated by Tcc instructions; the remaining quarter is reserved for future use.

A trap behaves like an unexpected procedure call. It causes the hardware to

(1) Save certain processor state (program counters, CWP, ASI, CCR, PSTATE, and the trap type) on a hardware register stack

(2) Enter privileged execution mode with a predefined PSTATE

(3) Begin executing trap handler code in the trap vector

When the trap handler has finished, it uses either a DONE or RETRY instruction to return.

A trap may be caused by a Tcc instruction, an SIR instruction, an instruction-induced exception, a reset, an asynchronous exception, or an interrupt request not directly related to a particular instruction. The processor must appear to behave as though, before executing each instruction, it determines if there are any pending exceptions or interrupt requests. If there are pending exceptions or interrupt requests, the processor selects the highest-priority exception or interrupt request and causes a trap.

Thus, an exception is a condition that makes it impossible for the processor to continue executing the current instruction stream without software intervention. A trap is the action taken by the processor when it changes the instruction flow in response to the presence of an exception, interrupt, or Tcc instruction.

A catastrophic error exception is due to the detection of a hardware malfunction from which, due to the nature of the error, the state of the machine at the time of the exception cannot be restored. Since the machine state cannot be restored, execution after such an exception may not be resumable. An example of such an error is an uncorrectable bus parity error.

IMPL. DEP. #31: The causes and effects of catastrophic errors are implementation-dependent. They may cause precise, deferred, or disrupting traps.

7.2 Processor States, Normal and Special Traps

The processor is always in one of three discrete states:

— execute_state, which is the normal execution state of the processor

— RED_state (Reset, Error, and Debug state), which is a restricted execution state reserved for processing traps that occur when TL = MAXTL – 1, and for processing hardware- and software-initiated resets

— error_state, which is a halted state that is entered as a result of a trap when TL = MAXTL, or due to an unrecoverable error

Traps processed in execute_state are called **normal traps**. Traps processed in RED_state are called **special traps**. Exceptions that cause the processor to enter error_state are recorded by the hardware and are made available in the TT field after the processor is reset.

Figure 37 shows the processor state diagram.

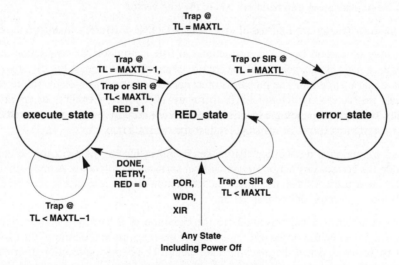

Figure 37—Processor State Diagram

7.2.1 RED_state

RED_state is an acronym for **R**eset, **E**rror, and **D**ebug state. The processor enters RED_ state under any one of the following conditions:

— A trap is taken when TL = MAXTL–1.

— Any of the four reset requests occurs (POR, WDR, XIR, SIR).

— An implementation-dependent trap, *internal_processor_error* exception, or *catastrophic_error* exception occurs.

— System software sets PSTATE.RED = 1.

RED_state serves two mutually exclusive purposes:

— During trap processing, it indicates that there are no more available trap levels; that is, if another nested trap is taken, the processor will enter error_state and halt. RED_state provides system software with a restricted execution environment.

— It provides the execution environment for all reset processing.

RED_state is indicated by PSTATE.RED. When this bit is set, the processor is in RED_state; when this bit is clear, the processor is not in RED_state, independent of the value of TL. Executing a DONE or RETRY instruction in RED_state restores the stacked copy of the PSTATE register, which clears the PSTATE.RED flag if the stacked copy had it cleared. System software can also set or clear the PSTATE.RED flag with a WRPR instruction, which also forces the processor to enter or exit RED_state, respectively. In this case, the WRPR instruction should be placed in the delay slot of a jump, so that the PC can be changed in concert with the state change.

Programming Note:

Setting TL = MAXTL with a WRPR instruction **does not** also set PSTATE.RED = 1; nor does it alter any other machine state. The values of PSTATE.RED and TL are independent.

7.2.1.1 RED_state Trap Table

Traps occurring in RED_state or traps that cause the processor to enter RED_state use an abbreviated trap vector. The RED_state trap vector is constructed so that it can overlay the normal trap vector if necessary. Figure 38 illustrates the RED_state trap vector.

Offset	TT	Reason
00_{16}	0	*Reserved* (SPARC-V8 reset)
20_{16}	1	Power-on reset (POR)
40_{16}	$2^\dagger$	Watchdog reset (WDR)
60_{16}	$3^\ddagger$	Externally initiated reset (XIR)
80_{16}	4	Software-initiated reset (SIR)
$A0_{16}$	*	All other exceptions in RED_state

† TT = 2 if a watchdog reset occurs while the processor is not in error_state; TT = trap type of the exception that caused entry into error_state if a watchdog reset (WDR) occurs in error_state.

‡ TT = 3 if an externally initiated reset (XIR) occurs while the processor is not in error_state; TT = trap type of the exception that caused entry into error_state if the externally initiated reset occurs in error_state.

* TT = trap type of the exception. See table 14 on page 100.

Figure 38—RED_state Trap Vector Layout

IMPL. DEP. #114: The RED_state trap vector is located at an implementation-dependent address referred to as RSTVaddr.

Implementation Note:

> The RED_state trap handlers should be located in trusted memory, for example, in ROM. The value of RSTVaddr may be hard-wired in an implementation, but it is suggested that it be externally setta- ble, for instance by scan, or read from pins at power-on reset.

7.2.1.2   RED_state Execution Environment

In RED_state the processor is forced to execute in a restricted environment by overriding the values of some processor controls and state registers.

Programming Note:

> The values are overridden, not set. This is to allow them to be switched atomically.

IMPL. DEP. #115: A processor's behavior in RED_state is implementation-dependent.

The following are recommended:

(1) Instruction address translation is a straight-through physical map; that is, the MMU is always suppressed for instruction access in RED_state.

(2) Data address translation is handled normally; that is, the MMU is used if it is enabled. However, any event that causes the processor to enter RED_state also dis- ables the MMU. The handler executing in RED_state can reenable the MMU.

(3) All references are uncached.

(4) Cache coherence in RED_state is the problem of the system designer and system programmer. Normally, cache enables are left unchanged by RED_state; thus, if a cache is enabled, it will continue to participate in cache coherence until explicitly disabled by recovery code. A cache may be disabled automatically if an error is detected in the cache.

(5) Unessential functional units (for example, the floating-point unit) and capabilities (for example, superscalar execution) should be disabled.

(6) If a store buffer is present, it should be emptied, if possible, before entering RED_ state.

(7) PSTATE.MM is set to TSO.

Programming Note:

> When RED_state is entered due to component failures, the handler should attempt to recover from potentially catastrophic error conditions or to disable the failing components. When RED_state is entered after a reset, the software should create the environment necessary to restore the system to a running state.

7.2.1.3 RED_state Entry Traps

The following traps are processed in RED_state in all cases

— **POR** (Power-on reset)

— **WDR** (Watchdog reset)

— **XIR** (Externally initiated reset)

In addition, the following trap is processed in RED_state if TL < MAXTL when the trap is taken. Otherwise it is processed in error_state.

— **SIR** (Software-initiated Reset)

An implementation also may elect to set PSTATE.RED = 1 after an *internal_processor_error* trap (impl. dep. #31), or any of the implementation-dependent traps (impl. dep. #35).

Implementation-dependent traps may force additional state changes, such as disabling failing components.

Traps that occur when TL = MAXTL − 1 also set PSTATE.RED = 1; that is, any trap handler entered with TL = MAXTL runs in RED_state.

Any nonreset trap that sets PSTATE.RED = 1 or that occurs when PSTATE.RED = 1, branches to a special entry in the RED_state trap vector at RSTVaddr + A0$_{16}$.

In systems in which it is desired that traps not enter RED_state, the RED_state handler may transfer to the normal trap vector by executing the following code:

```
! Assumptions:
!    -- In RED_state handler, therefore we know that
!       PSTATE.RED = 1, so a WRPR can directly toggle it to 0
!       and, we don't have to worry about intervening traps.
!    -- Registers %g1 and %g2 are available as scratch registers.
...
#define PSTATE_RED     0x0020         ! PSTATE.RFD is bit 5
...
rdpr     %tt,%g1                      ! Get the normal trap vector
rdpr     %tba,%g2                     ! address in %g2.
add      %g1,%g2,%g2
rdpr     %pstate,%g1                  ! Read PSTATE into %g1.
jmpl     %g2                          ! Jump to normal trap vector,
wrpr     %g1,PSTATE_RED,%pstate       ! toggling PSTATE.RED to 0.
```

7.2.1.4 RED_state Software Considerations

In effect, RED_state reserves one level of the trap stack for recovery and reset processing. Software should be designed to require only MAXTL − 1 trap levels for normal processing. That is, any trap that causes TL = MAXTL is an exceptional condition that should cause entry to RED_state.

Since the minimum value for MAXTL is 4, typical usage of the trap levels is as follows:

TL	Usage
0	Normal execution
1	System calls; interrupt handlers; instruction emulation
2	Window spill / fill
3	Page-fault handler
4	RED_state handler

Programming Note:

> In order to log the state of the processor, RED_state-handler software needs either a spare register or a preloaded pointer to a save area. To support recovery, the operating system might reserve one of the alternate global registers, (for example, %a7) for use in RED_state.

7.2.2 Error_state

The processor enters error_state when a trap occurs while the processor is already at its maximum supported trap level, that is, when TL = MAXTL.

IMPL. DEP. #39: The processor may enter error_state when an implementation-dependent error condition occurs.

IMPL. DEP. #40: Effects when error_state is entered are implementation-dependent, but it is recommended that as much processor state as possible be preserved upon entry to error_state.

In particular:

(1) The processor should present an external indication that it has entered error_state.

(2) The processor should halt, that is, make no further changes to system state.

(3) The processor should be restarted by a watchdog reset (WDR). Alternatively, it may be restarted by an externally initiated reset (XIR) or a power-on reset (POR).

After a reset that brings the processor out of error_state, the processor enters RED_state with TL set as defined in table 18 on page 104; the trap state describes the state at the time of entry into error_state. In particular, for WDR and XIR, TT is set to the value of the original trap that caused entry to error_state, not the normal TT value for the WDR or XIR.

7.3 Trap Categories

An exception or interrupt request can cause any of the following trap types:

— A precise trap

— A deferred trap

— A disrupting trap

— A reset trap

7.3.1 Precise Traps

A **precise trap** is induced by a particular instruction and occurs before any program-visible state has been changed by the trap-inducing instruction. When a precise trap occurs, several conditions must be true.

— The PC saved in TPC[TL] points to the instruction that induced the trap, and the nPC saved in NTPC[TL] points to the instruction that was to be executed next.

— All instructions issued before the one that induced the trap have completed execution.

— Any instructions issued after the one that induced the trap remain unexecuted.

Programming Note:

Among the actions the trap handler software might take after a precise trap are:

— Return to the instruction that caused the trap and reexecute it, by executing a RETRY instruction (PC ← old PC, nPC ← old nPC)

— Emulate the instruction that caused the trap and return to the succeeding instruction by executing a DONE instruction (PC ← old nPC, nPC ← old nPC + 4)

— Terminate the program or process associated with the trap

7.3.2 Deferred Traps

A **deferred trap** is also induced by a particular instruction, but unlike a precise trap, a deferred trap may occur after program-visible state has been changed. Such state may have been changed by the execution of either the trap-inducing instruction itself or by one or more other instructions.

If an instruction induces a deferred trap and a precise trap occurs simultaneously, the deferred trap may not be deferred past the precise trap, except that a floating-point exception may be deferred past a precise trap.

Associated with a particular deferred-trap implementation, there must exist:

— An instruction that causes a potentially outstanding deferred-trap exception to be taken as a trap.

— Privileged instructions that access the deferred-trap queues. This queue contains the state information needed by supervisor software to emulate the deferred-trap-inducing instruction, and to resume execution of the trapped instruction stream. See 5.2.13, "IU Deferred-Trap Queue.")

Note that resuming execution may require the emulation of instructions that had not completed execution at the time of the deferred trap, that is, those instructions in the deferred-trap queue.

IMPL. DEP. #32: Whether any deferred traps (and associated deferred-trap queues) are present is implementation-dependent.

Note that to avoid deferred traps entirely, an implementation would need to execute all implemented floating-point instructions synchronously with the execution of integer instructions, causing all generated exceptions to be precise. A deferred-trap queue (e.g., FQ) would be superfluous in such an implementation.

Programming Note:

> Among the actions software can take after a deferred trap are:
>
> — Emulate the instruction that caused the exception, emulate or cause to execute any other execution-deferred instructions that were in an associated deferred-trap state queue, and use RETRY to return control to the instruction at which the deferred trap was invoked, or
>
> — Terminate the program or process associated with the trap.

7.3.3 Disrupting Traps

A **disrupting trap** is neither a precise trap nor a deferred trap. A disrupting trap is caused by a **condition** (e.g., an interrupt), rather than directly by a particular instruction; this distinguishes it from precise and deferred traps. When a disrupting trap has been serviced, program execution resumes where it left off. This differentiates disrupting traps from reset traps, which resume execution at the unique reset address.

Disrupting traps are controlled by a combination of the Processor Interrupt Level (PIL) register and the Interrupt Enable (IE) field of PSTATE. A disrupting trap condition is ignored when interrupts are disabled (PSTATE.IE = 0) or when the condition's interrupt level is lower than that specified in PIL.

A disrupting trap may be due to either an interrupt request not directly related to a previously executed instruction, or to an exception related to a previously executed instruction. Interrupt requests may be either internal or external. An interrupt request can be induced by the assertion of a signal not directly related to any particular processor or memory state. Examples of this are the assertion of an "I/O done" signal or setting external interrupt request lines.

A disrupting trap related to an earlier instruction causing an exception is similar to a deferred trap in that it occurs after instructions following the trap-inducing instruction have modified the processor or memory state. The difference is that the condition which caused the instruction to induce the trap may lead to unrecoverable errors, since the implementation may not preserve the necessary state. An example of this is an ECC data-access error reported after the corresponding load instruction has completed.

Disrupting trap conditions should persist until the corresponding trap is taken.

Programming Note:
> Among the actions that trap-handler software might take after a disrupting trap are:
>
> — Use RETRY to return to the instruction at which the trap was invoked
>
>> (PC ← old PC, nPC ← old nPC), or
>
> — Terminate the program or process associated with the trap.

7.3.4 Reset Traps

A **reset trap** occurs when supervisor software or the implementation's hardware determines that the machine must be reset to a known state. Reset traps differ from disrupting traps, since they do not resume execution of the program that was running when the reset trap occurred.

IMPL. DEP. #37: Some of a processor's behavior during a reset trap is implementation-dependent. See 7.6.2, "Special Trap Processing," for details.

The following reset traps are defined for SPARC-V9:

Software-initiated reset (SIR):
> Initiated by software by executing the SIR instruction.

Power-on reset (POR):
> Initiated when power is applied (or reapplied) to the processor.

Watchdog reset (WDR):
> Initiated in response to error_state or expiration of a watchdog timer.

Externally initiated reset (XIR):
> Initiated in response to an external signal. This reset trap is normally used for critical system events, such as power failure.

7.3.5 Uses of the Trap Categories

The SPARC-V9 **trap model** stipulates that:

(1) Reset traps, except *software_initiated_reset* traps, occur asynchronously to program execution.

(2) When recovery from an exception can affect the interpretation of subsequent instructions, such exceptions shall be precise. These exceptions are:

— *software_initiated_reset*

— *instruction_access_exception*

— *privileged_action*

— *privileged_opcode*

— *trap_instruction*

— *instruction_access_error*

— *clean_window*

— *fp_disabled*

— *LDDF_mem_address_not_aligned*

— *STDF_mem_address_not_aligned*

— *tag_overflow*

— *unimplemented_LDD*

— *unimplemented_STD*

— *spill_n_normal*

— *spill_n_other*

— *fill_n_normal*

— *fill_n_other*

(3) **IMPL. DEP. #33**: Exceptions that occur as the result of program execution may be precise or deferred, although it is recommended that such exceptions be precise. Examples: *mem_address_not_aligned*, *division_by_zero*.

(4) An exception caused after the initial access of a multiple-access load or store instruction (load-store doubleword, LDSTUB, CASA, CASXA, or SWAP) that causes a catastrophic exception may be precise, deferred, or disrupting. Thus, a trap due to the second memory access can occur after the processor or memory state has been modified by the first access.

(5) Implementation-dependent catastrophic exceptions may cause precise, deferred, or disrupting traps (impl. dep. #31).

(6) Exceptions caused by external events unrelated to the instruction stream, such as interrupts, are disrupting.

For the purposes of this subsection, we must distinguish between the dispatch of an instruction and its execution by some functional unit. An instruction is deemed to have been **dispatched** when the software-visible PC advances beyond that instruction in the instruction stream. An instruction is deemed to have been **executed** when the results of that instruction are available to subsequent instructions.

For most instructions, dispatch and execution appear to occur simultaneously; when the PC has advanced beyond the instruction, its results are immediately available to subsequent instructions. For floating-point instructions, however, the PC may advance beyond the instruction as soon as the IU places the instruction into a floating-point queue; the instruction itself may not have completed (or even begun) execution, and results may not be available to subsequent instructions for some time. In particular, the fact that a floating-point instruction will generate an exception may not be noticed by the hardware until additional floating-point instructions have been placed into the queue by the IU. This creates the condition for a deferred trap.

A deferred trap may occur one or more instructions after the trap-inducing instruction is dispatched. However, a deferred trap must occur before the execution (but not necessarily the dispatch) of any instruction that depends on the trap-inducing instruction. That is, a deferred trap may not be deferred past the execution of an instruction that specifies source registers, destination registers, condition codes, or any software-visible machine state that could be modified by the trap-inducing instruction.

In the case of floating-point instructions, if a floating-point exception is currently deferred, an attempt to dispatch a floating-point instruction (FPop, FBfcc, FBPfcc, or floating-point load/store) invokes or causes the outstanding *fp_exception_ieee_754* trap.

Implementation Note:

> To provide the capability to terminate a user process on the occurrence of a catastrophic exception that can cause a deferred or disrupting trap, an implementation should provide one or more instructions that provoke an outstanding exception to be taken as a trap. For example, an outstanding floating-point exception might cause an *fp_exception_ieee_754* trap when any of an FPop, load or store floating-point register (including the FSR), FBfcc, or FBPfcc instruction is executed.

7.4 Trap Control

Several registers control how any given trap is processed:

— The interrupt enable (IE) field in PSTATE and the processor interrupt level (PIL) register control interrupt processing.

— The enable floating-point unit (FEF) field in FPRS, the floating-point unit enable (PEF) field in PSTATE, and the trap enable mask (TEM) in the FSR control floating-point traps.

— The TL register, which contains the current level of trap nesting, controls whether a trap causes entry to execute_state, RED_state, or error_state.

— PSTATE.TLE determines whether implicit data accesses in the trap routine will be performed using the big- or little-endian byte order.

7.4.1 PIL Control

Between the execution of instructions, the IU prioritizes the outstanding exceptions and interrupt requests according to table 15. At any given time, only the highest priority exception or interrupt request is taken as a trap.[1] When there are multiple outstanding exceptions or interrupt requests, SPARC-V9 assumes that lower-priority interrupt requests

---

1. The highest priority exception or interrupt is the one with the lowest priority value in table 15. For example, a priority 2 exception is processed before a priority 3 exception.

will persist and lower-priority exceptions will recur if an exception-causing instruction is reexecuted.

For interrupt requests, the IU compares the interrupt request level against the processor interrupt level (PIL) register. If the interrupt request level is greater than PIL, the processor takes the interrupt request trap, assuming there are no higher-priority exceptions outstanding

IMPL. DEP. #34: How quickly a processor responds to an interrupt request and the method by which an interrupt request is removed are implementation-dependent.

7.4.2 TEM Control

The occurrence of floating-point traps of type *IEEE_754_exception* can be controlled with the user-accessible trap enable mask (TEM) field of the FSR. If a particular bit of TEM is 1, the associated *IEEE_754_exception* can cause an *fp_exception_ieee_754* trap.

If a particular bit of TEM is 0, the associated *IEEE_754_exception* does not cause an *fp_exception_ieee_754* trap. Instead, the occurrence of the exception is recorded in the FSR's accrued exception field (*aexc*).

If an *IEEE_754_exception* results in an *fp_exception_ieee_754* trap, then the destination *f* register, *fccn*, and *aexc* fields remain unchanged. However, if an *IEEE_754_exception* does not result in a trap, then the *f* register, *fccn*, and *aexc* fields are updated to their new values.

7.5 Trap-Table Entry Addresses

Privileged software initializes the trap base address (TBA) register to the upper 49 bits of the trap-table base address. Bit 14 of the vector address (the "TL>0" field) is set based on the value of TL at the time the trap is taken; that is, to 0 if TL = 0 and to 1 if TL > 0. Bits 13..5 of the trap vector address are the contents of the TT register. The lowest five bits of the trap address, bits 4..0, are always 0 (hence each trap-table entry is at least 2^5 or 32 bytes long). Figure 39 illustrates this.

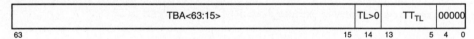

TBA<63:15>	TL>0	TT$_{TL}$	00000

63   15   14   13   5   4   0

Figure 39—Trap Vector Address

7.5.1 Trap Table Organization

The trap table layout is as illustrated in figure 40.

	Trap Table Contents	Trap Type
Value of TL **Before the Trap** **TL = 0**	Hardware traps	$000_{16}..07F_{16}$
	Spill/fill traps	$080_{16}..0FF_{16}$
	Software traps	$100_{16}..17F_{16}$
	Reserved	$180_{16}..1FF_{16}$
TL > 0	Hardware traps	$200_{16}..27F_{16}$
	Spill/fill traps	$280_{16}..2FF_{16}$
	Software traps	$300_{16}..37F_{16}$
	Reserved	$380_{16}..3FF_{16}$

Figure 40—Trap Table Layout

The trap table for TL = 0 comprises 512 32-byte entries; the trap table for TL > 0 comprises 512 more 32-byte entries. Therefore, the total size of a full trap table is $512 \times 32 \times 2$, or 32K bytes. However, if privileged software does not use software traps (Tcc instructions) at TL > 0, the table can be made 24K bytes long.

7.5.2 Trap Type (TT)

When a normal trap occurs, a value that uniquely identifies the trap is written into the current 9-bit TT register (TT[TL]) by hardware. Control is then transferred into the trap table to an address formed by the TBA register ("TL>0") and TT[TL] (see 5.2.8, "Trap Base Address (TBA)"). Since the lowest five bits of the address are always zero, each entry in the trap table may contain the first eight instructions of the corresponding trap handler.

Programming Note:
> The spill/fill and *clean_window* trap types are spaced such that their trap table entries are 128 bytes (32 instructions) long. This allows the complete code for one spill/fill or *clean_window* routine to reside in one trap table entry.

When a special trap occurs, the TT register is set as described in 7.2.1, "RED_state." Control is then transferred into the RED_state trap table to an address formed by the RST-Vaddr and an offset depending on the condition.

TT values $000_{16}..0FF_{16}$ are reserved for hardware traps. TT values $100_{16}..17F_{16}$ are reserved for software traps (traps caused by execution of a Tcc instruction). TT values $180_{16}..1FF_{16}$ are reserved for future uses. The assignment of TT values to traps is shown in table 14; table 15 lists the traps in priority order. Traps marked with an open bullet 'O' are optional and possibly implementation-dependent. Traps marked with a closed bullet '●' are mandatory; that is, hardware must detect and trap these exceptions and interrupts and must set the defined TT values.

The trap type for the *clean_window* exception is 024_{16}. Three subsequent trap vectors ($025_{16}..027_{16}$) are reserved to allow for an inline (branchless) trap handler. Window spill/fill traps are described in 7.5.2.1. Three subsequent trap vectors are reserved for each spill/fill vector, to allow for an inline (branchless) trap handler.

Table 14—Exception and Interrupt Requests, Sorted by TT Value

M / O	Exception or interrupt request	TT	Priority
●	Reserved	000_{16}	n/a
●	power_on_reset	001_{16}	0
○	watchdog_reset	002_{16}	1
○	externally_initiated_reset	003_{16}	1
●	software_initiated_reset	004_{16}	1
●	RED_state_exception	005_{16}	1
●	Reserved	$006_{16}..007_{16}$	n/a
●	instruction_access_exception	008_{16}	5
○	instruction_access_MMU_miss	009_{16}	2
○	instruction_access_error	$00A_{16}$	3
●	Reserved	$00B_{16}..00F_{16}$	n/a
●	illegal_instruction	010_{16}	7
●	privileged_opcode	011_{16}	6
○	unimplemented_LDD	012_{16}	6
○	unimplemented_STD	013_{16}	6
●	Reserved	$014_{16}..01F_{16}$	n/a
●	fp_disabled	020_{16}	8
○	fp_exception_ieee_754	021_{16}	11
○	fp_exception_other	022_{16}	11
●	tag_overflow	023_{16}	14
○	clean_window	$024_{16}..027_{16}$	10
●	division_by_zero	028_{16}	15
○	internal_processor_error	029_{16}	4
●	Reserved	$02A_{16}..02F_{16}$	n/a
●	data_access_exception	030_{16}	12
○	data_access_MMU_miss	031_{16}	12
○	data_access_error	032_{16}	12
○	data_access_protection	033_{16}	12
●	mem_address_not_aligned	034_{16}	10
○	LDDF_mem_address_not_aligned (impl. dep. #109)	035_{16}	10
○	STDF_mem_address_not_aligned (impl. dep. #110)	036_{16}	10
●	privileged_action	037_{16}	11
○	LDQF_mem_address_not_aligned (impl. dep. #111)	038_{16}	10
○	STQF_mem_address_not_aligned (impl. dep. #112)	039_{16}	10
●	Reserved	$03A_{16}..03F_{16}$	n/a
○	async_data_error	040_{16}	2
●	interrupt_level_n ($n = 1..15$)	$041_{16}..04F_{16}$	$32-n$
●	Reserved	$050_{16}..05F_{16}$	n/a
○	implementation_dependent_exception_n (impl. dep. #35)	$060_{16}..07F_{16}$	impl.-dep.
●	spill_n_normal ($n = 0..7$)	$080_{16}..09F_{16}$	9
●	spill_n_other ($n = 0..7$)	$0A0_{16}..0BF_{16}$	9
●	fill_n_normal ($n = 0..7$)	$0C0_{16}..0DF_{16}$	9
●	fill_n_other ($n = 0..7$)	$0E0_{16}..0FF_{16}$	9
●	trap_instruction	$100_{16}..17F_{16}$	16
●	Reserved	$180_{16}..1FF_{16}$	n/a

Table 15—Exception and Interrupt Requests, Sorted by Priority (0 = Highest; 31 = Lowest)

M / O	Exception or Interrupt Request	TT	Priority
●	*power_on_reset*	001_{16}	0
○	*watchdog_reset*	002_{16}	1
○	*externally_initiated_reset*	003_{16}	1
●	*software_initiated_reset*	004_{16}	1
●	*RED_state_exception*	005_{16}	1
○	*instruction_access_MMU_miss*	009_{16}	2
○	*async_data_error*	040_{16}	2
○	*instruction_access_error*	$00A_{16}$	3
○	*internal_processor_error*	029_{16}	4
●	*instruction_access_exception*	008_{16}	5
●	*privileged_opcode*	011_{16}	6
○	*unimplemented_LDD*	012_{16}	6
○	*unimplemented_STD*	013_{16}	6
●	*illegal_instruction*	010_{16}	7
●	*fp_disabled*	020_{16}	8
●	*spill_n_normal* ($n = 0..7$)	$080_{16}..09F_{16}$	9
●	*spill_n_other* ($n = 0..7$)	$0A0_{16}..0BF_{16}$	9
●	*fill_n_normal* ($n = 0..7$)	$0C0_{16}..0DF_{16}$	9
●	*fill_n_other* ($n = 0..7$)	$0E0_{16}..0FF_{16}$	9
○	*clean_window*	$024_{16}..027_{16}$	10
●	*mem_address_not_aligned*	034_{16}	10
○	*LDDF_mem_address_not_aligned* (impl. dep. #109)	035_{16}	10
○	*STDF_mem_address_not_aligned* (impl. dep. #110)	036_{16}	10
○	*LDQF_mem_address_not_aligned* (impl. dep. #111)	038_{16}	10
○	*STQF_mem_address_not_aligned* (impl. dep. #112)	039_{16}	10
○	*fp_exception_ieee_754*	021_{16}	11
○	*fp_exception_other*	022_{16}	11
●	*privileged_action*	037_{16}	11
●	*data_access_exception*	030_{16}	12
○	*data_access_MMU_miss*	031_{16}	12
○	*data_access_error*	032_{16}	12
○	*data_access_protection*	033_{16}	12
●	*tag_overflow*	023_{16}	14
●	*division_by_zero*	028_{16}	15
●	*trap_instruction*	$100_{16}..17F_{16}$	16
●	*interrupt_level_n* ($n = 1..15$)	$041_{16}..04F_{16}$	$32-n$
○	*implementation_dependent_exception_n* (impl. dep. #35)	$060_{16}..07F_{16}$	*impl.-dep.*

Compatibility Note:

> Support for some trap types is optional because they are associatred with specific instruction(s), which, in a given implementation, might be implemented purely in software. In such a case, hardware would never generate that type of trap; therefore, support for it would be superfluous. Examples of trap types to which this applies are *fp_exception_ieee_754* and *fp_exception_other*.

Since the assignment of exceptions and interrupt requests to particular trap vector addresses and the priority levels are not visible to a user program, an implementation is allowed to define additional hardware traps.

IMPL. DEP. #35: TT values 060_{16} TO $07F_{16}$ are reserved for implementation-dependent exceptions. The existence of *implementation_dependent_n* traps and whether any that do exist are precise, deferred, or disrupting is implementation-dependent. See Appendix C, "SPARC-V9 Implementation Dependencies."

Trap Type values marked "*Reserved*" in table 14 are reserved for future versions of the architecture.

7.5.2.1 Trap Type for Spill/Fill Traps

The trap type for window spill/fill traps is determined based on the contents of the OTHERWIN and WSTATE registers as follows:

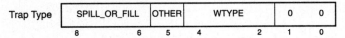

Trap Type	SPILL_OR_FILL	OTHER	WTYPE	0	0
	8	6 5	4 2	1	0

The fields have the following values:

SPILL_OR_FILL:

010_2 for spill traps; 011_2 for fill traps

OTHER:

(OTHERWIN≠0)

WTYPE:

If (OTHER) then WSTATE.OTHER else WSTATE.NORMAL

7.5.3 Trap Priorities

Table 14 shows the assignment of traps to TT values and the relative priority of traps and interrupt requests. Priority 0 is highest, priority 31 is lowest; that is, if $X < Y$, a pending exception or interrupt request with priority X is taken instead of a pending exception or interrupt request with priority Y.

IMPL. DEP. #36: The priorities of particular traps are relative and are implementation-dependent, because a future version of the architecture may define new traps, and an implementation may define implementation-dependent traps that establish new relative priorities.

However, the TT values for the exceptions and interrupt requests shown in table 14 must remain the same for every implementation.

7.6 Trap Processing

The processor's action during trap processing depends on the trap type, the current level of trap nesting (given in the TL register), and the processor state. All traps use normal trap processing, except those due to reset requests, catastrophic errors, traps taken when TL = MAXTL − 1, and traps taken when the processor is in RED_state. These traps use special RED_state trap processing.

During normal operation, the processor is in execute_state. It processes traps in execute_state and continues.

When a normal trap or software-initiated reset (SIR) occurs with TL = MAXTL, there are no more levels on the trap stack, so the processor enters error_state and halts. In order to avoid this catastrophic failure, SPARC-V9 provides the RED_state processor state. Traps processed in RED_state use a special trap vector and a special trap-vectoring algorithm. RED_state vectoring and the setting of the TT value for RED_state traps are described in 7.2.1, "RED_state."

Traps that occur with TL = MAXTL − 1 are processed in RED_state. In addition, reset traps are also processed in RED_state. Reset trap processing is described in 7.6.2, "Special Trap Processing." Finally, supervisor software can force the processor into RED_state by setting the PSTATE.RED flag to one.

Once the processor has entered RED_state, no matter how it got there, all subsequent traps are processed in RED_state until software returns the processor to execute_state or a normal or SIR trap is taken when TL = MAXTL, which puts the processor in error_state. Tables 16, 17, and 18 describe the processor mode and trap level transitions involved in handling traps:

Table 16—Trap Received While in execute_state

| Original state | New State, after receiving trap type | | | |
	Normal trap or interrupt	POR	WDR, XIR, Impl. Dep.	SIR
execute_state	execute_state	RED_state	RED_state	RED_state
TL < MAXTL − 1	TL + 1	MAXTL	TL + 1	TL + 1
execute_state	RED_state	RED_state	RED_state	RED_state
TL = MAXTL − 1	MAXTL	MAXTL	MAXTL	MAXTL
execute_state[†]	error_state	RED_state	RED_state	error_state
TL = MAXTL	MAXTL	MAXTL	MAXTL	MAXTL

[†]This state occurs when software changes TL to MAXTL and does not set PSTATE.RED, or if it clears PSTATE.RED while at MAXTL.

Table 17—Trap Received While in RED_state

Original state	New State, after receiving trap type			
	Normal trap or interrupt	POR	WDR, XIR, Impl. Dep.	SIR
RED_state TL < MAXTL – 1	RED_state TL + 1	RED_state MAXTL	RED_state TL + 1	RED_state TL + 1
RED_state TL = MAXTL – 1	RED_state MAXTL	RED_state MAXTL	RED_state MAXTL	RED_state MAXTL
RED_state TL = MAXTL	error_state MAXTL	RED_state MAXTL	RED_state MAXTL	error_state MAXTL

Table 18—Reset Received While in error_state

Original state	New State, after receiving trap type			
	Normal trap or interrupt	POR	WDR, XIR, Impl. Dep.	SIR
error_state TL < MAXTL – 1	—	RED_state MAXTL	RED_state TL + 1	—
error_state TL = MAXTL – 1	—	RED_state MAXTL	RED_state MAXTL	—
error_state TL = MAXTL	—	RED_state MAXTL	RED_state MAXTL	—

Implementation Note:
> The processor shall not recognize interrupts while it is in error_state.

7.6.1 Normal Trap Processing

A normal trap causes the following state changes to occur:

— If the processor is already in RED_state, the new trap is processed in RED_state unless TL = MAXTL. See 7.6.2.6, "Normal Traps When the Processor is in RED_state."

— If the processor is in execute_state and the trap level is one less than its maximum value, that is, TL = MAXTL–1, the processor enters RED_state. See 7.2.1, "RED_state," and 7.6.2.1, "Normal Traps with TL = MAXTL – 1."

— If the processor is in either execute_state or RED_state, and the trap level is already at its maximum value, that is, TL = MAXTL, the processor enters error_state. See 7.2.2, "Error_state."

Otherwise, the trap uses normal trap processing, and the following state changes occur:

— The trap level is set. This provides access to a fresh set of privileged trap-state registers used to save the current state, in effect, pushing a frame on the trap stack.
TL ← TL + 1

— Existing state is preserved

TSTATE[TL].CCR	← CCR
TSTATE[TL].ASI	← ASI
TSTATE[TL].PSTATE	← PSTATE
TSTATE[TL].CWP	← CWP
TPC[TL]	← PC
TNPC[TL]	← nPC

— The trap type is preserved.

TT[TL] ← the trap type

— The PSTATE register is updated to a predefined state

PSTATE.MM	is unchanged
PSTATE.RED	← 0
PSTATE.PEF	← 1 if FPU is present, 0 otherwise
PSTATE.AM	← 0 (address masking is turned off)
PSTATE.PRIV	← 1 (the processor enters privileged mode)
PSTATE.IE	← 0 (interrupts are disabled)
PSTATE.AG	← 1 (global regs are replaced with alternate globals)
PSTATE.CLE	← PSTATE.TLE (set endian mode for traps)

— For a register-window trap only, CWP is set to point to the register window that must be accessed by the trap-handler software, that is:

- If TT[TL] = 024_{16} (a *clean_window* trap), then CWP ← CWP + 1.

- If (080_{16} ≤ TT[TL] ≤ $0BF_{16}$) (window spill trap), then CWP ← CWP + CANSAVE + 2.

- If ($0C0_{16}$ ≤ TT[TL] ≤ $0FF_{16}$) (window fill trap), then CWP ← CWP–1.

For non-register-window traps, CWP is not changed.

— Control is transferred into the trap table:

$$PC \leftarrow TBA<63:15> \square (TL>0) \square TT[TL] \square 0\ 0000$$

$$nPC \leftarrow TBA<63:15> \square (TL>0) \square TT[TL] \square 0\ 0100$$

where "(TL>0)" is 0 if TL = 0, and 1 if TL > 0.

Interrupts are ignored as long as PSTATE.IE = 0.

Programming Note:

State in TPC[*n*], TNPC[*n*], TSTATE[*n*], and TT[*n*] is only changed autonomously by the processor when a trap is taken while TL = *n*−1, however, software can change any of these values with a WRPR instruction when TL = *n*.

7.6.2 Special Trap Processing

The following conditions invoke special trap processing:

— Traps taken with TL = MAXTL – 1

— Power-on reset traps

— Watchdog reset traps

— Externally initiated reset traps

— Software-initiated reset traps

— Traps taken when the processor is already in RED_state

— Implementation-dependent traps

IMPL. DEP. #38: Implementation-dependent registers may or may not be affected by the various reset traps.

7.6.2.1 Normal Traps with TL = MAXTL – 1

Normal traps that occur when TL = MAXTL – 1 are processed in RED_state. The following state changes occur:

— The trap level is advanced.
   TL ← MAXTL

— Existing state is preserved
   TSTATE[TL].CCR   ← CCR
   TSTATE[TL].ASI   ← ASI
   TSTATE[TL].PSTATE   ← PSTATE
   TSTATE[TL].CWP   ← CWP
   TPC[TL]   ← PC
   TNPC[TL]   ← nPC

— The trap type is preserved.
   TT[TL] ← the trap type

— The PSTATE register is set as follows:
   PSTATE.MM   ← 00_2 (TSO)
   PSTATE.RED   ← 1 (enter RED_state)
   PSTATE.PEF   ← 1 if FPU is present, 0 otherwise
   PSTATE.AM   ← 0 (address masking is turned off)
   PSTATE.PRIV   ← 1 (the processor enters privileged mode)
   PSTATE.IE   ← 0 (interrupts are disabled)
   PSTATE.AG   ← 1 (global regs are replaced with alternate globals)
   PSTATE.CLE   ← PSTATE.TLE (set endian mode for traps)

— For a register-window trap only, CWP is set to point to the register window that must be accessed by the trap-handler software, that is:

   • If TT[TL] = 024_{16} (a *clean_window* trap), then CWP ← CWP + 1.

- If $(080_{16} \leq TT[TL] \leq 0BF_{16})$ (window spill trap), then CWP ← CWP + CANSAVE + 2.
- If $(0C0_{16} \leq TT[TL] \leq 0FF_{16})$ (window fill trap), then CWP ← CWP–1.
For non-register-window traps, CWP is not changed.

— Implementation-specific state changes; for example, disabling an MMU

— Control is transferred into the RED_state trap table

> PC ← RSTVaddr<63:8> ⫿ 1010 0000$_2$
>
> nPC ← RSTVaddr<63:8> ⫿ 1010 0100$_2$

7.6.2.2 Power-On Reset (POR) Traps

Initiated when power is applied to the processor. If the processor is in error_state, a power-on reset (POR) brings the processor out of error_state and places it in RED_state. Processor state is undefined after POR, except for the following:

— The trap level is set.
TL ← MAXTL

— The trap type is set.
TT[TL] ← 001_{16}

— The PSTATE register is set as follows:

PSTATE.MM	←	00_2 (TSO)
PSTATE.RED	←	1 (enter RED_state)
PSTATE.PEF	←	1 if FPU is present, 0 otherwise
PSTATE.AM	←	0 (address masking is turned off)
PSTATE.PRIV	←	1 (the processor enters privileged mode)
PSTATE.IE	←	0 (interrupts are disabled)
PSTATE.AG	←	1 (global regs are replaced with alternate globals)
PSTATE.TLE	←	0 (big-endian mode for traps)
PSTATE.CLE	←	0 (big-endian mode for non-traps)

— The TICK register is protected.
TICK.NPT ← 1 (TICK unreadable by nonprivileged software)

— Implementation-specific state changes; for example, disabling an MMU

— Control is transferred into the RED_state trap table

> PC ← RSTVaddr<63:8> ⫿ 0010 0000$_2$
>
> nPC ← RSTVaddr<63:8> ⫿ 0010 0100$_2$

For any reset when TL = MAXTL, for all n<MAXTL, the values in TPC[n], TNPC[n], and TSTATE[n] are undefined.

7.6.2.3 Watchdog Reset (WDR) Traps

WDR traps are initiated by an external signal. Typically, this is generated in response to error_state or expiration of a watchdog timer. WDR clears error_state and hung states, and performs a system reset; pending and in-progress hardware operations (for example, loads and stores) may be cancelled or aborted. Architecturally defined registers (e. g., floating-point registers, integer registers, etc.) and state are unchanged from before the WDR, but they may be in an inconsistent state if operations are aborted. If the processor is in error_ state, a watchdog reset (WDR) brings the processor out of error_state and places it in RED_state.

The following state changes occur:

— The trap level is set.
   $TL \leftarrow MIN(TL + 1, MAXTL)$

— Existing state is preserved.
   TSTATE[TL].CCR $\leftarrow$ CCR
   TSTATE[TL].ASI $\leftarrow$ ASI
   TSTATE[TL].PSTATE $\leftarrow$ PSTATE
   TSTATE[TL].CWP $\leftarrow$ CWP
   TPC[TL] $\leftarrow$ PC
   TNPC[TL] $\leftarrow$ nPC

— TT[TL] is set as described below.

— The PSTATE register is set as follows:
   PSTATE.MM $\leftarrow 00_2$ (TSO)
   PSTATE.RED $\leftarrow 1$ (enter RED_state)
   PSTATE.PEF $\leftarrow 1$ if FPU is present, 0 otherwise
   PSTATE.AM $\leftarrow 0$ (address masking is turned off)
   PSTATE.PRIV $\leftarrow 1$ (the processor enters privileged mode)
   PSTATE.IE $\leftarrow 0$ (interrupts are disabled)
   PSTATE.AG $\leftarrow 1$ (global regs are replaced with alternate globals)
   PSTATE.CLE $\leftarrow$ PSTATE.TLE (set endian mode for traps)

— Implementation-specific state changes; for example, disabling an MMU.

— Control is transferred into the RED_state trap table.
   PC $\leftarrow$ RSTVaddr<63:8> $\Vert$ 0100 0000$_2$
   nPC $\leftarrow$ RSTVaddr<63:8> $\Vert$ 0100 0100$_2$

If a watchdog reset occurs when the processor is in error_state, the TT field gives the type of the trap that caused entry into error_state. If a watchdog reset occurs with the processor in execute_state, TT is set to 2 (WDR).

For any reset when TL = MAXTL, for all n<MAXTL, the values in TPC[n], TNPC[n], and TSTATE[n] are undefined.

7.6.2.4 Externally Initiated Reset (XIR) Traps

XIR traps are initiated by an external signal. They behave like an interrupt that cannot be masked by IE = 0 or PIL. Typically, XIR is used for critical system events such as power failure, reset button pressed, failure of external components that does not require a WDR (which aborts operations), or system-wide reset in a multiprocessor. If the processor is in error_state, an externally initiated reset (XIR) brings the processor out of error_state and places it in RED_state.

The following state changes occur:

— The trap level is set.
$TL \leftarrow MIN(TL + 1, MAXTL)$

— Existing state is preserved.

TSTATE[TL].CCR	$\leftarrow$ CCR
TSTATE[TL].ASI	$\leftarrow$ ASI
TSTATE[TL].PSTATE	$\leftarrow$ PSTATE
TSTATE[TL].CWP	$\leftarrow$ CWP
TPC[TL]	$\leftarrow$ PC
TNPC[TL]	$\leftarrow$ nPC

— TT[TL] is set as described below.

— The PSTATE register is set as follows:

PSTATE.MM	$\leftarrow 00_2$ (TSO)
PSTATE.RED	$\leftarrow$ 1 (enter RED_state)
PSTATE.PEF	$\leftarrow$ 1 if FPU is present, 0 otherwise
PSTATE.AM	$\leftarrow$ 0 (address masking is turned off)
PSTATE.PRIV	$\leftarrow$ 1 (the processor enters privileged mode)
PSTATE.IE	$\leftarrow$ 0 (interrupts are disabled)
PSTATE.AG	$\leftarrow$ 1 (global regs are replaced with alternate globals)
PSTATE.CLE	$\leftarrow$ PSTATE.TLE (set endian mode for traps)

— Implementation-specific state changes; for example, disabling an MMU.

— Control is transferred into the RED_state trap table.

$PC \leftarrow$ RSTVaddr<63:8> ⚬ $0110\ 0000_2$

$nPC \leftarrow$ RSTVaddr<63:8> ⚬ $0110\ 0100_2$

TT is set in the same manner as for watchdog reset. If the processor is in execute_state when the externally initiated reset (XIR) occurs, TT = 3. If the processor is in error_state when the XIR occurs, TT identifies the exception that caused entry into error_state.

For any reset when TL = MAXTL, for all n<MAXTL, the values in TPC[n], TNPC[n], and TSTATE[n] are undefined.

7.6.2.5 Software-Initiated Reset (SIR) Traps

SIR traps are initiated by executing an SIR instruction. This is used by supervisor software as a panic operation, or a meta-supervisor trap.

The following state changes occur:

— If TL = MAXTL, then enter error_state. Otherwise, do the following:

— The trap level is set.
$TL \leftarrow TL + 1$

— Existing state is preserved

TSTATE[TL].CCR	← CCR
TSTATE[TL].ASI	← ASI
TSTATE[TL].PSTATE	← PSTATE
TSTATE[TL].CWP	← CWP
TPC[TL]	← PC
TNPC[TL]	← nPC

— The trap type is set.

$$TT[TL] \leftarrow 04_{16}$$

— The PSTATE register is set as follows:

PSTATE.MM	← 00_2 (TSO)
PSTATE.RED	← 1 (enter RED_state)
PSTATE.PEF	← 1 if FPU is present, 0 otherwise
PSTATE.AM	← 0 (address masking is turned off)
PSTATE.PRIV	← 1 (the processor enters privileged mode)
PSTATE.IE	← 0 (interrupts are disabled)
PSTATE.AG	← 1 (global regs are replaced with alternate globals)
PSTATE.CLE	← PSTATE.TLE (set endian mode for traps)

— Implementation-specific state changes; for example, disabling an MMU.

— Control is transferred into the RED_state trap table

$$PC \leftarrow RSTVaddr{<}63{:}8{>} \ \square \ 1000\ 0000_2$$

$$nPC \leftarrow RSTVaddr{<}63{:}8{>} \ \square \ 1000\ 0100_2$$

For any reset when TL = MAXTL, for all n < MAXTL, the values in TPC[n], TNPC[n], and TSTATE[n] are undefined.

7.6.2.6 Normal Traps When the Processor is in RED_state

Normal traps taken when the processor is already in RED_state are also processed in RED_state, unless TL = MAXTL, in which case the processor enters error_state.

The processor state shall be set as follows:

— The trap level is set.

$$TL \leftarrow TL + 1$$

— Existing state is preserved.

TSTATE[TL].CCR	← CCR
TSTATE[TL].ASI	← ASI
TSTATE[TL].PSTATE	← PSTATE
TSTATE[TL].CWP	← CWP
TPC[TL]	← PC
TNPC[TL]	← nPC

— The trap type is preserved.

$$TT[TL] \leftarrow trap\ type$$

— The PSTATE register is set as follows:

PSTATE.MM	$\leftarrow$ 00_2 (TSO)
PSTATE.RED	$\leftarrow$ 1 (enter RED_state)
PSTATE.PEF	$\leftarrow$ 1 if FPU is present, 0 otherwise
PSTATE.AM	$\leftarrow$ 0 (address masking is turned off)
PSTATE.PRIV	$\leftarrow$ 1 (the processor enters privileged mode)
PSTATE.IE	$\leftarrow$ 0 (interrupts are disabled)
PSTATE.AG	$\leftarrow$ 1 (global regs are replaced with alternate globals)
PSTATE.CLE	$\leftarrow$ PSTATE.TLE (set endian mode for traps)

— For a register-window trap only, CWP is set to point to the register window that must be accessed by the trap-handler software, that is:

- If TT[TL] = 024_{16} (a *clean_window* trap), then CWP $\leftarrow$ CWP + 1.

- If ($080_{16} \leq$ TT[TL] $\leq 0BF_{16}$) (window spill trap), then
  CWP $\leftarrow$ CWP + CANSAVE + 2.

- If ($0C0_{16} \leq$ TT[TL] $\leq 0FF_{16}$) (window fill trap), then CWP $\leftarrow$ CWP − 1.

For non-register-window traps, CWP is not changed.

— Implementation-specific state changes; for example, disabling an MMU

— Control is transferred into the RED_state trap table

PC $\leftarrow$ RSTVaddr<63:8> ⫿ 1010 0000$_2$

nPC $\leftarrow$ RSTVaddr<63:8> ⫿ 1010 0100$_2$

7.6.2.7 Implementation-Dependent Traps

The operation of the processor for *implementation_dependent_exception_n* traps is implementation-dependent (impl. dep. #35).

7.7 Exception and Interrupt Descriptions

The following paragraphs describe the various exceptions and interrupt requests and the conditions that cause them. Each exception and interrupt request describes the corresponding trap type as defined by the trap model. An open bullet 'O' identifies optional and possibly implementation-dependent traps; traps marked with a closed bullet '●' are mandatory. Each trap is marked as precise, deferred, disrupting, or reset. Example exception conditions are included for each exception type. Appendix A, "Instruction Definitions," enumerates which traps can be generated by each instruction.

O **async_data_error** [*tt* = 040_{16}] (Disrupting)

An asynchronous data error occurred on a data access. Examples: an ECC error occurred while writing data from a cache store buffer to memory, or an ECC error occurred on an MMU hardware table walk. When an *async_data_error* occurs, the TPC and TNPC stacked by the trap are not necessarily related to the instruction or data access that caused the error; that is, *async_data_error* causes a disrupting trap.

Compatibility Note:

> The SPARC-V9 *async_data_error* exception supersedes the less general SPARC-V8 *data_store_error* exception.

○ **clean_window** [$tt = 024_{16}..027_{16}$] (Precise)

> A SAVE instruction discovered that the window about to be used contains data from another address space; the window must be cleaned before it can be used.
>
> **IMPL. DEP. #102:** An implementation may choose either to implement automatic cleaning of register windows in hardware, or to generate a *clean_window* trap, when needed, so that window(s) can be cleaned by software. If an implementation chooses the latter option, then support for this trap type is mandatory.

○ **data_access_error** [$tt = 032_{16}$] (Precise, Deferred, or Disrupting)

> A catastrophic error exception occurred on a data access from/to memory (for example, a parity error on a data cache access, or an uncorrectable ECC memory error) (impl. dep. #31).

● **data_access_exception** [$tt = 030_{16}$] (Precise or Deferred)

> An exception occurred on a data access. For example, an MMU indicated that a page was invalid or protected (impl. dep. #33).

○ **data_access_MMU_miss** [$tt = 031_{16}$] (Precise or Deferred)

> A miss in an MMU occurred on a data access from/to memory. For example, a page descriptor cache or translation lookaside buffer did not contain a translation for the virtual address. (impl. dep. #33)

○ **data_access_protection** [$tt = 033_{16}$] (Precise or Deferred)

> A protection fault occurred on a data access; for example, an MMU indicated that the page was write-protected (impl. dep. #33).

● **division_by_zero** [$tt = 028_{16}$] (Precise or Deferred)

> An integer divide instruction attempted to divide by zero (impl. dep. #33).

○ **externally_initiated_reset** [$tt = 003_{16}$] (Reset)

> An external signal was asserted. This trap is used for catastrophic events such as power failure, reset button pressed, and system-wide reset in multiprocessor systems.

● **fill_*n*_normal** [$tt = 0C0_{16}..0DF_{16}$] (Precise)

● **fill_*n*_other** [$tt = 0E0_{16}..0FF_{16}$] (Precise)

> A RESTORE or RETURN instruction has determined that the contents of a register window must be restored from memory.

Compatibility Note:

> The SPARC-V9 *fill_n_** exceptions supersede the SPARC-V8 *window_underflow* exception.

● **fp_disabled** [$tt = 020_{16}$] (Precise)

> An attempt was made to execute an FPop, a floating-point branch, or a floating-point load/store instruction while an FPU was not present, PSTATE.PEF = 0, or FPRS.FEF = 0.

○ **fp_exception_ieee_754** [$tt = 021_{16}$] (Precise or Deferred (impl. dep. #23))

An FPop instruction generated an IEEE_754_exception and its corresponding trap enable mask (TEM) bit was 1. The floating-point exception type, *IEEE_754_exception*, is encoded in the FSR.*ftt*, and specific *IEEE_754_exception* information is encoded in FSR.*cexc*.

○ **fp_exception_other** [$tt = 022_{16}$] (Precise or Deferred (impl. dep. #23))

An FPop instruction generated an exception other than an *IEEE_754_exception*. For example, the FPop is unimplemented, or the FPop did not complete, or there was a sequence or hardware error in the FPU. The floating-point exception type is encoded in the FSR's *ftt* field.

● **illegal_instruction** [$tt = 010_{16}$] (Precise or Deferred)

An attempt was made to execute an instruction with an unimplemented opcode, an ILLTRAP instruction, an instruction with invalid field usage, or an instruction that would result in illegal processor state. Note that unimplemented FPop instructions generate *fp_exception_other* traps.

○ **implementation_dependent_exception_*n*** [$tt = 060_{16}..07F_{16}$] (Pre, Def, or Dis)

These exceptions are implementation-dependent (impl. dep. #35).

○ **instruction_access_error** [$tt = 00A_{16}$] (Precise, Deferred, or Disrupting)

A catastrophic error exception occurred on an instruction access. For example, a parity error on an instruction cache access (impl. dep. #31).

● **instruction_access_exception** [$tt = 008_{16}$] (Precise)

An exception occurred on an instruction access. For example, an MMU indicated that the page was invalid or not executable.

○ **instruction_access_MMU_miss** [$tt = 009_{16}$] (Precise, Deferred, or Disrupting)

A miss in an MMU occurred on an instruction access from memory. For example, a PDC or TLB did not contain a translation for the virtual address. (impl. dep. #33)

○ **internal_processor_error** [$tt = 029_{16}$] (Precise, Deferred, or Disrupting)

A catastrophic error exception occurred in the main processor. For example, a parity or uncorrectable ECC error on an internal register or bus (impl. dep. #31).

Compatibility Note:

The SPARC-V9 *internal_processor_error* exception supersedes the less general SPARC-V8 *r_register_access_error* exception.

● **interrupt_level_*n*** [$tt = 041_{16}..04F_{16}$] (Disrupting)

An interrupt request level of *n* was presented to the IU, while PSTATE.IE = 1 and (interrupt request level > PIL).

○ **LDDF_mem_address_not_aligned** [$tt = 035_{16}$] (Precise)

An attempt was made to execute an LDDF instruction and the effective address was word-aligned but not doubleword-aligned. Use of this exception is implementation-dependent (impl. dep. #109). A separate trap entry for this exception supports fast software emulation of the LDDF instruction when the effective address is word-aligned but not doubleword-aligned. See A.25, "Load Floating-Point."

○ **LDQF_mem_address_not_aligned** [$tt = 038_{16}$] (Precise)

An attempt was made to execute an LDQF instruction and the effective address was word-aligned but not quadword-aligned. Use of this exception is implementation-dependent (impl. dep. #111). A separate trap entry for this exception supports fast software emulation of the LDQF instruction when the effective address is word-aligned but not quadword-aligned. See A.25, "Load Floating-Point."

● **mem_address_not_aligned** [$tt = 034_{16}$] (Precise or Deferred)

A load/store instruction generated a memory address that was not properly aligned according to the instruction, or a JMPL or RETURN instruction generated a non-word-aligned address (impl. dep. #33).

● **power_on_reset** [$tt = 001_{16}$] (Reset)

An external signal was asserted. This trap isused to bring a system reliably from the power-off to the power-on state.

● **privileged_action** [$tt = 037_{16}$] (Precise)

An action defined to be privileged has been attempted while PSTATE.PRIV = 0. Examples: a data access by nonprivileged software using an ASI value with its most significant bit = 0 (a restricted ASI), or an attempt to read the TICK register by nonprivileged software when TICK.NPT = 1.

● **privileged_opcode** [$tt = 011_{16}$] (Precise)

An attempt was made to execute a privileged instruction while PSTATE.PRIV = 0.

Compatibility Note:
This trap type is identical to the SPARC-V8 *privileged_instruction* trap. The name was changed to distinguish it from the new *privileged_action* trap type.

● **software_initiated_reset** [$tt = 004_{16}$] (Reset)

Caused by the execution of the SIR, Software-Initiated Reset, instruction. It allows system software to reset the processor.

● **spill_*n*_normal** [$tt = 080_{16}..09F_{16}$] (Precise)
● **spill_*n*_other** [$tt = 0A0_{16}..0BF_{16}$] (Precise)

A SAVE or FLUSHW instruction has determined that the contents of a register window must be saved to memory.

Compatibility Note:
The SPARC-V9 spill_*n*_* exceptions supersede the SPARC-V8 *window_overflow* exception.

○ **STDF_mem_address_not_aligned** [$tt = 036_{16}$] (Precise)

An attempt was made to execute an STDF instruction and the effective address was word-aligned but not doubleword-aligned. Use of this exception is implementation-dependent (impl. dep. #110). A separate trap entry for this exception supports fast software emulation of the STDF instruction when the effective address is word-aligned but not doubleword-aligned. See A.51, "Store Floating-Point."

○ **STQF_mem_address_not_aligned** [$tt = 039_{16}$] (Precise)

An attempt was made to execute an STQF instruction and the effective address was word-aligned but not quadword-aligned. Use of this exception is implementation-dependent (impl. dep. #112). A separate trap entry for this exception supports fast software emulation of the STQF instruction when the effective address is word-aligned but not quadword-aligned. See A.51, "Store Floating-Point."

- **tag_overflow** [$tt = 023_{16}$] (Precise)

  A TADDccTV or TSUBccTV instruction was executed, and either 32-bit arithmetic overflow occurred or at least one of the tag bits of the operands was nonzero.

- **trap_instruction** [$tt = 100_{16}..17F_{16}$] (Precise)

  A Tcc instruction was executed and the trap condition evaluated to TRUE.

○ **unimplemented_LDD** [$tt = 012_{16}$] (Precise)

  An attempt was made to execute an LDD instruction, which is not implemented in hardware on this implementation (impl. dep. #107).

○ **unimplemented_STD** [$tt = 013_{16}$] (Precise)

  An attempt was made to execute an STD instruction which is not implemented in hardware on this implementation (impl. dep. #108).

- **watchdog_reset** [$tt = 002_{16}$] (Precise)

  An external signal was asserted. This trap exists to break a system deadlock created when an expected external event does not happen within the expected time. In simple systems it is also used to bring a system out of error_state, through RED_ state, and ultimately back to execute_state.

All other trap types are reserved.

8 Memory Models

8.1 Introduction

The SPARC-V9 **memory models** define the semantics of memory operations. The instruction set semantics require that loads and stores seem to be performed in the order in which they appear in the dynamic control flow of the program. The actual order in which they are processed by the memory may be different. The purpose of the memory models is to specify what constraints, if any, are placed on the order of memory operations.

The memory models apply both to uniprocessor and to shared-memory multiprocessors. Formal memory models are necessary in order to precisely define the interactions between multiple processors and input/output devices in a shared-memory configuration. Programming shared-memory multiprocessors requires a detailed understanding of the operative memory model and the ability to specify memory operations at a low level in order to build programs that can safely and reliably coordinate their activities. See Appendix J, "Programming With the Memory Models," for additional information on the use of the models in programming real systems.

The SPARC-V9 architecture is a **model** that specifies the behavior observable by software on SPARC-V9 systems. Therefore, access to memory can be implemented in any manner, as long as the behavior observed by software conforms to that of the models described here and formally defined in Appendix D, "Formal Specification of the Memory Models."

The SPARC-V9 architecture defines three different memory models: **Total Store Order (TSO)**, **Partial Store Order (PSO)**, and **Relaxed Memory Order (RMO)**. All SPARC-V9 processors must provide Total Store Order (or a more strongly ordered model, for example, Sequential Consistency) to ensure SPARC-V8 compatibility.

IMPL. DEP. 113: Whether the PSO or RMO models are supported is implementation-dependent.

Figure 41 shows the relationship of the various SPARC-V9 memory models, from the least restrictive to the most restrictive. Programs written assuming one model will function correctly on any included model.

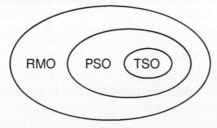

Figure 41—Memory Models from Least Restrictive (RMO) to Most Restrictive (TSO)

SPARC-V9 provides multiple memory models so that:

— Implementations can schedule memory operations for high performance.

— Programmers can create synchronization primitives using shared memory.

These models are described informally in this subsection and formally in Appendix D, "Formal Specification of the Memory Models." If there is a conflict in interpretation between the informal description provided here and the formal models, the formal models supersede the informal description.

There is no preferred memory model for SPARC-V9. Programs written for Relaxed Memory Order will work in Partial Store Order and Total Store Order as well. Programs written for Partial Store Order will work in Total Store Order. Programs written for a weak model, such as RMO, may execute more quickly, since the model exposes more scheduling opportunities, but may also require extra instructions to ensure synchronization. Multiprocessor programs written for a stronger model will behave unpredictably if run in a weaker model.

Machines that implement **sequential consistency** (also called strong ordering or strong consistency) automatically support programs written for TSO, PSO, and RMO. Sequential consistency is not a SPARC-V9 memory model. In sequential consistency, the loads, stores, and atomic load-stores of all processors are performed by memory in a serial order that conforms to the order in which these instructions are issued by individual processors. A machine that implements sequential consistency may deliver lower performance than an equivalent machine that implements a weaker model. Although particular SPARC-V9 implementations may support sequential consistency, portable software must not rely on having this model available.

8.2 Memory, Real Memory, and I/O Locations

Memory is the collection of locations accessed by the load and store instructions (described in Appendix A, "Instruction Definitions"). Each location is identified by an address consisting of two elements: an **address space identifier** (ASI), which identifies an address space, and a 64-bit **address,** which is a byte offset into that address space. Memory addresses may be interpreted by the memory subsystem to be either physical addresses or virtual addresses; addresses may be remapped and values cached, provided that memory properties are preserved transparently and coherency is maintained.

When two or more data addresses refer to the same datum, the address is said to be **aliased**. In this case, the processor and memory system must cooperate to maintain consistency; that is, a store to an aliased address must change all values aliased to that address.

Memory addresses identify either real memory or I/O locations.

Real memory stores information without side effects. A load operation returns the value most recently stored. Operations are side-effect-free in the sense that a load, store, or atomic load-store to a location in real memory has no program-observable effect, except upon that location.

I/O locations may not behave like memory and may have side effects. Load, store, and atomic load-store operations performed on I/O locations may have observable side effects and loads may not return the value most recently stored. The value semantics of operations on I/O locations are **not** defined by the memory models, but the constraints on the order in which operations are performed is the same as it would be if the I/O locations were real memory. The storage properties, contents, semantics, ASI assignments, and addresses of I/O registers are implementation-dependent (impl. dep. #6) (impl. dep. #7) (impl. dep. #123).

IMPL. DEP. #118: The manner in which I/O locations are identified is implementation-dependent.

See F.3.2, "Attributes the MMU Associates with Each Mapping," for example.

IMPL. DEP #120: The coherence and atomicity of memory operations between processors and I/O DMA memory accesses are implementation-dependent.

Compatibility Note:

> Operations to I/O locations are **not** guaranteed to be sequentially consistent between themselves, as they are in SPARC-V8.

> SPARC-V9 does not distinguish real memory from I/O locations in terms of ordering. All references, both to I/O locations and real memory, conform to the memory model's order constraints. References to I/O locations may need to be interspersed with MEMBAR instructions to guarantee the desired ordering. Loads following stores to locations with side effects may return unexpected results due to lookaside into the processor's store buffer, which may subsume the memory transaction. This can be avoided by using a MEMBAR #LookAside.

> Systems supporting SPARC-V8 applications that use memory mapped I/O locations must ensure that SPARC-V8 sequential consistency of I/O locations can be maintained when those locations are referenced by a SPARC-V8 application. The MMU either must enforce such consistency or cooperate with system software and/or the processor to provide it.

IMPL. DEP #121: An implementation may choose to identify certain addresses and use an implementation-dependent memory model for references to them.

For example, an implementation might choose to process addresses tagged with a flag bit in the memory management unit (see Appendix F, "SPARC-V9 MMU Requirements"), or to treat those that utilize a particular ASI (see 8.3, "Addressing and Alternate Address Spaces," below) as using a sequentially consistent model.

8.3 Addressing and Alternate Address Spaces

An address in SPARC-V9 is a tuple consisting of an 8-bit address space identifier (ASI) and a 64-bit byte-address offset in the specified address space. Memory is byte-addressed, with halfword accesses aligned on 2-byte boundaries, word accesses (which include instruction fetches) aligned on 4-byte boundaries, extended-word and doubleword accesses aligned on 8-byte boundaries, and quadword quantities aligned on 16-byte boundaries. With the possible exception of the cases described in 6.3.1.1, "Memory Alignment Restrictions," an improperly aligned address in a load, store, or load-store instruction always causes a trap to occur. The largest datum that is guaranteed to be atomically read or written is an aligned doubleword. Also, memory references to different bytes, halfwords, and words in a given doubleword are treated for ordering purposes as references to the same location. Thus, the unit of ordering for memory is a doubleword.

Programming Note:

> While the doubleword is the coherency unit for update, programmers should not assume that doubleword floating-point values are updated as a unit unless they are doubleword-aligned and always updated using double-precision loads and stores. Some programs use pairs of single-precision operations to load and store double-precision floating-point values when the compiler cannot determine that they are doubleword-aligned. Also, while quad-precision operations are defined in the SPARC-V9 architecture, the granularity of loads and stores for quad-precision floating-point values may be word or doubleword.

The processor provides an address space identifier with every address. This ASI may serve several purposes:

— To identify which of several distinguished address spaces the 64-bit address offset is to be interpreted as addressing

— To provide additional access control and attribute information, for example, the processing which is to be taken if an access fault occurs or to specify the endianness of the reference

— To specify the address of an internal control register in the processor, cache, or memory management hardware

The memory management hardware can associate an independent 2^{64}-byte memory address space with each ASI. If this is done, it becomes possible to allow system software easy access to the address space of the faulting program when processing exceptions, or to implement access to a client program's memory space by a server program.

The architecturally specified ASIs are listed in table 12 on page 72. ASIs need not be fully decoded by the hardware (impl. dep. #30). In particular, specifying an architecturally undefined ASI value in a memory reference instruction or in the ASI register may produce unexpected implementation-dependent results.

When TL = 0, normal accesses by the processor to memory when fetching instructions and performing loads and stores implicitly specify ASI_PRIMARY or ASI_PRIMARY_LITTLE, depending on the setting of the PSTATE.CLE bit.

IMPL. DEP. #124: When TL > 0, the implicit ASI for instruction fetches, loads, and stores is implementation-dependent.

Implementation Note:

> Implementations that support the nucleus context should use ASI_NUCLEUS{_LITTLE}; those that do not should use ASI_PRIMARY{_LITTLE}. See F.4.4, "Contexts," for more information about the nucleus context.

Accesses to other address spaces use the load/store alternate instructions. For these accesses, the ASI is either contained in the instruction (for the register-register addressing mode) or taken from the ASI register (for register-immediate addressing).

ASIs are either unrestricted or restricted. An unrestricted ASI is one that may be used independent of the privilege level (PSTATE.PRIV) at which the processor is running. Restricted ASIs require that the processor be in privileged mode for a legal access to occur. Restricted ASIs have their high-order bit equal to zero. The relationship between processor state and ASI restriction is shown in table 11 on page 71.

Several restricted ASIs must be provided: ASI_AS_IF_USER_PRIMARY{_LITTLE} and ASI_AS_IF_USER_SECONDARY{_LITTLE}. The intent of these ASIs is to give system software efficient access to the memory space of a program.

The normal address space is primary address space, which is accessed by the unrestricted ASI_PRIMARY{_LITTLE}. The secondary address space, which is accessed by the unrestricted ASI_SECONDARY{_LITTLE}, is provided to allow a server program to access a client program's address space.

ASI_PRIMARY_NOFAULT{_LITTLE} and ASI_SECONDARY_NOFAULT{_LITTLE} support **nonfaulting loads.** These ASIs are aliased to ASI_PRIMARY{_LITTLE} and ASI_SECONDARY{_LITTLE}, respectively, and have exactly the same action. They may be used to color (that is, distinguish into classes) loads in the instruction stream so that, in combination with a judicious mapping of low memory and a specialized trap handler, an optimizing compiler can move loads outside of conditional control structures.

Programming Note:

> Nonfaulting loads allow optimizations that move loads ahead of conditional control structures which guard their use; thus, they can minimize the effects of load latency by improving instruction scheduling. The semantics of nonfaulting load are the same as for any other load, except when non-recoverable catastrophic faults occur (for example, address-out-of-range errors). When such a fault occurs, it is ignored and the hardware and system software cooperate to make the load appear to complete normally, returning a zero result. The compiler's optimizer generates load-alternate instructions with the ASI field or register set to ASI_PRIMARY_NOFAULT{_LITTLE} or ASI_SECONDARY_NOFAULT{_LITTLE} for those loads it determines should be nonfaulting. To minimize unnecessary processing if a fault does occur, it is desirable to map low addresses (especially address zero) to a page of all zeros, so that references through a NULL pointer do not cause unnecessary traps.

Implementation Note:

> An implementation, through a combination of hardware and system software, must prevent non-faulting loads on memory locations that have side effects; otherwise, such accesses produce undefined results.

8.4 The SPARC-V9 Memory Model

The SPARC-V9 processor architecture specifies the organization and structure of a SPARC-V9 central processing unit, but does not specify a memory system architecture. Appendix F, "SPARC-V9 MMU Requirements," summarizes the MMU support required by a SPARC-V9 central processing unit.

The memory models specify the possible order relationships between memory-reference instructions issued by a processor and the order and visibility of those instructions as seen by other processors. The memory model is intimately intertwined with the program execution model for instructions.

8.4.1 The SPARC-V9 Program Execution Model

The SPARC-V9 processor model consists of three units: an issue unit, a reorder unit, and an execute unit, as shown in figure 42.

The issue unit reads instructions over the instruction path from memory and issues them in **program order**. Program order is precisely the order determined by the control flow of the program and the instruction semantics, under the assumption that each instruction is performed independently and sequentially.

Issued instructions are collected, reordered, and then dispatched to the execute unit. Instruction reordering allows an implementation to perform some operations in parallel and to better allocate resources. The reordering of instructions is constrained to ensure that the results of program execution are the same as they would be if the instructions were performed in program order. This property is called **processor self-consistency**.

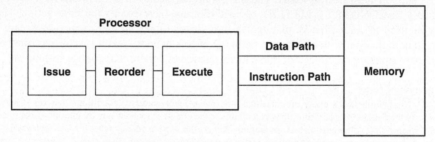

Figure 42—Processor Model: Uniprocessor System

Processor self-consistency requires that the result of execution, in the absence of any shared memory interaction with another processor, be identical to the result that would be observed if the instructions were performed in program order. In the model in figure 42, instructions are issued in program order and placed in the reorder buffer. The processor is allowed to reorder instructions, provided it does not violate any of the data-flow constraints for registers or for memory.

The data-flow order constraints for register reference instructions are:

— An instruction cannot be performed until all earlier instructions that set a register it uses have been performed (read-after-write hazard; write-after-write hazard).

— An instruction cannot be performed until all earlier instructions that use a register it sets have been performed (write-after-read hazard).

An implementation can avoid blocking instruction execution in the second case by using a renaming mechanism which provides the old value of the register to earlier instructions and the new value to later uses.

The data-flow order constraints for memory-reference instructions are those for register reference instructions, plus the following additional constraints:

(1) A memory-reference instruction that sets (stores to) a location cannot be performed until all previous instructions that use (load from) the location have been performed (write-after-read hazard).

(2) A memory-reference instruction that uses (loads) the value at a location cannot be performed until all earlier memory-reference instructions that set (store to) the location have been performed (read-after-write hazard).

As with the case for registers, implementations can avoid blocking instructions in case (2) by providing an additional mechanism, in this case, a write buffer which guarantees that the value returned by a load is that which would be returned by the most recent store, even though the store has not completed. As a result, the value associated with an address may appear to be different when observed from a processor that has written the location and is holding the value in its write buffer than it would be when observed from a processor that references memory (or its own write buffer). Moreover, the load that was satisfied by the write buffer never appears at the memory.

Memory-barrier instructions (MEMBAR and STBAR) and the active memory model specified by PSTATE.MM also constrain the issue of memory-reference instructions. See 8.4.3, "The MEMBAR Instruction," and 8.4.4, "Memory Models," for a detailed description.

The constraints on instruction execution assert a partial ordering on the instructions in the reorder buffer. Every one of the several possible orderings is a legal execution ordering for the program. See Appendix D, "Formal Specification of the Memory Models," for more information.

8.4.2 The Processor/Memory Interface Model

Each processor in a multiprocessor system is modelled as shown in figure 43; that is, having two independent paths to memory: one for instructions and one for data. Caches and mappings are considered to be part of the memory. Data caches are maintained by hardware to be consistent (coherent). Instruction caches need not be kept consistent with data caches and, therefore, require explicit program action to ensure consistency when a program modifies an executing instruction stream. Memory is shared in terms of address space, but may be inhomogeneous and distributed in an implementation. Mapping and caches are ignored in the model, since their functions are transparent to the memory model.[1]

In real systems addresses may have attributes that the processor must respect. The processor executes loads, stores, and atomic load-sotres in whatever order it chooses, as constrained by program order and the current memory model. The ASI address-couples it generates are translated by a memory management unit (MMU), which associates attributes with the address and may, in some instances, abort the memory transaction and signal an exception to the CPU. For example, a region of memory may be marked as non-prefetchable, non-cacheable, read-only, or restricted. It is the MMU's responsibility, working in conjunction with system software, to ensure that memory attribute constraints are not violated. See Appendix F, "SPARC-V9 MMU Requirements," for more information.

Instructions are performed in an order constrained by local dependencies. Using this dependency ordering, an execution unit submits one or more pending memory transactions to the memory. The memory performs transactions in **memory order**. The memory

---

1. The model described here is only a model. Implementations of SPARC-V9 systems are unsonstrained so long as their observable behaviors match those of the model.

unit may perform transactions submitted to it out of order; hence, the execution unit must not submit two or more transactions concurrently that are required to be ordered.

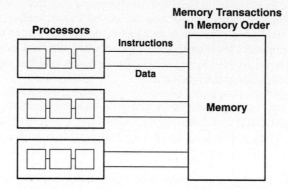

Figure 43—Data Memory Paths: Multiprocessor System

The memory accepts transactions, performs them, and then acknowledges their completion. Multiple memory operations may be in progress at any time and may be initiated in a nondeterministic fashion in any order, provided that all transactions to a location preserve the per-processor partial orders. Memory transactions may complete in any order. Once initiated, all memory operations are performed atomically: loads from one location all see the same value, and the result of stores are visible to all potential requestors at the same instant.

The order of memory operations observed at a single location is a **total order** that preserves the partial orderings of each processor's transactions to this address. There may be many legal total orders for a given program's execution.

8.4.3 The MEMBAR Instruction

MEMBAR serves two distinct functions in SPARC-V9. One variant of the MEMBAR, the ordering MEMBAR, provides a way for the programmer to control the order of loads and stores issued by a processor. The other variant of MEMBAR, the sequencing MEMBAR, allows the programmer to explicitly control order and completion for memory operations. Sequencing MEMBARs are needed only when a program requires that the effect of an operation become globally visible, rather than simply being scheduled.[2] As both forms are bit-encoded into the instruction, a single MEMBAR can function both as an ordering MEMBAR and as a sequencing MEMBAR.

---

2. Sequencing MEMBARs are needed for some input/output operations, forcing stores into specialized stable storage, context switching, and occasional other systems functions. Using a Sequencing MEMBAR when one is not needed may cause a degradation of performance. See Appendix J, "Programming With the Memory Models," for examples of their use.

8.4.3.1 Ordering MEMBAR Instructions

Ordering MEMBAR instructions induce an ordering in the instruction stream of a single processor. Sets of loads and stores that appear before the MEMBAR in program order are ordered with respect to sets of loads and stores that follow the MEMBAR in program order. Atomic operations (LDSTUB(A), SWAP(A), CASA, and CASXA) are ordered by MEMBAR as if they were both a load and a store, since they share the semantics of both. An STBAR instruction, with semantics that are a subset of MEMBAR, is provided for SPARC-V8 compatibility. MEMBAR and STBAR operate on all pending memory operations in the reorder buffer, independent of their address or ASI, ordering them with respect to all future memory operations. This ordering applies only to memory-reference instructions issued by the processor issuing the MEMBAR. Memory-reference instructions issued by other processors are unaffected.

The ordering relationships are bit-encoded as shown in table 19. For example, MEMBAR 01_{16}, written as "`membar #LoadLoad`" in assembly language, requires that all load operations appearing before the MEMBAR in program order complete before any of the load operations following the MEMBAR in program order complete. Store operations are unconstrained in this case. MEMBAR 08_{16} (`#StoreStore`) is equivalent to the STBAR instruction; it requires that the values stored by store instructions appearing in program order prior to the STBAR instruction be visible to other processors prior to issuing any store operations that appear in program order following the STBAR.

In table 19 these ordering relationships are specified by the '$<m$' symbol, which signifies memory order. See Appendix D, "Formal Specification of the Memory Models," for a formal description of the $<m$ relationship.

Table 19—Ordering Relationships Selected by Mask

Ordering relation, earlier < later	Suggested assembler tag	Mask value	*nmask* bit #
Load $<m$ Load	`#LoadLoad`	01_{16}	0
Store $<m$ Load	`#StoreLoad`	02_{16}	1
Load $<m$ Store	`#LoadStore`	04_{16}	2
Store $<m$ Store	`#StoreStore`	08_{16}	3

Selections may be combined to form more powerful barriers. For example, a MEMBAR instruction with a mask of 09_{16} (`#LoadLoad | #StoreStore`) orders loads with respect to loads and stores with respect to stores, but does not order loads with respect to stores or vice versa.

An ordering MEMBAR instruction does not guarantee any completion property; it only introduces an ordering constraint. For example, a program should not assume that a store preceding a MEMBAR instruction has completed following execution of the MEMBAR.

8.4.3.2 Sequencing MEMBAR Instructions

A sequencing MEMBAR exerts explicit control over the completion of operations. There are three sequencing MEMBAR options, each with a different degree of control and a different application.

Lookaside Barrier:

Ensures that loads following this MEMBAR are from memory and not from a lookaside into a write buffer. **Lookaside Barrier** requires that pending stores issued prior to the MEMBAR be completed before any load from that address following the MEMBAR may be issued. A **Lookaside Barrier** MEMBAR may be needed to provide lock fairness and to support some plausible I/O location semantics. See the example in J.14.1, "I/O Registers With Side Effects."

Memory Issue Barrier:

Ensures that all memory operations appearing in program order before the sequencing MEMBAR complete before any any new memory operation may be initiated. See the example in J.14.2, "The Control and Status Register (CSR)."

Synchronization Barrier:

Ensures that all instructions (memory reference and others) preceding the MEMBAR complete and the effects of any fault or error have become visible before any instruction following the MEMBAR in program order is initiated. A **Synchronization Barrier** MEMBAR fully synchronizes the processor that issues it.

Table 20 shows the encoding of these functions in the MEMBAR instruction.

Table 20—Sequencing Barrier Selected by Mask

Sequencing function	Assembler tag	Mask value	*cmask* bit #
Lookaside Barrier	#Lookaside	10_{16}	0
Memory Issue Barrier	#MemIssue	20_{16}	1
Synchronization Barrier	#Sync	40_{16}	2

8.4.4 Memory Models

The SPARC-V9 memory models are defined below in terms of order constraints placed upon memory-reference instruction execution, in addition to the minimal set required for self-consistency. These order constraints take the form of MEMBAR operations implicitly performed following some memory-reference instructions.

8.4.4.1 Relaxed Memory Order (RMO)

Relaxed Memory Order places no ordering constraints on memory references beyond those required for processor self-consistency. When ordering is required, it must be provided explicitly in the programs using MEMBAR instructions.

8.4.4.2 Partial Store Order (PSO)

Partial Store Order may be provided for compatibility with existing SPARC-V8 programs. Programs that execute correctly in the RMO memory model will execute correctly in the PSO model.

The rules for PSO are:

— Loads are blocking and ordered with respect to earlier loads.

— Atomic load-stores are ordered with respect to loads.

Thus, PSO ensures that:

— Each load and atomic load-store instruction behaves as if it were followed by a MEMBAR with a mask value of 05_{16}.

— Explicit MEMBAR instructions are required to order store and atomic load-store instructions with respect to each other.

8.4.4.3 Total Store Order (TSO)

Total Store Order must be provided for compatibility with existing SPARC-V8 programs. Programs that execute correctly in either RMO or PSO will execute correctly in the TSO model.

The rules for TSO are:

— Loads are blocking and ordered with respect to earlier loads.

— Stores are ordered with respect to stores.

— Atomic load-stores are ordered with respect to loads and stores.

Thus, TSO ensures that:

— Each load instruction behaves as if it were followed by a MEMBAR with a mask value of 05_{16}.

— Each store instruction behaves as if it were followed by a MEMBAR with a mask of 08_{16}.

— Each atomic load-store behaves as if it were followed by a MEMBAR with a mask of $0D_{16}$.

8.4.5 Mode Control

The memory model is specified by the two-bit state in PSTATE.MM, described in 5.2.1.3, "PSTATE_mem_model (MM)."

Writing a new value into PSTATE.MM causes subsequent memory reference instructions to be performed with the order constraints of the specified memory model.

SPARC-V9 processors need not provide all three memory models; undefined values of PSTATE.MM have implementation-dependent effects.

IMPL. DEP. #119: The effect of writing an unimplemented memory mode designation into PSTATE.MM is implementation-dependent.

Implementation Note:

> All SPARC-V9 implementations must provide TSO or a stronger model to maintain SPARC-V8 compatibility. An implementation may provide PSO, RMO, or neither.

Except when a trap enters RED_state, PSTATE.MM is left unchanged when a trap is entered and the old value is stacked. When entering RED_state, the value of PSTATE.MM is set to TSO.

8.4.6 Hardware Primitives for Mutual Exclusion

In addition to providing memory-ordering primitives that allow programmers to construct mutual-exclusion mechanisms in software, SPARC-V9 provides three hardware primitives for mutual exclusion:

— Compare and Swap (CASA, CASXA)

— Load Store Unsigned Byte (LDSTUB, LDSTUBA)

— Swap (SWAP, SWAPA)

Each of these instructions has the semantics of both a load and a store in all three memory models. They are all **atomic,** in the sense that no other store can be performed between the load and store elements of the instruction. All of the hardware mutual exclusion operations conform to the memory models and may require barrier instructions to ensure proper data visibility.

When the hardware mutual-exclusion primitives address I/O locations, the results are implementation-dependent (impl. dep. #123). In addition, the atomicity of hardware mutual-exclusion primitives is guaranteed only for processor memory references and not when the memory location is simultaneously being addressed by an I/O device such as a channel or DMA (impl. dep. #120).

8.4.6.1 Compare and Swap (CASA, CASXA)

Compare-and-swap is an atomic operation which compares a value in a processor register to a value in memory, and, if and only if they are equal, swaps the value in memory with the value in a second processor register. Both 32-bit (CASA) and 64-bit (CASXA) operations are provided. The compare-and-swap operation is atomic in the sense that once begun, no other processor can access the memory location specified until the compare has completed and the swap (if any) has also completed and is potentially visible to all other processors in the system.

Compare-and-swap is substantially more powerful than the other hardware synchronization primitives. It has an infinite consensus number; that is, it can resolve, in a wait-free fashion, an infinite number of contending processes. Because of this property, compare-and-swap can be used to construct wait-free algorithms that do not require the use of locks. See Appendix J, "Programming With the Memory Models," for examples.

8.4.6.2 Swap (SWAP)

SWAP atomically exchanges the lower 32 bits in a processor register with a word in memory. Swap has a consensus number of two; that is, it cannot resolve more than two contending processes in a wait-free fashion.

8.4.6.3 Load Store Unsigned Byte (LDSTUB)

LDSTUB loads a byte value from memory to a register and writes the value FF_{16} into the addressed byte atomically. LDSTUB is the classic test-and-set instruction. Like SWAP, it has a consensus number of two and so cannot resolve more than two contending processes in a wait-free fashion.

8.4.7 Synchronizing Instruction and Data Memory

The SPARC-V9 memory models do not require that instruction and data memory images be consistent at all times. The instruction and data memory images may become inconsistent if a program writes into the instruction stream. As a result, whenever instructions are modified by a program in a context where the data (that is, the instructions) in the memory and the data cache hierarchy may be inconsistent with instructions in the instruction cache hierarchy, some special programmatic action must be taken.

The FLUSH instruction will ensure consistency between the instruction stream and the data references across any local caches for a particular doubleword value in the processor executing the FLUSH. It will ensure eventual consistency across all caches in a multiprocessor system. The programmer must be careful to ensure that the modification sequence is robust under multiple updates and concurrent execution. Since, in the general case, loads and stores may be performed out of order, appropriate MEMBAR and FLUSH instructions must be interspersed as needed to control the order in which the instruction data is mutated.

The FLUSH instruction ensures that subsequent instruction fetches from the doubleword target of the FLUSH by the processor executing the FLUSH appear to execute after any loads, stores, and atomic load-stores issued by the processor to that address prior to the FLUSH. FLUSH acts as a barrier for instruction fetches in the processor that executes it and has the properties of a store with respect to MEMBAR operations.

FLUSH has no latency on the issuing processor; the modified instruction stream is immediately available.[3]

IMPL. DEP. #122: The latency between the execution of FLUSH on one processor and the point at which the modified instructions have replaced outdated instructions in a multiprocessor is implementation-dependent.

If all caches in a system (uniprocessor or multiprocessor) have a unified cache consistency protocol, FLUSH does nothing.

---

3. SPARC-V8 specified a five-instruction latency. Invalidation of instructions in execution in the instruction cache is likely to force an instruction-cache fault.

Use of FLUSH in a multiprocessor environment may cause unexpected performance degradation in some systems, because every processor that may have a copy of the modified data in its instruction cache must invalidate that data. In the worst case naive system, **all** processors must invalidate the data. The performance problem is compounded by the doubleword granularity of the FLUSH, which must be observed even when the actual invalidation unit is larger, for example, a cache line.

Programming Note:

> Because FLUSH is designed to act on a doubleword, and because, on some implementations, FLUSH may trap to system software, it is recommended that system software provide a user-callable service routine for flushing arbitrarily sized regions of memory. On some implementations, this routine would issue a series of FLUSH instructions; on others, it might issue a single trap to system software that would then flush the entire region.

A Instruction Definitions

A.1 Overview

This appendix describes each SPARC-V9 instruction. Related instructions are grouped into subsections. Each subsection consists of these parts:

(1) A table of the opcodes defined in the subsection with the values of the field(s) that uniquely identify the instruction(s).

(2) An illustration of the applicable instruction format(s). In these illustrations, a dash '—' indicates that the field is **reserved** for future versions of the architecture and shall be zero in any instance of the instruction. If a conforming SPARC-V9 implementation encounters nonzero values in these fields, its behavior is undefined. See Appendix I, "Extending the SPARC-V9 Architecture," for information about extending the SPARC-V9 instruction set.

(3) A list of the suggested assembly language syntax; the syntax notation is described in Appendix G, "Suggested Assembly Language Syntax."

(4) A description of the features, restrictions, and exception-causing conditions.

(5) A list of the exceptions that can occur as a consequence of attempting to execute the instruction(s). Exceptions due to an *instruction_access_error*, *instruction_access_ exception*, *instruction_access_MMU_miss*, *async_data_error*, or *internal_processor_ error*, and interrupt requests are not listed, since they can occur on any instruction. Also, any instruction that is not implemented in hardware shall generate an *illegal_ instruction* exception (or *fp_exception_other* exception with *ftt = unimplemented_FPop* for floating-point instructions) when it is executed.

This appendix does not include any timing information (in either cycles or clock time), since timing is implementation-dependent.

Table 22 summarizes the instruction set; the instruction definitions follow the table. Within table 22, throughout this appendix, and in Appendix E, "Opcode Maps," certain opcodes are marked with mnemonic superscripts. The superscripts and their meanings are defined in table 21:

Table 21—Opcode Superscripts

Superscript	Meaning
D	Deprecated instruction
P	Privileged opcode
P_{ASI}	Privileged action if bit 7 of the referenced ASI is zero
P_{ASR}	Privileged opcode if the referenced ASR register is privileged
P_{NPT}	Privileged action if PSTATE.PRIV = 0 and TICK.NPT = 1

Table 22—Instruction Set

Opcode	Name	Page
ADD (ADDcc)	Add (and modify condition codes)	135
ADDC (ADDCcc)	Add with carry (and modify condition codes)	135
AND (ANDcc)	And (and modify condition codes)	181
ANDN (ANDNcc)	And not (and modify condition codes)	181
BPcc	Branch on integer condition codes with prediction	146
Bicc[D]	Branch on integer condition codes	144
BPr	Branch on contents of integer register with prediction	136
CALL	Call and link	149
CASA[PASI]	Compare and swap word in alternate space	150
CASXA[PASI]	Compare and swap doubleword in alternate space	150
DONE[P]	Return from trap	155
FABS(s,d,q)	Floating-point absolute value	162
FADD(s,d,q)	Floating-point add	156
FBfcc[D]	Branch on floating-point condition codes	138
FBPfcc	Branch on floating-point condition codes with prediction	141
FCMP(s,d,q)	Floating-point compare	157
FCMPE(s,d,q)	Floating-point compare (exception if unordered)	157
FDIV(s,d,q)	Floating-point divide	163
FdMULq	Floating-point multiply double to quad	163
FiTO(s,d,q)	Convert integer to floating-point	161
FLUSH	Flush instruction memory	165
FLUSHW	Flush register windows	167
FMOV(s,d,q)	Floating-point move	162
FMOV(s,d,q)cc	Move floating-point register if condition is satisfied	185
FMOV(s,d,q)r	Move f-p reg. if integer reg. contents satisfy condition	189
FMUL(s,d,q)	Floating-point multiply	163
FNEG(s,d,q)	Floating-point negate	162
FsMULd	Floating-point multiply single to double	163
FSQRT(s,d,q)	Floating-point square root	164
F(s,d,q)TOi	Convert floating point to integer	159
F(s,d,q)TO(s,d,q)	Convert between floating-point formats	160
F(s,d,q)TOx	Convert floating point to 64-bit integer	159
FSUB(s,d,q)	Floating-point subtract	156
FxTO(s,d,q)	Convert 64-bit integer to floating-point	161
ILLTRAP	Illegal instruction	168
IMPDEP1	Implementation-dependent instruction	169
IMPDEP2	Implementation-dependent instruction	169
JMPL	Jump and link	170
LDD[D]	Load doubleword	175
LDDA[D, PASI]	Load doubleword from alternate space	177
LDDF	Load double floating-point	171
LDDFA[PASI]	Load double floating-point from alternate space	173
LDF	Load floating-point	171
LDFA[PASI]	Load floating-point from alternate space	173
LDFSR[D]	Load floating-point state register lower	171

Table 22—Instruction Set (Continued)

Opcode	Name	Page
LDQF	Load quad floating-point	171
LDQFA^{PASI}	Load quad floating-point from alternate space	173
LDSB	Load signed byte	175
LDSBA^{PASI}	Load signed byte from alternate space	177
LDSH	Load signed halfword	175
LDSHA^{PASI}	Load signed halfword from alternate space	177
LDSTUB	Load-store unsigned byte	179
LDSTUBA^{PASI}	Load-store unsigned byte in alternate space	180
LDSW	Load signed word	175
LDSWA^{PASI}	Load signed word from alternate space	177
LDUB	Load unsigned byte	175
LDUBA^{PASI}	Load unsigned byte from alternate space	177
LDUH	Load unsigned halfword	175
LDUHA^{PASI}	Load unsigned halfword from alternate space	177
LDUW	Load unsigned word	175
LDUWA^{PASI}	Load unsigned word from alternate space	177
LDX	Load extended	175
LDXA^{PASI}	Load extended from alternate space	177
LDXFSR	Load floating-point state register	171
MEMBAR	Memory barrier	183
MOVcc	Move integer register if condition is satisfied	191
MOVr	Move integer register on contents of integer register	195
MULScc^D	Multiply step (and modify condition codes)	199
MULX	Multiply 64-bit integers	196
NOP	No operation	201
OR (ORcc)	Inclusive-or (and modify condition codes)	181
ORN (ORNcc)	Inclusive-or not (and modify condition codes)	181
POPC	Population count	202
PREFETCH	Prefetch data	203
PREFETCHA^{PASI}	Prefetch data from alternate space	203
RDASI	Read ASI register	211
RDASR^{PASR}	Read ancillary state register	211
RDCCR	Read condition codes register	211
RDFPRS	Read floating-point registers state register	211
RDPC	Read program counter	211
RDPR^P	Read privileged register	208
RDTICK^{PNPT}	Read TICK register	211
RDY^D	Read Y register	211
RESTORE	Restore caller's window	214
RESTORED^P	Window has been restored	216
RETRY^P	Return from trap and retry	155
RETURN	Return	213
SAVE	Save caller's window	214
SAVED^P	Window has been saved	216
SDIV^D (SDIVcc^D)	32-bit signed integer divide (and modify condition codes)	152
SDIVX	64-bit signed integer divide	196

Table 22—Instruction Set (*Continued*)

Opcode	Name	Page
SETHI	Set high 22 bits of low word of integer register	217
SIR	Software-initiated reset	220
SLL	Shift left logical	218
SLLX	Shift left logical, extended	218
SMUL^D (SMULcc^D)	Signed integer multiply (and modify condition codes)	197
SRA	Shift right arithmetic	218
SRAX	Shift right arithmetic, extended	218
SRL	Shift right logical	218
SRLX	Shift right logical, extended	218
STB	Store byte	226
STBA^{PASI}	Store byte into alternate space	228
STBAR^D	Store barrier	221
STD^D	Store doubleword	226
STDA$^{D, PASI}$	Store doubleword into alternate space	226
STDF	Store double floating-point	222
STDFA^{PASI}	Store double floating-point into alternate space	224
STF	Store floating-point	222
STFA^{PASI}	Store floating-point into alternate space	224
STFSR^D	Store floating-point state register	222
STH	Store halfword	226
STHA^{PASI}	Store halfword into alternate space	228
STQF	Store quad floating-point	222
STQFA^{PASI}	Store quad floating-point into alternate space	224
STW	Store word	226
STWA^{PASI}	Store word into alternate space	228
STX	Store extended	226
STXA^{PASI}	Store extended into alternate space	228
STXFSR	Store extended floating-point state register	222
SUB (SUBcc)	Subtract (and modify condition codes)	230
SUBC (SUBCcc)	Subtract with carry (and modify condition codes)	230
SWAP^D	Swap integer register with memory	231
SWAPA$^{D, PASI}$	Swap integer register with memory in alternate space	232
TADDcc (TADDccTV^D)	Tagged add and modify condition codes (trap on overflow)	234
Tcc	Trap on integer condition codes	237
TSUBcc (TSUBccTV^D)	Tagged subtract and modify condition codes (trap on overflow)	235
UDIV^D (UDIVcc^D)	Unsigned integer divide (and modify condition codes)	152
UDIVX	64-bit unsigned integer divide	196
UMUL^D (UMULcc^D)	Unsigned integer multiply (and modify condition codes)	197
WRASI	Write ASI register	241
WRASR^{PASR}	Write ancillary state register	241
WRCCR	Write condition codes register	241
WRFPRS	Write floating-point registers state register	241
WRPR^P	Write privileged register	239
WRY^D	Write Y register	241
XNOR (XNORcc)	Exclusive-nor (and modify condition codes)	181
XOR (XORcc)	Exclusive-or (and modify condition codes)	181

A.2 Add

Opcode	Op3	Operation
ADD	00 0000	Add
ADDcc	01 0000	Add and modify cc's
ADDC	00 1000	Add with Carry
ADDCcc	01 1000	Add with Carry and modify cc's

Format (3):

10	rd	op3	rs1	i=0	—	rs2

10	rd	op3	rs1	i=1	simm13

31 30 29   25 24   19 18   14 13 12   5 4   0

Suggested Assembly Language Syntax	
add	reg_{rs1}, reg_or_imm, reg_{rd}
addcc	reg_{rs1}, reg_or_imm, reg_{rd}
addc	reg_{rs1}, reg_or_imm, reg_{rd}
addccc	reg_{rs1}, reg_or_imm, reg_{rd}

Description:

ADD and ADDcc compute "$r[rs1] + r[rs2]$" if $i = 0$, or "$r[rs1] + \text{sign\_ext}(simm13)$" if $i = 1$, and write the sum into $r[rd]$.

ADDC and ADDCcc ("ADD with carry") also add the CCR register's 32-bit carry ($icc.c$) bit; that is, they compute "$r[rs1] + r[rs2] + icc.c$" or "$r[rs1] + \text{sign\_ext}(simm13) + icc.c$" and write the sum into $r[rd]$.

ADDcc and ADDCcc modify the integer condition codes (CCR.icc and CCR.xcc). Overflow occurs on addition if both operands have the same sign and the sign of the sum is different.

Programming Note:
ADDC and ADDCcc read the 32-bit condition codes' carry bit (CCR.icc.c), not the 64-bit condition codes' carry bit (CCR.xcc.c).

Compatibility Note:
ADDC and ADDCcc were named ADDX and ADDXcc, respectively, in SPARC-V8.

Exceptions:
(none)

A.3 Branch on Integer Register with Prediction (BPr)

Opcode	rcond	Operation	Register contents test
—	000	*Reserved*	—
BRZ	001	Branch on Register Zero	$r[rs1] = 0$
BRLEZ	010	Branch on Register Less Than or Equal to Zero	$r[rs1] \leq 0$
BRLZ	011	Branch on Register Less Than Zero	$r[rs1] < 0$
—	100	*Reserved*	—
BRNZ	101	Branch on Register Not Zero	$r[rs1] \neq 0$
BRGZ	110	Branch on Register Greater Than Zero	$r[rs1] > 0$
BRGEZ	111	Branch on Register Greater Than or Equal to Zero	$r[rs1] \geq 0$

Format (2):

00	a	0	rcond	011	d16hi	p	rs1	d16lo

31 30 29 28 27   25 24   22 21 20 19 18   14 13   0

Suggested Assembly Language Syntax	
brz{,a}{,pt|,pn}	reg_{rs1}, *label*
brlez{,a}{,pt|,pn}	reg_{rs1}, *label*
brlz{,a}{,pt|,pn}	reg_{rs1}, *label*
brnz{,a}{,pt|,pn}	reg_{rs1}, *label*
brgz{,a}{,pt|,pn}	reg_{rs1}, *label*
brgez{,a}{,pt|,pn}	reg_{rs1}, *label*

Programming Note:

To set the annul bit for BPr instructions, append ",a" to the opcode mnemonic. For example, use "brz,a %i3,*label*." The preceding table indicates that the ",a" is optional by enclosing it in braces. To set the branch prediction bit "p," append either ",pt" for predict taken or ",pn" for predict not taken to the opcode mnemonic. If neither ",pt" nor ",pn" is specified, the assembler shall default to ",pt".

Description:

These instructions branch based on the contents of $r[rs1]$. They treat the register contents as a signed integer value.

A BPr instruction examines all 64 bits of $r[rs1]$ according to the *rcond* field of the instruction, producing either a TRUE or FALSE result. If TRUE, the branch is taken; that is, the instruction causes a PC-relative, delayed control transfer to the address "PC + (4 * sign_ext(*d16hi* ⬚ *d16lo*))." If FALSE, the branch is not taken.

If the branch is taken, the delay instruction is always executed, regardless of the value of the annul bit. If the branch is not taken and the annul bit (*a*) is 1, the delay instruction is annulled (not executed).

The predict bit (p) is used to give the hardware a hint about whether the branch is expected to be taken. A 1 in the p bit indicates that the branch is expected to be taken; a 0 indicates that the branch is expected not to be taken.

Annulment, delay instructions, prediction, and delayed control transfers are described further in Chapter 6, "Instructions."

Implementation Note:

If this instruction is implemented by tagging each register value with an N (negative) bit and Z (zero) bit, the following table can be used to determine if *rcond* is TRUE:

Branch	Test
BRNZ	not Z
BRZ	Z
BRGEZ	not N
BRLZ	N
BRLEZ	N or Z
BRGZ	not (N or Z)

Exceptions:

illegal_instruction (if *rcond* = 000_2 or 100_2)

A.4   Branch on Floating-Point Condition Codes (FBfcc)

> The FBfcc instructions are deprecated; they are provided only for compatibility with previous versions of the architecture. They should not be used in new SPARC-V9 software. It is recommended that the FBPfcc instructions be used in their place.

Opcode	cond	Operation	*fcc* test
FBA[D]	1000	Branch Always	1
FBN[D]	0000	Branch Never	0
FBU[D]	0111	Branch on Unordered	U
FBG[D]	0110	Branch on Greater	G
FBUG[D]	0101	Branch on Unordered or Greater	G or U
FBL[D]	0100	Branch on Less	L
FBUL[D]	0011	Branch on Unordered or Less	L or U
FBLG[D]	0010	Branch on Less or Greater	L or G
FBNE[D]	0001	Branch on Not Equal	L or G or U
FBE[D]	1001	Branch on Equal	E
FBUE[D]	1010	Branch on Unordered or Equal	E or U
FBGE[D]	1011	Branch on Greater or Equal	E or G
FBUGE[D]	1100	Branch on Unordered or Greater or Equal	E or G or U
FBLE[D]	1101	Branch on Less or Equal	E or L
FBULE[D]	1110	Branch on Unordered or Less or Equal	E or L or U
FBO[D]	1111	Branch on Ordered	E or L or G

Format (2):

00	a	cond	110	disp22

31 30 29 28   25 24   22 21   0

Suggested Assembly Language Syntax		
fba{,a}	*label*	
fbn{,a}	*label*	
fbu{,a}	*label*	
fbg{,a}	*label*	
fbug{,a}	*label*	
fbl{,a}	*label*	
fbul{,a}	*label*	
fblg{,a}	*label*	
fbne{,a}	*label*	(*synonym*: fbnz)
fbe{,a}	*label*	(*synonym*: fbz)
fbue{,a}	*label*	
fbge{,a}	*label*	
fbuge{,a}	*label*	
fble{,a}	*label*	
fbule{,a}	*label*	
fbo{,a}	*label*	

Programming Note:

To set the annul bit for FBfcc instructions, append ",a" to the opcode mnemonic. For example, use "fbl,a *label*." The preceding table indicates that the ",a" is optional by enclosing it in braces .

Description:

Unconditional Branches (FBA, FBN):

If its annul field is 0, an FBN (Branch Never) instruction acts like a NOP. If its annul field is 1, the following (delay) instruction is annulled (not executed) when the FBN is executed. In neither case does a transfer of control take place.

FBA (Branch Always) causes a PC-relative, delayed control transfer to the address "PC + (4 × sign_ext(*disp22*))," regardless of the value of the floating-point condition code bits. If the annul field of the branch instruction is 1, the delay instruction is annulled (not executed). If the annul field is 0, the delay instruction is executed.

Fcc-Conditional Branches:

Conditional FBfcc instructions (except FBA and FBN) evaluate floating-point condition code zero (*fcc0*) according to the *cond* field of the instruction. Such evaluation produces either a TRUE or FALSE result. If TRUE, the branch is taken, that is, the instruction causes a PC-relative, delayed control transfer to the address "PC + (4 × sign_ext(*disp22*))." If FALSE, the branch is not taken.

If a conditional branch is taken, the delay instruction is always executed, regardless of the value of the annul field. If a conditional branch is not taken and the *a* (annul) field is 1, the delay instruction is annulled (not executed). Note that the annul bit has a **different** effect on conditional branches than it does on unconditional branches.

Annulment, delay instructions, and delayed control transfers are described further in Chapter 6, "Instructions."

Compatibility Note:
Unlike SPARC-V8, SPARC-V9 does not require an instruction between a floating-point compare operation and a floating-point branch (FBfcc, FBPfcc).

If FPRS.FEF = 0 or PSTATE.PEF = 0, or if an FPU is not present, the FBfcc instruction is not executed and instead, generates an *fp_disabled* exception.

Exceptions:
fp_disabled

A.5   Branch on Floating-Point Condition Codes with Prediction (FBPfcc)

Opcode	cond	Operation	*fcc* test
FBPA	1000	Branch Always	1
FBPN	0000	Branch Never	0
FBPU	0111	Branch on Unordered	U
FBPG	0110	Branch on Greater	G
FBPUG	0101	Branch on Unordered or Greater	G or U
FBPL	0100	Branch on Less	L
FBPUL	0011	Branch on Unordered or Less	L or U
FBPLG	0010	Branch on Less or Greater	L or G
FBPNE	0001	Branch on Not Equal	L or G or U
FBPE	1001	Branch on Equal	E
FBPUE	1010	Branch on Unordered or Equal	E or U
FBPGE	1011	Branch on Greater or Equal	E or G
FBPUGE	1100	Branch on Unordered or Greater or Equal	E or G or U
FBPLE	1101	Branch on Less or Equal	E or L
FBPULE	1110	Branch on Unordered or Less or Equal	E or L or U
FBPO	1111	Branch on Ordered	E or L or G

Format (2):

00	a	cond	101	cc1	cc0	p	disp19

31 30 29 28   25 24   22 21 20 19 18   0

cc1 □ cc0	Condition code
00	*fcc0*
01	*fcc1*
10	*fcc2*
11	*fcc3*

Suggested Assembly Language Syntax		
fba{,a}{,pt|,pn}	%fcc*n, label*	
fbn{,a}{,pt|,pn}	%fcc*n, label*	
fbu{,a}{,pt|,pn}	%fcc*n, label*	
fbg{,a}{,pt|,pn}	%fcc*n, label*	
fbug{,a}{,pt|,pn}	%fcc*n, label*	
fbl{,a}{,pt|,pn}	%fcc*n, label*	
fbul{,a}{,pt|,pn}	%fcc*n, label*	
fblg{,a}{,pt|,pn}	%fcc*n, label*	
fbne{,a}{,pt|,pn}	%fcc*n, label*	(*synonym:* fbnz)
fbe{,a}{,pt|,pn}	%fcc*n, label*	(*synonym:* fbz)
fbue{,a}{,pt|,pn}	%fcc*n, label*	
fbge{,a}{,pt|,pn}	%fcc*n, label*	
fbuge{,a}{,pt|,pn}	%fcc*n, label*	
fble{,a}{,pt|,pn}	%fcc*n, label*	
fbule{,a}{,pt|,pn}	%fcc*n, label*	
fbo{,a}{,pt|,pn}	%fcc*n, label*	

Programming Note:

To set the annul bit for FBPfcc instructions, append ",a" to the opcode mnemonic. For example, use "fbl,a %fcc3,label." The preceding table indicates that the ",a" is optional by enclosing it in braces. To set the branch prediction bit, append either ",pt" (for predict taken) or "pn" (for predict not taken) to the opcode mnemonic. If neither ",pt" nor ",pn" is specified, the assembler shall default to ",pt". To select the appropriate floating-point condition code, include "%fcc0", "%fcc1", "%fcc2", or "%fcc3" before the label.

Description:

Unconditional Branches (FBPA, FBPN):

If its annul field is 0, an FBPN (Floating-Point Branch Never with Prediction) instruction acts like a NOP. If the Branch Never's annul field is 0, the following (delay) instruction is executed; if the annul field is 1, the following instruction is annulled (not executed). In no case does an FBPN cause a transfer of control to take place.

FBPA (Floating-Point Branch Always with Prediction) causes an unconditional PC-relative, delayed control transfer to the address "PC + $(4 \times$ sign_ext(*disp19*))." If the annul field of the branch instruction is 1, the delay instruction is annulled (not executed). If the annul field is 0, the delay instruction is executed.

Fcc-Conditional Branches:

Conditional FBPfcc instructions (except FBPA and FBPN) evaluate one of the four floating-point condition codes (*fcc0, fcc1, fcc2, fcc3*) as selected by *cc0* and *cc1*, according to the *cond* field of the instruction, producing either a TRUE or FALSE result. If TRUE, the branch is taken, that is, the instruction causes a PC-relative, delayed control transfer to the address "PC + $(4 \times$ sign_ext(*disp19*))." If FALSE, the branch is not taken.

If a conditional branch is taken, the delay instruction is always executed, regardless of the value of the annul field. If a conditional branch is not taken and the *a* (annul) field is 1, the delay instruction is annulled (not executed). Note that the annul bit has a **different** effect on conditional branches than it does on unconditional branches.

The predict bit (*p*) is used to give the hardware a hint about whether the branch is expected to be taken. A 1 in the *p* bit indicates that the branch is expected to be taken. A 0 indicates that the branch is expected not to be taken.

Annulment, delay instructions, and delayed control transfers are described further in Chapter 6, "Instructions."

If FPRS.FEF = 0 or PSTATE.PEF = 0, or if an FPU is not present, an FBPfcc instruction is not executed and instead, generates an *fp_disabled* exception.

Compatibility Note:

Unlike SPARC-V8, SPARC-V9 does not require an instruction between a floating-point compare operation and a floating-point branch (FBfcc, FBPfcc).

Exceptions:

fp_disabled

A.6   Branch on Integer Condition Codes (Bicc)

> The Bicc instructions are deprecated; they are provided only for compatibility with previous versions of the architecture. They should not be used in new SPARC-V9 software. It is recommended that the BPcc instructions be used in their place.

Opcode	cond	Operation	*icc* test
BA^D	1000	Branch Always	1
BN^D	0000	Branch Never	0
BNE^D	1001	Branch on Not Equal	**not** Z
BE^D	0001	Branch on Equal	Z
BG^D	1010	Branch on Greater	**not** (Z **or** (N **xor** V))
BLE^D	0010	Branch on Less or Equal	Z **or** (N **xor** V)
BGE^D	1011	Branch on Greater or Equal	**not** (N **xor** V)
BL^D	0011	Branch on Less	N **xor** V
BGU^D	1100	Branch on Greater Unsigned	**not** (C **or** Z)
BLEU^D	0100	Branch on Less or Equal Unsigned	C **or** Z
BCC^D	1101	Branch on Carry Clear (Greater than or Equal, Unsigned)	**not** C
BCS^D	0101	Branch on Carry Set (Less than, Unsigned)	C
BPOS^D	1110	Branch on Positive	**not** N
BNEG^D	0110	Branch on Negative	N
BVC^D	1111	Branch on Overflow Clear	**not** V
BVS^D	0111	Branch on Overflow Set	V

Format (2):

00	a	cond	010	disp22

31 30 29 28   25 24   22 21   0

Suggested Assembly Language Syntax		
ba{,a}	*label*	
bn{,a}	*label*	
bne{,a}	*label*	(*synonym*: bnz)
be{,a}	*label*	(*synonym*: bz)
bg{,a}	*label*	
ble{,a}	*label*	
bge{,a}	*label*	
bl{,a}	*label*	
bgu{,a}	*label*	
bleu{,a}	*label*	
bcc{,a}	*label*	(*synonym*: bgeu)
bcs{,a}	*label*	(*synonym*: blu)
bpos{,a}	*label*	
bneg{,a}	*label*	
bvc{,a}	*label*	
bvs{,a}	*label*	

Programming Note:

To set the annul bit for Bicc instructions, append "`,a`" to the opcode mnemonic. For example, use "`bgu,a` *label*." The preceding table indicates that the "`,a`" is optional by enclosing it in braces.

Description:

Unconditional Branches (BA, BN):

If its annul field is 0, a BN (Branch Never) instruction acts like a NOP. If its annul field is 1, the following (delay) instruction is annulled (not executed). In neither case does a transfer of control take place.

BA (Branch Always) causes an unconditional PC-relative, delayed control transfer to the address "PC + (4 × sign_ext(*disp22*))." If the annul field of the branch instruction is 1, the delay instruction is annulled (not executed). If the annul field is 0, the delay instruction is executed.

Icc-Conditional Branches:

Conditional Bicc instructions (all except BA and BN) evaluate the 32-bit integer condition codes (*icc*), according to the *cond* field of the instruction, producing either a TRUE or FALSE result. If TRUE, the branch is taken, that is, the instruction causes a PC-relative, delayed control transfer to the address "PC + (4 × sign_ ext(*disp22*))." If FALSE, the branch is not taken.

If a conditional branch is taken, the delay instruction is always executed regardless of the value of the annul field. If a conditional branch is not taken and the *a* (annul) field is 1, the delay instruction is annulled (not executed). Note that the annul bit has a **different** effect on conditional branches than it does on unconditional branches.

Annulment, delay instructions, and delayed control transfers are described further in Chapter 6, "Instructions."

Exceptions:

(none)

A.7 Branch on Integer Condition Codes with Prediction (BPcc)

Opcode	cond	Operation	*icc* test
BPA	1000	Branch Always	1
BPN	0000	Branch Never	0
BPNE	1001	Branch on Not Equal	**not** Z
BPE	0001	Branch on Equal	Z
BPG	1010	Branch on Greater	**not (Z or (N xor V))**
BPLE	0010	Branch on Less or Equal	Z or (N xor V)
BPGE	1011	Branch on Greater or Equal	**not (N xor V)**
BPL	0011	Branch on Less	N xor V
BPGU	1100	Branch on Greater Unsigned	**not (C or Z)**
BPLEU	0100	Branch on Less or Equal Unsigned	C or Z
BPCC	1101	Branch on Carry Clear (Greater Than or Equal, Unsigned)	**not** C
BPCS	0101	Branch on Carry Set (Less than, Unsigned)	C
BPPOS	1110	Branch on Positive	**not** N
BPNEG	0110	Branch on Negative	N
BPVC	1111	Branch on Overflow Clear	**not** V
BPVS	0111	Branch on Overflow Set	V

Format (2):

00	a	cond	001	cc1	cc0	p	disp19

31 30 29 28   25 24   22 21 20 19 18   0

cc1 $\Box$ cc0	Condition code
00	*icc*
01	—
10	*xcc*
11	—

Suggested Assembly Language Syntax		
ba{,a}{,ptl,pn}	*i_or_x_cc, label*	
bn{,a}{,ptl,pn}	*i_or_x_cc, label*	(*or*: `iprefetch` *label*)
bne{,a}{,ptl,pn}	*i_or_x_cc, label*	(*synonym*: bnz)
be{,a}{,ptl,pn}	*i_or_x_cc, label*	(*synonym*: bz)
bg{,a}{,ptl,pn}	*i_or_x_cc, label*	
ble{,a}{,ptl,pn}	*i_or_x_cc, label*	
bge{,a}{,ptl,pn}	*i_or_x_cc, label*	
bl{,a}{,ptl,pn}	*i_or_x_cc, label*	
bgu{,a}{,ptl,pn}	*i_or_x_cc, label*	
bleu{,a}{,ptl,pn}	*i_or_x_cc, label*	
bcc{,a}{,ptl,pn}	*i_or_x_cc, label*	(*synonym*: bgeu)
bcs{,a}{,ptl,pn}	*i_or_x_cc, label*	(*synonym*: blu)
bpos{,a}{,ptl,pn}	*i_or_x_cc, label*	
bneg{,a}{,ptl,pn}	*i_or_x_cc, label*	
bvc{,a}{,ptl,pn}	*i_or_x_cc, label*	
bvs{,a}{,ptl,pn}	*i_or_x_cc, label*	

Programming Note:

To set the annul bit for BPcc instructions, append ",a" to the opcode mnemonic. For example, use "bgu,a %icc,label." The preceding table indicates that the ",a" is optional by enclosing it in braces. To set the branch prediction bit, append to an opcode mnemonic either ",pt" for predict taken or ",pn" for predict not taken. If neither ",pt" nor ",pn" is specified, the assembler shall default to ",pt". To select the appropriate integer condition code, include "%icc" or "%xcc" before the label.

Description:

Unconditional Branches (BPA, BPN):

A BPN (Branch Never with Prediction) instruction for this branch type (*op2* = 1) is used in SPARC-V9 as an instruction prefetch; that is, the effective address (PC + (4 × sign_ext(*disp19*))) specifies an address of an instruction that is expected to be executed soon. The processor may use this information to begin prefetching instructions from that address. Like the PREFETCH instruction, this instruction may be treated as a NOP by an implementation. If the Branch Never's annul field is 1, the following (delay) instruction is annulled (not executed). If the annul field is 0, the following instruction is executed. In no case does a Branch Never cause a transfer of control to take place.

BPA (Branch Always with Prediction) causes an unconditional PC-relative, delayed control transfer to the address "PC + (4 × sign_ext(*disp19*))." If the annul field of the branch instruction is 1, the delay instruction is annulled (not executed). If the annul field is 0, the delay instruction is executed.

Conditional Branches:

Conditional BPcc instructions (except BPA and BPN) evaluate one of the two integer condition codes (*icc* or *xcc*), as selected by *cc0* and *cc1*, according to the *cond* field of the instruction, producing either a TRUE or FALSE result. If TRUE, the branch is taken; that is, the instruction causes a PC-relative, delayed control transfer to the address "PC + (4 × sign_ext(*disp19*))." If FALSE, the branch is not taken.

If a conditional branch is taken, the delay instruction is always executed regardless of the value of the annul field. If a conditional branch is not taken and the *a* (annul) field is 1, the delay instruction is annulled (not executed). Note that the annul bit has a **different** effect for conditional branches than it does for unconditional branches.

The predict bit (*p*) is used to give the hardware a hint about whether the branch is expected to be taken. A 1 in the *p* bit indicates that the branch is expected to be taken; a 0 indicates that the branch is expected not to be taken.

Annulment, delay instructions, prediction, and delayed control transfers are described further in Chapter 6, "Instructions."

Exceptions:

illegal_instruction (*cc1* ☐ *cc0* = 01_2 or 11_2)

A.8 Call and Link

Opcode	op	Operation
CALL	01	Call and Link

Format (1):

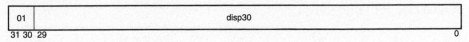

01	disp30

31 30 29   0

Suggested Assembly Language Syntax
call   *label*

Description:

The CALL instruction causes an unconditional, delayed, PC-relative control transfer to address PC + (4 × sign_ext(*disp30*)). Since the word displacement (*disp30*) field is 30 bits wide, the target address lies within a range of -2^{31} to $+2^{31} - 4$ bytes. The PC-relative displacement is formed by sign-extending the 30-bit word displacement field to 62 bits and appending two low-order zeros to obtain a 64-bit byte displacement.

The CALL instruction also writes the value of PC, which contains the address of the CALL, into $r[15]$ (*out* register 7). The high-order 32-bits of the PC value stored in $r[15]$ are implementation-dependent when PSTATE.AM = 1 (impl. dep. #125). The value written into $r[15]$ is visible to the instruction in the delay slot.

Exceptions:
        (none)

A.9 Compare and Swap

Opcode	op3	Operation
CASA^{PASI}	11 1100	Compare and Swap Word from Alternate space
CASXA^{PASI}	11 1110	Compare and Swap Extended from Alternate space

Format (3):

11	rd	op3	rs1	i=0	imm_asi	rs2

11	rd	op3	rs1	i=1	—	rs2

31 30 29   25 24   19 18   14 13 12   5 4   0

Suggested Assembly Language Syntax	
casa	[reg_{rs1}] imm_asi, reg_{rs2}, reg_{rd}
casa	[reg_{rs1}] %asi, reg_{rs2}, reg_{rd}
casxa	[reg_{rs1}] imm_asi, reg_{rs2}, reg_{rd}
casxa	[reg_{rs1}] %asi, reg_{rs2}, reg_{rd}

Description:

These instructions are used for synchronization and memory updates by concurrent processes. Uses of compare-and-swap include spin-lock operations, updates of shared counters, and updates of linked-list pointers. The latter two can use wait-free (nonlocking) protocols.

The CASXA instruction compares the value in register $r[rs2]$ with the doubleword in memory pointed to by the doubleword address in $r[rs1]$. If the values are equal, the value in $r[rd]$ is swapped with the doubleword pointed to by the doubleword address in $r[rs1]$. If the values are not equal, the contents of the doubleword pointed to by $r[rs1]$ replaces the value in $r[rd]$, but the memory location remains unchanged.

The CASA instruction compares the low-order 32 bits of register $r[rs2]$ with a word in memory pointed to by the word address in $r[rs1]$. If the values are equal, the low-order 32 bits of register $r[rd]$ are swapped with the contents of the memory word pointed to by the address in $r[rs1]$ and the high-order 32 bits of register $r[rd]$ are set to zero. If the values are not equal, the memory location remains unchanged, but the zero-extended contents of the memory word pointed to by $r[rs1]$ replace the low-order 32 bits of $r[rd]$ and the high-order 32 bits of register $r[rd]$ are set to zero.

A compare-and-swap instruction comprises three operations: a load, a compare, and a swap. The overall instruction is atomic; that is, no intervening interrupts or deferred traps are recognized by the processor, and no intervening update resulting from a compare-and-swap, swap, load, load-store unsigned byte, or store instruction to the doubleword containing the addressed location, or any portion of it, is performed by the memory system.

A compare-and-swap operation does **not** imply any memory barrier semantics. When compare-and-swap is used for synchronization, the same consideration should be given to memory barriers as if a load, store, or swap instruction were used.

A compare-and-swap operation behaves as if it performs a store, either of a new value from *r*[*rd*] or of the previous value in memory. The addressed location must be writable, even if the values in memory and *r*[*rs2*] are not equal.

If $i = 0$, the address space of the memory location is specified in the *imm_asi* field; if $i = 1$, the address space is specified in the ASI register.

A *mem_address_not_aligned* exception is generated if the address in *r*[*rs1*] is not properly aligned. CASXA and CASA cause a *privileged_action* exception if PSTATE.PRIV = 0 and bit 7 of the ASI is zero.

The coherence and atomicity of memory operations between processors and I/O DMA memory accesses are implementation-dependent (impl. dep #120).

Implementation Note:
> An implementation might cause an exception due to an error during the store memory access, even though there was no error during the load memory access.

Programming Note:
> Compare and Swap (CAS) and Compare and Swap Extended (CASX) synthetic instructions are available. See G.3, "Synthetic Instructions," for the correct syntax.

The compare-and-swap instructions do not affect the condition codes.

Exceptions:
> *privileged_action*
> *mem_address_not_aligned*
> *data_access_exception*
> *data_access_MMU_miss*
> *data_access_protection*
> *data_access_error*
> *async_data_error*

A.10   Divide (64-bit / 32-bit)

> The UDIV, UDIVcc, SDIV, and SDIVcc instructions are deprecated; they are provided only for compatibility with previous versions of the architecture. They should not be used in new SPARC-V9 software. It is recommended that the UDIVX and SDIVX instructions be used in their place.

Opcode	op3	Operation
UDIV[D]	00 1110	Unsigned Integer Divide
SDIV[D]	00 1111	Signed Integer Divide
UDIVcc[D]	01 1110	Unsigned Integer Divide and modify cc's
SDIVcc[D]	01 1111	Signed Integer Divide and modify cc's

Format (3):

10	rd	op3	rs1	i=0	—	rs2

10	rd	op3	rs1	i=1	simm13

31 30 29   25 24   19 18   14 13 12   5   4   0

Suggested Assembly Language Syntax	
udiv	reg_{rs1}, reg_or_imm, reg_{rd}
sdiv	reg_{rs1}, reg_or_imm, reg_{rd}
udivcc	reg_{rs1}, reg_or_imm, reg_{rd}
sdivcc	reg_{rs1}, reg_or_imm, reg_{rd}

Description:

The divide instructions perform 64-bit by 32-bit division, producing a 32-bit result. If $i = 0$, they compute "$(Y \square$ *lower 32 bits of r[rs1]) ÷ lower 32 bits of r[rs2]*." Otherwise (i.e., if $i = 1$), the divide instructions compute "$(Y \square$ *lower 32 bits of r[rs1]) ÷ lower 32 bits of* sign_ext(*simm13*)." In either case, if overflow does not occur, the less significant 32 bits of the integer quotient are sign-or zero-extended to 64 bits and are written into *r[rd]*.

The contents of the Y register are undefined after any 64-bit by 32-bit integer divide operation.

Unsigned Divide:

Unsigned divide (UDIV, UDIVcc) assumes an unsigned integer doubleword dividend $(Y \square$ *lower 32 bits of r[rs1]*) and an unsigned integer word divisor (*lower 32 bits of r[rs2]* or *lower 32 bits of* sign_ext(*simm13*)) and computes an unsigned integer word quotient (*r[rd]*). Immediate values in *simm13* are in the ranges $0..2^{12} - 1$ and $2^{32} - 2^{12}..2^{32} - 1$ for unsigned divide instructions.

Unsigned division rounds an inexact rational quotient toward zero .

Programming Note:

> The **rational quotient** is the infinitely precise result quotient. It includes both the integer part and the fractional part of the result. For example, the rational quotient of 11/4 = 2.75 (Integer part = 2, fractional part = .75).

The result of an unsigned divide instruction can overflow the low-order 32 bits of the destination register $r[rd]$ under certain conditions. When overflow occurs the largest appropriate unsigned integer is returned as the quotient in $r[rd]$. The condition under which overflow occurs and the value returned in $r[rd]$ under this condition is specified in the following table.

Table 23—UDIV / UDIVcc Overflow Detection and Value Returned

Condition under which overflow occurs	Value returned in $r[rd]$
Rational quotient $\geq 2^{32}$	$2^{32}-1$ (0000 0000 FFFF FFFF$_{16}$)

When no overflow occurs, the 32-bit result is zero-extended to 64 bits and written into register $r[rd]$.

UDIV does not affect the condition code bits. UDIVcc writes the integer condition code bits as shown in the following table. Note that negative (N) and zero (Z) are set according to the value of $r[rd]$ after it has been set to reflect overflow, if any.

Bit	UDIVcc
icc.N	Set if $r[rd]$<31> = 1
icc.Z	Set if $r[rd]$<31:0> = 0
icc.V	Set if overflow (*per table 23*)
icc.C	Zero
xcc.N	Set if $r[rd]$<63]> = 1
xcc.Z	Set if $r[rd]$<63:0> = 0
xcc.V	Zero
xcc.C	Zero

Signed Divide:

Signed divide (SDIV, SDIVcc) assumes a signed integer doubleword dividend (Y □ *lower 32 bits of r[rs1]*) and a signed integer word divisor (*lower 32 bits of r[rs2]* or *lower 32 bits of* sign_ext(*simm13*)) and computes a signed integer word quotient (*r[rd]*).

Signed division rounds an inexact quotient toward zero. For example, $-7 \div 4$ equals the rational quotient of -1.75, which rounds to -1 (not -2) when rounding toward zero.

The result of a signed divide can overflow the low-order 32 bits of the destination register $r[rd]$ under certain conditions. When overflow occurs the largest appropriate signed integer is returned as the quotient in $r[rd]$. The conditions under which overflow occurs and the value returned in $r[rd]$ under those conditions are specified in the following table.

Table 24—SDIV / SDIVcc Overflow Detection and Value Returned

Condition under which overflow occurs	Value returned in *r[rd]*
Rational quotient $\geq 2^{31}$	$2^{31}-1$ (0000 0000 7FFF FFFF$_{16}$)
Rational quotient $\leq -2^{31}-1$	-2^{31} (FFFF FFFF 8000 0000$_{16}$)

When no overflow occurs, the 32-bit result is sign-extended to 64 bits and written into register *r[rd]*.

SDIV does not affect the condition code bits. SDIVcc writes the integer condition code bits as shown in the following table. Note that negative (N) and zero (Z) are set according to the value of *r[rd]* after it has been set to reflect overflow, if any.

Bit	SDIVcc
icc.N	Set if *r[rd]*<31> = 1
icc.Z	Set if *r[rd]*<31:0> = 0
icc.V	Set if overflow (*per table 24*)
icc.C	Zero
xcc.N	Set if *r[rd]*<63]> = 1
xcc.Z	Set if *r[rd]*<63:0> = 0
xcc.V	Zero
xcc.C	Zero

Exceptions:
> *division_by_zero*

A.11 DONE and RETRY

Opcode	op3	fcn	Operation
DONE[P]	11 1110	0	Return from Trap (skip trapped instruction)
RETRY[P]	11 1110	1	Return from Trap (retry trapped instruction)
—	11 1110	2..31	*Reserved*

Format (3):

10	fcn	op3	—

31 30 29   25 24   19 18   0

Suggested Assembly Language Syntax
done
retry

Description:

The DONE and RETRY instructions restore the saved state from TSTATE (CWP, ASI, CCR, and PSTATE), set PC and nPC, and decrement TL.

The RETRY instruction resumes execution with the trapped instruction by setting PC←TPC[TL] (the saved value of PC on trap) and nPC←TNPC[TL] (the saved value of nPC on trap).

The DONE instruction skips the trapped instruction by setting PC←TNPC[TL] and nPC←TNPC[TL]+4.

Execution of a DONE or RETRY instruction in the delay slot of a control-transfer instruction produces undefined results.

Programming Note:
    The DONE and RETRY instructions should be used to return from privileged trap handlers.

Exceptions:
    privileged_opcode
    illegal_instruction (if TL = 0 or *fcn* = 2..31)

A.12 Floating-Point Add and Subtract

Opcode	op3	opf	Operation
FADDs	11 0100	0 0100 0001	Add Single
FADDd	11 0100	0 0100 0010	Add Double
FADDq	11 0100	0 0100 0011	Add Quad
FSUBs	11 0100	0 0100 0101	Subtract Single
FSUBd	11 0100	0 0100 0110	Subtract Double
FSUBq	11 0100	0 0100 0111	Subtract Quad

Format (3):

10	rd	op3	rs1	opf	rs2
31 30 29	25 24	19 18	14 13	5 4	0

Suggested Assembly Language Syntax	
fadds	$freg_{rs1}$, $freg_{rs2}$, $freg_{rd}$
faddd	$freg_{rs1}$, $freg_{rs2}$, $freg_{rd}$
faddq	$freg_{rs1}$, $freg_{rs2}$, $freg_{rd}$
fsubs	$freg_{rs1}$, $freg_{rs2}$, $freg_{rd}$
fsubd	$freg_{rs1}$, $freg_{rs2}$, $freg_{rd}$
fsubq	$freg_{rs1}$, $freg_{rs2}$, $freg_{rd}$

Description:

The floating-point add instructions add the floating-point register(s) specified by the *rs1* field and the floating-point register(s) specified by the *rs2* field, and write the sum into the floating-point register(s) specified by the *rd* field.

The floating-point subtract instructions subtract the floating-point register(s) specified by the *rs2* field from the floating-point register(s) specified by the *rs1* field, and write the difference into the floating-point register(s) specified by the *rd* field.

Rounding is performed as specified by the FSR.RD field.

Exceptions:
> *fp_disabled*
> *fp_exception_ieee_754* (OF, UF, NX, NV)
> *fp_exception_other* (*invalid_fp_register* (only FADDQ and FSUBQ))

A.13 Floating-Point Compare

Opcode	op3	opf	Operation
FCMPs	11 0101	0 0101 0001	Compare Single
FCMPd	11 0101	0 0101 0010	Compare Double
FCMPq	11 0101	0 0101 0011	Compare Quad
FCMPEs	11 0101	0 0101 0101	Compare Single and Exception if Unordered
FCMPEd	11 0101	0 0101 0110	Compare Double and Exception if Unordered
FCMPEq	11 0101	0 0101 0111	Compare Quad and Exception if Unordered

Format (3):

10	000	cc1	cc0	op3	rs1	opf	rs2
31 30 29		27 26	25 24	19 18	14 13	5 4	0

Suggested Assembly Language Syntax	
fcmps	%fccn, $freg_{rs1}$, $freg_{rs2}$
fcmpd	%fccn, $freg_{rs1}$, $freg_{rs2}$
fcmpq	%fccn, $freg_{rs1}$, $freg_{rs2}$
fcmpes	%fccn, $freg_{rs1}$, $freg_{rs2}$
fcmped	%fccn, $freg_{rs1}$, $freg_{rs2}$
fcmpeq	%fccn, $freg_{rs1}$, $freg_{rs2}$

cc1 ☐ cc0	Condition code
00	$fcc0$
01	$fcc1$
10	$fcc2$
11	$fcc3$

Description:

These instructions compare the floating-point register(s) specified by the *rs1* field with the floating-point register(s) specified by the *rs2* field, and set the selected floating-point condition code (fccn) according to the following table:

fcc value	Relation
0	$freg_{rs1} = freg_{rs2}$
1	$freg_{rs1} < freg_{rs2}$
2	$freg_{rs1} > freg_{rs2}$
3	$freg_{rs1}$? $freg_{rs2}$ (unordered)

The "?" in the above table indicates that the comparison is unordered. The unordered condition occurs when one or both of the operands to the compare is a signaling or quiet NaN.

The "compare and cause exception if unordered" (FCMPEs, FCMPEd, and FCMPEq) instructions cause an invalid (NV) exception if either operand is a NaN.

FCMP causes an invalid (NV) exception if either operand is a signaling NaN.

Compatibility Note:
> Unlike SPARC-V8, SPARC-V9 does not require an instruction between a floating-point compare operation and a floating-point branch (FBfcc, FBPfcc).

Compatibility Note:
> SPARC-V8 floating-point compare instructions are required to have a zero in the $r[rd]$ field. In SPARC-V9, bits 26 and 25 of the $r[rd]$ field are used to specify the floating-point condition code to be set. Legal SPARC-V8 code will work on SPARC-V9 because the zeroes in the $r[rd]$ field are interpreted as $fcc0$, and the FBfcc instruction branches based on $fcc0$.

Exceptions:

> *fp_disabled*
> *fp_exception_ieee_754* (NV)
> *fp_exception_other* (*invalid_fp_register* (FCMPq, FCMPEq only))

A.14 Convert Floating-Point to Integer

Opcode	op3	opf	Operation
FsTOx	11 0100	0 1000 0001	Convert Single to 64-bit Integer
FdTOx	11 0100	0 1000 0010	Convert Double to 64-bit Integer
FqTOx	11 0100	0 1000 0011	Convert Quad to 64-bit Integer
FsTOi	11 0100	0 1101 0001	Convert Single to 32-bit Integer
FdTOi	11 0100	0 1101 0010	Convert Double to 32-bit Integer
FqTOi	11 0100	0 1101 0011	Convert Quad to 32-bit Integer

Format (3):

10	rd	op3	—	opf	rs2
31 30 29	25 24	19 18	14 13	5 4	0

Suggested Assembly Language Syntax	
fstox	$freg_{rs2}$, $freg_{rd}$
fdtox	$freg_{rs2}$, $freg_{rd}$
fqtox	$freg_{rs2}$, $freg_{rd}$
fstoi	$freg_{rs2}$, $freg_{rd}$
fdtoi	$freg_{rs2}$, $freg_{rd}$
fqtoi	$freg_{rs2}$, $freg_{rd}$

Description:

FsTOx, FdTOx, and FqTOx convert the floating-point operand in the floating-point register(s) specified by *rs2* to a 64-bit integer in the floating-point register(s) specified by *rd*.

FsTOi, FdTOi, and FqTOi convert the floating-point operand in the floating-point register(s) specified by *rs2* to a 32-bit integer in the floating-point register specified by *rd*.

The result is always rounded toward zero; that is, the rounding direction (RD) field of the FSR register is ignored.

If the floating-point operand's value is too large to be converted to an integer of the specified size, or is a NaN or infinity, an invalid (NV) exception occurs. The value written into the floating-point register(s) specified by *rd* in these cases is defined in B.5, "Integer Overflow Definition."

Exceptions:

    fp_disabled
    fp_exception_ieee_754 (NV, NX)
    fp_exception_other (*invalid_fp_register* (FqTOi, FqTOx only))

A.15 Convert Between Floating-Point Formats

Opcode	op3	opf	Operation
FsTOd	11 0100	0 1100 1001	Convert Single to Double
FsTOq	11 0100	0 1100 1101	Convert Single to Quad
FdTOs	11 0100	0 1100 0110	Convert Double to Single
FdTOq	11 0100	0 1100 1110	Convert Double to Quad
FqTOs	11 0100	0 1100 0111	Convert Quad to Single
FqTOd	11 0100	0 1100 1011	Convert Quad to Double

Format (3):

10	rd	op3	—	opf	rs2
31 30 29	25 24	19 18	14 13	5 4	0

Suggested Assembly Language Syntax	
fstod	$freg_{rs2}$, $freg_{rd}$
fstoq	$freg_{rs2}$, $freg_{rd}$
fdtos	$freg_{rs2}$, $freg_{rd}$
fdtoq	$freg_{rs2}$, $freg_{rd}$
fqtos	$freg_{rs2}$, $freg_{rd}$
fqtod	$freg_{rs2}$, $freg_{rd}$

Description:

These instructions convert the floating-point operand in the floating-point register(s) specified by *rs2* to a floating-point number in the destination format. They write the result into the floating-point register(s) specified by *rd*.

Rounding is performed as specified by the FSR.RD field.

FqTOd, FqTOs, and FdTOs (the "narrowing" conversion instructions) can raise OF, UF, and NX exceptions. FdTOq, FsTOq, and FsTOd (the "widening" conversion instructions) cannot.

Any of these six instructions can trigger an NV exception if the source operand is a signaling NaN.

B.2.1, "Untrapped Result in Different Format Than Operands," defines the rules for converting NaNs from one floating-point format to another.

Exceptions:
> *fp_disabled*
> *fp_exception_ieee_754* (OF, UF, NV, NX)
> *fp_exception_other* (*invalid_fp_register*) (FsTOq, FdTOq, FqTOs, FqTOd)

A.16 Convert Integer to Floating-Point

Opcode	op3	opf	Operation
FxTOs	11 0100	0 1000 0100	Convert 64-bit Integer to Single
FxTOd	11 0100	0 1000 1000	Convert 64-bit Integer to Double
FxTOq	11 0100	0 1000 1100	Convert 64-bit Integer to Quad
FiTOs	11 0100	0 1100 0100	Convert 32-bit Integer to Single
FiTOd	11 0100	0 1100 1000	Convert 32-bit Integer to Double
FiTOq	11 0100	0 1100 1100	Convert 32-bit Integer to Quad

Format (3):

10	rd	op3	—	opf	rs2

31 30   29   25 24   19 18   14 13   5 4   0

Suggested Assembly Language Syntax	
fxtos	$freg_{rs2}$, $freg_{rd}$
fxtod	$freg_{rs2}$, $freg_{rd}$
fxtoq	$freg_{rs2}$, $freg_{rd}$
fitos	$freg_{rs2}$, $freg_{rd}$
fitod	$freg_{rs2}$, $freg_{rd}$
fitoq	$freg_{rs2}$, $freg_{rd}$

Description:

FxTOs, FxTOd, and FxTOq convert the 64-bit signed integer operand in the floating-point register(s) specified by *rs2* into a floating-point number in the destination format. The source register, floating-point register(s) specified by *rs2*, must be an even-numbered (that is, double-precision) floating-point register.

FiTOs, FiTOd, and FiTOq convert the 32-bit signed integer operand in floating-point register(s) specified by *rs2* into a floating-point number in the destination format. All write their result into the floating-point register(s) specified by *rd*.

FiTOs, FxTOs, and FxTOd round as specified by the FSR.RD field.

Exceptions:
> *fp_disabled*
> *fp_exception_ieee_754* (NX (FiTOs, FxTOs, FxTOd only))
> *fp_exception_other* (*invalid_fp_register* (FiTOq, FxTOq only))

A.17 Floating-Point Move

Opcode	op3	opf	Operation
FMOVs	11 0100	0 0000 0001	Move Single
FMOVd	11 0100	0 0000 0010	Move Double
FMOVq	11 0100	0 0000 0011	Move Quad
FNEGs	11 0100	0 0000 0101	Negate Single
FNEGd	11 0100	0 0000 0110	Negate Double
FNEGq	11 0100	0 0000 0111	Negate Quad
FABSs	11 0100	0 0000 1001	Absolute Value Single
FABSd	11 0100	0 0000 1010	Absolute Value Double
FABSq	11 0100	0 0000 1011	Absolute Value Quad

Format (3):

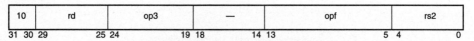

10	rd	op3	—	opf	rs2

31 30 29   25 24   19 18   14 13   5 4   0

Suggested Assembly Language Syntax	
fmovs	$freg_{rs2}$, $freg_{rd}$
fmovd	$freg_{rs2}$, $freg_{rd}$
fmovq	$freg_{rs2}$, $freg_{rd}$
fnegs	$freg_{rs2}$, $freg_{rd}$
fnegd	$freg_{rs2}$, $freg_{rd}$
fnegq	$freg_{rs2}$, $freg_{rd}$
fabss	$freg_{rs2}$, $freg_{rd}$
fabsd	$freg_{rs2}$, $freg_{rd}$
fabsq	$freg_{rs2}$, $freg_{rd}$

Description:

The single-precision versions of these instructions copy the contents of a single-precision floating-point register to the destination. The double-precision forms copy the contents of a double-precision floating-point register to the destination. The quad-precision versions copy a quad-precision value in floating-point registers to the destination.

FMOV copies the source to the destination unaltered.

FNEG copies the source to the destination with the sign bit complemented.

FABS copies the source to the destination with the sign bit cleared.

These instructions do not round.

Exceptions:

fp_disabled
fp_exception_other (*invalid_fp_register*(FMOVq, FNEGq, FABSq only))

A.18 Floating-Point Multiply and Divide

Opcode	op3	opf	Operation
FMULs	11 0100	0 0100 1001	Multiply Single
FMULd	11 0100	0 0100 1010	Multiply Double
FMULq	11 0100	0 0100 1011	Multiply Quad
FsMULd	11 0100	0 0110 1001	Multiply Single to Double
FdMULq	11 0100	0 0110 1110	Multiply Double to Quad
FDIVs	11 0100	0 0100 1101	Divide Single
FDIVd	11 0100	0 0100 1110	Divide Double
FDIVq	11 0100	0 0100 1111	Divide Quad

Format (3):

10	rd	op3	rs1	opf	rs2
31 30 29	25 24	19 18	14 13	5 4	0

Suggested Assembly Language Syntax	
fmuls	$freg_{rs1}$, $freg_{rs2}$, $freg_{rd}$
fmuld	$freg_{rs1}$, $freg_{rs2}$, $freg_{rd}$
fmulq	$freg_{rs1}$, $freg_{rs2}$, $freg_{rd}$
fsmuld	$freg_{rs1}$, $freg_{rs2}$, $freg_{rd}$
fdmulq	$freg_{rs1}$, $freg_{rs2}$, $freg_{rd}$
fdivs	$freg_{rs1}$, $freg_{rs2}$, $freg_{rd}$
fdivd	$freg_{rs1}$, $freg_{rs2}$, $freg_{rd}$
fdivq	$freg_{rs1}$, $freg_{rs2}$, $freg_{rd}$

Description:

The floating-point multiply instructions multiply the contents of the floating-point register(s) specified by the *rs1* field by the contents of the floating-point register(s) specified by the *rs2* field, and write the product into the floating-point register(s) specified by the *rd* field.

The FsMULd instruction provides the exact double-precision product of two single-precision operands, without underflow, overflow, or rounding error. Similarly, FdMULq provides the exact quad-precision product of two double-precision operands.

The floating-point divide instructions divide the contents of the floating-point register(s) specified by the *rs1* field by the contents of the floating-point register(s) specified by the *rs2* field, and write the quotient into the floating-point register(s) specified by the *rd* field.

Rounding is performed as specified by the FSR.RD field.

Exceptions:

> *fp_disabled*
> *fp_exception_ieee_754* (OF, UF, DZ (FDIV only), NV, NX)
> *fp_exception_other* (*invalid_fp_register* (FMULq, FdMULq, and FDIVq only))

A.19 Floating-Point Square Root

Opcode	op3	opf	Operation
FSQRTs	11 0100	0 0010 1001	Square Root Single
FSQRTd	11 0100	0 0010 1010	Square Root Double
FSQRTq	11 0100	0 0010 1011	Square Root Quad

Format (3):

10	rd	op3	—	opf	rs2

31 30 29   25 24   19 18   14 13   5 4   0

Suggested Assembly Language Syntax
fsqrts $freg_{rs2}$, $freg_{rd}$
fsqrtd $freg_{rs2}$, $freg_{rd}$
fsqrtq $freg_{rs2}$, $freg_{rd}$

Description:

These instructions generate the square root of the floating-point operand in the floating-point register(s) specified by the *rs2* field, and place the result in the destination floating-point register(s) specified by the *rd* field.

Rounding is performed as specified by the FSR.RD field.

Implementation Note:
> See *Implementation Characteristics of Current SPARC-V9-based Products, Revision 9.x,* a document available from SPARC International, for information on whether the FSQRT instructions are implemented in hardware or software in the various SPARC-V9 implementations.

Exceptions:
> *fp_disabled*
> *fp_exception_ieee_754* (*IEEE_754_exception* (NV, NX))
> *fp_exception_other* (*invalid_fp_register* (FSQRTq))

A.20 Flush Instruction Memory

Opcode	op3	Operation
FLUSH	11 1011	Flush Instruction Memory

Format (3):

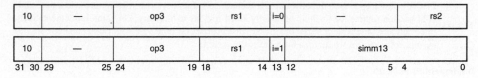

10	—	op3	rs1	i=0	—	rs2

10	—	op3	rs1	i=1	simm13

31 30 29   25 24   19 18   14 13 12   5 4   0

Suggested Assembly Language Syntax
flush   *address*

Description:

FLUSH ensures that the doubleword specified as the effective address is consistent across any local caches and, in a multiprocessor system, will eventually become consistent everywhere.

In the following discussion P_{FLUSH} refers to the processor that executed the FLUSH instruction. FLUSH ensures that instruction fetches from the specified effective address by P_{FLUSH} appear to execute after any loads, stores, and atomic load-stores to that address issued by P_{FLUSH} prior to the FLUSH. In a multiprocessor system, FLUSH also ensures that these values will eventually become visible to the instruction fetches of all other processors. FLUSH behaves as if it were a store with respect to MEMBAR-induced orderings. See A.31, "Memory Barrier."

FLUSH operates on at least the doubleword containing the addressed location.

The effective address operand for the FLUSH instruction is "$r[rs1] + r[rs2]$" if $i = 0$, or "$r[rs1]$ + sign_ext(*simm13*)" if $i = 1$. The least significant two address bits of the effective address are unused and should be supplied as zeros by software. Bit 2 of the address is ignored, because FLUSH operates on at least a doubleword.

Programming Notes:

(1) Typically, FLUSH is used in self-modifying code. See H.1.6, "Self-Modifying Code," for information about use of the FLUSH instruction in portable self-modifying code. The use of self-modifying code is discouraged.

(2) The order in which memory is modified can be controlled by using FLUSH and MEMBAR instructions interspersed appropriately between stores and atomic load-stores. FLUSH is needed only between a store and a subsequent instruction fetch from the modified location. When multiple processes may concurrently modify live (that is, potentially executing) code, care must be taken to ensure that the order of update maintains the program in a semantically correct form at all times.

(3) The memory model guarantees in a uniprocessor that **data** loads observe the results of the most recent store, even if there is no intervening FLUSH.

(4) FLUSH may be time-consuming. Some implementations may trap rather than implement FLUSH in hardware. In a multiprocessor configuration, FLUSH requires all processors that may be referencing the addressed doubleword to flush their instruction caches, a potentially disruptive activity.

(5) In a multiprocessor system, the time it takes for a FLUSH to take effect is implementation-dependent (impl. dep. #122). No mechanism is provided to ensure or test completion.

(6) Because FLUSH is designed to act on a doubleword, and because, on some implementations, FLUSH may trap to system software, it is recommended that system software provide a user-callable service routine for flushing arbitrarily sized regions of memory. On some implementations, this routine would issue a series of FLUSH instructions; on others, it might issue a single trap to system software that would then flush the entire region.

Implementation Notes:

(1) **IMPL. DEP. #42**: If FLUSH is not implemented in hardware, it causes an *illegal_instruction* exception and the function of FLUSH is performed by system software. Whether FLUSH traps is implementation-dependent.

(2) The effect of a FLUSH instruction as observed from P_{FLUSH} is immediate. Other processors in a multiprocessor system eventually will see the effect of the FLUSH, but the latency is implementation-dependent (impl. dep. #122).

Exceptions:

(none)

A.21   Flush Register Windows

Opcode	op3	Operation
FLUSHW	10 1011	Flush Register Windows

Format (3):

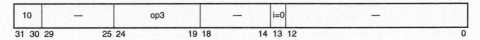

10	—	op3	—	i=0	—

31 30 29   25 24   19 18   14 13 12   0

Suggested Assembly Language Syntax
flushw

Description:

FLUSHW causes all active register windows except the current window to be flushed to memory at locations determined by privileged software. FLUSHW behaves as a NOP if there are no active windows other than the current window. At the completion of the FLUSHW instruction, the only active register window is the current one.

Programming Note:
> The FLUSHW instruction can be used by application software to switch memory stacks or examine register contents for previous stack frames.

FLUSHW acts as a NOP if CANSAVE = NWINDOWS − 2. Otherwise, there is more than one active window, so FLUSHW causes a spill exception. The trap vector for the spill exception is based on the contents of OTHERWIN and WSTATE. The spill trap handler is invoked with the CWP set to the window to be spilled (that is, (CWP + CANSAVE + 2) **mod** NWINDOWS). See 6.3.6, "Register Window Management Instructions."

Programming Note:
> Typically, the spill handler will save a window on a memory stack and return to reexecute the FLUSHW instruction. Thus, FLUSHW will trap and reexecute until all active windows other than the current window have been spilled.

Exceptions:
> *spill_n_normal*
> *spill_n_other*

A.22 Illegal Instruction Trap

Opcode	op	op2	Operation
ILLTRAP	00	000	*illegal_instruction* trap

Format (2):

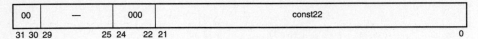

00	—	000	const22

31 30 29   25 24   22 21   0

Suggested Assembly Language Syntax
illtrap   *const22*

Description:

The ILLTRAP instruction causes an *illegal_instruction* exception. The *const22* value is ignored by the hardware; specifically, this field is **not** reserved by the architecture for any future use.

Compatibility Note:
Except for its name, this instruction is identical to the SPARC-V8 UNIMP instruction.

Exceptions:
illegal_instruction

A.23   Implementation-Dependent Instructions

Opcode	op3	Operation
IMPDEP1	11 0110	Implementation-Dependent Instruction 1
IMPDEP2	11 0111	Implementation-Dependent Instruction 2

Format (3):

10	impl-dep	op3	impl-dep

31 30 29   25 24   19 18   0

Description:

IMPL. DEP. #106: The IMPDEP1 and IMPDEP2 instructions are completely implementation-dependent. Implementation-dependent aspects include their operation, the interpretation of bits 29..25 and 18..0 in their encodings, and which (if any) exceptions they may cause.

See I.1.2, "Implementation-Dependent and Reserved Opcodes," for information about extending the SPARC-V9 instruction set using the implementation-dependent instructions.

Compatibility Note:
   These instructions replace the CPop*n* instructions in SPARC-V8.

Exceptions:
   illegal_instruction (if the implementation does not define the instructions)
   implementation-dependent (if the implementation defines the instructions)

A.24 Jump and Link

Opcode	op3	Operation
JMPL	11 1000	Jump and Link

Format (3):

10	rd	op3	rs1	i=0	—	rs2

10	rd	op3	rs1	i=1	simm13

```
31  30 29        25 24        19 18      14 13 12            5  4           0
```

Suggested Assembly Language Syntax
jmpl   *address, reg* $_{rd}$

Description:

The JMPL instruction causes a register-indirect delayed control transfer to the address given by "$r[rs1] + r[rs2]$" if i field = 0, or "$r[rs1]$ + sign_ext(*simm13*)" if $i = 1$.

The JMPL instruction copies the PC, which contains the address of the JMPL instruction, into register $r[rd]$. The high-order 32-bits of the PC value stored in $r[rd]$ are implementation-dependent when PSTATE.AM = 1 (impl. dep. #125). The value written into $r[rd]$ is visible to the instruction in the delay slot.

If either of the low-order two bits of the jump address is nonzero, a *mem_address_not_aligned* exception occurs.

Programming Note:

A JMPL instruction with rd = 15 functions as a register-indirect call using the standard link register.

JMPL with rd = 0 can be used to return from a subroutine. The typical return address is "$r[31] + 8$," if a nonleaf routine (one that uses the SAVE instruction) is entered by a CALL instruction, or "$r[15] + 8$" if a leaf routine (one that does not use the SAVE instruction) is entered by a CALL instruction or by a JMPL instruction with rd = 15.

Exceptions:

mem_address_not_aligned

A.25 Load Floating-Point

> The LDFSR instruction is deprecated; it is provided only for compatibility with previous versions of the architecture. It should not be used in new SPARC-V9 software. It is recommended that the LDXFSR instruction be used in its place.

Opcode	op3	rd	Operation
LDF	10 0000	0..31	Load Floating-Point Register
LDDF	10 0011	†	Load Double Floating-Point Register
LDQF	10 0010	†	Load Quad Floating-Point Register
LDFSR^D	10 0001	0	Load Floating-Point State Register Lower
LDXFSR	10 0001	1	Load Floating-Point State Register
—	10 0001	2..31	*Reserved*

† Encoded floating-point register value, as described in 5.1.4.1

Format (3):

11	rd	op3	rs1	i=0	—	rs2

11	rd	op3	rs1	i=1	simm13

31 30 29   25 24   19 18   14 13 12   5 4   0

Suggested Assembly Language Syntax	
ld	[*address*], *freg*_{rd}
ldd	[*address*], *freg*_{rd}
ldq	[*address*], *freg*_{rd}
ld	[*address*], %fsr
ldx	[*address*], %fsr

Description:

The load single floating-point instruction (LDF) copies a word from memory into $f[rd]$.

The load doubleword floating-point instruction (LDDF) copies a word-aligned doubleword from memory into a double-precision floating-point register.

The load quad floating-point instruction (LDQF) copies a word-aligned quadword from memory into a quad-precision floating-point register.

The load floating-point state register lower instruction (LDFSR) waits for all FPop instructions that have not finished execution to complete, and then loads a word from memory into the lower 32 bits of the FSR.

The load floating-point state register instruction (LDXFSR) waits for all FPop instructions that have not finished execution to complete, and then loads a doubleword from memory into the FSR.

Compatibility Note:
> SPARC-V9 supports two different instructions to load the FSR; the SPARC-V8 LDFSR instruction is defined to load only the lower 32 bits into the FSR, whereas LDXFSR allows SPARC-V9 programs to load all 64 bits of the FSR.

Load floating-point instructions access the primary address space (ASI = 80_{16}). The effective address for these instructions is "$r[rs1] + r[rs2]$" if $i = 0$, or "$r[rs1]$ + sign_ext($simm13$)" if $i = 1$.

LDF, LDFSR, LDDF, and LDQF cause a *mem_address_not_aligned* exception if the effective memory address is not word-aligned; LDXFSR causes a *mem_address_not_aligned* exception if the address is not doubleword-aligned. If the floating-point unit is not enabled (per FPRS.FEF and PSTATE.PEF), or if no FPU is present, a load floating-point instruction causes an *fp_disabled* exception.

IMPL. DEP. #109(1): LDDF requires only word alignment. However, if the effective address is word-aligned but not doubleword-aligned, LDDF may cause an *LDDF_mem_address_not_aligned* exception. In this case the trap handler software shall emulate the LDDF instruction and return.

IMPL. DEP. #111(1): LDQF requires only word alignment. However, if the effective address is word-aligned but not quadword-aligned, LDQF may cause an *LDQF_mem_address_not_aligned* exception. In this case the trap handler software shall emulate the LDQF instruction and return.

Programming Note:
> In SPARC-V8, some compilers issued sequences of single-precision loads when they could not determine that double- or quadword operands were properly aligned. For SPARC-V9, since emulation of misaligned loads is expected to be fast, it is recommended that compilers issue sets of single-precision loads only when they can determine that double- or quadword operands are **not** properly aligned.

Implementation Note:
> **IMPL. DEP. #44:** If a load floating-point instruction traps with any type of access error, the contents of the destination floating-point register(s) remain unchanged or are undefined.

Exceptions:
> *async_data_error*
> *illegal_instruction* ($op3 = 21_{16}$ and $rd = 2..31$)
> *fp_disabled*
> *LDDF_mem_address_not_aligned* (LDDF only) (impl. dep. #109)
> *LDQF_mem_address_not_aligned* (LDQF only) (impl. dep. #111)
> *fp_exception_other* (*invalid_fp_register* (LDQF only))
> *mem_address_not_aligned*
> *data_access_MMU_miss*
> *data_access_exception*
> *data_access_error*
> *data_access_protection*

A.26 Load Floating-Point from Alternate Space

Opcode	op3	rd	Operation
LDFA^{PASI}	11 0000	0..31	Load Floating-Point Register from Alternate space
LDDFA^{PASI}	11 0011	†	Load Double Floating-Point Register from Alternate space
LDQFA^{PASI}	11 0010	†	Load QuadFloating-Point Register from Alternate space

† Encoded floating-point register value, as described in 5.1.4.1

Format (3):

11	rd	op3	rs1	i=0	imm_asi	rs2

11	rd	op3	rs1	i=1	simm13

31 30 29   25 24   19 18   14 13 12   5 4   0

Suggested Assembly Language Syntax	
lda	[regaddr] imm_asi, freg$_{rd}$
lda	[reg_plus_imm] %asi, freg$_{rd}$
ldda	[regaddr] imm_asi, freg$_{rd}$
ldda	[reg_plus_imm] %asi, freg$_{rd}$
ldqa	[regaddr] imm_asi, freg$_{rd}$
ldqa	[reg_plus_imm] %asi, freg$_{rd}$

Description:

The load single floating-point from alternate space instruction (LDFA) copies a word from memory into $f[rd]$.

The load doubleword floating-point from alternate space instruction (LDDFA) copies a word-aligned doubleword from memory into a double-precision floating-point register.

The load quad floating-point from alternate space instruction (LDQFA) copies a word-aligned quadword from memory into a quad-precision floating-point register.

Load floating-point from alternate space instructions contain the address space identifier (ASI) to be used for the load in the *imm_asi* field if $i = 0$, or in the ASI register if $i = 1$. The access is privileged if bit seven of the ASI is zero; otherwise, it is not privileged. The effective address for these instructions is "$r[rs1] + r[rs2]$" if $i = 0$, or "$r[rs1] + $ sign_ext($simm13$)" if $i = 1$.

LDFA, LDDFA, and LDQFA cause a *mem_address_not_aligned* exception if the effective memory address is not word-aligned; If the floating-point unit is not enabled (per FPRS.-FEF and PSTATE.PEF), or if no FPU is present, load floating-point from alternate space instructions cause an *fp_disabled* exception. LDFA, LDDFA and LDQFA cause a *privileged_action* exception if PSTATE.PRIV = 0 and bit 7 of the ASI is zero.

IMPL. DEP. #109(2): LDDFA requires only word alignment. However, if the effective address is word-aligned but not doubleword-aligned, LDDFA may cause an *LDDF_mem_address_not_* *aligned* exception. In this case the trap handler software shall emulate the LDDF instruction and return.

IMPL. DEP. #111(2): LDQFA requires only word alignment. however, if the effective address is word-aligned but not quadword-aligned, LDQFA may cause an *ldqf_mem_address_not_aligned* exception. In this case the trap handler software shall emulate the LDQF instruction and return.

Programming Note:

        In SPARC-V8, some compilers issued sequences of single-precision loads when they could not determine that double- or quadword operands were properly aligned. For SPARC-V9, since emulation of mis-aligned loads is expected to be fast, it is recommended that compilers issue sets of single-precision loads only when they can determine that double- or quadword operands are **not** properly aligned.

Implementation Note:

        If a load floating-point instruction traps with any type of access error, the destination floating-point register(s) either remain unchanged or are undefined. (impl. dep. #44)

Exceptions:

    async_data_error
    fp_disabled
    LDDF_mem_address_not_aligned (LDDFA only) (impl. dep. #109)
    LDQF_mem_address_not_aligned (LDQFA only) (impl. dep. #111)
    fp_exception_other (*invalid_fp_register* (LDQFA only))
    mem_address_not_aligned
    privileged_action
    data_access_MMU_miss
    data_access_exception
    data_access_error
    data_access_protection

A.27 Load Integer

> The LDD instruction is deprecated; it is provided only for compatibility with previous versions of the architecture. It should not be used in new SPARC-V9 software. It is recommended that the LDX instruction be used in its place.

Opcode	op3	Operation
LDSB	00 1001	Load Signed Byte
LDSH	00 1010	Load Signed Halfword
LDSW	00 1000	Load Signed Word
LDUB	00 0001	Load Unsigned Byte
LDUH	00 0010	Load Unsigned Halfword
LDUW	00 0000	Load Unsigned Word
LDX	00 1011	Load Extended Word
LDD[D]	00 0011	Load Doubleword

Format (3):

11	rd	op3	rs1	i=0	—	rs2

11	rd	op3	rs1	i=1	simm13

31 30 29   25 24   19 18   14 13 12   5 4   0

Suggested Assembly Language Syntax	
ldsb	[address], reg$_{rd}$
ldsh	[address], reg$_{rd}$
ldsw	[address], reg$_{rd}$
ldub	[address], reg$_{rd}$
lduh	[address], reg$_{rd}$
lduw	[address], reg$_{rd}$ (synonym: ld)
ldx	[address], reg$_{rd}$
ldd	[address], reg$_{rd}$

Description:

The load integer instructions copy a byte, a halfword, a word, an extended word, or a doubleword from memory. All except LDD copy the fetched value into $r[rd]$. A fetched byte, halfword, or word is right-justified in the destination register $r[rd]$; it is either sign-extended or zero-filled on the left, depending on whether the opcode specifies a signed or unsigned operation, respectively.

The load doubleword integer instructions (LDD) copy a doubleword from memory into an r-register pair. The word at the effective memory address is copied into the even r register. The word at the effective memory address + 4 is copied into the following odd-numbered *r* register. The upper 32 bits of both the even-numbered and odd-numbered *r* registers are zero-filled. Note that a load doubleword with *rd* = 0 modifies only *r*[1]. The least significant bit of the *rd* field in an LDD instruction is unused and should be set to zero by software. An attempt to execute a load doubleword instruction that refers to a misaligned (odd-numbered) destination register causes an *illegal_instruction* exception.

IMPL. DEP. #107(1): It is implementation-dependent whether LDD is implemented in hardware. If not, an attempt to execute it will cause an *unimplemented_ldd* exception.

Load integer instructions access the primary address space (ASI = 80_{16}). The effective address is "*r*[*rs1*] + *r*[*rs2*]" if *i* = 0, or "*r*[*rs1*] + sign_ext(*simm13*)" if *i* = 1.

A successful load (notably, load extended and load doubleword) instruction operates atomically.

LDUH and LDSH cause a *mem_address_not_aligned* exception if the address is not half-word-aligned. LDUW and LDSW cause a *mem_address_not_aligned* exception if the effective address is not word-aligned; LDX and LDD cause a *mem_address_not_aligned* exception if the address is not doubleword-aligned.

Programming Note:
> LDD is provided for compatibility with SPARC-V8. It may execute slowly on SPARC-V9 machines because of data path and register-access difficulties. In some systems it may trap to emulation code. It is suggested that programmers and compilers avoid using these instructions.
>
> If LDD is emulated in software, an LDX instruction should be used for the memory access in order to preserve atomicity.

Compatibility Note:
> The SPARC-V8 LD instruction has been renamed LDUW in SPARC-V9. The LDSW instruction is new in SPARC-V9.

Exceptions:
> *async_data_error*
> *unimplemented_LDD* (LDD only (impl. dep. #107))
> *illegal_instruction* (LDD with odd *rd*)
> *mem_address_not_aligned* (all except LDSB, LDUB)
> *data_access_exception*
> *data_access_protection*
> *data_access_MMU_miss*
> *data_access_error*

A.28 Load Integer from Alternate Space

> The LDDA instruction is deprecated; it is provided only for compatibility with previous versions of the architecture. It should not be used in new SPARC-V9 software. It is recommended that the LDXA instruction be used in its place.

Opcode	op3	Operation
LDSBA^{PASI}	01 1001	Load Signed Byte from Alternate space
LDSHA^{PASI}	01 1010	Load Signed Halfword from Alternate space
LDSWA^{PASI}	01 1000	Load Signed Word from Alternate space
LDUBA^{PASI}	01 0001	Load Unsigned Byte from Alternate space
LDUHA^{PASI}	01 0010	Load Unsigned Halfword from Alternate space
LDUWA^{PASI}	01 0000	Load Unsigned Word from Alternate space
LDXA^{PASI}	01 1011	Load Extended Word from Alternate space
LDDA$^{D, PASI}$	01 0011	Load Doubleword from Alternate space

Format (3):

11	rd	op3	rs1	i=0	imm_asi	rs2

11	rd	op3	rs1	i=1	simm13

```
31 30 29      25 24           19 18      14 13 12              5 4        0
```

Suggested Assembly Language Syntax		
ldsba	[*regaddr*] *imm_asi*, reg $_{rd}$	
ldsha	[*regaddr*] *imm_asi*, reg $_{rd}$	
ldswa	[*regaddr*] *imm_asi*, reg $_{rd}$	
lduba	[*regaddr*] *imm_asi*, reg $_{rd}$	
lduha	[*regaddr*] *imm_asi*, reg $_{rd}$	
lduwa	[*regaddr*] *imm_asi*, reg $_{rd}$	(*synonym:* lda)
ldxa	[*regaddr*] *imm_asi*, reg $_{rd}$	
ldda	[*regaddr*] *imm_asi*, reg $_{rd}$	
ldsba	[*reg_plus_imm*] %asi, reg $_{rd}$	
ldsha	[*reg_plus_imm*] %asi, reg $_{rd}$	
ldswa	[*reg_plus_imm*] %asi, reg $_{rd}$	
lduba	[*reg_plus_imm*] %asi, reg $_{rd}$	
lduha	[*reg_plus_imm*] %asi, reg $_{rd}$	
lduwa	[*reg_plus_imm*] %asi, reg $_{rd}$	(*synonym:* lda)
ldxa	[*reg_plus_imm*] %asi, reg $_{rd}$	
ldda	[*reg_plus_imm*] %asi, reg $_{rd}$	

Description:

The load integer from alternate space instructions copy a byte, a halfword, a word, an extended word, or a doubleword from memory. All except LDDA copy the fetched value into r[*rd*]. A fetched byte, halfword, or word is right-justified in the destination register *r*[*rd*]; it is either sign-extended or zero-filled on the left, depending on whether the opcode specifies a signed or unsigned operation, respectively.

The load doubleword integer from alternate space instruction (LDDA) copies a doubleword from memory into an *r*-register pair. The word at the effective memory address is copied into the even *r* register. The word at the effective memory address + 4 is copied into the following odd-numbered *r* register. The upper 32 bits of both the even-numbered and odd-numbered *r* registers are zero-filled. Note that a load doubleword with *rd* = 0 modifies only *r*[1]. The least significant bit of the *rd* field in an LDDA instruction is unused and should be set to zero by software. An attempt to execute a load doubleword instruction that refers to a misaligned (odd-numbered) destination register causes an *illegal_instruction* exception.

IMPL. DEP. #107(2): It is implementation-dependent whether LDDA is implemented in hardware. If not, an attempt to execute it will cause an *unimplemented_ldd* exception.

The load integer from alternate space instructions contain the address space identifier (ASI) to be used for the load in the *imm_asi* field if $i = 0$, or in the ASI register if $i = 1$. The access is privileged if bit seven of the ASI is zero; otherwise, it is not privileged. The effective address for these instructions is "*r*[*rs1*] + *r*[*rs2*]" if $i = 0$, or "*r*[*rs1*] + sign_ext(*simm13*)" if $i = 1$.

A successful load (notably, load extended and load doubleword) instruction operates atomically.

LDUHA, and LDSHA cause a *mem_address_not_aligned* exception if the address is not halfword-aligned. LDUWA and LDSWA cause a *mem_address_not_aligned* exception if the effective address is not word-aligned; LDXA and LDDA cause a *mem_address_not_aligned* exception if the address is not doubleword-aligned.

These instructions cause a *privileged_action* exception if PSTATE.PRIV = 0 and bit 7 of the ASI is zero.

Programming Note:
> LDDA is provided for compatibility with SPARC-V8. It may execute slowly on SPARC-V9 machines because of data path and register-access difficulties. In some systems it may trap to emulation code. It is suggested that programmers and compilers avoid using this instruction.

> If LDDA is emulated in software, an LDXA instruction should be used for the memory access in order to preserve atomicity.

Compatibility Note:
> The SPARC-V8 instruction LDA has been renamed LDUWA in SPARC-V9. The LDSWA instruction is new in SPARC-V9.

Exceptions:
> *async_data_error*
> *privileged_action*
> *unimplemented_LDD* (LDDA only (impl. dep. #107))
> *illegal_instruction* (LDDA with odd *rd*)
> *mem_address_not_aligned* (all except LDSBA and LDUBA)
> *data_access_exception*
> *data_access_protection*
> *data_access_MMU_miss*
> *data_access_error*

A.29   Load-Store Unsigned Byte

Opcode	op3	Operation
LDSTUB	00 1101	Load-Store Unsigned Byte

Format (3):

11	rd	op3	rs1	i=0	—	rs2

11	rd	op3	rs1	i=1	simm13

31 30 29   25 24   19 18   14 13 12   5 4   0

Suggested Assembly Language Syntax
ldstub   [*address*], *reg$_{rd}$*

Description:

The load-store unsigned byte instruction copies a byte from memory into $r[rd]$, and then rewrites the addressed byte in memory to all ones. The fetched byte is right-justified in the destination register $r[rd]$ and zero-filled on the left.

The operation is performed atomically, that is, without allowing intervening interrupts or deferred traps. In a multiprocessor system, two or more processors executing LDSTUB, LDSTUBA, CASA, CASXA, SWAP, or SWAPA instructions addressing all or parts of the same doubleword simultaneously are guaranteed to execute them in an undefined but serial order.

The effective address for these instructions is "$r[rs1] + r[rs2]$" if $i = 0$, or "$r[rs1]$ + sign_ext($simm13$)" if $i = 1$.

The coherence and atomicity of memory operations between processors and I/O DMA memory accesses are implementation-dependent (impl. dep #120).

Exceptions:
> *async_data_error*
> *data_access_exception*
> *data_access_error*
> *data_access_protection*
> *data_access_MMU_miss*

A.30 Load-Store Unsigned Byte to Alternate Space

Opcode	op3	Operation
LDSTUBA^{Pasi}	01 1101	Load-Store Unsigned Byte into Alternate space

Format (3):

11	rd	op3	rs1	i=0	imm_asi	rs2

11	rd	op3	rs1	i=1	simm13

31 30 29   25 24   19 18   14 13 12   5 4   0

Suggested Assembly Language Syntax
ldstuba   [regaddr] imm_asi, reg_{rd}
ldstuba   [reg_plus_imm] %asi, reg_{rd}

Description:

The load-store unsigned byte into alternate space instruction copies a byte from memory into $r[rd]$, then rewrites the addressed byte in memory to all ones. The fetched byte is right-justified in the destination register $r[rd]$ and zero-filled on the left.

The operation is performed atomically, that is, without allowing intervening interrupts or deferred traps. In a multiprocessor system, two or more processors executing LDSTUB, LDSTUBA, CASA, CASXA, SWAP, or SWAPA instructions addressing all or parts of the same doubleword simultaneously are guaranteed to execute them in an undefined, but serial order.

LDSTUBA contains the address space identifier (ASI) to be used for the load in the *imm_asi* field if $i = 0$, or in the ASI register if $i = 1$. The access is privileged if bit seven of the ASI is zero; otherwise, it is not privileged. The effective address is "$r[rs1] + r[rs2]$" if $i = 0$, or "$r[rs1]$ + sign_ext(*simm13*)" if $i = 1$.

LDSTUBA causes a *privileged_action* exception if PSTATE.PRIV = 0 and bit 7 of the ASI is zero.

The coherence and atomicity of memory operations between processors and I/O DMA memory accesses are implementation-dependent (impl. dep #120).

Exceptions:

> *async_data_error*
> *privileged_action*
> *data_access_exception*
> *data_access_error*
> *data_access_protection*
> *data_access_MMU_miss*

A.31 Logical Operations

Opcode	op3	Operation
AND	00 0001	And
ANDcc	01 0001	And and modify cc's
ANDN	00 0101	And Not
ANDNcc	01 0101	And Not and modify cc's
OR	00 0010	Inclusive Or
ORcc	01 0010	Inclusive Or and modify cc's
ORN	00 0110	Inclusive Or Not
ORNcc	01 0110	Inclusive Or Not and modify cc's
XOR	00 0011	Exclusive Or
XORcc	01 0011	Exclusive Or and modify cc's
XNOR	00 0111	Exclusive Nor
XNORcc	01 0111	Exclusive Nor and modify cc's

Format (3):

10	rd	op3	rs1	i=0	—	rs2

10	rd	op3	rs1	i=1	simm13

31 30 29   25 24   19 18   14 13 12   5 4   0

Suggested Assembly Language Syntax	
and	reg_{rs1}, reg_or_imm, reg_{rd}
andcc	reg_{rs1}, reg_or_imm, reg_{rd}
andn	reg_{rs1}, reg_or_imm, reg_{rd}
andncc	reg_{rs1}, reg_or_imm, reg_{rd}
or	reg_{rs1}, reg_or_imm, reg_{rd}
orcc	reg_{rs1}, reg_or_imm, reg_{rd}
orn	reg_{rs1}, reg_or_imm, reg_{rd}
orncc	reg_{rs1}, reg_or_imm, reg_{rd}
xor	reg_{rs1}, reg_or_imm, reg_{rd}
xorcc	reg_{rs1}, reg_or_imm, reg_{rd}
xnor	reg_{rs1}, reg_or_imm, reg_{rd}
xnorcc	reg_{rs1}, reg_or_imm, reg_{rd}

Description:

These instructions implement bitwise logical operations. They compute "$r[rs1]$ **op** $r[rs2]$" if $i = 0$, or "$r[rs1]$ **op** sign_ext($simm13$)" if $i = 1$, and write the result into $r[rd]$.

ANDcc, ANDNcc, ORcc, ORNcc, XORcc, and XNORcc modify the integer condition codes (icc and xcc). They set $icc.v$, $icc.c$, $xcc.v$, and $xcc.c$ to zero, $icc.n$ to bit 31 of the result, $xcc.n$ to bit 63 of the result, $icc.z$ to 1 if bits 31:0 of the result are zero (otherwise to 0), and $xcc.z$ to 1 if all 64 bits of the result are zero (otherwise to 0).

ANDN, ANDNcc, ORN, and ORNcc logically negate their second operand before applying the main (AND or OR) operation.

Programming Note:

XNOR and XNORcc are identical to the XOR-Not and XOR-Not-cc logical operations, respectively.

Exceptions:

(none)

A.31 Memory Barrier

Opcode	op3	Operation
MEMBAR	10 1000	Memory Barrier

Format (3):

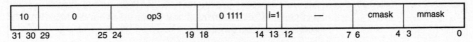

10	0	op3	0 1111	i=1	—	cmask	mmask

31 30 29   25 24   19 18   14 13 12   7 6   4 3   0

Suggested Assembly Language Syntax
membar   *membar_mask*

Description:

The memory barrier instruction, MEMBAR, has two complementary functions: to express order constraints between memory references and to provide explicit control of memory-reference completion. The *membar_mask* field in the suggested assembly language is the bitwise OR of the *cmask* and *mmask* instruction fields.

MEMBAR introduces an order constraint between classes of memory references appearing before the MEMBAR and memory references following it in a program. The particular classes of memory references are specified by the *mmask* field. Memory references are classified as loads (including load instructions, LDSTUB(A), SWAP(A), CASA, and CASXA) and stores (including store instructions, LDSTUB(A), SWAP(A), CASA, CASXA, and FLUSH). The *mmask* field specifies the classes of memory references subject to ordering, as described below. MEMBAR applies to all memory operations in all address spaces referenced by the issuing processor, but has no effect on memory references by other processors. When the *cmask* field is nonzero, completion as well as order constraints are imposed, and the order imposed can be more stringent than that specifiable by the *mmask* field alone.

A load has been performed when the value loaded has been transmitted from memory and cannot be modified by another processor. A store has been performed when the value stored has become visible, that is, when the previous value can no longer be read by any processor. In specifying the effect of MEMBAR, instructions are considered to be executed as if they were processed in a strictly sequential fashion, with each instruction completed before the next has begun.

The *mmask* field is encoded in bits 3 through 0 of the instruction. Table 25 specifies the order constraint that each bit of *mmask* (selected when set to 1) imposes on memory references appearing before and after the MEMBAR. From zero to four mask bits may be selected in the *mmask* field.

Table 25—MEMBAR *mmask* Encodings

Mask bit	Name	Description
mmask<3>	#StoreStore	The effects of all stores appearing prior to the MEMBAR instruction must be visible to all processors before the effect of any stores following the MEMBAR. Equivalent to the deprecated STBAR instruction
mmask<2>	#LoadStore	All loads appearing prior to the MEMBAR instruction must have been performed before the effect of any stores following the MEMBAR is visible to any other processor.
mmask<1>	#StoreLoad	The effects of all stores appearing prior to the MEMBAR instruction must be visible to all processors before loads following the MEMBAR may be performed.
mmask<0>	#LoadLoad	All loads appearing prior to the MEMBAR instruction must have been performed before any loads following the MEMBAR may be performed.

The *cmask* field is encoded in bits 6 through 4 of the instruction. Bits in the *cmask* field, illustrated in table 26, specify additional constraints on the order of memory references and the processing of instructions. If *cmask* is zero, then MEMBAR enforces the partial ordering specified by the *mmask* field; if *cmask* is nonzero, then completion as well as partial order constraints are applied.

Table 26—MEMBAR *cmask* Encodings

Mask bit	Function	Name	Description
cmask<2>	Synchronization barrier	#Sync	All operations (including nonmemory reference operations) appearing prior to the MEMBAR must have been performed and the effects of any exceptions become visible before any instruction after the MEMBAR may be initiated.
cmask<1>	Memory issue barrier	#MemIssue	All memory reference operations appearing prior to the MEMBAR must have been performed before any memory operation after the MEMBAR may be initiated.
cmask<0>	Lookaside barrier	#Lookaside	A store appearing prior to the MEMBAR must complete before any load following the MEMBAR referencing the same address can be initiated.

For information on the use of MEMBAR, see 8.4.3, "The MEMBAR Instruction," and Appendix J, "Programming With the Memory Models." Chapter 8, "Memory Models," and Appendix F, "SPARC-V9 MMU Requirements," contain additional information about the memory models themselves.

The encoding of MEMBAR is identical to that of the RDASR instruction, except that $rs1 = 15$, $rd = 0$, and $i = 1$.

The coherence and atomicity of memory operations between processors and I/O DMA memory accesses are implementation-dependent (impl. dep #120).

Compatibility Note:
> MEMBAR with $mmask = 8_{16}$ and $cmask = 0_{16}$ ("membar #StoreStore") is identical in function to the SPARC-V8 STBAR instruction, which is deprecated.

Exceptions:
> (none)

A.32 Move Floating-Point Register on Conditon (FMOVcc)

For Integer Condition Codes:

Opcode	op3	cond	Operation	*icc/xcc* test
FMOVA	11 0101	1000	Move Always	1
FMOVN	11 0101	0000	Move Never	0
FMOVNE	11 0101	1001	Move if Not Equal	not Z
FMOVE	11 0101	0001	Move if Equal	Z
FMOVG	11 0101	1010	Move if Greater	not (Z or (N xor V))
FMOVLE	11 0101	0010	Move if Less or Equal	Z or (N xor V)
FMOVGE	11 0101	1011	Move if Greater or Equal	not (N xor V)
FMOVL	11 0101	0011	Move if Less	N xor V
FMOVGU	11 0101	1100	Move if Greater Unsigned	not (C or Z)
FMOVLEU	11 0101	0100	Move if Less or Equal Unsigned	(C or Z)
FMOVCC	11 0101	1101	Move if Carry Clear (Greater or Equal, Unsigned)	not C
FMOVCS	11 0101	0101	Move if Carry Set (Less than, Unsigned)	C
FMOVPOS	11 0101	1110	Move if Positive	not N
FMOVNEG	11 0101	0110	Move if Negative	N
FMOVVC	11 0101	1111	Move if Overflow Clear	not V
FMOVVS	11 0101	0111	Move if Overflow Set	V

For Floating-Point Condition Codes:

Opcode	op3	cond	Operation	*fcc* test
FMOVFA	11 0101	1000	Move Always	1
FMOVFN	11 0101	0000	Move Never	0
FMOVFU	11 0101	0111	Move if Unordered	U
FMOVFG	11 0101	0110	Move if Greater	G
FMOVFUG	11 0101	0101	Move if Unordered or Greater	G or U
FMOVFL	11 0101	0100	Move if Less	L
FMOVFUL	11 0101	0011	Move if Unordered or Less	L or U
FMOVFLG	11 0101	0010	Move if Less or Greater	L or G
FMOVFNE	11 0101	0001	Move if Not Equal	L or G or U
FMOVFE	11 0101	1001	Move if Equal	E
FMOVFUE	11 0101	1010	Move if Unordered or Equal	E or U
FMOVFGE	11 0101	1011	Move if Greater or Equal	E or G
FMOVFUGE	11 0101	1100	Move if Unordered or Greater or Equal	E or G or U
FMOVFLE	11 0101	1101	Move if Less or Equal	E or L
FMOVFULE	11 0101	1110	Move if Unordered or Less or Equal	E or L or U
FMOVFO	11 0101	1111	Move if Ordered	E or L or G

Format (4):

10	rd	op3	0	cond	opf_cc	opf_low	rs2

31 30 29   25 24   19 18 17   14 13   11 10   5 4   0

Encoding of the *opf_cc* **field** (also see table 38 on page 267):

opf_cc	Condition code
000	fcc0
001	fcc1
010	fcc2
011	fcc3
100	icc
101	—
110	xcc
111	—

Encoding of *opf* **field (opf_cc ☐ opf_low):**

Instruction variation		opf_cc	opf_low	opf
FMOVScc	%fcc*n*, *rs2*, *rd*	0*nn*	00 0001	0 *nn*00 0001
FMOVDcc	%fcc*n*, *rs2*, *rd*	0*nn*	00 0010	0 *nn*00 0010
FMOVQcc	%fcc*n*, *rs2*, *rd*	0*nn*	00 0011	0 *nn*00 0011
FMOVScc	%icc, *rs2*, *rd*	100	00 0001	1 0000 0001
FMOVDcc	%icc, *rs2*, *rd*	100	00 0010	1 0000 0010
FMOVQcc	%icc, *rs2*, *rd*	100	00 0011	1 0000 0011
FMOVScc	%xcc, *rs2*, *rd*	110	00 0001	1 1000 0001
FMOVDcc	%xcc, *rs2*, *rd*	110	00 0010	1 1000 0010
FMOVQcc	%xcc, *rs2*, *rd*	110	00 0011	1 1000 0011

For Integer Condition Codes:

Suggested Assembly Language Syntax		
fmov{s,d,q}a	*i_or_x_cc, freg$_{rs2}$, freg$_{rd}$*	
fmov{s,d,q}n	*i_or_x_cc, freg$_{rs2}$, freg$_{rd}$*	
fmov{s,d,q}ne	*i_or_x_cc, freg$_{rs2}$, freg$_{rd}$*	(*synonyms*: fmov{s,d,q}nz)
fmov{s,d,q}e	*i_or_x_cc, freg$_{rs2}$, freg$_{rd}$*	(*synonyms*: fmov{s,d,q}z)
fmov{s,d,q}g	*i_or_x_cc, freg$_{rs2}$, freg$_{rd}$*	
fmov{s,d,q}le	*i_or_x_cc, freg$_{rs2}$, freg$_{rd}$*	
fmov{s,d,q}ge	*i_or_x_cc, freg$_{rs2}$, freg$_{rd}$*	
fmov{s,d,q}l	*i_or_x_cc, freg$_{rs2}$, freg$_{rd}$*	
fmov{s,d,q}gu	*i_or_x_cc, freg$_{rs2}$, freg$_{rd}$*	
fmov{s,d,q}leu	*i_or_x_cc, freg$_{rs2}$, freg$_{rd}$*	
fmov{s,d,q}cc	*i_or_x_cc, freg$_{rs2}$, freg$_{rd}$*	(*synonyms*: fmov{s,d,q}geu)
fmov{s,d,q}cs	*i_or_x_cc, freg$_{rs2}$, freg$_{rd}$*	(*synonyms*: fmov{s,d,q}lu)
fmov{s,d,q}pos	*i_or_x_cc, freg$_{rs2}$, freg$_{rd}$*	
fmov{s,d,q}neg	*i_or_x_cc, freg$_{rs2}$, freg$_{rd}$*	
fmov{s,d,q}vc	*i_or_x_cc, freg$_{rs2}$, freg$_{rd}$*	
fmov{s,d,q}vs	*i_or_x_cc, freg$_{rs2}$, freg$_{rd}$*	

Programming Note:
   To select the appropriate condition code, include "%icc" or "%xcc" before the registers.

For Floating-Point Condition Codes:

Suggested Assembly Language Syntax		
fmov{s,d,q}a	%fcc*n, freg$_{rs2}$, freg$_{rd}$*	
fmov{s,d,q}n	%fcc*n, freg$_{rs2}$, freg$_{rd}$*	
fmov{s,d,q}u	%fcc*n, freg$_{rs2}$, freg$_{rd}$*	
fmov{s,d,q}g	%fcc*n, freg$_{rs2}$, freg$_{rd}$*	
fmov{s,d,q}ug	%fcc*n, freg$_{rs2}$, freg$_{rd}$*	
fmov{s,d,q}l	%fcc*n, freg$_{rs2}$, freg$_{rd}$*	
fmov{s,d,q}ul	%fcc*n, freg$_{rs2}$, freg$_{rd}$*	
fmov{s,d,q}lg	%fcc*n, freg$_{rs2}$, freg$_{rd}$*	
fmov{s,d,q}ne	%fcc*n, freg$_{rs2}$, freg$_{rd}$*	(*synonyms*: fmov{s,d,q}nz)
fmov{s,d,q}e	%fcc*n, freg$_{rs2}$, freg$_{rd}$*	(*synonyms*: fmov{s,d,q}z)
fmov{s,d,q}ue	%fcc*n, freg$_{rs2}$, freg$_{rd}$*	
fmov{s,d,q}ge	%fcc*n, freg$_{rs2}$, freg$_{rd}$*	
fmov{s,d,q}uge	%fcc*n, freg$_{rs2}$, freg$_{rd}$*	
fmov{s,d,q}le	%fcc*n, freg$_{rs2}$, freg$_{rd}$*	
fmov{s,d,q}ule	%fcc*n, freg$_{rs2}$, freg$_{rd}$*	
fmov{s,d,q}o	%fcc*n, freg$_{rs2}$, freg$_{rd}$*	

Description:

These instructions copy the floating-point register(s) specified by *rs2* to the floating-point register(s) specified by *rd* if the condition indicated by the *cond* field is satisfied by the selected condition code. The condition code used is specified by the *opf_cc* field of the instruction. If the condition is FALSE, then the destination register(s) are not changed.

These instructions do not modify any condition codes.

Programming Note:

Branches cause most implementations' performance to degrade significantly. Frrequently, the MOVcc and FMOVcc instructions can be used to avoid branches. For example, the following C language segment:

```
double A, B, X;
if (A > B) then X  = 1.03; else X  = 0.0;
```

can be coded as

```
! assume A is in %f0; B is in %f2; %xx points to constant area
        ldd       [%xx+C_1.03],%f4  ! X  = 1.03
        fcmpd     %fcc3,%f0,%f2     ! A > B
        fble ,a   %fcc3,label
        ! following only executed if the branch is taken
        fsubd     %f4,%f4,%f4       ! X  = 0.0
label:...
```

This takes four instructions including a branch.

Using FMOVcc, this could be coded as

```
        ldd       [%xx+C_1.03],%f4  ! X  = 1.03
        fsubd     %f4,%f4,%f6       ! X' = 0.0
        fcmpd     %fcc3,%f0,%f2     ! A > B
        fmovdle   %fcc3,%f6,%f4     ! X  = 0.0
```

This also takes four instructions, but requires no branches and may boost performance significantly. It is suggested that MOVcc and FMOVcc be used instead of branches wherever they would improve performance.

Exceptions:

fp_disabled
fp_exception_other (*invalid_fp_register* (quad forms only))
fp_exception_other (*ftt = unimplemented_FPop* (*opf_cc* = 101_2 or 111_2))

A.33 Move F-P Register on Integer Register Condition (FMOVr)

Opcode	op3	rcond	Operation	Test
—	11 0101	000	*Reserved*	—
FMOVRZ	11 0101	001	Move if Register Zero	$r[rs1] = 0$
FMOVRLEZ	11 0101	010	Move if Register Less Than or Equal to Zero	$r[rs1] \leq 0$
FMOVRLZ	11 0101	011	Move if Register Less Than Zero	$r[rs1] < 0$
—	11 0101	100	*Reserved*	—
FMOVRNZ	11 0101	101	Move if Register Not Zero	$r[rs1] \neq 0$
FMOVRGZ	11 0101	110	Move if Register Greater Than Zero	$r[rs1] > 0$
FMOVRGEZ	11 0101	111	Move if Register Greater Than or Equal to Zero	$r[rs1] \geq 0$

Format (4):

10	rd	op3	rs1	0	rcond	opf_low	rs2

31 30 29   25 24   19 18   14 13 12   10 9   5 4   0

Encoding of *opf_low* field:

Instruction variation	opf_low
FMOVS*rcond* *rs1, rs2, rd*	0 0101
FMOVD*rcond* *rs1, rs2, rd*	0 0110
FMOVQ*rcond* *rs1, rs2, rd*	0 0111

Suggested Assembly Language Syntax		
fmovr{s,d,q}e	$reg_{rs1}, freg_{rs2}, freg_{rd}$	(*synonym:* fmovr{s,d,q}z)
fmovr{s,d,q}lez	$reg_{rs1}, freg_{rs2}, freg_{rd}$	
fmovr{s,d,q}lz	$reg_{rs1}, freg_{rs2}, freg_{rd}$	
fmovr{s,d,q}ne	$reg_{rs1}, freg_{rs2}, freg_{rd}$	(*synonym:* fmovr{s,d,q}nz)
fmovr{s,d,q}gz	$reg_{rs1}, freg_{rs2}, freg_{rd}$	
fmovr{s,d,q}gez	$reg_{rs1}, freg_{rs2}, freg_{rd}$	

Description:

If the contents of integer register $r[rs1]$ satisfy the condition specified in the *rcond* field, these instructions copy the contents of the floating-point register(s) specified by the *rs2* field to the floating-point register(s) specified by the *rd* field. If the contents of $r[rs1]$ do not satisfy the condition, the floating-point register(s) specified by the *rd* field are not modified.

These instructions treat the integer register contents as a signed integer value; they do not modify any condition codes.

Implementation Note:

If this instruction is implemented by tagging each register value with an N (negative) and a Z (zero) bit, use the following table to determine whether *rcond* is TRUE:

Branch	Test
FMOVRNZ	**not** Z
FMOVRZ	Z
FMOVGEZ	**not** N
FMOVRLZ	N
FMOVRLEZ	N **or** Z
FMOVRGZ	N **nor** Z

Exceptions:

fp_disabled

fp_exception_other (*invalid_fp_register* (quad forms only))

fp_exception_other (*unimplemented_FPop* (*rcond* = 000_2 or 100_2))

A.34 Move Integer Register on Condition (MOVcc)

For Integer Condition Codes:

Opcode	op3	cond	Operation	*icc/xcc* test
MOVA	10 1100	1000	Move Always	1
MOVN	10 1100	0000	Move Never	0
MOVNE	10 1100	1001	Move if Not Equal	not Z
MOVE	10 1100	0001	Move if Equal	Z
MOVG	10 1100	1010	Move if Greater	not (Z or (N xorV))
MOVLE	10 1100	0010	Move if Less or Equal	Z or (N xorV)
MOVGE	10 1100	1011	Move if Greater or Equal	not (N xorV)
MOVL	10 1100	0011	Move if Less	N xorV
MOVGU	10 1100	1100	Move if Greater Unsigned	not (C orZ)
MOVLEU	10 1100	0100	Move if Less or Equal Unsigned	(C orZ)
MOVCC	10 1100	1101	Move if Carry Clear (Greater or Equal, Unsigned)	not C
MOVCS	10 1100	0101	Move if Carry Set (Less than, Unsigned)	C
MOVPOS	10 1100	1110	Move if Positive	not N
MOVNEG	10 1100	0110	Move if Negative	N
MOVVC	10 1100	1111	Move if Overflow Clear	not V
MOVVS	10 1100	0111	Move if Overflow Set	V

For Floating-Point Condition Codes:

Opcode	op3	cond	Operation	*fcc* test
MOVFA	10 1100	1000	Move Always	1
MOVFN	10 1100	0000	Move Never	0
MOVFU	10 1100	0111	Move if Unordered	U
MOVFG	10 1100	0110	Move if Greater	G
MOVFUG	10 1100	0101	Move if Unordered or Greater	G or U
MOVFL	10 1100	0100	Move if Less	L
MOVFUL	10 1100	0011	Move if Unordered or Less	L or U
MOVFLG	10 1100	0010	Move if Less or Greater	L or G
MOVFNE	10 1100	0001	Move if Not Equal	L or G or U
MOVFE	10 1100	1001	Move if Equal	E
MOVFUE	10 1100	1010	Move if Unordered or Equal	E or U
MOVFGE	10 1100	1011	Move if Greater or Equal	E or G
MOVFUGE	10 1100	1100	Move if Unordered or Greater or Equal	E or G or U
MOVFLE	10 1100	1101	Move if Less or Equal	E or L
MOVFULE	10 1100	1110	Move if Unordered or Less or Equal	E or L or U
MOVFO	10 1100	1111	Move if Ordered	E or L or G

Format (4):

10	rd	op3	cc2	cond	i=0	cc1	cc0	—	rs2

10	rd	op3	cc2	cond	i=1	cc1	cc0	simm11

31 30 29   25 24   19 18 17   14 13 12 11 10   5 4   0

cc2 □ cc1 □ cc0	Condition code
000	fcc0
001	fcc1
010	fcc2
011	fcc3
100	icc
101	*Reserved*
110	xcc
111	*Reserved*

For Integer Condition Codes:

Suggested Assembly Language Syntax	
mova	*i_or_x_cc, reg_or_imm11, reg$_{rd}$*
movn	*i_or_x_cc, reg_or_imm11, reg$_{rd}$*
movne	*i_or_x_cc, reg_or_imm11, reg$_{rd}$* (*synonym:* movnz)
move	*i_or_x_cc, reg_or_imm11, reg$_{rd}$* (*synonym:* movz)
movg	*i_or_x_cc, reg_or_imm11, reg$_{rd}$*
movle	*i_or_x_cc, reg_or_imm11, reg$_{rd}$*
movge	*i_or_x_cc, reg_or_imm11, reg$_{rd}$*
movl	*i_or_x_cc, reg_or_imm11, reg$_{rd}$*
movgu	*i_or_x_cc, reg_or_imm11, reg$_{rd}$*
movleu	*i_or_x_cc, reg_or_imm11, reg$_{rd}$*
movcc	*i_or_x_cc, reg_or_imm11, reg$_{rd}$* (*synonym:* movgeu)
movcs	*i_or_x_cc, reg_or_imm11, reg$_{rd}$* (*synonym:* movlu)
movpos	*i_or_x_cc, reg_or_imm11, reg$_{rd}$*
movneg	*i_or_x_cc, reg_or_imm11, reg$_{rd}$*
movvc	*i_or_x_cc, reg_or_imm11, reg$_{rd}$*
movvs	*i_or_x_cc, reg_or_imm11, reg$_{rd}$*

Programming Note:

To select the appropriate condition code, include "%icc" or "%xcc" before the register or immediate field.

For Floating-Point Condition Codes:

	Suggested Assembly Language Syntax	
mova	%fccn, reg_or_imm11, reg_rd	
movn	%fccn, reg_or_imm11, reg_rd	
movu	%fccn, reg_or_imm11, reg_rd	
movg	%fccn, reg_or_imm11, reg_rd	
movug	%fccn, reg_or_imm11, reg_rd	
movl	%fccn, reg_or_imm11, reg_rd	
movul	%fccn, reg_or_imm11, reg_rd	
movlg	%fccn, reg_or_imm11, reg_rd	
movne	%fccn, reg_or_imm11, reg_rd	(*synonym*: movnz)
move	%fccn, reg_or_imm11, reg_rd	(*synonym*: movz)
movue	%fccn, reg_or_imm11, reg_rd	
movge	%fccn, reg_or_imm11, reg_rd	
movuge	%fccn, reg_or_imm11, reg_rd	
movle	%fccn, reg_or_imm11, reg_rd	
movule	%fccn, reg_or_imm11, reg_rd	
movo	%fccn, reg_or_imm11, reg_rd	

Programming Note:

> To select the appropriate condition code, include "%fcc0," "%fcc1," "%fcc2," or "%fcc3" before the register or immediate field.

Description:

These instructions test to see if *cond* is TRUE for the selected condition codes. If so, they copy the value in $r[rs2]$ if i field = 0, or "sign_ext(*simm11*)" if i = 1 into $r[rd]$. The condition code used is specified by the $cc2$, $cc1$, and $cc0$ fields of the instruction. If the condition is FALSE, then $r[rd]$ is not changed.

These instructions copy an integer register to another integer register if the condition is TRUE. The condition code that is used to determine whether the move will occur can be either integer condition code (*icc* or *xcc*) or any floating-point condition code (*fcc0*, *fcc1*, *fcc2*, or *fcc3*).

These instructions do not modify any condition codes.

Programming Note:

> Branches cause many implementations' performance to degrade significantly. Frequently, the MOVcc and FMOVcc instructions can be used to avoid branches. For example, the C language if-then-else statement
>
> ```
> if (A > B) then X = 1; else X = 0;
> ```
>
> can be coded as
>
> ```
>       cmp     %i0,%i2
>       bg,a    %xcc,label
>       or      %g0,1,%i3        ! X = 1
>       or      %g0,0,%i3        ! X = 0
> label:...
> ```

This takes four instructions including a branch. Using MOVcc this could be coded as

```
cmp      %i0,%i2
or       %g0,1,%i3              ! assume X = 1
movle    %xcc,0,%i3             ! overwrite with X = 0
```

This takes only three instructions and no branches and may boost performance significantly. It is suggested that MOVcc and FMOVcc be used instead of branches wherever they would increase performance.

Exceptions:

illegal_instruction ($cc2 \square cc1 \square cc0 = 101_2$ or 111_2)

fp_disabled ($cc2 \square cc1 \square cc0 = 000_2$, 001_2, 010_2, or 011_2 and the FPU is disabled)

A.35   Move Integer Register on Register Condition (MOVR)

Opcode	op3	rcond	Operation	Test
—	10 1111	000	*Reserved*	—
MOVRZ	10 1111	001	Move if Register Zero	$r[rs1] = 0$
MOVRLEZ	10 1111	010	Move if Register Less Than or Equal to Zero	$r[rs1] \leq 0$
MOVRLZ	10 1111	011	Move if Register Less Than Zero	$r[rs1] < 0$
—	10 1111	100	*Reserved*	—
MOVRNZ	10 1111	101	Move if Register Not Zero	$r[rs1] \neq 0$
MOVRGZ	10 1111	110	Move if Register Greater Than Zero	$r[rs1] > 0$
MOVRGEZ	10 1111	111	Move if Register Greater Than or Equal to Zero	$r[rs1] \geq 0$

Format (3):

10	rd	op3	rs1	i=0	rcond	—	rs2

10	rd	op3	rs1	i=1	rcond	simm10

```
31 30 29        25 24         19 18      14 13 12   10 9         5 4          0
```

Suggested Assembly Language Syntax	
`movrne`	reg_{rs1}, reg_or_imm10, reg_{rd} (*synonym:* `movrnz`)
`movre`	reg_{rs1}, reg_or_imm10, reg_{rd} (*synonym:* `movrz`)
`movrgez`	reg_{rs1}, reg_or_imm10, reg_{rd}
`movrlz`	reg_{rs1}, reg_or_imm10, reg_{rd}
`movrlez`	reg_{rs1}, reg_or_imm10, reg_{rd}
`movrgz`	reg_{rs1}, reg_or_imm10, reg_{rd}

Description:

If the contents of integer register $r[rs1]$ satisfies the condition specified in the *rcond* field, these instructions copy $r[rs2]$ (if $i = 0$) or sign_ext(*simm10*) (if $i = 1$) into $r[rd]$. If the contents of $r[rs1]$ does not satisfy the condition then $r[rd]$ is not modified. These instructions treat the register contents as a signed integer value; they do not modify any condition codes.

Implementation Note:

If this instruction is implemented by tagging each register value with an N (negative) and a Z (zero) bit, use the following table to determine if *rcond* is TRUE:

Branch	Test
MOVRNZ	**not** Z
MOVRZ	Z
MOVRGEZ	**not** N
MOVRLZ	N
MOVRLEZ	N **or** Z
MOVRGZ	N **nor** Z

Exceptions:

illegal_instruction (*rcond* = 000_2 or 100_2)

A.36 Multiply and Divide (64-bit)

Opcode	op3	Operation
MULX	00 1001	Multiply (signed or unsigned)
SDIVX	10 1101	Signed Divide
UDIVX	00 1101	Unsigned Divide

Format (3):

10	rd	op3	rs1	i=0	—	rs2

10	rd	op3	rs1	i=1	simm13

31 30 29   25 24   19 18   14 13 12   5   4   0

Suggested Assembly Language Syntax	
mulx	reg_{rs1}, reg_or_imm, reg_{rd}
sdivx	reg_{rs1}, reg_or_imm, reg_{rd}
udivx	reg_{rs1}, reg_or_imm, reg_{rd}

Description:

MULX computes "$r[rs1] \times r[rs2]$" if $i = 0$ or "$r[rs1] \times$ sign_ext(*simm13*)" if $i = 1$, and writes the 64-bit product into $r[rd]$. MULX can be used to calculate the 64-bit product for signed or unsigned operands (the product is the same).

SDIVX and UDIVX compute "$r[rs1] \div r[rs2]$" if $i = 0$ or "$r[rs1] \div$ sign_ext(*simm13*)" if $i = 1$, and write the 64-bit result into $r[rd]$. SDIVX operates on the operands as signed integers and produces a corresponding signed result. UDIVX operates on the operands as unsigned integers and produces a corresponding unsigned result.

For SDIVX, if the largest negative number is divided by -1, the result should be the largest negative number. That is:

$$8000\ 0000\ 0000\ 0000_{16} \div FFFF\ FFFF\ FFFF\ FFFF_{16} = 8000\ 0000\ 0000\ 0000_{16}.$$

These instructions do not modify any condition codes.

Exceptions:
    division_by_zero

A.37 Multiply (32-bit)

> The UMUL, UMULcc, SMUL, and SMULcc instructions are deprecated; they are provided only for compatibility with previous versions of the architecture. They should not be used in new SPARC-V9 software. It is recommended that the MULX instruction be used in their place.

Opcode	op3	Operation
UMUL^D	00 1010	Unsigned Integer Multiply
SMUL^D	00 1011	Signed Integer Multiply
UMULcc^D	01 1010	Unsigned Integer Multiply and modify cc's
SMULcc^D	01 1011	Signed Integer Multiply and modify cc's

Format (3):

10	rd	op3	rs1	i=0	—	rs2

10	rd	op3	rs1	i=1	simm13

31 30 29   25 24   19 18   14 13 12   5 4   0

Suggested Assembly Language Syntax	
umul	reg_{rs1}, reg_or_imm, reg_{rd}
smul	reg_{rs1}, reg_or_imm, reg_{rd}
umulcc	reg_{rs1}, reg_or_imm, reg_{rd}
smulcc	reg_{rs1}, reg_or_imm, reg_{rd}

Description:

The multiply instructions perform 32-bit by 32-bit multiplications, producing 64-bit results. They compute "$r[rs1]$<31:0> × $r[rs2]$<31:0>" if $i = 0$, or "$r[rs1]$<31:0> × sign_ ext($simm13$)<31:0>" if $i = 1$. They write the 32 most significant bits of the product into the Y register and all 64 bits of the product into $r[rd]$.

Unsigned multiply (UMUL, UMULcc) operates on unsigned integer word operands and computes an unsigned integer doubleword product. Sgned multiply (SMUL, SMULcc) operates on signed integer word operands and computes a signed integer doubleword product.

UMUL and SMUL do not affect the condition code bits. UMULcc and SMULcc write the integer condition code bits, *icc* and *xcc*, as follows. Note that 32-bit negative (*icc*.N) and zero (*icc*.Z) condition codes are set according to the **less** significant word of the product, and not according to the full 64-bit result.

Bit	UMULcc / SMULcc
icc.N	Set if product[31] = 1
icc.Z	Set if product[31:0] = 0
icc.V	Zero
icc.C	Zero
xcc.N	Set if product[63] = 1
xcc.Z	Set if product[63:0] = 0
xcc.V	Zero
xcc.C	Zero

Programming Note:

32-bit overflow after UMUL / UMULcc is indicated by $Y \neq 0$.

32-bit overflow after SMUL / SMULcc is indicated by $Y \neq (r[rd] >> 31)$, where ">>" indicates 32-bit arithmetic right shift.

Implementation Note:

An implementation may assume that the smaller operand typically will be *r[rs2]* or *simm13*.

Implementation Note:

See *Implementation Characteristics of Current SPARC-V9-based Products, Revision 9.x*, a document available from SPARC International, for information on whether these instructions are implemented by hardware or software in the various SPARC-V9 implementations.

Exceptions:

(none)

A.38 Multiply Step

> The MULScc instruction is deprecated; it is provided only for compatibility with previous versions of the architecture. It should not be used in new SPARC-V9 software. It is recommended that the MULX instruction be used in its place.

Opcode	op3	Operation
MULScc^D	10 0100	Multiply Step and modify cc's

Format (3):

10	rd	op3	rs1	i=0	—	rs2

10	rd	op3	rs1	i=1	simm13

31 30 29   25 24   19 18   14 13 12   5 4   0

Suggested Assembly Language Syntax
mulscc reg_{rs1}, reg_or_imm, reg_{rd}

Description:

MULScc treats the lower 32 bits of both $r[rs1]$ and the Y register as a single 64-bit, right-shiftable doubleword register. The least significant bit of $r[rs1]$ is treated as if it were adjacent to bit 31 of the Y register. The MULScc instruction adds, based on the least significant bit of Y.

Multiplication assumes that the Y register initially contains the multiplier, $r[rs1]$ contains the most significant bits of the product, and $r[rs2]$ contains the multiplicand. Upon completion of the multiplication, the Y register contains the least significant bits of the product.

Note that a standard MULScc instruction has $rs1 = rd$.

MULScc operates as follows:

(1) The multiplicand is $r[rs2]$ if $i = 0$, or sign_ext($simm13$) if $i = 1$.

(2) A 32-bit value is computed by shifting $r[rs1]$ right by one bit with "CCR.$icc.n$ **xor** CCR.$icc.v$" replacing bit 31 of $r[rs1]$. (This is the proper sign for the previous partial product.)

(3) If the least significant bit of Y = 1, the shifted value from step (2) and the multiplicand are added. If the least significant bit of the Y = 0, then 0 is added to the shifted value from step (2).

(4) The sum from step (3) is written into $r[rd]$. The upper 32-bits of $r[rd]$ are undefined. The integer condition codes are updated according to the addition performed
in step (3). The values of the extended condition codes are undefined.

(5) The Y register is shifted right by one bit, with the least significant bit of the
unshifted $r[rs1]$ replacing bit 31of Y.

Exceptions:
(none)

A.39 No Operation

Opcode	op	op2	Operation
NOP	00	100	No Operation

Format (2):

00	op	on2	0000000000000000000000000

31 30 29   25 24   22 21   0

Suggested Assembly Language Syntax
nop

Description:

The NOP instruction changes no program-visible state (except the PC and nPC).

Note that NOP is a special case of the SETHI instruction, with $imm22 = 0$ and $rd = 0$.

Exceptions:

(none)

A.40   Population Count

Opcode	op3	Operation
POPC	10 1110	Population Count

Format (3):

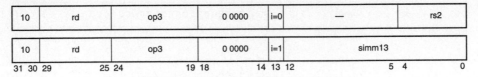

| 10 | rd | op3 | 0 0000 | i=0 | — | rs2 |

| 10 | rd | op3 | 0 0000 | i=1 | simm13 |

31 30 29   25 24   19 18   14 13 12   5   4   0

Suggested Assembly Language Syntax	
popc	reg_or_imm, reg_{rd}

Description:

POPC counts the number of one bits in $r[rs2]$ if $i = 0$, or the number of one bits in sign_
ext($simm13$) if $i = 1$, and stores the count in $r[rd]$. This instruction does not modify the
condition codes.

Implementation Note:
>   Instruction bits 18 through 14 must be zero for POPC. Other encodings of this field ($rs1$) may be
>   used in future versions of the SPARC architecture for other instructions.

Programming Note:
>   POPC can be used to "find first bit set" in a register. A C program illustrating how POPC can be
>   used for this purpose follows:

```
int ffs(zz)    /* finds first 1 bit, counting from the LSB */
unsigned zz;
{
        return popc ( zz ^ (~ (−zz)));  /* for nonzero zz */
}
```

>   Inline assembly language code for `ffs( )` is

```
neg      %IN, %M_IN             ! −zz( 2's complement)
xnor     %IN, %M_IN, %TEMP      ! ^ ~ −zz (exclusive nor)
popc     %TEMP,%RESULT          ! result  = popc( zz ^ ~ −zz)
movrz    %IN,%g0,%RESULT        ! %RESULT should be 0 for %IN=0
```

>   where IN, M_IN, TEMP, and RESULT are integer registers.

Example:

```
IN                    = ...001010000! 1st 1 bit from rt is 4th bit
−IN                   = ...11011000
~ −IN                 = ...00100111
IN ^ ~ −IN            = ...00001111
popc(IN ^ ~ −IN)      = 4
```

Exceptions:
>   *illegal_instruction* (instruction<18:14> ≠ 0)

A.41 Prefetch Data

Opcode	op3	Operation
PREFETCH	10 1101	Prefetch Data
PREFETCHA^{PASI}	11 1101	Prefetch Data from Alternate Space

Format (3) PREFETCH:

11	fcn	op3	rs1	i=0	—	rs2

11	fcn	op3	rs1	i=1	simm13

31 30 29   25 24   19 18   14 13 12   5 4   0

Format (3) PREFETCHA:

11	fcn	op3	rs1	i=0	imm_asi	rs2

11	fcn	op3	rs1	i=1	simm13

31 30 29   25 24   19 18   14 13 12   5 4   0

fcn	Prefetch function
0	Prefetch for several reads
1	Prefetch for one read
2	Prefetch for several writes
3	Prefetch for one write
4	Prefetch page
5–15	*Reserved*
16–31	*Implementation-dependent*

Suggested Assembly Language Syntax		
prefetch	[*address*],	*prefetch_fcn*
prefetcha	[*regaddr*] *imm_asi*,	*prefetch_fcn*
prefetcha	[*reg_plus_imm*] %asi,	*prefetch_fcn*

Description:

In nonprivileged code, a prefetch instruction has the same observable effect as a NOP; its execution is nonblocking and cannot cause an observable trap. In particular, a prefetch instruction shall not trap if it is applied to an illegal or nonexistent memory address.

IMPL. DEP. #103(1): Whether the execution of a PREFETCH instruction has observable effects in privileged code is implementation-dependent.

IMPL. DEP. #103(2): Whether the execution of a PREFETCH instruction can cause a *data_access_mmu_miss* exception is implementation-dependent.

Whether prefetch always succeeds when the MMU is disabled is implementation-dependent (impl. dep. # 117).

Implementation Note:
> Any effects of prefetch in privileged code should be reasonable (e.g., handling ECC errors, no page prefetching allowed within code that handles page faults). The benefits of prefetching should be available to most privileged code.

Execution of a prefetch instruction initiates data movement (or preparation for future data movement or address mapping) to reduce the latency of subsequent loads and stores to the specified address range.

A successful prefetch initiates movement of a block of data containing the addressed byte from memory toward the processor.

IMPL. DEP. #103(3): The size and alignment in memory of the data block is implementation-dependent; the minimum size is 64 bytes and the minimum alignment is a 64-byte boundary.

Programming Note:
> Software may prefetch 64 bytes beginning at an arbitrary address *address* by issuing the instructions

> | prefetch | [*address*], *prefetch_fcn* |
> |---|---|
> | prefetch | [*address* + 63], *prefetch_fcn* |

Implementation Note:
> Prefetching may be used to help manage memory cache(s). A prefetch from a nonprefetchable location has no effect. It is up to memory management hardware to determine how locations are identified as not prefetchable.

Prefetch instructions that do **not** load from an alternate address space access the primary address space (ASI_PRIMARY{_LITTLE}). Prefetch instructions that **do** load from an alternate address space contain the address space identifier (ASI) to be used for the load in the *imm_asi* field if $i = 0$, or in the ASI register if $i = 1$. The access is privileged if bit seven of the ASI is zero; otherwise, it is not privileged. The effective address for these instructions is "$r[rs1] + r[rs2]$" if $i = 0$, or "$r[rs1] + \text{sign\_ext}(simm13)$" if $i = 1$.

Variants of the prefetch instruction can be used to prepare the memory system for different types of accesses.

IMPL. DEP. #103(4): An implementation may implement none, some, or all of these variants. A variant not implemented shall execute as a nop. An implemented variant may support its full semantics, or may support just the simple common-case prefetching semantics.

A.41.1 Prefetch Variants

The prefetch variant is selected by the *fcn* field of the instruction. *fcn* values 5..15 are reserved for future extensions of the architecture.

IMPL. DEP. #103(5): PREFETCH *fcn* values of 16..31 are implementation-dependent.

Each prefetch variant reflects an intent on the part of the compiler or programmer. This is different from other instructions in SPARC-V9 (except BPN), all of which specify specific actions. An implementation may implement a prefetch variant by any technique, as long as the intent of the variant is achieved.

The prefetch instruction is designed to treat the common cases well. The variants are intended to provide scalability for future improvements in both hardware and compilers. If a variant is implemented, then it should have the effects described below. In case some of the variants listed below are implemented and some are not, there is a recommended overloading of the unimplemented variants (see the Implementation Note labeled "Recommended Overloadings" in A.41.2).

A.41.1.1 Prefetch for Several Reads (*fcn* = 0)

The intent of this variant is to cause movement of data into the data cache nearest the processor, with "reasonable" efforts made to obtain the data.

Implementation Note:
> If, for example, some TLB misses are handled in hardware, then they should be handled. On the other hand, a multiple ECC error is reasonable cause for cancellation of a prefetch.

This is the most important case of prefetching.

If the addressed data is already present (and owned, if necessary) in the cache, then this variant has no effect.

A.41.1.2 Prefetch for One Read (*fcn* = 1)

This variant indicates that, if possible, the data cache should be minimally disturbed by the data read from the given address, because that data is expected to be read once and not reused (read or written) soon after that.

If the data is already present in the cache, then this variant has no effect.

Programming Note:
> The intended use of this variant is in streaming large amounts of data into the processor without overwriting data in cache memory.

A.41.1.3 Prefetch for Several Writes (and Possibly Reads) (*fcn* = 2)

The intent of this variant is to cause movement of data in preparation for writing.

If the addressed data is already present in the data cache, then this variant has no effect.

Programming Note:
> An example use of this variant is to write a dirty cache line back to memory, or to initialize a cache line in preparation for a partial write.

Implementation Note:
> On a multiprocessor, this variant indicates that exclusive ownership of the addressed data is needed, so it may have the additional effect of obtaining exclusive ownership of the addressed cache line.

Implementation Note:
> On a uniprocessor, there is no distinction between Prefetch for Several Reads and this variant.

A.41.1.4   Prefetch for One Write (*fcn* = 3)

This variant indicates that, if possible, the data cache should be minimally disturbed by the data written to this address, because that data is not expected to be reused (read or written) soon after it has been written once.

If the data is already present in the cache, then this variant has no effect.

A.41.1.5   Prefetch Page (*fcn* = 4)

In a virtual-memory system, the intended action of this variant is for the supervisor software or hardware to initiate asynchronous mapping of the referenced virtual address, assuming that it is legal to do so.

Programming Note:
> The desire is to avoid a later page fault for the given address, or at least to shorten the latency of a page fault.

In a nonvirtual-memory system, or if the addressed page is already mapped, this variant has no effect.

The referenced page need not be mapped when the instruction completes. Loads and stores issued before the page is mapped should block just as they would if the prefetch had never been issued. When the activity associated with the mapping has completed, the loads and stores may proceed.

Implementation Note:
> An example of mapping activity is DMA from secondary storage.

Implementation Note:
> Use of this variant may be disabled or restricted in privileged code that is not permitted to cause page faults.

A.41.1.6   Implementation-Dependent Prefetch (*fcn* = 16..31)

These values are available for implementations to use. An implementation shall treat any unimplemented prefetch *fcn* values as NOPs (impl. dep. #103).

A.41.2   General Comments

There is no variant of PREFETCH for instruction prefetching. Instruction prefetching should be encoded using the Branch Never (BPN) form of the BPcc instruction (see A.7, "Branch on Integer Condition Codes with Prediction (BPcc)").

One error to avoid in thinking about prefetch instructions is that they should have "no cost to execute." As long as the cost of executing a prefetch instruction is well less than one-third the cost of a cache miss, use of prefetching is a net win. It does not appear that prefetching causes a significant number of useless fetches from memory, though it may increase the rate of **useful** fetches (and hence the bandwidth), because it more efficiently overlaps computing with fetching.

Implementation Note:

Recommended Overloadings. There are four recommended sets of overloadings for the prefetch variants, based on a simplistic classification of SPARC-V9 systems into cost (low-cost *vs.* high-cost) and processor multiplicity (uniprocessor *vs.* multiprocessor) categories. These overloadings are chosen to help ensure efficient portability of software across a range of implementations.

In a uniprocessor, there is no need to support multiprocessor cache protocols; hence, Prefetch for Several Reads and Prefetch for Several Writes may behave identically. In a low-cost implementation, Prefetch for One Read and Prefetch for One Write may be identical to Prefetch for Several Reads and Prefetch for Several Writes, respectively.

Multiplicity	Cost	Prefetch for ..	Could be overloaded to mean the same as Prefetch for ..
Uniprocessor	Low	One read	Several writes
		Several reads	Several writes
		One write	Several writes
		Several writes	—
Uniprocessor	High	One read	—
		Several reads	Several writes
		One write	—
		Several writes	—
Multiprocessor	Low	One read	Several reads
		Several reads	—
		One write	Several writes
		Several writes	—
Multiprocessor	High	One read	—
		Several reads	—
		One write	—
		Several writes	—

Programming Note:

A SPARC-V9 compiler that generates PREFETCH instructions should generate each of the four variants where it is most appropriate. The overloadings suggested in the previous Implementation Note ensure that such code will be portable and reasonably efficient across a range of hardware configurations.

Implementation Note:

The Prefetch for One Read and Prefetch for One Write variants assume the existence of a "bypass cache," so that the bulk of the "real cache" remains undisturbed. If such a bypass cache is used, it should be large enough to properly shield the processor from memory latency. Such a cache should probably be small, highly associative, and use a FIFO replacement policy.

Exceptions:

data_access_MMU_miss (implementation-dependent (impl. dep. #103))
illegal_instruction ($fcn=5..15$)

A.42 Read Privileged Register

Opcode	op3	Operation
RDPR[P]	10 1010	Read Privileged Register

Format (3):

10	rd	op3	rs1	—

31 30 29   25 24   19 18   14 13   0

rs1	Privileged register
0	TPC
1	TNPC
2	TSTATE
3	TT
4	TICK
5	TBA
6	PSTATE
7	TL
8	PIL
9	CWP
10	CANSAVE
11	CANRESTORE
12	CLEANWIN
13	OTHERWIN
14	WSTATE
15	FQ
16..30	—
31	VER

Suggested Assembly Language Syntax
rdpr   %tpc, reg_{rd}
rdpr   %tnpc, reg_{rd}
rdpr   %tstate, reg_{rd}
rdpr   %tt, reg_{rd}
rdpr   %tick, reg_{rd}
rdpr   %tba, reg_{rd}
rdpr   %pstate, reg_{rd}
rdpr   %tl, reg_{rd}
rdpr   %pil, reg_{rd}
rdpr   %cwp, reg_{rd}
rdpr   %cansave, reg_{rd}
rdpr   %canrestore, reg_{rd}
rdpr   %cleanwin, reg_{rd}
rdpr   %otherwin, reg_{rd}
rdpr   %wstate, reg_{rd}
rdpr   %fq, reg_{rd}
rdpr   %ver, reg_{rd}

Description:

The *rs1* field in the instruction determines the privileged register that is read. There are MAXTL copies of the TPC, TNPC, TT, and TSTATE registers. A read from one of these registers returns the value in the register indexed by the current value in the trap level register (TL). A read of TPC, TNPC, TT, or TSTATE when the trap level is zero (TL = 0) causes an *illegal_instruction* exception.

RDPR instructions with *rs1* in the range 16..30 are reserved; executing a RDPR instruction with *rs1* in that range causes an *illegal_instruction* exception.

A read from the FQ (Floating-Point Deferred-Trap Queue) register copies the front doubleword of the queue into *r[rd]*. The semantics of reading the FQ and the data returned are implementation-dependent (impl. dep. #24). However, the address of a trapping floating-point instruction must be available to the privileged trap handler. On an implementation with a floating-point queue, an attempt to execute RDPR of FQ when the queue is empty (FSR.*qne* = 0) shall cause an *fp_exception* exception with FSR.*ftt* set to 4 (*sequence_error*). In an implementation without a floating-point queue, an attempt to execute RDPR of FQ shall cause either an *illegal_instruction* exception or an *fp_exception_other* exception with FSR.*ftt* set to 3 (*unimplemented_FPop*) (impl. dep. #25).

Programming Note:
> On an implementation with precise floating-point traps, the address of a trapping instruction will be in the TPC[TL] register when the trap code begins execution. On an implementation with deferred floating-point traps, the address of the trapping instruction might be a value obtained from the FQ.

Exceptions:
> *privileged_opcode*
> *illegal_instruction* ((*rs1* = 16..30) or ((rs1 ≤3) and (TL = 0)))

fp_exception_other (*sequence_error*) (RDPR of FQ when FSR.*qne* = 0 in a system
    with an FQ; (impl. dep. #25)
illegal_instruction (RDPR of FQ in a system without an FQ; (impl. dep. #25)

A.43   Read State Register

> The RDY instruction is deprecated; it is provided only for compatibility with previous versions of the architecture. It should not be used in new SPARC-V9 software. It is recommended that all instructions which reference the Y register be avoided.

Opcode	op3	rs1	Operation
RDY^D	10 1000	0	Read Y Register
—	10 1000	1	*reserved*
RDCCR	10 1000	2	Read Condition Codes Register
RDASI	10 1000	3	Read ASI Register
RDTICK^{Pnpt}	10 1000	4	Read Tick Register
RDPC	10 1000	5	Read Program Counter
RDFPRS	10 1000	6	Read Floating-Point Registers Status Register
RDASR^{Pasr}	10 1000	7–14	Read Ancillary State Register (*reserved*)
See text	10 1000	15	*See text*
RDASR^{Pasr}	10 1000	16–31	*Implementation-dependent* (impl. dep. #47)

Format (3):

10	rd	op3	rs1	i=0	—

31 30 29   25 24   19 18   14 13 12   0

Suggested Assembly Language Syntax
rd   %y, *reg*$_{rd}$
rd   %ccr, *reg*$_{rd}$
rd   %asi, *reg*$_{rd}$
rd   %tick, *reg*$_{rd}$
rd   %pc, *reg*$_{rd}$
rd   %fprs, *reg*$_{rd}$
rd   *asr_reg*$_{rs1}$, *reg*$_{rd}$

Description:

These instructions read the specified state register into $r[rd]$.

Note that RDY, RDCCR, RDASI, RDPC, RDTICK, RDFPRS, and RDASR are distinguished only by the value in the $rs1$ field.

If $rs1 \geq 7$, an ancillary state register is read. Values of $rs1$ in the range 7..14 are reserved for future versions of the architecture; values in the range 16..31 are available for implementations to use (impl. dep. #8). A RDASR instruction with $rs1 = 15$, $rd = 0$, and $i = 0$ is defined to be an STBAR instruction (see A.50). An RDASR instruction with $rs1 = 15$, $rd = 0$, and $i = 1$ is defined to be a MEMBAR instruction (see A.31). RDASR with *rs1* = 15 and *rd*≠0 is reserved for future versions of the architecture; it causes an *illegal_ instruction* exception.

RDTICK causes a *privileged_action* exception if PSTATE.PRIV = 0 and TICK.NPT = 1.

For RDPC, the high-order 32-bits of the PC value stored in *r*[*rd*] are implementation-dependent when PSTATE.AM = 1 (impl. dep. #125).

RDFPRS waits for all pending FPops to complete before reading the FPRS register.

IMPL. DEP. #47: RDASR instructions with *rd* in the range 16..31 are available for implementation-dependent uses (impl. dep. #8). For a RDASR instruction with *rs1* in the range 16..31, the following are implementation-dependent: the interpretation of bits 13:0 and 29:25 in the instruction, whether the instruction is privileged (impl. dep. #9), and whether the instruction causes an *illegal_ instruction* exception.

See I.1.1, "Read/Write Ancillary State Registers (ASRs)," for a discussion of extending the SPARC-V9 instruction set using read/write ASR instructions.

Implementation Note:
> Ancillary state registers may include (for example) timer, counter, diagnostic, self-test, and trap-control registers. See *Implementation Characteristics of Current SPARC-V9-based Products, Revision 9.x*, a document available from SPARC International, for information on implemented ancillary state registers.

Compatibility Note:
> The SPARC-V8 RDPSR, RDWIM, and RDTBR instructions do not exist in SPARC-V9 osince the PSR, WIM, and TBR registers do not exist in SPARC-V9.

Exceptions:
> *privileged_opcode* (RDASR only; implementation-dependent (impl. dep. #47))
> *illegal_instruction* (RDASR with *rs1* = 1 or 7..14; RDASR with *rs1* = 15 and *rd*≠0;
>   RDASR with *rs1* = 16..31 and the implementation does not define the instruction as an extension; implementation-dependent (impl. dep. #47))
> *privileged_action* (RDTICK only)

A.44 RETURN

Opcode	op3	Operation
RETURN	11 1001	RETURN

Format (3):

10	—	op3	rs1	i=0	—	rs2

10	—	op3	rs1	i=1	simm13

31 30 29   25 24   19 18   14 13 12   5 4   0

Suggested Assembly Language Syntax
return   *address*

Description:

The RETURN instruction causes a delayed transfer of control to the target address and has the window semantics of a RESTORE instruction; that is, it restores the register window prior to the last SAVE instruction. The target address is "$r[rs1] + r[rs2]$" if $i = 0$, or "$r[rs1] + $ sign_ext($simm13$)" if $i = 1$. Registers $r[rs1]$ and $r[rs2]$ come from the **old** window.

The RETURN instruction may cause an exception. It may cause a *window_fill* exception as part of its RESTORE semantics or it may cause a *mem_address_not_aligned* exception if either of the two low-order bits of the target address are nonzero.

Programming Note:

To reexecute the trapped instruction when returning from a user trap handler, use the RETURN instruction in the delay slot of a JMPL instruction, for example:

```
jmpl     %l6,%g0   ! Trapped PC supplied to user trap handler
return   %l7       ! Trapped nPC supplied to user trap handler
```

Programming Note:

A routine that uses a register window may be structured either as

```
save     %sp,-framesize, %sp
. . .
ret                ! Same as jmpl %i7 + 8, %g0
restore            ! Something useful like "restore %o2,%l2,%o0"
```

or as

```
save     %sp,-framesize, %sp
. . .
return   %i7 + 8
nop                ! Could do some useful work in the caller's
                   ! window e.g. "or %o1, %o2,%o0"
```

Exceptions:

mem_address_not_aligned
fill_n_normal ($n = 0..7$)
fill_n_other ($n = 0..7$)

A.45 SAVE and RESTORE

Opcode	op3	Operation
SAVE	11 1100	Save caller's window
RESTORE	11 1101	Restore caller's window

Format (3):

10	rd	op3	rs1	i=0	—	rs2

10	rd	op3	rs1	i=1	simm13

```
31  30 29        25 24        19 18       14 13 12              5 4        0
```

Suggested Assembly Language Syntax	
save	reg_{rs1}, reg_or_imm, reg_{rd}
restore	reg_{rs1}, reg_or_imm, reg_{rd}

Description (Effect on Nonprivileged State):

The SAVE instruction provides the routine executing it with a new register window. The *out* registers from the old window become the *in* registers of the new window. The contents of the *out* and the *local* registers in the new window are zero or contain values from the executing process; that is, the process sees a clean window.

The RESTORE instruction restores the register window saved by the last SAVE instruction executed by the current process. The *in* registers of the old window become the *out* registers of the new window. The *in* and *local* registers in the new window contain the previous values.

Furthermore, if and only if a spill or fill trap is not generated, SAVE and RESTORE behave like normal ADD instructions, except that the source operands $r[rs1]$ and/or $r[rs2]$ are read from the **old** window (that is, the window addressed by the original CWP) and the sum is written into $r[rd]$ of the **new** window (that is, the window addressed by the new CWP).

Note that CWP arithmetic is performed modulo the number of implemented windows, NWINDOWS.

Programming Note:
> Typically, if a SAVE (RESTORE) instruction traps, the spill (fill) trap handler returns to the trapped instruction to reexecute it. So, although the ADD operation is not performed the first time (when the instruction traps), it is performed the second time the instruction executes. The same applies to changing the CWP.

Programming Note:
> The SAVE instruction can be used to atomically allocate a new window in the register file and a new software stack frame in memory. See H.1.2, "Leaf-Procedure Optimization," for details.

Programming Note:
> There is a performance tradeoff to consider between using SAVE/RESTORE and saving and restoring selected registers explicitly.

Description (effect on privileged state):

If the SAVE instruction does not trap, it increments the CWP (**mod** NWINDOWS) to provide a new register window and updates the state of the register windows by decrementing CANSAVE and incrementing CANRESTORE.

If the new register window is occupied (that is, CANSAVE = 0), a spill trap is generated. The trap vector for the spill trap is based on the value of OTHERWIN and WSTATE. The spill trap handler is invoked with the CWP set to point to the window to be spilled (that is, old CWP + 2).

If CANSAVE ≠ 0, the SAVE instruction checks whether the new window needs to be cleaned. It causes a *clean_window* trap if the number of unused clean windows is zero, that is, (CLEANWIN − CANRESTORE) = 0. The *clean_window* trap handler is invoked with the CWP set to point to the window to be cleaned (that is, old CWP + 1).

If the RESTORE instruction does not trap, it decrements the CWP (**mod** NWINDOWS) to restore the register window that was in use prior to the last SAVE instruction executed by the current process. It also updates the state of the register windows by decrementing CANRESTORE and incrementing CANSAVE.

If the register window to be restored has been spilled (CANRESTORE = 0), a fill trap is generated. The trap vector for the fill trap is based on the values of OTHERWIN and WSTATE, as described in 7.5.2.1, "Trap Type for Spill/Fill Traps." The fill trap handler is invoked with CWP set to point to the window to be filled, that is, old CWP − 1.

Programming Note:
> The vectoring of spill and fill traps can be controlled by setting the value of the OTHERWIN and WSTATE registers appropriately. For details, see the unnumbered subsection titled "Splitting the Register Windows" in H.2.3, "Client-Server Model."

Programming Note:
> The spill (fill) handler normally will end with a SAVED (RESTORED) instruction followed by a RETRY instruction.

Exceptions:
> *clean_window* (SAVE only)
> *fill_n_normal* (RESTORE only, $n = 0..7$)
> *fill_n_other* (RESTORE only, $n = 0..7$)
> *spill_n_normal* (SAVE only, $n = 0..7$)
> *spill_n_other* (SAVE only, $n = 0..7$)

A.46 SAVED and RESTORED

Opcode	op3	fcn	Operation
SAVED[P]	11 0001	0	Window has been Saved
RESTORED[P]	11 0001	1	Window has been Restored
—	11 0001	2..31	*Reserved*

Format (3):

10	fcn	op3	—

31 30 29   25 24   19 18   0

Suggested Assembly Language Syntax
saved
restored

Description:

SAVED and RESTORED adjust the state of the register-windows control registers.

SAVED increments CANSAVE. If OTHERWIN = 0, it decrements CANRESTORE. If OTHERWIN≠0, it decrements OTHERWIN.

RESTORED increments CANRESTORE. If OTHERWIN = 0, it decrements CANSAVE. If OTHERWIN ≠ 0, it decrements OTHERWIN. In addition, if CLEANWIN ≠ NWINDOWS, RESTORED increments CLEANWIN.

Programming Note:
> The spill (fill) handlers use the SAVED (RESTORED) instruction to indicate that a window has been spilled (filled) successfully. See H.2.2, "Example Code for Spill Handler," for details.

Programming Note:
> Normal privileged software would probably not do a SAVED or RESTORED from trap level zero (TL = 0). However, it is not illegal to do so, and does not cause a trap.

Programming Note:
> Executing a SAVED (RESTORED) instruction outside of a window spill (fill) trap handler is likely to create an inconsistent window state. Hardware will not signal an exception, however, since maintaining a consistent window state is the responsibility of privileged software.

Exceptions:
privileged_opcode
illegal_instruction (fcn=2..31)

A.47 SETHI

Opcode	op	op2	Operation
SETHI	00	100	Set High 22 Bits of Low Word

Format (2):

00	rd	100	imm22

31 30 29   25 24   22 21   0

Suggested Assembly Language Syntax	
sethi	$const22$, reg_{rd}
sethi	$\%hi\,(value)$, reg_{rd}

Description:

SETHI zeroes the least significant 10 bits and the most significant 32 bits of $r[rd]$, and replaces bits 31 through 10 of $r[rd]$ with the value from its *imm22* field.

SETHI does not affect the condition codes.

A SETHI instruction with $rd = 0$ and $imm22 = 0$ is defined to be a NOP instruction, which is defined in A.39.

Programming Note:

The most common form of 64-bit constant generation is creating stack offsets whose magnitude is less than 2^{32}. The code below can be used to create the constant 0000 0000 ABCD 1234_{16}:

```
sethi    %hi(0xabcd1234),%o0
or       %o0, 0x234, %o0
```

The following code shows how to create a negative constant. Note that the immediate field of the xor instruction is sign extended and can be used to get 1s in all of the upper 32 bits. For example, to set the negative constant FFFF FFFF ABCD 1234_{16}:

```
sethi    %hi(0x5432edcb),%o0 ! note 0x5432EDCB, not 0xABCD1234
xor      %o0, 0x1e34, %o0    ! part of imm. overlaps upper bits
```

Exceptions:

(none)

A.48 Shift

Opcode	op3	x	Operation
SLL	10 0101	0	Shift Left Logical - 32 Bits
SRL	10 0110	0	Shift Right Logical - 32 Bits
SRA	10 0111	0	Shift Right Arithmetic - 32 Bits
SLLX	10 0101	1	Shift Left Logical - 64 Bits
SRLX	10 0110	1	Shift Right Logical - 64 Bits
SRAX	10 0111	1	Shift Right Arithmetic - 64 Bits

Format (3):

10	rd	op3	rs1	i=0	x	—	rs2

10	rd	op3	rs1	i=1	x=0	—	shcnt32

10	rd	op3	rs1	i=1	x=1	—	shcnt64

31 30 29   25 24   19 18   14 13 12   6 5 4   0

Suggested Assembly Language Syntax	
sll	reg_{rs1}, reg_or_shcnt, reg_{rd}
srl	reg_{rs1}, reg_or_shcnt, reg_{rd}
sra	reg_{rs1}, reg_or_shcnt, reg_{rd}
sllx	reg_{rs1}, reg_or_shcnt, reg_{rd}
srlx	reg_{rs1}, reg_or_shcnt, reg_{rd}
srax	reg_{rs1}, reg_or_shcnt, reg_{rd}

Description:

When $i = 0$ and $x = 0$, the shift count is the least significant five bits of $r[rs2]$. When $i = 0$ and $x = 1$, the shift count is the least significant six bits of $r[rs2]$. When $i = 1$ and $x = 0$, the shift count is the immediate value specified in bits 0 through 4 of the instruction. When $i = 1$ and $x = 1$, the shift count is the immediate value specified in bits 0 through 5 of the instruction.

i	x	Shift count
0	0	bits 4..0 of $r[rs2]$
0	1	bits 5..0 of $r[rs2]$
1	0	bits 4..0 of instruction
1	1	bits 5..0 of instruction

SLL and SLLX shift all 64 bits of the value in $r[rs1]$ left by the number of bits specified by the shift count, replacing the vacated positions with zeroes, and write the shifted result to $r[rd]$.

SRL shifts the low 32 bits of the value in $r[rs1]$ right by the number of bits specified by the shift count. Zeroes are shifted into bit 31. The upper 32 bits are set to zero, and the result is written to $r[rd]$.

SRLX shifts all 64 bits of the value in $r[rs1]$ right by the number of bits specified by the shift count. Zeroes are shifted into the vacated high-order bit positions, and the shifted result is written to $r[rd]$.

SRA shifts the low 32 bits of the value in $r[rs1]$ right by the number of bits specified by the shift count, and replaces the vacated positions with bit 31 of $r[rs1]$. The high order 32 bits of the result are all set with bit 31 of $r[rs1]$, and the result is written to $r[rd]$.

SRAX shifts all 64 bits of the value in $r[rs1]$ right by the number of bits specified by the shift count, and replaces the vacated positions with bit 63 of $r[rs1]$. The shifted result is written to $r[rd]$.

No shift occurs when the shift count is zero, but the high-order bits are affected by the 32-bit shifts as noted above.

These instructions do not modify the condition codes.

Programming Note:
"Arithmetic left shift by 1 (and calculate overflow)" can be effected with the ADDcc instruction.

Programming Note:
The instruction "sra $rs1$, 0 , rd" can be used to convert a 32-bit value to 64 bits, with sign extension into the upper word. "srl $rs1$, 0 , rd" can be used to clear the upper 32 bits of $r[rd]$.

Exceptions:
(none)

A.49   Software-Initiated Reset

Opcode	op3	rd	Operation
SIR	11 0000	15	Software-initiated reset

Format (3):

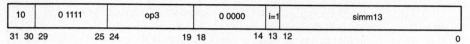

10	0 1111	op3	0 0000	i=1	simm13

31 30 29   25 24   19 18   14 13 12   0

Suggested Assembly Language Syntax
sir   *simm13*

Description:

SIR is used to generate a software-initiated reset (SIR). It may be executed in either privileged or nonprivileged mode, with slightly different effect. As with other traps, a software-initiated reset performs different actions when TL = MAXTL than it does when TL < MAXTL.

When executed in user mode, the action of SIR is conditional on the SIR_enable control flag.

IMPL. DEP. #116: The location of the and means of accessing the SIR_enable control flag are implementation-dependent. In some implementations it may be permanently zero.

When SIR_enable is 0, SIR executes without effect (as a NOP) in user mode. When SIR is executed in privileged mode or in user mode with SIR_enable = 1, the processor performs a software-initiated reset. See 7.6.2.5, "Software-Initiated Reset (SIR) Traps," for more information about software-initiated resets.

Programming Note:
> This instruction is never illegal. It is not a privileged instruction, even though its action in privileged mode is different than in user mode.

Exceptions:
> *software_initiated_reset*

A.50 Store Barrier

> The STBAR instruction is deprecated; it is provided only for compatibility with previous versions of the architecture. It should not be used in new SPARC-V9 software. It is recommended that the MEMBAR instruction be used in its place.

Opcode	op3	Operation
STBAR^D	10 1000	Store Barrier

Format (3):

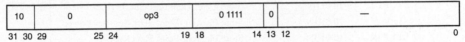

10	0	op3	0 1111	0	—

31 30 29   25 24   19 18   14 13 12   0

Suggested Assembly Language Syntax
stbar

Description:

The store barrier instruction (STBAR) forces **all** store and atomic load-store operations issued by a processor prior to the STBAR to complete their effects on memory before **any** store or atomic load-store operations issued by that processor subsequent to the STBAR are executed by memory.

Note that the encoding of STBAR is identical to that of the RDASR instruction except that $rs1 = 15$ and $rd = 0$, and is identical to that of the MEMBAR instruction except that bit 13 $(i) = 0$.

The coherence and atomicity of memory operations between processors and I/O DMA memory accesses are implementation-dependent (impl. dep #120).

Compatibility Note:

STBAR is identical in function to a MEMBAR instruction with $mmask = 8_{16}$. STBAR is retained for compatibility with SPARC-V8.

Implementation Note:

For correctness, it is sufficient for a processor to stop issuing new store and atomic load-store operations when an STBAR is encountered and resume after all stores have completed and are observed in memory by all processors. More efficient implementations may take advantage of the fact that the processor is allowed to issue store and load-store operations after the STBAR, as long as those operations are guaranteed not to become visible before all the earlier stores and atomic load-stores have become visible to all processors.

Exceptions:

(none)

A.51   Store Floating-Point

> The STFSR instruction is deprecated; it is provided only for compatibility with previous versions of the architecture. It should not be used in new SPARC-V9 software. It is recommended that the STXFSR instruction be used in its place.

Opcode	op3	rd	Operation
STF	10 0100	0..31	Store Floating-Point Register
STDF	10 0111	†	Store Double Floating-Point Register
STQF	10 0110	†	Store Quad Floating-Point Register
STFSR^D	10 0101	0	Store Floating-Point State Register Lower
STXFSR	10 0101	1	Store Floating-Point State Register
—	10 0101	2..31	*Reserved*

† Encoded floating-point register value, as described in 5.1.4.1

Format (3):

11	rd	op3	rs1	i=0	—	rs2

11	rd	op3	rs1	i=1	simm13

31 30 29   25 24   19 18   14 13 12   5   4   0

Suggested Assembly Language Syntax	
st	$freg_{rd}$, [*address*]
std	$freg_{rd}$, [*address*]
stq	$freg_{rd}$, [*address*]
st	%fsr, [*address*]
stx	%fsr, [*address*]

Description:

The store single floating-point instruction (STF) copies $f[rd]$ into memory.

The store double floating-point instruction (STDF) copies a doubleword from a double floating-point register into a word-aligned doubleword in memory.

The store quad floating-point instruction (STQF) copies the contents of a quad floating-point register into a word-aligned quadword in memory.

The store floating-point state register lower instruction (STFSR) waits for any currently executing FPop instructions to complete, and then writes the lower 32 bits of the FSR into memory.

The store floating-point state register instruction (STXFSR) waits for any currently executing FPop instructions to complete, and then writes all 64 bits of the FSR into memory.

Compatibility Note:
> SPARC-V9 needs two store-FSR instructions, since the SPARC-V8 STFSR instruction is defined to store only 32 bits of the FSR into memory. STXFSR allows SPARC-V9 programs to store all 64 bits of the FSR.

STFSR and STXFSR zero FSR.*ftt* after writing the FSR to memory.

Implementation Note:
> FSR.*ftt* should not be zeroed until it is known that the store will not cause a precise trap.

The effective address for these instructions is "$r[rs1] + r[rs2]$" if $i = 0$, or "$r[rs1] + \text{sign\_ext}(simm13)$" if $i = 1$.

STF, STFSR, STDF, and STQF cause a *mem_address_not_aligned* exception if the effective memory address is not word-aligned; STXFSR causes a *mem_address_not_aligned* exception if the address is not doubleword-aligned. If the floating-point unit is not enabled for the source register *rd* (per FPRS.FEF and PSTATE.PEF), or if the FPU is not present, a store floating-point instruction causes an *fp_disabled* exception.

IMPL. DEP. #110(1): STDF requires only word alignment in memory. If the effective address is word-aligned but not doubleword-aligned, it may cause an *STDF_mem_address_not_aligned* exception. In this case the trap handler software shall emulate the STDF instruction and return.

IMPL. DEP. #112(1): STQF requires only word alignment in memory. If the effective address is word-aligned but not quadword-aligned, it may cause an *STQF_mem_address_not_aligned* exception. In this case the trap handler software shall emulate the STQF instruction and return.

Programming Note:
> In SPARC-V8, some compilers issued sets of single-precision stores when they could not determine that double- or quadword operands were properly aligned. For SPARC-V9, since emulation of misaligned stores is expected to be fast, it is recommended that compilers issue sets of single-precision stores only when they can determine that double- or quadword operands are **not** properly aligned.

Exceptions:

> *async_data_error*
> *fp_disabled*
> *mem_address_not_aligned*
> *STDF_mem_address_not_aligned* (STDF only) (impl. dep. #110)
> *STQF_mem_address_not_aligned* (STQF only) (impl. dep. #112)
> *data_access_exception*
> *data_access_protection*
> *data_access_MMU_miss*
> *data_access_error*
> *illegal_instruction* ($op3 = 25_{16}$ and $rd = 2..31$)
> *fp_exception_other* (*invalid_fp_register* (STQF only))

A.52 Store Floating-Point into Alternate Space

Opcode	op3	rd	Operation
STFA^{PASI}	11 0100	0..31	Store Floating-Point Register to Alternate Space
STDFA^{PASI}	11 0111	†	Store Double Floating-Point Register to Alternate Space
STQFA^{PASI}	11 0110	†	Store Quad Floating-Point Register to Alternate Space

† Encoded floating-point register value, as described in 5.1.4.1

Format (3):

11	rd	op3	rs1	i=0	imm_asi	rs2

11	rd	op3	rs1	i=1	simm13

31 30   29   25 24   19 18   14 13 12   5 4   0

Suggested Assembly Language Syntax	
sta	$freg_{rd}$, [regaddr] imm_asi
sta	$freg_{rd}$, [reg_plus_imm] %asi
stda	$freg_{rd}$, [regaddr] imm_asi
stda	$freg_{rd}$, [reg_plus_imm] %asi
stqa	$freg_{rd}$, [regaddr] imm_asi
stqa	$freg_{rd}$, [reg_plus_imm] %asi

Description:

The store single floating-point into alternate space instruction (STFA) copies $f[rd]$ into memory.

The store double floating-point into alternate space instruction (STDFA) copies a double-word from a double floating-point register into a word-aligned doubleword in memory.

The store quad floating-point into alternate space instruction (STQFA) copies the contents of a quad floating-point register into a word-aligned quadword in memory.

Store floating-point into alternate space instructions contain the address space identifier (ASI) to be used for the load in the *imm_asi* field if $i = 0$, or in the ASI register if $i = 1$. The access is privileged if bit seven of the ASI is zero; otherwise, it is not privileged. The effective address for these instructions is "$r[rs1] + r[rs2]$" if $i = 0$, or "$r[rs1] + $ sign_ext($simm13$)" if $i = 1$.

STFA, STDFA, and STQFA cause a *mem_address_not_aligned* exception if the effective memory address is not word-aligned. If the floating-point unit is not enabled for the source register *rd* (per FPRS.FEF and PSTATE.PEF), or if the FPU is not present, store floating-point into alternate space instructions cause an *fp_disabled* exception.

STFA, STDFA, and STQFA cause a *privileged_action* exception if PSTATE.PRIV = 0 and bit 7 of the ASI is zero.

IMPL. DEP. #110(2): STDFA requires only word alignment in memory. If the effective address is word-aligned but not doubleword-aligned, it may cause an *STDF_mem_address_not_aligned* exception. In this case the trap handler software shall emulate the STDFA instruction and return.

IMPL. DEP. #112(2): STQFA requires only word alignment in memory. If the effective address is word-aligned but not quadword-aligned, it may cause an *STQF_mem_address_not_aligned* exception. In this case the trap handler software shall emulate the STQFA instruction and return.

Programming Note:

In SPARC-V8, some compilers issued sets of single-precision stores when they could not determine that double- or quadword operands were properly aligned. For SPARC-V9, since emulation of misaligned stores is expected to be fast, it is recommended that compilers issue sets of single-precision stores only when they can determine that double- or quadword operands are **not** properly aligned.

Exceptions:

async_data_error
fp_disabled
mem_address_not_aligned
STDF_mem_address_not_aligned (STDFA only) (impl. dep. #110)
STQF_mem_address_not_aligned (STQFA only) (impl. dep. #112)
privileged_action
data_access_exception
data_access_protection
data_access_MMU_miss
data_access_error
fp_exception_other (invalid_fp_register (STQFA only))

A.53 Store Integer

> The STD instruction isdeprecated; it is provided only for compatibility with previous versions of the architecture. It should not be used in new SPARC-V9 software. It is recommended that the STX instruction be used in its place.

Opcode	op3	Operation
STB	00 0101	Store Byte
STH	00 0110	Store Halfword
STW	00 0100	Store Word
STX	00 1110	Store Extended Word
STD^D	00 0111	Store Doubleword

Format (3):

11	rd	op3	rs1	i=0	—	rs2

11	rd	op3	rs1	i=1	simm13

31 30 29   25 24   19 18   14 13 12   5 4   0

	Suggested Assembly Language Syntax	
stb	reg_{rd}, [address]	(synonyms: stub, stsb)
sth	reg_{rd}, [address]	(synonyms: stuh, stsh)
stw	reg_{rd}, [address]	(synonyms: st, stuw, stsw)
stx	reg_{rd}, [address]	
std	reg_{rd}, [address]	

Description:

The store integer instructions (except store doubleword) copy the whole extended (64-bit) integer, the less-significant word, the least significant halfword, or the least significant byte of $r[rd]$ into memory.

The store doubleword integer instruction (STD) copies two words from an r register pair into memory. The least significant 32 bits of the even-numbered r register are written into memory at the effective address, and the least significant 32 bits of the following odd-numbered r register are written into memory at the "effective address + 4." The least significant bit of the rd field of a store doubleword instruction is unused and should always be set to zero by software. An attempt to execute a store doubleword instruction that refers to a misaligned (odd-numbered) rd causes an *illegal_instruction* exception.

IMPL. DEP. #108(1): IT is implementation-dependent whether STD is implemented in hardware. if not, an attempt to execute it will cause an *unimplemented_STD* exception.

The effective address for these instructions is "$r[rs1] + r[rs2]$" if $i = 0$, or "$r[rs1] + $ sign_ext($simm13$)" if $i = 1$.

A successful store (notably, store extended and store doubleword) instruction operates atomically.

STH causes a *mem_address_not_aligned* exception if the effective address is not halfword-aligned. STW causes a *mem_address_not_aligned* exception if the effective address is not word-aligned. STX, and STD causes a *mem_address_not_aligned* exception if the effective address is not doubleword-aligned.

Programming Note:

STD is provided for compatibility with SPARC-V8. It may execute slowly on SPARC-V9 machines because of data path and register-access difficulties. In some SPARC-V9 systems it may cause a trap to emulation code; therefore, STD should be avoided.

If STD is emulated in software, STX should be used in order to preserve atomicity.

Compatibility Note:

The SPARC-V8 ST instruction has been renamed STW in SPARC-V9.

Exceptions:

async_data_error
unimplemented_STD (STD only) (impl. dep. #108)
illegal_instruction (STD with odd *rd*)
mem_address_not_aligned (all except STB)
data_access_exception
data_access_error
data_access_protection
data_access_MMU_miss

A.54 Store Integer into Alternate Space

> The STDA instruction is deprecated; it is provided only for compatibility with previous versions of the architecture. It should not be used in new SPARC-V9 software. It is recommended that the STXA instruction be used in its place.

Opcode	op3	Operation
STBA^{PASI}	01 0101	Store Byte into Alternate space
STHA^{PASI}	01 0110	Store Halfword into Alternate space
STWA^{PASI}	01 0100	Store Word into Alternate space
STXA^{PASI}	01 1110	Store Extended Word into Alternate space
STDA$^{D, PASI}$	01 0111	Store Doubleword into Alternate space

Format (3):

11	rd	op3	rs1	i=0	imm_asi	rs2

11	rd	op3	rs1	i=1	simm13

31 30 29   25 24   19 18   14 13 12   5 4   0

Suggested Assembly Language Syntax		
stba	reg_{rd}, [regaddr] imm_asi	(synonyms: stuba, stsba)
stha	reg_{rd}, [regaddr] imm_asi	(synonyms: stuha, stsha)
stda	reg_{rd}, [regaddr] imm_asi	
stwa	reg_{rd}, [regaddr] imm_asi	(synonyms: sta, stuwa, stswa)
stxa	reg_{rd}, [regaddr] imm_asi	
stba	reg_{rd}, [reg_plus_imm] %asi	(synonyms: stuba, stsba)
stha	reg_{rd}, [reg_plus_imm] %asi	(synonyms: stuha, stsha)
stwa	reg_{rd}, [reg_plus_imm] %asi	(synonyms: sta, stuwa, stswa)
stxa	reg_{rd}, [reg_plus_imm] %asi	
stda	reg_{rd}, [reg_plus_imm] %asi	

Description:

The store integer into alternate space instructions (except store doubleword) copy the whole extended (64-bit) integer, the less-significant word, the least-significant halfword, or the least-significant byte of $r[rd]$ into memory.

The store doubleword integer instruction (STDA) copies two words from an r register pair into memory. The least-significant 32 bits of the even-numbered r register are written into memory at the effective address, and the least-significant 32 bits of the following odd-numbered r register are written into memory at the "effective address + 4." The least significant bit of the rd field of a store doubleword instruction is unused and should always be set to zero by software. An attempt to execute a store doubleword instruction that refers to a misaligned (odd-numbered) rd causes an *illegal_instruction* exception.

IMPL. DEP. #108(2): It is implementation-dependent whether STDA is implemented in hardware. If not, an attempt to execute it will cause an *unimplemented_STD* exception.

Store integer to alternate space instructions contain the address space identifier (ASI) to be used for the load in the *imm_asi* field if $i = 0$, or in the ASI register if $i = 1$. The access is privileged if bit seven of the ASI is zero; otherwise, it is not privileged. The effective address for these instructions is "$r[rs1] + r[rs2]$" if $i = 0$, or "$r[rs1]+\text{sign\_ext}(simm13)$" if $i = 1$.

A successful store (notably, store extended and store doubleword) instruction operates atomically.

STHA causes a *mem_address_not_aligned* exception if the effective address is not half-word-aligned. STWA causes a *mem_address_not_aligned* exception if the effective address is not word-aligned. STXA and STDA cause a *mem_address_not_aligned* exception if the effective address is not doubleword-aligned.

A store integer into alternate space instruction causes a *privileged_action* exception if PSTATE.PRIV = 0 and bit 7 of the ASI is zero.

Programming Note:
> STDA is provided for compatibility with SPARC-V8. It may execute slowly on SPARC-V9 machines because of data path and register-access difficulties. In some SPARC-V9 systems it may cause a trap to emulation code; therefore, STDA should be avoided.
>
> If STDA is emulated in software, STXA should be used in order to preserve atomicity.

Compatibility Note:
> The SPARC-V8 STA instruction is renamed STWA in SPARC-V9.

Exceptions:
> *async_data_error*
> *unimplemented_STD* (STDA only) (impl. dep. #108)
> *illegal_instruction* (STDA with odd *rd*)
> *privileged_action*
> *mem_address_not_aligned* (all except STBA)
> *data_access_exception*
> *data_access_error*
> *data_access_protection*
> *data_access_MMU_miss*

A.55 Subtract

Opcode	op3	Operation
SUB	00 0100	Subtract
SUBcc	01 0100	Subtract and modify cc's
SUBC	00 1100	Subtract with Carry
SUBCcc	01 1100	Subtract with Carry and modify cc's

Format (3):

10	rd	op3	rs1	i=0	—	rs2

10	rd	op3	rs1	i=1	simm13

31 30 29   25 24   19 18   14 13 12   5 4   0

Suggested Assembly Language Syntax	
sub	reg_{rs1}, reg_or_imm, reg_{rd}
subcc	reg_{rs1}, reg_or_imm, reg_{rd}
subc	reg_{rs1}, reg_or_imm, reg_{rd}
subccc	reg_{rs1}, reg_or_imm, reg_{rd}

Description:

These instructions compute "$r[rs1] - r[rs2]$" if $i = 0$, or "$r[rs1] - $ sign_ext($simm13$)" if $i = 1$, and write the difference into $r[rd]$.

SUBC and SUBCcc ("SUBtract with carry") also subtract the CCR register's 32-bit carry ($icc.c$) bit; that is, they compute "$r[rs1] - r[rs2] - icc.c$" or "$r[rs1] - $ sign_ext($simm13$) $- icc.c$," and write the difference into $r[rd]$.

SUBcc and SUBCcc modify the integer condition codes (CCR.icc and CCR.xcc). 32-bit overflow (CCR.$icc.v$) occurs on subtraction if bit 31 (the sign) of the operands differ and bit 31 (the sign) of the difference differs from $r[rs1]<31>$. 64-bit overflow (CCR.$xcc.v$) occurs on subtraction if bit 63 (the sign) of the operands differ and bit 63 (the sign) of the difference differs from $r[rs1]<63>$.

Programming Note:
A SUBcc with $rd = 0$ can be used to effect a signed or unsigned integer comparison. See the CMP synthetic instruction in Appendix G.

Programming Note:
SUBC and SUBCcc read the 32-bit condition codes' carry bit (CCR.icc.c), not the 64-bit condition codes' carry bit (CCR.xcc.c).

Compatibility Note:
SUBC and SUBCcc were named SUBX and SUBXcc, respectively, in SPARC-V8.

Exceptions:
(none)

A.56 Swap Register with Memory

> The SWAP instruction is deprecated; it is provided only for compatibility with pre-
> vious versions of the architecture. It should not be used in new SPARC-V9 soft-
> ware. It is recommended that the CASX instruction be used in its place.

Opcode	op3	Operation
SWAP^D	00 1111	SWAP register with memory

Format (3):

11	rd	op3	rs1	i=0	—	rs2

11	rd	op3	rs1	i=1	simm13

31 30 29   25 24   19 18   14 13 12   5 4   0

Suggested Assembly Language Syntax
swap   [*address*], *reg$_{rd}$*

Description:

SWAP exchanges the lower 32 bits of *r*[*rd*] with the contents of the word at the addressed
memory location. The upper 32 bits of *r*[*rd*] are set to zero. The operation is performed
atomically, that is, without allowing intervening interrupts or deferred traps. In a multiprocessor system, two or more processors executing CASA, CASXA, SWAP, SWAPA,
LDSTUB, or LDSTUBA instructions addressing any or all of the same doubleword simultaneously are guaranteed to execute them in an undefined but serial order.

The effective address for these instructions is "*r*[*rs1*] + *r*[*rs2*]" if *i* = 0, or "*r*[*rs1*] + sign_
ext(*simm13*)" if *i* = 1. This instruction causes a *mem_address_not_aligned* exception if the
effective address is not word-aligned.

The coherence and atomicity of memory operations between processors and I/O DMA
memory accesses are implementation-dependent (impl. dep #120).

Implementation Note:

> See *Implementation Characteristics of Current SPARC V9 based Products, Revision 9.x*, a docu-
> ment available from SPARC International, for information on the presence of hardware support for
> these instructions in the various SPARC-V9 implementations.

Exceptions:

> *mem_address_not_aligned*
> *data_access_exception*
> *data_access_error*
> *data_access_protection*
> *data_access_MMU_miss*
> *async_data_error*

A.57   Swap Register with Alternate Space Memory

The SWAPA instruction is deprecated; it is provided only for compatibility with previous versions of the architecture. It should not be used in new SPARC-V9 software. It is recommended that the CASXA instruction be used in its place.

Opcode	op3	Operation
SWAPA$^{D, P_{ASI}}$	01 1111	SWAP register with Alternate space memory

Format (3):

11	rd	op3	rs1	i=0	imm_asi	rs2

11	rd	op3	rs1	i=1	simm13

31 30 29   25 24   19 18   14 13 12   5   4   0

Suggested Assembly Language Syntax	
swapa	[regaddr] imm_asi, reg$_{rd}$
swapa	[reg_plus_imm] %asi, reg$_{rd}$

Description:

SWAPA exchanges the lower 32 bits of $r[rd]$ with the contents of the word at the addressed memory location. The upper 32 bits of $r[rd]$ are set to zero. The operation is performed atomically, that is, without allowing intervening interrupts or deferred traps. In a multiprocessor system, two or more processors executing CASA, CASXA, SWAP, SWAPA, LDSTUB, or LDSTUBA instructions addressing any or all of the same double-word simultaneously are guaranteed to execute them in an undefined, but serial order.

The SWAPA instruction contains the address space identifier (ASI) to be used for the load in the *imm_asi* field if $i = 0$, or in the ASI register if $i = 1$. The access is privileged if bit seven of the ASI is zero; otherwise, it is not privileged. The effective address for this instruction is "$r[rs1] + r[rs2]$" if $i = 0$, or "$r[rs1] + \text{sign\_ext}(simm13)$" if $i = 1$.

This instruction causes a *mem_address_not_aligned* exception if the effective address is not word-aligned. It causes a *privileged_action* exception if PSTATE.PRIV = 0 and bit 7 of the ASI is zero.

The coherence and atomicity of memory operations between processors and I/O DMA memory accesses are implementation-dependent (impl. dep #120).

Implementation Note:

See *Implementation Characteristics of Current SPARC-V9-based Products, Revision 9.x*, a document available from SPARC International, for information on the presence of hardware support for this instruction in the various SPARC-V9 implementations.

Exceptions:

mem_address_not_aligned
privileged_action
data_access_exception
data_access_error
data_access_protection
data_access_MMU_miss
async_data_error

A.58 Tagged Add

> The TADDccTV instruction is deprecated; it is provided only for compatibility with previous versions of the architecture. It should not be used in new SPARC-V9 software. It is recommended that TADDcc followed by BPVS be used in its place (with instructions to save the pre-TADDcc integer condition codes, if necessary).

Opcode	op3	Operation
TADDcc	10 0001	Tagged Add and modify cc's
TADDccTV^D	10 0011	Tagged Add and modify cc's, or Trap on Overflow

Format (3):

10	rd	op3	rs1	i=0	—	rs2

10	rd	op3	rs1	i=1	simm13

31 30 29   25 24   19 18   14 13 12   5 4   0

Suggested Assembly Language Syntax	
taddcc	reg_{rs1}, reg_or_imm, reg_{rd}
taddcctv	reg_{rs1}, reg_or_imm, reg_{rd}

Description:

These instructions compute a sum that is "$r[rs1] + r[rs2]$" if $i = 0$, or "$r[rs1] + \text{sign\_ext}(simm13)$" if $i = 1$.

TADDcc modifies the integer condition codes (icc and xcc), and TADDccTV does so also, if it does not trap.

A *tag_overflow* exception occurs if bit 1 or bit 0 of either operand is nonzero, or if the addition generates 32-bit arithmetic overflow (i.e., both operands have the same value in bit 31, and bit 31 of the sum is different).

If TADDccTV causes a tag overflow, a *tag_overflow* exception is generated, and $r[rd]$ and the integer condition codes remain unchanged. If a TADDccTV does not cause a tag overflow, the sum is written into $r[rd]$, and the integer condition codes are updated. CCR.*icc.v* is set to 0 to indicate no 32-bit overflow. If a TADDcc causes a tag overflow, the 32-bit overflow bit (CCR.*icc.v*) is set to 1; if it does not cause a tag overflow, CCR.*icc.v* is cleared.

In either case, the remaining integer condition codes (both the other CCR.*icc* bits and all the CCR.*xcc* bits) are also updated as they would be for a normal ADD instruction. In particular, the setting of the CCR.*xcc.v* bit is not determined by the tag overflow condition (tag overflow is used only to set the 32-bit overflow bit). CCR.*xcc.v* is set only based on the normal 64-bit arithemetic overflow condition, like a normal 64-bit add.

Compatibility Note:

TADDccTV traps based on the 32-bit overflow condition, just as in SPARC-V8. Although the tagged-add instructions set the 64-bit condition codes CCR.*xcc*, there is no form of the instruction that traps the 64-bit overflow condition.

Exceptions:

tag_overflow (TADDccTV only)

A.59   Tagged Subtract

> The TSUBccTV instruction is deprecated; it is provided only for compatibility with previous versions of the architecture. It should not be used in new SPARC-V9 software. It is recommended that TSUBcc followed by BPVS be used in its place (with instructions to save the pre-TSUBcc integer condition codes, if necessary).

Opcode	op3	Operation
TSUBcc	10 0001	Tagged Subtract and modify cc's
TSUBccTV^D	10 0011	Tagged Subtract and modify cc's, or Trap on Overflow

Format (3):

10	rd	op3	rs1	i=0	—	rs2

10	rd	op3	rs1	i=1	simm13

31 30 29   25 24   19 18   14 13 12   5 4   0

Suggested Assembly Language Syntax	
tsubcc	reg_{rs1}, reg_or_imm, reg_{rd}
tsubcctv	reg_{rs1}, reg_or_imm, reg_{rd}

Description:

These instructions compute "$r[rs1] - r[rs2]$" if $i = 0$, or "$r[rs1] - \text{sign\_ext}(simm13)$" if $i = 1$.

TSUBcc modifies the integer condition codes (*icc* and *xcc*); TSUBccTV also modifies the integer condition codes, if it does not trap.

A tag overflow occurs if bit 1 or bit 0 of either operand is nonzero, or if the subtraction generates 32-bit arithmetic overflow; that is, the operands have different values in bit 31 (the 32-bit sign bit) and the sign of the 32-bit difference in bit 31 differs from bit 31 of $r[rs1]$.

If TSUBccTV causes a tag overflow, a *tag overflow* exception is generated and $r[rd]$ and the integer condition codes remain unchanged. If a TSUBccTV does not cause a tag overflow condition, the difference is written into $r[rd]$, and the integer condition codes are updated. CCR.*icc.v* is set to 0 to indicate no 32-bit overflow. If a TSUBcc causes a tag overflow, the 32-bit overflow bit (CCR.*icc.v*) is set to 1; if it does not cause a tag overflow, CCR.*icc.v* is cleared.

In either case, the remaining integer condition codes (both the other CCR.*icc* bits and all the CCR.*xcc* bits) are also updated as they would be for a normal subtract instruction. In particular, the setting of the CCR.*xcc.v* bit is not determined by the tag overflow condition (tag overflow is used only to set the 32-bit overflow bit). CCR.*xcc.v* is set only based on the normal 64-bit arithmetic overflow condition, like a normal 64-bit subtract.

Compatibility Note:

TSUBccTV traps are based on the 32-bit overflow condition, just as in SPARC-V8. Although the tagged-subtract instructions set the 64-bit condition codes CCR.*xcc*, there is no form of the instruction that traps on 64-bit overflow.

Exceptions:

tag_overflow (TSUBccTV only)

A.60 Trap on Integer Condition Codes (Tcc)

Opcode	op3	cond	Operation	*icc* test
TA	11 1010	1000	Trap Always	1
TN	11 1010	0000	Trap Never	0
TNE	11 1010	1001	Trap on Not Equal	**not** Z
TE	11 1010	0001	Trap on Equal	Z
TG	11 1010	1010	Trap on Greater	**not** (Z **or** (N **xor** V))
TLE	11 1010	0010	Trap on Less or Equal	Z (N **xor** V)
TGE	11 1010	1011	Trap on Greater or Equal	**not** (N **xor** V)
TL	11 1010	0011	Trap on Less	N **xor** V
TGU	11 1010	1100	Trap on Greater Unsigned	**not** (C **or** Z)
TLEU	11 1010	0100	Trap on Less or Equal Unsigned	(C **or** Z)
TCC	11 1010	1101	Trap on Carry Clear (Greater than or Equal, Unsigned)	**not** C
TCS	11 1010	0101	Trap on Carry Set (Less Than, Unsigned)	C
TPOS	11 1010	1110	Trap on Positive or zero	**not** N
TNEG	11 1010	0110	Trap on Negative	N
TVC	11 1010	1111	Trap on Overflow Clear	**not** V
TVS	11 1010	0111	Trap on Overflow Set	V

Format (4):

10	—	cond	op3	rs1	i=0	cc1	cc0	—	rs2

10	—	cond	op3	rs1	i=1	cc1	cc0	—	sw_trap_#

31 30 29 28   25 24   19 18   14 13 12 11 10   7 6 5 4   0

cc1 ☐ cc0	Condition codes
00	icc
01	—
10	xcc
11	—

	Suggested Assembly Language Syntax	
ta	*i_or_x_cc, software_trap_number*	
tn	*i_or_x_cc, software_trap_number*	
tne	*i_or_x_cc, software_trap_number*	(*synonym:* tnz)
te	*i_or_x_cc, software_trap_number*	(*synonym:* tz)
tg	*i_or_x_cc, software_trap_number*	
tle	*i_or_x_cc, software_trap_number*	
tge	*i_or_x_cc, software_trap_number*	
tl	*i_or_x_cc, software_trap_number*	
tgu	*i_or_x_cc, software_trap_number*	
tleu	*i_or_x_cc, software_trap_number*	
tcc	*i_or_x_cc, software_trap_number*	(*synonym:* tgeu)
tcs	*i_or_x_cc, software_trap_number*	(*synonym:* tlu)
tpos	*i_or_x_cc, software_trap_number*	
tneg	*i_or_x_cc, software_trap_number*	
tvc	*i_or_x_cc, software_trap_number*	
tvs	*i_or_x_cc, software_trap_number*	

Description:

The Tcc instruction evaluates the selected integer condition codes (*icc* or *xcc*) according to the *cond* field of the instruction, producing either a TRUE or FALSE result. If TRUE and no higher-priority exceptions or interrupt requests are pending, then a *trap_instruction* exception is generated. If FALSE, a *trap_instruction* exception does not occur and the instruction behaves like a NOP.

The software trap number is specified by the least significant seven bits of "$r[rs1] + r[rs2]$" if $i = 0$, or the least significant seven bits of "$r[rs1] + sw\_trap\_\#$" if $i = 1$.

When $i = 1$, bits 7 through 10 are reserved and should be supplied as zeros by software. When $i = 0$, bits 5 through 10 are reserved, and the most significant 57 bits of "$r[rs1] + r[rs2]$" are unused, and both should be supplied as zeros by software.

Description (Effect on Privileged State):

If a *trap_instruction* traps, 256 plus the software trap number is written into TT[TL]. Then the trap is taken, and the processor performs the normal trap entry procedure, as described in Chapter 7, "Traps."

Programming Note:
> Tcc can be used to implement breakpointing, tracing, and calls to supervisor software. It can also be used for run-time checks, such as out-of-range array indexes, integer overflow, etc.

Compatibility Note:
> Tcc is upward compatible with the SPARC-V8 Ticc instruction, with one qualification: a Ticc with $i = 1$ and $simm13 < 0$ may execute differently on a SPARC-V9 processor. Use of the $i = 1$ form of Ticc is believed to be rare in SPARC-V8 software, and $simm13 < 0$ is probably not used at all, so it is believed that, in practice, full software compatibillity will be achieved.

Exceptions:
> *trap_instruction*
> *illegal_instruction* ($cc1$ ☐ $cc0 = 01_2$ or 11_2)

A.61 Write Privileged Register

Opcode	op3	Operation
WRPR[P]	11 0010	Write Privileged Register

Format (3):

10	rd	op3	rs1	i=0	—	rs2

10	rd	op3	rs1	i=1	simm13

31 30 29   25 24   19 18   14 13 12   5 4   0

rd	Privileged register
0	TPC
1	TNPC
2	TSTATE
3	TT
4	TICK
5	TBA
6	PSTATE
7	TL
8	PIL
9	CWP
10	CANSAVE
11	CANRESTORE
12	CLEANWIN
13	OTHERWIN
14	WSTATE
15..31	*Reserved*

Suggested Assembly Language Syntax		
wrpr	reg_{rs1}, reg_or_imm,	%tpc
wrpr	reg_{rs1}, reg_or_imm,	%tnpc
wrpr	reg_{rs1}, reg_or_imm,	%tstate
wrpr	reg_{rs1}, reg_or_imm,	%tt
wrpr	reg_{rs1}, reg_or_imm,	%tick
wrpr	reg_{rs1}, reg_or_imm,	%tba
wrpr	reg_{rs1}, reg_or_imm,	%pstate
wrpr	reg_{rs1}, reg_or_imm,	%tl
wrpr	reg_{rs1}, reg_or_imm,	%pil
wrpr	reg_{rs1}, reg_or_imm,	%cwp
wrpr	reg_{rs1}, reg_or_imm,	%cansave
wrpr	reg_{rs1}, reg_or_imm,	%canrestore
wrpr	reg_{rs1}, reg_or_imm,	%cleanwin
wrpr	reg_{rs1}, reg_or_imm,	%otherwin
wrpr	reg_{rs1}, reg_or_imm,	%wstate

Description:

This instruction stores the value "$r[rs1]$ **xor** $r[rs2]$" if $i = 0$, or "$r[rs1]$ **xor** sign_ext($simm13$)" if $i = 1$ to the writable fields of the specified privileged state register. Note the exclusive-or operation.

The *rd* field in the instruction determines the privileged register that is written. There are at least four copies of the TPC, TNPC, TT, and TSTATE registers, one for each trap level. A write to one of these registers sets the register indexed by the current value in the trap level register (TL). A write to TPC, TNPC, TT, or TSTATE when the trap level is zero (TL = 0) causes an *illegal_instruction* exception.

A WRPR of TL does not cause a trap or return from trap; it does not alter any other machine state.

Programming Note:
> A WRPR of TL can be used to read the values of TPC, TNPC, and TSTATE for any trap level, however, care must be taken that traps do not occur while the TL register is modified.

The WRPR instruction is a **non**delayed-write instruction. The instruction immediately following the WRPR observes any changes made to processor state made by the WRPR.

WRPR instructions with *rd* in the range 15..31 are reserved for future versions of the architecture; executing a WRPR instruction with *rd* in that range causes an *illegal_instruction* exception.

Programming Note:
> On an implementation that provides a floating-point queue, supervisor software should be aware of the state of the FQ before disabling the floating-point unit (changing PSTATE.PEF from 1 to 0 with a WRPR instruction) (impl. dep. #24). Typically, supervisor software ensures that the FQ is empty (FSR.*qne* = 0) before disabling the floating-point unit.

Exceptions:
privileged_opcode
illegal_instruction (($rd = 15..31$) or (($rd \leq 3$) and (TL = 0)))

A.62 Write State Register

> The WRY instruction is deprecated; it is provided only for compatibility with previous versions of the architecture. It should not be used in new SPARC-V9 software. It is recommended that all instructions which reference the Y register be avoided.

Opcode	op3	rd	Operation
WRY^D	11 0000	0	Write Y register
—	11 0000	1	*Reserved*
WRCCR	11 0000	2	Write Condition Codes Register
WRASI	11 0000	3	Write ASI register
WRASR^{PASR}	11 0000	4, 5	Write Ancillary State Register (*reserved*)
WRFPRS	11 0000	6	Write Floating-Point Registers Status register
WRASR^{PASR}	11 0000	7..14	Write Ancillary State Register (*reserved*)
See text	11 0000	15	*See text*
WRASR^{PASR}	11 0000	16..31	*Implementation-dependent* (impl. dep. #48)

Format (3):

10	rd	op3	rs1	i=0	—	rs2

10	rd	op3	rs1	i=1	simm13

31 30 29   25 24   19 18   14 13 12   5 4   0

Suggested Assembly Language Syntax	
wr	reg_{rs1}, *reg_or_imm*, %y
wr	reg_{rs1}, *reg_or_imm*, %ccr
wr	reg_{rs1}, *reg_or_imm*, %asi
wr	reg_{rs1}, *reg_or_imm*, %fprs
wr	reg_{rs1}, *reg_or_imm*, asr_reg_{rd}

Description:

WRY, WRCCR, WRFPRS, and WRASI stores the value "$r[rs1]$ **xor** $r[rs2]$" if $i = 0$, or "$r[rs1]$ **xor** sign_ext($simm13$)" if $i = 1$, to the writable fields of the specified state register. Note the exclusive-or operation.

Note that WRY, WRCCR, WRASI, WRFPRS, and WRASR are distinguished only by the *rd* field.

WRASR writes a value to the ancillary state register (ASR) indicated by *rd*. The operation performed to generate the value written may be *rd*-dependent or implementation-dependent (see below). A WRASR instruction is indicated by $op = 2_{16}$, $rd = 4$, 5, or ≥ 7 and $op3 = 30_{16}$.

An instruction with $op = 2_{16}$, $op3 = 30_{16}$, $rd = 15$, $rs1 = 0$, and $i = 1$ is defined as a SIR instruction. See A.49, "Software-Initiated Reset." When $op = 2_{16}$, $op3 = 30_{16}$, and $rd = 15$, if either $rs1 \neq 0$ or $i \neq 1$, then an *illegal_instruction* exception shall be generated.

IMPL. DEP. #48: WRASR instructions with *rd* in the range 16..31 are available for implementation-dependent uses (impl. dep. #8). For a WRASR instruction with *rd* in the range 16..31, the following are implementation-dependent: the interpretation of bits 18:0 in the instruction, the operation(s) performed (for example, XOR) to generate the value written to the ASR, whether the instruction is privileged (impl. dep. #9), and whether the instruction causes an *illegal_instruction* exception.

See I.1.1, "Read/Write Ancillary State Registers (ASRs)," for a discussion of extending the SPARC-V9 instruction set using read/write ASR instructions.

The WRY, WRCCR, WRFPRS, and WRASI instructions are **not** delayed-write instructions. The instruction immediately following a WRY, WRCCR, WRFPRS, or WRASI observes the new value of the Y, CCR, FPRS, or ASI register.

WRFPRS waits for any pending floating-point operations to complete before writing the FPRS register.

Implementation Note:
> Ancillary state registers may include (for example) timer, counter, diagnostic, self-test, and trap-control registers. See *Implementation Characteristics of Current SPARC-V9-based Products, Revision 9.x*, a document available from SPARC International, for information on ancillary state registers provided by specific implementations.

Compatibility Note:
> The SPARC-V8 WRIER, WRPSR, WRWIM, and WRTBR instructions do not exist in SPARC-V9, since the IER, PSR, TBR, and WIM registers do not exist in SPARC-V9.

Exceptions:
> *privileged_opcode* (WRASR only; implementation-dependent (impl. dep. #48))
> *illegal_instruction* (WRASR with $rs1 = 16..31$ and the implementation does not define the instruction as an extension; implementation-dependent (impl. dep. #48), or WRASR with *rd* equal to 1, 4, 5, or in the range 7..14), WRASR with *rd* equal to 15 and $rs1 \neq 0$ or $i \neq 1$

B IEEE Std 754-1985 Requirements for SPARC-V9

The IEEE Std 754-1985 floating-point standard contains a number of implementation-dependencies. This appendix specifies choices for these implementation-dependencies, to ensure that SPARC-V9 implementations are as consistent as possible.

B.1 Traps Inhibit Results

As described in 5.1.7, "Floating-Point State Register (FSR)," and elsewhere, when a floating-point trap occurs:

— The destination floating-point register(s) (the f registers) are unchanged.

— The floating-point condition codes ($fcc0$, $fcc1$, $fcc2$, and $fcc3$) are unchanged.

— The FSR.$aexc$ (accrued exceptions) field is unchanged.

— The FSR.$cexc$ (current exceptions) field is unchanged except for *IEEE_754_exceptions*; in that case, $cexc$ contains a bit set to "1" corresponding to the exception that caused the trap. Only one bit shall be set in $cexc$.

Instructions causing an *fp_exception_other* trap due to unfinished or unimplemented FPops execute as if by hardware; that is, a trap is undetectable by user software, except that timing may be affected. A user-mode trap handler invoked for an *IEEE_754_exception*, whether as a direct result of a hardware *fp_exception_ieee_754* trap or as an indirect result of supervisor handling of an *unfinished_FPop* or *unimplemented_FPop*, can rely on the following:

— The address of the instruction that caused the exception will be available to it.

— The destination floating-point register(s) are unchanged from their state prior to that instruction's execution.

— The floating-point condition codes ($fcc0$, $fcc1$, $fcc2$, and $fcc3$) are unchanged.

— The FSR $aexc$ field is unchanged.

— The FSR $cexc$ field contains exactly one bit set to 1, corresponding to the exception that caused the trap.

— The FSR *ftt*, *qne*, and *reserved* fields are zero.

Supervisor software is responsible for enforcing these requirements if the hardware trap mechanism does not.

B.2   NaN Operand and Result Definitions

An untrapped floating-point result can be in a format that is either the same as, or different from, the format of the source operands. These two cases are described separately below.

B.2.1   Untrapped Result in Different Format from Operands

F[sdq]TO[sdq] with a quiet NaN operand:

No exception caused; result is a quiet NaN. The operand is transformed as follows:

NaN transformation: The most significant bits of the operand fraction are copied to the most significant bits of the result fraction. When converting to a narrower format, excess low-order bits of the operand fraction are discarded. When converting to a wider format, excess low-order bits of the result fraction are set to 0. The quiet bit (the most significant bit of the result fraction) is always set to 1, so the NaN transformation always produces a quiet NaN. The sign bit is copied from the operand to the result without modification.

F[sdq]TO[sdq] with a signaling NaN operand:

Invalid exception; result is the signaling NaN operand processed by the **NaN transformation** above to produce a quiet NaN.

FCMPE[sdq] with any NaN operand:

Invalid exception; the selected floating-point condition code is set to unordered.

FCMP[sdq] with any signaling NaN operand:

Invalid exception; the selected floating-point condition code is set to unordered.

FCMP[sdq] with any quiet NaN operand but no signaling NaN operand:

No exception; the selected floating-point condition code is set to unordered.

B.2.2   Untrapped Result in Same Format as Operands

No NaN operand:

For an invalid operation such as **sqrt**(−1.0) or 0.0 ÷ 0.0, the result is the quiet NaN with sign = zero, exponent = all ones, and fraction = all ones. The sign is zero to distinguish such results from storage initialized to all ones.

One operand, a quiet NaN:

No exception; result is the quiet NaN operand.

One operand, a signaling NaN:

Invalid exception; result is the signaling NaN with its quiet bit (most significant bit of fraction field) set to 1.

Two operands, both quiet NaNs:

No exception; result is the *rs2* (second source) operand.

Two operands, both signaling NaNs:

Invalid exception; result is the *rs2* operand with the quiet bit set to 1.

Two operands, only one a signaling NaN:
Invalid exception; result is the signaling NaN operand with the quiet bit set to 1.

Two operands, neither a signaling NaN, only one a quiet NaN:
No exception; result is the quiet NaN operand.

In table 27 NaNn means that the NaN is in rs$n$, Q means quiet, S signaling.

Table 27—Untrapped Floating-Point Results

		rs2 operand		
		Number	QNaN2	SNaN2
rs1 operand	**None**	IEEE 754	QNaN2	QSNaN2
	Number	IEEE 754	QNaN2	QSNaN2
	QNaN1	QNaN1	QNaN2	QSNaN2
	SNaN1	QSNaN1	QSNaN1	QSNaN2

QSNaNn means a quiet NaN produced by the **NaN transformation** on a signaling NaN from rs$n$; the invalid exception is always indicated. The QNaNn results in the table never generate an exception, but IEEE 754 specifies several cases of invalid exceptions, and QNaN results from operands that are both numbers.

B.3   Trapped Underflow Definition (UFM = 1)

Underflow occurs if the exact unrounded result has magnitude between zero and the smallest normalized number in the destination format.

IMPL. DEP. #55: Whether tininess (in IEEE 754 terms) is detected before or after rounding is implementation-dependent. It is recommended that tininess be detected before rounding.

Note that the wrapped exponent results intended to be delivered on trapped underflows and overflows in IEEE 754 are irrelevant to SPARC-V9 at the hardware and supervisor software levels; if they are created at all, it would be by user software in a user-mode trap handler.

B.4   Untrapped Underflow Definition (UFM = 0)

Underflow occurs if the exact unrounded result has magnitude between zero and the smallest normalized number in the destination format, **and** the correctly rounded result in the destination format is inexact.

Table 28 summarizes what happens when an exact **unrounded** value u satisfying

$$0 \leq |u| \leq smallest\ normalized\ number$$

would round, if no trap intervened, to a **rounded** value r which might be zero, subnormal, or the smallest normalized value. "UF" means underflow trap (with ufc set in $cexc$), "NX" means inexact trap (with nxc set in $cexc$), "uf" means untrapped underflow exception (with ufc set in $cexc$ and ufa in $aexc$), and "nx" means untrapped inexact exception (with nxc set in $cexc$ and nxa in $aexc$).

Table 28—Untrapped Floating-Point Underflow

Underflow trap: Inexact trap:		UFM = 1 NXM = ?	UFM = 0 NXM = 1	UFM = 0 NXM = 0
u = r	*r* is minimum normal	*None*	*None*	*None*
	r is subnormal	UF	*None*	*None*
	r is zero	*None*	*None*	*None*
u ≠ r	*r* is minimum normal	UF [†]	NX	uf nx
	r is subnormal	UF	NX	uf nx
	r is zero	UF	NX	uf nx

[†] If tininess is detected after rounding and NXM = 1, then NX, otherwise *"None"* (impl. dep. #55).

B.5 Integer Overflow Definition

F[sdq]TOi:

When a NaN, infinity, large positive argument ≥ 2147483648.0, or large negative argument ≤ –2147483649.0 is converted to an integer, the invalid_current (*nvc*) bit of FSR.*cexc* should be set and *fp_exception_IEEE_754* should be raised. If the floating-point invalid trap is disabled (FSR.TEM.NVM = 0), no trap occurs and a numerical result is generated: if the sign bit of the operand is 0, the result is 2147483647; if the sign bit of the operand is 1, the result is –2147483648.

F[sdq]TOx:

When a NaN, infinity, large positive argument ≥ 2^{63}, or large negative argument ≤ $-(2^{63} + 1)$, is converted to an extended integer, the invalid_current (*nvc*) bit of FSR.*cexc* should be set and *fp_exception_IEEE_754* should be raised. If the floating-point invalid trap is disabled (FSR.TEM.NVM = 0), no trap occurs and a numerical result is generated: if the sign bit of the operand is 0, the result is $2^{63} - 1$; if the sign bit of the operand is 1, the result is -2^{63}.

B.6 Floating-Point Nonstandard Mode

SPARC-V9 implementations are permitted but not encouraged to deviate from IEEE Std 754-1985 requirements when the nonstandard mode (NS) bit of the FSR is set (impl. dep. #18).

C SPARC-V9 Implementation Dependencies

This appendix provides a summary of all implementation dependencies in the SPARC-V9 standard. The notation "**IMPL. DEP. #nn:**" is used to identify the definition of an implementation dependency; the notation "(impl. dep. #nn)" is used to identify a reference to an implementation dependency. The number *nn* provides an index into table 29 on page 249.

SPARC International maintains a document, *Implementation Characteristics of Current SPARC-V9-based Products, Revision 9.x*, which describes the implementation-dependent design features of SPARC-V9-compliant implementations. Contact SPARC International for this document at

SPARC International
535 Middlefield Rd, Suite 210
Menlo Park, CA 94025
(415) 321-8692

C.1 Definition of an Implementation Dependency

The SPARC-V9 architecture is a **model** that specifies unambiguously the behavior observed by **software** on SPARC-V9 systems. Therefore, it does not necessarily describe the operation of the **hardware** of any actual implementation.

An implementation is **not** required to execute every instruction in hardware. An attempt to execute a SPARC-V9 instruction that is not implemented in hardware generates a trap. Whether an instruction is implemented directly by hardware, simulated by software, or emulated by firmware is implementation-dependent (impl. dep. #1).

The two levels of SPARC-V9 compliance are described in 1.2.6, "SPARC-V9 Compliance."

Some elements of the architecture are defined to be implementation-dependent. These elements include certain registers and operations that may vary from implementation to implementation, and are explicitly identified as such in this appendix.

Implementation elements (such as instructions or registers) that appear in an implementation but are not defined in this document (or its updates) are not considered to be SPARC-V9 elements of that implementation.

C.2 Hardware Characteristics

Hardware characteristics that do not affect the behavior observed by software on SPARC-V9 systems are not considered architectural implementation dependencies. A hardware characteristic may be relevant to the user system design (for example, the speed of execution of an instruction) or may be transparent to the user (for example, the method used for achieving cache consistency). The SPARC International document, *Implementation Characteristics of Current SPARC-V9-based Products, Revision 9.x*, provides a useful list of these hardware characteristics, along with the list of implementation-dependent design features of SPARC-V9-compliant implementations.

In general, hardware characteristics deal with

— Instruction execution speed

— Whether instructions are implemented in hardware

— The nature and degree of concurrency of the various hardware units comprising a SPARC-V9 implementation.

C.3   Implementation Dependency Categories

Many of the implementation dependencies can be grouped into four categories, abbreviated by their first letters throughout this appendix:

Value (v):
   The semantics of an architectural feature are well-defined, except that a value associated with it may differ across implementations. A typical example is the number of implemented register windows (Implementation dependency #2).

Assigned Value (a):
   The semantics of an architectural feature are well-defined, except that a value associated with it may differ across implementations and the actual value is assigned by SPARC International. Typical examples are the *impl* field of Version register (VER) (Implementtentation dependency #13) and the FSR.*ver* field (Implementation dependency #19).

Functional Choice (f):
   The SPARC-V9 architecture allows implementors to choose among several possible semantics related to an architectural function. A typical example is the treatment of a catastrophic error exception, which may cause either a deferred or a disrupting trap (Implementation dependency #31).

Total Unit (t):
   The existence of the architectural unit or function is recognized, but details are left to each implementation. Examples include the handling of I/O registers (Implementation dependency #7) and some alternate address spaces (Implementation dependency #29).

C.4   List of Implementation Dependencies

Table 29 provides a complete list of the implementation dependencies in the architecture, the definition of each, and references to the page numbers in the standard where each is defined or referenced. Most implementation dependencies occur because of the address spaces, I/O registers, registers (including ASRs), the type of trapping used for an exception, the handling of errors, or miscellaneous non-SPARC-V9-architectural units such as the MMU or caches (which affect the FLUSH instruction).

Table 29—Implementation Dependencies

Number	Category	*Def* / Ref page #	Description
1	f	*8*, 247	**Software emulation of instructions** Whether an instruction is implemented directly by hardware, simulated by software, or emulated by firmware is implementation-dependent.
2	v	*15*, 30, 32, 57	**Number of IU registers** An implementation of the IU may contain from 64 to 528 general-purpose 64-bit *r* registers. This corresponds to a grouping of the registers into two sets of eight global *r* registers, plus a circular stack of from three to 32 sets of 16 registers each, known as register windows. Since the number of register windows present (NWINDOWS) is implementation-dependent, the total number of registers is also implementation-dependent.
3	f	*82*	**Incorrect IEEE Std 754-1985 results** An implementation may indicate that a floating-point instruction did not produce a correct ANSI/IEEE Standard 754-1985 result by generating a special floating-point unfinished or unimplemented exception. In this case, privileged mode software shall emulate any functionality not present in the hardware.
4-5	—	—	*Reserved*
6	f	*18*, 119	**I/O registers privileged status** Whether I/O registers can be accessed by nonprivileged code is implementation-dependent.
7	t	*18*, 119	**I/O register definitions** The contents and addresses of I/O registers are implementation-dependent.
8	t	*20*, 30, 35, 60, 211, 212, 242, 252, 252	**RDASR/WRASR target registers** Software can use read/write ancillary state register instructions to read/write implementation-dependent processor registers (ASRs 16-31).
9	f	*20*, 36, 60, 242, 252, 252	**RDASR/WRASR privileged status** Whether each of the implementation-dependent read/write ancillary state register instructions (for ASRs 16-31) is privileged is implementation-dependent.
10-12	—	—	*Reserved*
13	a	*57*	**VER.*impl*** VER.*impl* uniquely identifies an implementation or class of software-compatible implementations of the architecture. Values $FFF0_{16}..FFFF_{16}$ are reserved and are not available for assignment.
14-15	—	—	*Reserved*
16	t	*30*	**IU deferred-trap queue** The existence, contents, and operation of an IU deferred-trap queue are implementation-dependent; it is not visible to user application programs under normal operating conditions.
17	—	—	*Reserved*

Table 29—Implementation Dependencies (*Continued*)

Number	Category	*Def* / Ref page #	Description
18	f	*44*, 246	**Nonstandard IEEE 754-1985 results** Bit 22 of the FSR, FSR_nonstandard_fp (NS), when set to 1, causes the FPU to produce implementation-defined results that may not correspond to IEEE Standard 754-1985.
19	a	*45*	**FPU version, FSR.ver** Bits 19:17 of the FSR, FSR.*ver*, identify one or more implementations of the FPU architecture.
20-21	—	—	*Reserved*
22	f	*50*	**FPU TEM, cexc, and aexc** An implementation may choose to implement the TEM, *cexc*, and *aexc* fields in hardware in either of two ways (see 5.1.7.11 for details).
23	f	*60*, 113, 113	**Floating-point traps** Floating-point traps may be precise or deferred. If deferred, a floating-point deferred-trap queue (FQ) must be present.
24	t	*30*, 209	**FPU deferred-trap queue (FQ)** The presence, contents of, and operations on the floating-point deferred-trap queue (FQ) are implementation-dependent.
25	f	*47*, 209, 210, 210	**RDPR of FQ with nonexistent FQ** On implementations without a floating-point queue, an attempt to read the FQ with an RDPR instruction shall cause either an *illegal_instruction* exception or an *fp_exception_other* exception with FSR.*ftt* set to 4 (*sequence_error*).
26-28	—	—	*Reserved*
29	t	18, *71*, 72	**Address space identifier (ASI) definitions** The following ASI assignments are implementation-dependent: restricted ASIs $00_{16}..03_{16}$, $05_{16}..0B_{16}$, $0D_{16}..0F_{16}$, $12_{16}..17_{16}$, and $1A_{16}..7F_{16}$; and unrestricted ASIs $C0_{16}..FF_{16}$.
30	f	*71*	**ASI address decoding** An implementation may choose to decode only a subset of the 8-bit ASI specifier; however, it shall decode at least enough of the ASI to distinguish ASI_PRIMARY, ASI_PRIMARY_LITTLE, ASI_AS_IF_USER_PRIMARY, ASI_AS_IF_USER_PRIMARY_LITTLE, ASI_PRIMARY_NOFAULT, ASI_PRIMARY_NOFAULT_LITTLE, ASI_SECONDARY, ASI_SECONDARY_LITTLE, ASI_AS_IF_USER_SECONDARY, ASI_AS_IF_USER_SECONDARY_LITTLE, ASI_SECONDARY_NOFAULT, and ASI_SECONDARY_NOFAULT_LITTLE. If ASI_NUCLEUS and ASI_NUCLEUS_LITTLE are supported (impl. dep. #124), they must be decoded also. Finally, an implementation must always decode ASI bit<7> while PSTATE.PRIV = 0, so that an attempt by nonprivileged software to access a restricted ASI will always cause a *privileged_action* exception.
31	f	*88*, 91, 112, 113, 113	**Catastrophic error exceptions** The causes and effects of catastrophic error exceptions are implementation-dependent. They may cause precise, deferred, or disrupting traps.
32	t	*94*	**Deferred traps** Whether any deferred traps (and associated deferred-trap queues) are present is implementation-dependent.

Table 29—Implementation Dependencies (*Continued*)

Number	Category	*Def* / Ref page #	Description
33	f	*96*, 112, 112, 112, 112, 113, 114	**Trap precision** Exceptions that occur as the result of program execution may be precise or deferred, although it is recommended that such exceptions be precise. Examples include *mem_address_not_aligned* and *division_by_zero*.
34	f	*98*	**Interrupt clearing** How quickly a processor responds to an interrupt request and the method by which an interrupt request is removed are implementation-dependent.
35	t	91, 100, 101, *102*, 111, 113	**Implementation-dependent traps** Trap type (TT) values $060_{16}..07F_{16}$ are reserved for implementation-dependent exceptions. The existence of *implementation_ dependent_n* traps and whether any that do exist are precise, deferred, or disrupting is implementation-dependent.
36	f	*102*	**Trap priorities** The priorities of particular traps are relative and are implementation-dependent, because a future version of the architecture may define new traps, and implementations may define implementation-dependent traps that establish new relative priorities.
37	f	*95*	**Reset trap** Some of a processor's behavior during a reset trap is implementation-dependent.
38	f	*106*	**Effect of reset trap on implementation-dependent registers** Implementation-dependent registers may or may not be affected by the various reset traps.
39	f	*92*	**Entering error_state on implementation-dependent errors** The processor may enter error_state when an implementation-dependent error condition occurs.
40	f	*92*	**Error_state processor state** What occurs after error_state is entered is implementation-dependent, but it is recommended that as much processor state as possible be preserved upon entry to error_state.
41	—	—	*Reserved*
42	t,f,v	*166*	**FLUSH instruction** If FLUSH is not implemented in hardware, it causes an *illegal_ instruction* exception and its function is performed by system software. Whether FLUSH traps is implementation-dependent.
43	—	—	*Reserved*
44	f	*172*, 174	**Data access FPU trap** If a load floating-point instruction traps with any type of access error exception, the contents of the destination floating-point register(s) either remain unchanged or are undefined.
45 - 46	—	—	*Reserved*

Table 29—Implementation Dependencies (*Continued*)

Number	Category	*Def* / Ref page #	Description
47	t	211, *212*, 212, 212	**RDASR** RDASR instructions with *rd* in the range 16..31 are available for implementation-dependent uses (impl. dep. #8). For an RDASR instruction with *rs1* in the range 16..31, the following are implementation-dependent: the interpretation of bits 13:0 and 29:25 in the instruction, whether the instruction is privileged (impl. dep. #9), and whether it causes an *illegal_instruction* trap.
48	t	241, *242*, 242, 242	**WRASR** WRASR instructions with *rd* in the range 16..31 are available for implementation-dependent uses (impl. dep. #8). For a WRASR instruction with *rd* in the range 16..31, the following are implementation-dependent: the interpretation of bits 18:0 in the instruction, the operation(s) performed (for example, **xor**) to generate the value written to the ASR, whether the instruction is privileged (impl. dep. #9), and whether it causes an *illegal_instruction* trap.
49-54	—	—	*Reserved*
55	f	49, 49, *245*, 246	**Floating-point underflow detection** Whether "tininess" (in IEEE 754 terms) is detected before or after rounding is implementation-dependent. It is recommended that tininess be detected before rounding.
56-100	—	—	*Reserved*
101	v	21, *54*, 55, 55, 56, 57	**Maximum trap level** It is implementation-dependent how many additional levels, if any, past level 4 are supported.
102	f	*112*	**Clean windows trap** An implementation may choose either to implement automatic "cleaning" of register windows in hardware, or generate a *clean_window* trap, when needed, for window(s) to be cleaned by software.
103	f	*203, 203, 204, 204, 204*, 206, 207	**Prefetch instructions** The following aspects of the PREFETCH and PREFETCHA instructions are implementation-dependent: (1) whether they have an observable effect in privileged code; (2) whether they can cause a *data_access_MMU_miss* exception; (3) the attributes of the block of memory prefetched: its size (minimum = 64 bytes) and its alignment (minimum = 64-byte alignment); (4) whether each variant is implemented as a NOP, with its full semantics, or with common-case prefetching semantics; (5) whether and how variants 16..31 are implemented.
104	a	*57*	**VER.manuf** VER.*manuf* contains a 16-bit semiconductor manufacturer code. This field is optional, and if not present reads as zero. VER.*manuf* may indicate the original supplier of a second-sourced chip in cases involving mask-level second-sourcing. It is intended that the contents of VER.*manuf* track the JEDEC semiconductor manufacturer code as closely as possible. If the manufacturer does not have a JEDEC semiconductor manufacturer code, SPARC International will assign a VER.*manuf* value.

Table 29—Implementation Dependencies (*Continued*)

Number	Category	*Def* / Ref page #	Description
105	f	*51*	**TICK register** The difference between the values read from the TICK register on two reads should reflect the number of processor cycles executed between the reads. If an accurate count cannot always be returned, any inaccuracy should be small, bounded, and documented. An implementation may implement fewer than 63 bits in TICK.-*counter*; however, the counter as implemented must be able to count for at least 10 years without overflowing. Any upper bits not implemented must read as zero.
106	f	82, *169*	**IMPDEP*n* instructions** The IMPDEP1 and IMPDEP2 instructions are completely implementation-dependent. Implementation-dependent aspects include their operation, the interpretation of bits 29:25 and 18:0 in their encodings, and which (if any) exceptions they may cause.
107	f	*176*, 176, *178*, 178	**Unimplemented LDD trap** It is implementation-dependent whether LDD and LDDA are implemented in hardware. If not, an attempt to execute either will cause an *unimplemented_LDD* trap.
108	f	115, *226*, 227, *229*, 229	**Unimplemented STD trap** It is implementation-dependent whether STD and STDA are implemented in hardware. If not, an attempt to execute either will cause an *unimplemented_STD* trap.
109	f	113, *172*, 172, *173*	**LDDF_mem_address_not_aligned** LDDF and LDDFA require only word alignment. However, if the effective address is word-aligned but not doubleword-aligned, either may cause an *LDDF_mem_address_not_aligned* trap, in which case the trap handler software shall emulate the LDDF (or LDDFA) instruction and return.
110	f	114, *223*, 223, *225*, 225	**STDF_mem_address_not_aligned** STDF and STDFA require only word alignment in memory. However, if the effective address is word-aligned but not doubleword-aligned, either may cause an *STDF_mem_address_not_aligned* trap, in which case the trap handler software shall emulate the STDF or STDFA instruction and return.
111	f	114, *172*, 172, *174*	**LDQF_mem_address_not_aligned** LDQF and LDQFA require only word alignment. However, if the effective address is word-aligned but not quadword-aligned, either may cause an *LDQF_mem_address_not_aligned* trap, in which case the trap handler software shall emulate the LDQF (or LDQFA) instruction and return.
112	f	115, *223*, 223, *225*, 225	**STQF_mem_address_not_aligned** STQF and STQFA require only word alignment in memory. However, if the effective address is word-aligned but not quadword-aligned, either may cause an *STQF_mem_address_not_aligned* trap, in which case the trap handler software shall emulate the STQF or STQFA instruction and return.
113	f	52, *117*	**Implemented memory models** Whether the Partial Store Order (PSO) or Relaxed Memory Order (RMO) models are supported is implementation-dependent.

Table 29—Implementation Dependencies (*Continued*)

Number	Category	*Def* / Ref page #	Description
114	f	*90*	**RED_state trap vector address (RSTVaddr)** The RED_state trap vector is located at an implementation-dependent address referred to as RSTVaddr.
115	f	*90*	**RED_state processor state** What occurs after the processor enters RED_state is implementation-dependent.
116	f	*220*	**SIR_enable control flag** The location of and the means of accessing the SIR_enable control flag are implementation-dependent. In some implementations, it may be permanently zero.
117	f	204, *276*	**MMU disabled prefetch behavior** Whether Prefetch and Non-faulting Load always succeed when the MMU is disabled is implementation-dependent.
118	f	*119*	**Identifying I/O locations** The manner in which I/O locations are identified is implementation-dependent.
119	f	52, *127*	**Unimplemented values for PSTATE.MM** The effect of writing an unimplemented memory-mode designation into PSTATE.MM is implementation-dependent.
120	f	*119*, 128, 151, 179, 184, 221, 231, 232	**Coherence and atomicity of memory operations** The coherence and atomicity of memory operations between processors and I/O DMA memory accesses are implementation-dependent.
121	f	*119*	**Implementation-dependent memory model** An implementation may choose to identify certain addresses and use an implementation-dependent memory model for references to them.
122	f	*129*, 166, 166	**FLUSH latency** The latency between the execution of FLUSH on one processor and the point at which the modified instructions have replaced outdated instructions in a multiprocessor is implementation-dependent.
123	f	*18*, 119, 128	**Input/output (I/O) semantics** The semantic effect of accessing input/output (I/O) registers is implementation-dependent.
124	v	72, 71, *120*, 250	**Implicit ASI when TL > 0** When TL > 0, the implicit ASI for instruction fetches, loads, and stores is implementation-dependent. See F.4.4, "Contexts," for more information.
125	f	*53*, 77, 149, 170, 212	**Address masking** When PSTATE.AM = 1, the value of the high-order 32-bits of the PC transmitted to the specified destination register(s) by CALL, JMPL, RDPC, and on a trap is implementation-dependent.

D Formal Specification of the Memory Models

This appendix provides a formal description of the SPARC-V9 processor's interaction with memory. The formal description is more complete and more precise than the description of Chapter 8, "Memory Models," and therefore represents the definitive specification. Implementations must conform to this model, and programmers must use this description to resolve any ambiguity.

This formal specification is not intended to be a description of an actual implementation, only to describe in a precise and rigorous fashion the behavior that any conforming implementation must provide.

D.1 Processors and Memory

The system model consists of a collection of processors, P_0, P_1,..P_{n-1}. Each processor executes its own instruction stream.[1] Processors may share address space and access to real memory and I/O locations.

To improve performance, processors may interpose a **cache** or caches in the path between the processor and memory. For data and I/O references, caches are required to be transparent. The memory model specifies the functional behavior of the entire memory subsystem, which includes any form of caching. Implementations must use appropriate cache coherency mechanisms to achieve this transparency.[2]

The SPARC-V9 memory model requires that all data references be consistent but does not require that instruction references or input/output references be maintained consistent. The FLUSH instruction or an appropriate operating system call may be used to ensure that instruction and data spaces are consistent. Likewise, system software is needed to manage the consistency of I/O operations.

The memory model is a local property of a processor that determines the order properties of memory references. The ordering properties have global implications when memory is shared, since the memory model determines what data is visible to observing processors and in what order. Moreover, the operative memory model of the observing processor affects the apparent order of shared data reads and writes that it observes.

---

1. Processors are equivalent to their software abstraction, processes, provided that context switching is properly performed. See Appendix J, "Programming With the Memory Models," for an example of context switch code.

2. Philip Bitar and Alvin M. Despain, "Multiprocessor Cache Synchronization: Issues, Innovations, Evolution," *Proc. 13th Annual International Symposium on Computer Architecture*, Computer Architecture News 14:2, June 1986, pp.424-433.

D.2   An Overview of the Memory Model Specification

The underlying goal of the memory model is to place the weakest possible constraints on the processor implementations and to provide a precise specification of the possible orderings of memory operations so that shared-memory multiprocessors can be constructed.

An **execution trace** is a sequence of instructions with a specified initial instruction. An execution trace constitutes one possible execution of a program and may involve arbitrary reorderings and parallel execution of instructions. A **self-consistent** execution trace is one that generates precisely the same results as those produced by a program order execution trace.

A **program order execution trace** is an execution trace that begins with a specified initial instruction and executes one instruction at a time in such a fashion that all the semantic effects of each instruction take effect before the next instruction is begun. The execution trace this process generates is defined to be **program order**.

A **program** is defined by the collection of all possible program order execution traces.

Dependence order is a partial order on the instructions in an execution trace that is adequate to ensure that the execution trace is self-consistent. Dependence order can be constructed using conventional data dependence analysis techniques. Dependence order holds only between instructions in the instruction trace of a single processor; instructions that are part of execution traces on different processors are never dependence-ordered.

Memory order is a total order on the memory reference instructions (loads, stores, and atomic load/stores) which satisfies the dependence order and, possibly, other order constraints such as those introduced implicitly by the choice of memory model or explicitly by the appearance of memory barrier (MEMBAR) instructions in the execution trace. The existence of a global memory order on the performance of all stores implies that memory access is write-atomic.[3]

A **memory model** is a set of rules that constrain the order of memory references. The SPARC-V9 architecture supports three memory models: total store order (TSO), partial store order (PSO), and relaxed memory order (RMO). The memory models are defined only for memory and not for I/O locations. See 8.2, "Memory, Real Memory, and I/O Locations," for more information.

The formal definition used in the SPARC-V8 specification[4] remains valid for the definition of PSO and TSO, except for the FLUSH instruction, which has been modified slightly.[5] The SPARC-V9 architecture introduces a new memory model, RMO, which differs from TSO and PSO in that it allows load operations to be reordered as long as single thread programs remain self-consistent.

---

3. W.W. Collier, "Reasoning About Parallel Architectures", Prentice-Hall, 1992 includes an excellent discussion of write-atomicity and related memory model topics.

4. Pradeep Sindhu, Jean-Marc Frailong, and Michel Ceklov. "Formal Specification of Memory Models," Xerox Palo Alto Research Center Report CSL-91-11, December 1991.

5. In SPARC-V8, a FLUSH instruction needs at least five instruction execution cycles before it is guaranteed to have local effects; in SPARC-V9 this five-cycle requirement has been removed.

D.3 Memory Transactions

D.3.1 Memory Transactions

A memory transaction is one of the following:

Store:
> A request by a processor to replace the value of a specified memory location. The address and new value are bound to the store transaction when the processor initiates the store transaction. A store is complete when the new value is visible to all processors in the system.

Load:
> A request by a processor to retrieve the value of the specified memory location. The address is bound to the load transaction when the processor initiates the load transaction. A load is complete when the value being returned cannot be modified by a store made by another processor.

Atomic:
> A *load/store* pair with the guarantee that no other memory transaction will alter the state of the memory between the load and the store. The SPARC-V9 instruction set includes three atomic instructions: LDSTUB, SWAP and CAS.[6] An atomic transaction is considered to be both a load and a store.[7]

Flush:
> A request by a processor to force changes in the data space aliased to the instruction space to become consistent. Flush transactions are considered to be store operations for memory model purposes.

Memory transactions are referred to by capital letters: $X_n a$, which denotes a specific memory transaction X by processor n to memory address a. The processor index and the address are specified only if needed. The predicate $S(X)$ is true if and only if X has store semantics. The predicate $L(X)$ is true if and only if X has load semantics.

MEMBAR instructions are not memory transactions; rather they convey order information above and beyond the implicit ordering implied by the memory model in use. MEMBAR instructions are applied in program order.

D.3.2 Program Order

The **program order** is a per-processor total order that denotes the sequence in which processor n logically executes instructions. The program order relation is denoted by $<p$ such

---

6. There are three generic forms. CASA and CASXA reference 32-bit and 64-bit objects respectively. Both normal and alternate ASI forms exist for LDSTUB and SWAP. CASA and CASXA only have alternate forms, however, a CASA (CASXA) with ASI = ASI_PRIMARY{_LITTLE} is equivalent to CAS (CASX). Synthetic instructions for CAS and CASX are suggested in G.3, "Synthetic Instructions."

7. Even though the store part of a CASA is conditional, it is assumed that the store will always take place whether it does or not in a particular implementation. Since the value stored when the condition fails is the value already present, and since the CASA operation is atomic, no observing processor can determine whether the store occurred or not.

that $X_n <p Y_n$ is true if and only if the memory transaction X_n is caused by an instruction that is executed before the instruction that caused memory transaction Y_n.

Program order specifies a unique total order for all memory transactions initiated by one processor.

Memory barrier (MEMBAR) instructions executed by the processor are ordered with respect to $<p$. The predicate $M(X,Y)$ is true if and only if $X <p Y$ and there exists a MEM-BAR instruction that orders X and Y (that is, it appears in program order between X and Y). MEMBAR instructions can be either ordering or sequencing and may be combined into a single instruction using a bit-encoded mask.[8]

Ordering MEMBAR instructions impose constraints on the order in which memory transactions are performed.

Sequencing MEMBARs introduce additional constraints that are required in cases where the memory transaction has side-effects beyond storing data. Such side-effects are beyond the scope of the memory model, which is limited to order and value semantics for memory.[9]

This definition of program order is equivalent to the definition given in the SPARC-V8 memory model specification.

D.3.3 Dependence Order

Dependence order is a partial order that captures the constraints that hold between instructions that access the same processor register or memory location. In order to allow maximum concurrency in processor implementations, dependence order assumes that registers are dynamically renamed to avoid false dependences arising from register reuse.

Two memory transaction X and Y are dependence ordered, denoted by $X <d Y$, if and only if they are program ordered, $X <p Y$, **and** at least one of the following conditions is true:

(1) Y is a condition that depends on X and $S(Y)$ is true.

(2) Y reads a register that is written by X.

(3) X and Y access the same memory location and $S(X)$ and $L(Y)$ are both true.

The dependence order also holds between the memory transactions associated with the instructions. It is important to remember that partial ordering is transitive.

Rule (1) includes all control dependences that arise from the dynamic execution of programs. In particular, a store or atomic memory transaction that is executed after a condi-

---

8. The Ordering MEMBAR instruction uses 4 bits of its argument to specify the existence of an order relation depending on whether X and Y have load or store semantics. The Sequencing MEMBAR uses three bits to specify completion conditions. The MEMBAR encoding is specified in A.31.

9. Sequencing constraints have other effects, such as controlling when a memory error is recognized or when an I/O access reaches global visibility. The need for sequencing constraints is always associated with I/O and kernel level programming and not usually with normal, user-level application programming.

tional branch will depend on the outcome of that branch instruction, which in turn will depend on one or more memory transactions that precede the branch instruction. Loads after an unresolved conditional branch may proceed, that is, a conditional branch does not dependence order subsequent loads. Control dependences always order the initiation of subsequent instructions to the performance of the preceding instructions.[10]

Rule (2) captures dependences arising from register use. It is not necessary to include an ordering when X reads a register that is later written by Y, because register renaming will allow out-of-order execution in this case. Register renaming is equivalent to having an infinite pool of registers and requiring all registers to be write-once. Observe that the condition code register is set by some arithmetic and logical instructions and used by conditional branch instructions thus introducing a dependence order.

Rule (3) captures ordering constraints resulting from memory accesses to the same location and require that the dependence order reflect the program order for store-load pairs, but not for load-store or store-store pairs. A load may be executed speculatively, since loads are side-effect free, provided that Rule (3) is eventually satisfied.

An actual processor implementation will maintain dependence order by score-boarding, hardware interlocks, data flow techniques, compiler directed code scheduling, and so forth, or, simply, by sequential program execution. The means by which the dependence order is derived from a program is irrelevant to the memory model, which has to specify which possible memory transaction sequences are legal for a given set of data dependences. Practical implementations will not necessarily use the minimal set of constraints: adding unnecessary order relations from the program order to the dependence order only reduces the available concurrency, but does not impair correctness.

D.3.4 Memory Order

The sequence in which memory transactions are performed by the memory is called **memory order**, which is a total order on all memory transactions.

In general, the memory order cannot be known *a priori*. Instead, the memory order is specified as a set of constraints that are imposed on the memory transactions. The requirement that memory transaction X must be performed before memory transaction Y is denoted by $X <m Y$. Any memory order that satisfies these constraints is legal. The memory subsystem may choose arbitrarily among legal memory orders, hence multiple executions of the same programs may result in different memory orders.

D.4 Specification of Relaxed Memory Order (RMO)

D.4.1 Value Atomicity

Memory transactions will atomically set or retrieve the value of a memory location as long as the size of the value is less than or equal to eight bytes, the unit of coherency.

---

10. Self modifying code (use of FLUSH instructions) also causes control dependences.

D.4.2 Store Atomicity

All possible execution traces are consistent with the existence of a memory order that totally orders all transactions including all store operations.

This does not imply that the memory order is observable. Nor does it imply that RMO requires any central serialization mechanism.

D.4.3 Atomic Memory Transactions

The atomic memory transactions SWAP, LDSTUB, and CAS are performed as one memory transaction that is both a load and a store with respect to memory order constraints. No other memory transaction can separate the load and store actions of an atomic memory transaction. The semantics of atomic instructions are defined in Appendix A, "Instruction Definitions."

D.4.4 Memory Order Constraints

A memory order is legal in RMO if and only if:

(1) $X <d\ Y\ \&\ L(X) \Rightarrow X <m\ Y$

(2) $M(X,Y) \Rightarrow X <m\ Y$

(3) $Xa <p\ Ya\ \&\ S(Y) \Rightarrow X <m\ Y$

Rule (1) states that the RMO model will maintain dependence when the preceding transaction is a load. Preceding stores may be delayed in the implementation, so their order may not be preserved globally.

Rule (2) states that MEMBAR instructions order the performance of memory transactions.

Rule (3) states that stores to the same address are performed in program order. This is necessary for processor self-consistency

D.4.5 Value of Memory Transactions

The value of a load Ya is the value of the most recent store that was performed with respect to memory order or the value of the most recently initiated store by the same processor. Assuming Y is a load to memory location a:

$$Value(La)\ =\ Value(\ Max_{<m}\ \{\ S\ |\ Sa <m\ La\ \text{or}\ Sa <p\ La\ \}\ )$$

where $Max_{<m}\{..\}$ selects the most recent element with respect to the memory order and where *Value()* yields the value of a particular memory transaction. This states that the value returned by a load is either the result of the most recent store to that address which has been performed by any processor or which has been initiated by the processor issuing the load. The distinction between local and remote stores permits use of store-buffers, which are explicitly supported in all SPARC-V9 memory models.

D.4.6 Termination of Memory Transactions

Any memory transaction will eventually be performed. This is formalized by the requirement that only a finite number of memory ordered loads can be performed before a pending store is completed.

D.4.7 Flush Memory Transaction

Flush instructions are treated as store memory transactions as far as the memory order is concerned. Their semantics are defined in A.20, "Flush Instruction Memory." Flush instructions introduce a control dependence to any subsequent (in program order) execution of the instruction that was addressed by the flush.

D.5 Specification of Partial Store Order (PSO)

The specification of Partial Store Order (PSO) is that of Relaxed Memory Order (RMO) with the additional requirement that all memory transactions with load semantics are followed by an implied MEMBAR #LoadLoad | #LoadStore.

D.6 Specification of Total Store Order (TSO)

The specification of Total Store Order (TSO) is that of Partial Store Order (PSO) with the additional requirement that all memory transactions with store semantics are followed by an implied MEMBAR #StoreStore.

D.7 Examples Of Program Executions

This subsection lists several code sequences and an exhaustive list of all possible execution sequences under RMO, PSO and TSO. For each example, the code is followed by the list of order relations between the corresponding memory transactions. The memory transactions are referred to by numbers. In each case, the program is executed once for each memory model.

D.7.1 Observation of Store Atomicity

The code example below demonstrates how store atomicity prevents multiple processors from observing inconsistent sequences of events. In this case, processors 2 and 3 observe changes to the shared variables A and B, which are being modified by processor 1. Initially both variables are 0. The stores by processor 1 do not use any form of synchronization, and they may in fact be issued by two independent processors.

Should processor 2 find A to have the new value (1) and B to have the old value (0), it can infer that A was updated before B. Likewise, processor 3 may find $B = 1$ and $A = 0$, which implies that B was changed before A. It is impossible for both to occur in all SPARC-V9 memory models since there cannot exist a total order on all stores. This property of the memory models has been encoded in the assertion A1.

However, in RMO, the observing processor must separate the load operations with membar instructions. Otherwise, the loads may be reordered and no inference on the update order can be made.

Figure 44 is taken from the output of the SPARC-V9 memory model simulator, which enumerates all possible outcomes of short code sequences and which can be used to prove assertions about such programs.

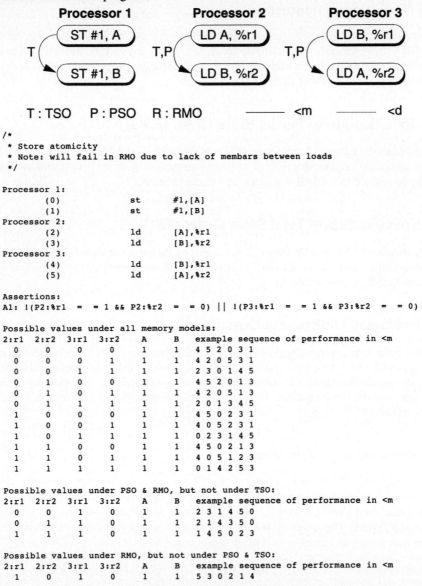

```
/*
 * Store atomicity
 * Note: will fail in RMO due to lack of membars between loads
 */

Processor 1:
        (0)             st      #1,[A]
        (1)             st      #1,[B]
Processor 2:
        (2)             ld      [A],%r1
        (3)             ld      [B],%r2
Processor 3:
        (4)             ld      [B],%r1
        (5)             ld      [A],%r2

Assertions:
A1: !(P2:%r1 = = 1 && P2:%r2 = = 0) || !(P3:%r1 = = 1 && P3:%r2 = = 0)

Possible values under all memory models:
2:r1  2:r2  3:r1  3:r2     A     B    example sequence of performance in <m
  0     0     0     0       1     1    4 5 2 0 3 1
  0     0     0     1       1     1    4 2 0 5 3 1
  0     0     1     1       1     1    2 3 0 1 4 5
  0     1     0     0       1     1    4 5 2 0 1 3
  0     1     0     1       1     1    4 2 0 5 1 3
  0     1     1     1       1     1    2 0 1 3 4 5
  1     0     0     0       1     1    4 5 0 2 3 1
  1     0     0     1       1     1    4 0 5 2 3 1
  1     0     1     1       1     1    0 2 3 1 4 5
  1     1     0     0       1     1    4 5 0 2 1 3
  1     1     0     1       1     1    4 0 5 1 2 3
  1     1     1     1       1     1    0 1 4 2 5 3

Possible values under PSO & RMO, but not under TSO:
2:r1  2:r2  3:r1  3:r2     A     B    example sequence of performance in <m
  0     0     1     0       1     1    2 3 1 4 5 0
  0     1     1     0       1     1    2 1 4 3 5 0
  1     1     1     0       1     1    1 4 5 0 2 3

Possible values under RMO, but not under PSO & TSO:
2:r1  2:r2  3:r1  3:r2     A     B    example sequence of performance in <m
  1     0     1     0       1     1    5 3 0 2 1 4
```

Figure 44—Store Atomicity Example

D.7.2 Dekker's Algorithm

The essence of Dekker's algorithm is shown in figure 45 on page 263.[11] To assure mutual exclusion, each processor signals its intent to enter a critical region by asserting a dedicated variable (*A* for processor 1 and *B* for processor 2). It then checks that the other processor does not want to enter and, if it finds the other signal variable is deasserted, it enters the critical region. This code does not guarantee that any processor can enter (that requires a retry mechanism which is omitted here), but it does guarantee mutual exclusion, which means that it is impossible that each processor finds the other's lock idle (= 0) when it enters cthe ritical section.

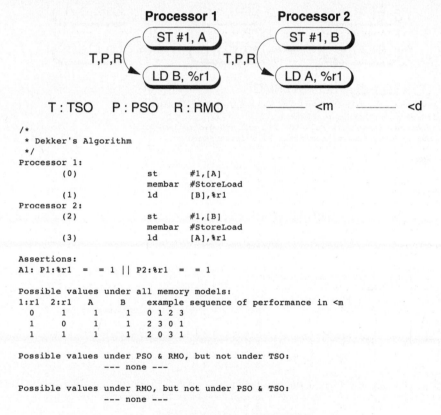

```
/*
 * Dekker's Algorithm
 */
Processor 1:
        (0)                 st      #1,[A]
                            membar  #StoreLoad
        (1)                 ld      [B],%r1
Processor 2:
        (2)                 st      #1,[B]
                            membar  #StoreLoad
        (3)                 ld      [A],%r1


Assertions:
A1: P1:%r1  =  = 1 || P2:%r1  =  = 1

Possible values under all memory models:
1:r1  2:r1    A      B     example sequence of performance in <m
  0     1     1      1     0 1 2 3
  1     0     1      1     2 3 0 1
  1     1     1      1     2 0 3 1

Possible values under PSO & RMO, but not under TSO:
                --- none ---

Possible values under RMO, but not under PSO & TSO:
                --- none ---
```

Figure 45—Dekker's Algorithm

D.7.3 Indirection Through Processors

Another property of the SPARC-V9 memory models is that causal update relations are preserved, which is a side-effect of the existence of a total memory order. In the example

---

11. See also DEC Litmus Test 8 described in the *Alpha Architecture Handbook*, Digital Equipment Corporation, 1992, p. 5-14.

below, processor 3 observes updates made by processor 1. Processor 2 simply copies B to C, which does not impact the causal chain of events.

Again, this example intentionally exposes two potential error sources. In PSO (and RMO), the stores by processor 1 are not ordered automatically and may be performed out of program order. The correct code would need to insert a MEMBAR #StoreStore between these stores. In RMO (but not in PSO), the observation process 3 needs to separate the two load instructions by a MEMBAR #LoadLoad.

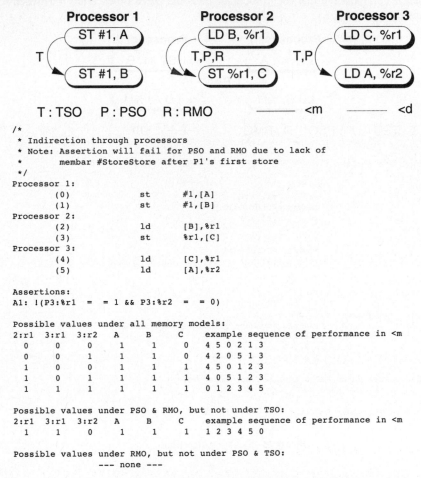

```
/*
 * Indirection through processors
 * Note: Assertion will fail for PSO and RMO due to lack of
 *       membar #StoreStore after P1's first store
 */
Processor 1:
        (0)             st      #1,[A]
        (1)             st      #1,[B]
Processor 2:
        (2)             ld      [B],%r1
        (3)             st      %r1,[C]
Processor 3:
        (4)             ld      [C],%r1
        (5)             ld      [A],%r2

Assertions:
A1: !(P3:%r1 = = 1 && P3:%r2 = = 0)

Possible values under all memory models:
2:r1  3:r1  3:r2    A     B     C     example sequence of performance in <m
  0     0     0     1     1     0     4 5 0 2 1 3
  0     0     1     1     1     0     4 2 0 5 1 3
  1     0     0     1     1     1     4 5 0 1 2 3
  1     0     1     1     1     1     4 0 5 1 2 3
  1     1     1     1     1     1     0 1 2 3 4 5

Possible values under PSO & RMO, but not under TSO:
2:r1  3:r1  3:r2    A     B     C     example sequence of performance in <m
  1     1     0     1     1     1     1 2 3 4 5 0

Possible values under RMO, but not under PSO & TSO:
                    --- none ---
```

Figure 46—Indirection Through Processors

D.7.4 PSO Behavior

The code in figure 47 on page 265 shows how different results can be obtained by allowing out of order performance of two stores in PSO and RMO models. A store to B is allowed to be performed before a store to A. If two loads of processor 2 are performed between the two stores, then the assertion below is satisfied for the PSO and RMO models.

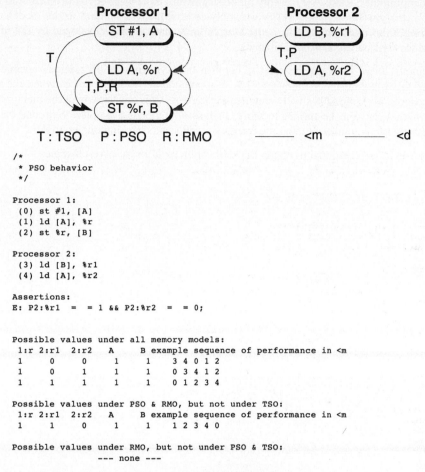

/*
 * PSO behavior
 */

```
Processor 1:
 (0) st #1, [A]
 (1) ld [A], %r
 (2) st %r, [B]

Processor 2:
 (3) ld [B], %r1
 (4) ld [A], %r2

Assertions:
E: P2:%r1  =  = 1 && P2:%r2  =  = 0;


Possible values under all memory models:
1:r 2:r1  2:r2    A    B example sequence of performance in <m
 1     0     0     1    1    3 4 0 1 2
 1     0     1     1    1    0 3 4 1 2
 1     1     1     1    1    0 1 2 3 4

Possible values under PSO & RMO, but not under TSO:
1:r 2:r1  2:r2    A    B example sequence of performance in <m
 1     1     0     1    1    1 2 3 4 0

Possible values under RMO, but not under PSO & TSO:
                  --- none ---
```

Figure 47—PSO Behavior

D.7.5 Application to Compilers

A significant problem in a multiprocessor environment arises from the fact that normal compiler optimizations which reorder code can subvert programmer intent. The SPARC-V9 memory model can be applied to the program, rather than an execution, in order to identify transformations that can be applied, provided that the program has a proper set of MEMBARs in place. In this case, the dependence order is a program dependence order, rather than a trace dependence order, and must include the dependences from all possible executions.

D.7.6 Verifying Memory Models

While defining the SPARC-V9 memory models, software tools were developed that auto-matically analyze and formally verify assembly-code sequences running in the models. The core of this collection of tools is the Murphi finite-state verifier developed by David Dill and his students at Stanford University.

For example, these tools can be used to confirm that synchronization routines operate properly in various memory models and to generate counter example traces when they fail. The tools work by exhaustively enumerating system states in a version of the memory model, so they can only be applied to fairly small assembly code examples. We found the tools to be helpful in understanding the memory models and checking our examples.[12]

Contact SPARC International to obtain the verification tools and a set of examples.

---

12. For a discussion of an earlier application of similar tools to TSO and PSO, see David Dill, Seungjoon Park, and Andreas G. Nowatzyk, "Formal Specification of Abstract Memory Models" in *Research on Integrated Systems: Proceedings of the 1993 Symposium*, Ed. Gaetano Borriello and Carl Ebeling, MIT Press, 1993.

E Opcode Maps

E.1 Overview

This appendix contains the SPARC-V9 instruction opcode maps.

Opcodes marked with a dash '—' are reserved; an attempt to execute a reserved opcode shall cause a trap, unless it is an implementation-specific extension to the instruction set. See 6.3.11, "Reserved Opcodes and Instruction Fields," for more information.

In this appendix and in Appendix A, "Instruction Definitions," certain opcodes are marked with mnemonic superscripts. These superscripts and their meanings are defined in table 21 on page 131. For deprecated opcodes, see the appropriate instruction pages in Appendix A, "Instruction Definitions," for preferred substitute instructions.

E.2 Tables

Table 30—*op*[1:0]

op [1:0]			
0	**1**	**2**	**3**
Branches & SETHI *See table 31*	CALL	Arithmetic & Misc. *See table 32*	Loads/Stores *See table 33*

Table 31—*op2*[2:0] (*op* = 0)

op2 [2:0]							
0	**1**	**2**	**3**	**4**	**5**	**6**	**7**
ILLTRAP	BPcc *See table 36*	Bicc^D *See table 36*	BPr *See table 37*	SETHI NOP†	FBPfcc *See table 36*	FBfcc^D *See table 36*	—

†*rd* = 0, *imm22* = 0

Table 32—*op3*[5:0] (*op* = 2)

		op3 [5:4]			
		0	**1**	**2**	**3**
op3 [3:0]	**0**	ADD	ADDcc	TADDcc	WRY^D (*rd* = 0) — (*rd*=1) WRCCR (*rd*=2) WRASI (*rd*=3) WRASR^{PASR} (*see* A.62) WRFPRS (*rd*=6) SIR (*rd*=15, *rs1*=0, *i*=1)
	1	AND	ANDcc	TSUBcc	SAVED^P (*fcn* = 0), RESTORED^P (*fcn* = 1)
	2	OR	ORcc	TADDccTV^D	WRPR^P
	3	XOR	XORcc	TSUBccTV^D	—
	4	SUB	SUBcc	MULScc^D	FPop1 *See table 34*
	5	ANDN	ANDNcc	SLL (*x* = 0), SLLX (*x* = 1)	FPop2 *See table 35*
	6	ORN	ORNcc	SRL (*x* = 0), SRLX (*x* = 1)	IMPDEP1
	7	XNOR	XNORcc	SRA (*x* = 0), SRAX (*x* = 1)	IMPDEP2
	8	ADDC	ADDCcc	RDY^D (*rs1* = 0) — (*rs1* = 1) RDCCR (*rs1*=2) RDASI (*rs1*=3) RDTICK^{PNPT} (*rs1*=4) RDPC (*rs1*=5) RDFPRS (*rs1*=6) RDASR^{PASR} (*see* A.43) MEMBAR (*rs1* = 15, *rd*=0, *i* = 1) STBAR^D (*rs1* = 15, *rd*=0, *i* = 0)	JMPL
	9	MULX	—	—	RETURN
	A	UMUL^D	UMULcc^D	RDPR	Tcc *See table 36*
	B	SMUL^D	SMULcc^D	FLUSHW	FLUSH
	C	SUBC	SUBCcc	MOVcc	SAVE
	D	UDIVX	—	SDIVX	RESTORE
	E	UDIV^D	UDIVcc^D	POPC (*rs1* = 0) — (*rs1*>0)	DONE^P (*fcn* = 0) RETRY^P (*fcn* = 1)
	F	SDIV^D	SDIVcc^D	MOVr *See table 37*	—

Table 33—*op3*[5:0] (*op* = 3)

		op3 [5:4]			
		0	**1**	**2**	**3**
op3 [3:0]	**0**	LDUW	LDUWA[PASI]	LDF	LDFA[PASI]
	1	LDUB	LDUBA[PASI]	LDFSR[D], LDXFSR	—
	2	LDUH	LDUHA[PASI]	LDQF	LDQFA[PASI]
	3	LDD[D]	LDDA[D, PASI]	LDDF	LDDFA[PASI]
	4	STW	STWA[PASI]	STF	STFA[PASI]
	5	STB	STBA[PASI]	STFSR[D], STXFSR	—
	6	STH	STHA[PASI]	STQF	STQFA[PASI]
	7	STD[D]	STDA[PASI]	STDF	STDFA[PASI]
	8	LDSW	LDSWA[PASI]	—	—
	9	LDSB	LDSBA[PASI]	—	—
	A	LDSH	LDSHA[PASI]	—	—
	B	LDX	LDXA[PASI]	—	—
	C	—	—	—	CASA[PASI]
	D	LDSTUB	LDSTUBA[PASI]	PREFETCH	PREFETCHA[PASI]
	E	STX	STXA[PASI]	—	CASXA[PASI]
	F	SWAP[D]	SWAPA[D, PASI]	—	—

Table 34—opf[8:0] (*op* = 2, *op3* = 34_{16} = FPop1)

opf[8:4]	0	1	2	3	4	5	6	7	8	9	A	B	C	D	E	F
00	—	FMOVs	FMOVd	FMOVq	—	FNEGs	FNEGd	FNEGq	—	FABSs	FABSd	FABSq	—	—	—	—
01	—	—	—	—	—	—	—	—	—	—	—	—	—	—	—	—
02	—	—	—	—	—	—	—	—	—	FSQRTs	FSQRTd	FSQRTq	—	—	—	—
03	—	—	—	—	—	—	—	—	—	—	—	—	—	—	—	—
04	—	FADDs	FADDd	FADDq	—	FSUBs	FSUBd	FSUBq	—	FMULs	FMULd	FMULq	—	FDIVs	FDIVd	FDIVq
05	—	—	—	—	—	—	—	—	—	—	—	—	—	—	—	—
06	—	—	—	—	—	—	—	—	—	FsMULd	—	—	—	—	FdMULq	—
07	—	—	—	—	—	—	—	—	—	—	—	—	—	—	—	—
08	—	FsTOx	FdTOx	FqTOx	FxTOs	—	—	—	FxTOd	—	—	—	FxTOq	—	—	—
09	—	—	—	—	—	—	—	—	—	—	—	—	—	—	—	—
0A	—	—	—	—	—	—	—	—	—	—	—	—	—	—	—	—
0B	—	—	—	—	—	—	—	—	—	—	—	—	—	—	—	—
0C	—	—	—	—	FiTOs	—	FdTOs	FqTOs	FiTOd	FsTOd	—	FqTOd	FiTOq	FsTOq	FdTOq	—
0D	—	FsTOi	FdTOi	FqTOi	—	—	—	—	—	—	—	—	—	—	—	—
0E..1F	—	—	—	—	—	—	—	—	—	—	—	—	—	—	—	—

Table 35—opf[8:0] (op = 2, op3 = 35₁₆ = FPop2)

opf [8:4]	opf[3:0]								
	0	1	2	3	4	5	6	7	8..F
00	—	FMOVs (fcc0)	FMOVd (fcc0)	FMOVq (fcc0)	—	†	†	†	—
01	—	—	—	—	—	—	—	—	—
02	—	—	—	—	—	FMOVRsZ	FMOVRdZ	FMOVRqZ	—
03	—	—	—	—	—	—	—	—	—
04	—	FMOVs (fcc1)	FMOVd (fcc1)	FMOVq (fcc1)	—	FMOVRsLEZ	FMOVRdLEZ	FMOVRqLEZ	—
05	—	FCMPs	FCMPd	FCMPq	—	FCMPEs	FCMPEd	FCMPEq	—
06	—	—	—	—	—	FMOVRsLZ	FMOVRdLZ	FMOVRqLZ	—
07	—	—	—	—	—	—	—	—	—
08	—	FMOVs (fcc2)	FMOVd (fcc2)	FMOVq (fcc2)	—	†	†	†	—
09	—	—	—	—	—	—	—	—	—
0A	—	—	—	—	—	FMOVRsNZ	FMOVRdNZ	FMOVRqNZ	—
0B	—	—	—	—	—	—	—	—	—
0C	—	FMOVs (fcc3)	FMOVd (fcc3)	FMOVq (fcc3)	—	FMOVRsGZ	FMOVRdGZ	FMOVRqGZ	—
0D	—	—	—	—	—	—	—	—	—
0E	—	—	—	—	—	FMOVRsGEZ	FMOVRdGEZ	FMOVRqGEZ	—
0F	—	—	—	—	—	—	—	—	—
10	—	FMOVs (icc)	FMOVd (icc)	FMOVq (icc)	—	—	—	—	—
11..17	—	—	—	—	—	—	—	—	—
18	—	FMOVs (xcc)	FMOVd (xcc)	FMOVq (xcc)	—	—	—	—	—
19..1F	—	—	—	—	—	—	—	—	—

† Undefined variation of FMOVR

Table 36—*cond*[3:0]

		BPcc	Bicc[D]	FBPfcc	FBfcc[D]	Tcc
		op = 0 op2 = 1	op = 0 op2 = 2	op = 0 op2 = 5	op = 0 op2 = 6	op = 2 op3 = $3A_{16}$
cond [3:0]	0	BPN	BN[D]	FBPN	FBN[D]	TN
	1	BPE	BE[D]	FBPNE	FBNE[D]	TE
	2	BPLE	BLE[D]	FBPLG	FBLG[D]	TLE
	3	BPL	BL[D]	FBPUL	FBUL[D]	TL
	4	BPLEU	BLEU[D]	FBPL	FBL[D]	TLEU
	5	BPCS	BCS[D]	FBPUG	FBUG[D]	TCS
	6	BPNEG	BNEG[D]	FBPG	FBG[D]	TNEG
	7	BPVS	BVS[D]	FBPU	FBU[D]	TVS
	8	BPA	BA[D]	FBPA	FBA[D]	TA
	9	BPNE	BNE[D]	FBPE	FBE[D]	TNE
	A	BPG	BG[D]	FBPUE	FBUE[D]	TG
	B	BPGE	BGE[D]	FBPGE	FBGE[D]	TGE
	C	BPGU	BGU[D]	FBPUGE	FBUGE[D]	TGU
	D	BPCC	BCC[D]	FBPLE	FBLE[D]	TCC
	E	BPPOS	BPOS[D]	FBPULE	FBULE[D]	TPOS
	F	BPVC	BVC[D]	FBPO	FBO[D]	TVC

Table 37—Encoding of *rcond*[2:0] Instruction Field

		BPr	MOVr	FMOVr
		op = 0 op2 = 3	op = 2 op3 = $2F_{16}$	op = 2 op3 = 35_{16}
rcond [2:0]	0	—	—	—
	1	BRZ	MOVRZ	FMOVZ
	2	BRLEZ	MOVRLEZ	FMOVLEZ
	3	BRLZ	MOVRLZ	FMOVLZ
	4	—	—	—
	5	BRNZ	MOVRNZ	FMOVNZ
	6	BRGZ	MOVRGZ	FMOVGZ
	7	BRGEZ	MOVRGEZ	FMOVGEZ

Table 38—*cc/opf_cc* Fields (MOVcc and FMOVcc)

opf_cc			Condition code selected
cc2	cc1	cc0	
0	0	0	fcc0
0	0	1	fcc1
0	1	0	fcc2
0	1	1	fcc3
1	0	0	icc
1	0	1	—
1	1	0	xcc
1	1	1	—

Table 39—*cc* Fields (FBPfcc, FCMP and FCMPE)

cc1	cc0	Condition code selected
0	0	fcc0
0	1	fcc1
1	0	fcc2
1	1	fcc3

Table 40—*cc* Fields (BPcc and Tcc)

cc1	cc0	Condition code selected
0	0	icc
0	1	—
1	0	xcc
1	1	—

F SPARC-V9 MMU Requirements

F.1 Introduction

This appendix describes the boundary conditions that all SPARC-V9 MMUs must satisfy. The appendix does not define the architecture of any specific memory management unit. It is possible to build a SPARC-V9-compliant system without an MMU.

F.1.1 Definitions

address space:
> A range of locations accessible with a 64-bit virtual address. Different address spaces may use the same virtual address to refer to different physical locations.

aliases:
> Two virtual addresses are aliases of each other if they refer to the same physical address.

context:
> A set of translations used to support a particular address space.

page:
> The range of virtual addresses translated by a single translation element. The size of a page is the size of the range translated by a single translation element. Different pages may have different sizes. Associated with a page or with a translation element are attributes (e.g., restricted, permission, etc.) and statistics (e.g., referenced, modified, etc.)

translation element:
> Used to translate a range of virtual addresses to a range of physical addresses.

F.2 Overview

All SPARC-V9 MMUs must provide the following basic functions:

— Translate 64-bit virtual addresses to physical addresses. This translation may be implemented with one or more page sizes.

— Provide the RED_state operation, as defined in 7.2.1, "RED_state."

— Provide a method for disabling the MMU. When the MMU is disabled, no translation occurs: Physical Address<*N*:0> = Virtual Address<*N*:0>, where *N* is implementation-dependent. Furthermore, the disabled MMU will not perform any
memory protection (see F.4.2, "Memory Protection") or prefetch and non-faulting
load violation (see F.4.3, "Prefetch and Non-Faulting Load Violation") checks.

IMPL. DEP. #117: Whether PREFETCH and non-faulting load always succeed when the
MMU is disabled is implementation-dependent.

— Provide page-level protections. Conventional protections (Read, Write, Execute)
for both privileged and nonprivileged accesses may be provided.

— Provide page-level enabling and disabling of prefetch and non-faulting load operation. The MMU, however, need not provide separate protection mechanisms for
prefetch and non-faulting load.

— Support multiple address spaces (ASIs). The MMU must support the address
spaces as defined in F.3.1, "Information the MMU Expects from the Processor."

— Provide page-level statistics such as referenced and modified.

The above requirements apply only to those systems that include SPARC-V9 MMUs. See
F.8, "SPARC-V9 Systems without an MMU."

F.3   The Processor-MMU Interface

A SPARC-V9 MMU must support at least two types of addresses:

(1) **Virtual Addresses**, which map all system-wide, program-visible memory. A
SPARC-V9 MMU may choose not to support translation for the entire 64-bit virtual address space, as long as addresses outside the supported virtual address range
are treated either as No_translation or Translation_not_valid (see F.3.3, "Information the MMU Sends to the Processor").

(2) **Physical Addresses**, which map real physical memory and I/O device space.
There is no minimum requirement for how many physical address bits a SPARC-
V9 MMU must support.

A SPARC-V9 MMU translates virtual addresses from the processor into physical
addresses, as illustrated in figure 48.

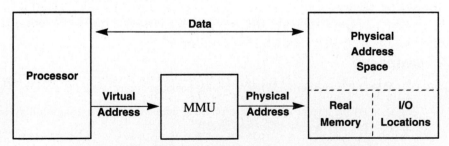

Figure 48—Logical Diagram of a SPARC-V9 System with an MMU

Figure 48 shows only the address and data paths between the processor and the MMU. The control interface between the processor and the MMU is discussed in F.3.1, "Information the MMU Expects from the Processor," and F.3.3, "Information the MMU Sends to the Processor."

F.3.1 Information the MMU Expects from the Processor

A SPARC-V9 MMU expects the following information to accompany each virtual address from the processor:

RED_state:
> Indicates whether the MMU should operate in RED_state, as defined in 7.2.1, "RED_state."

Data / Instruction:
> Indicates whether the access is an instruction fetch or data access (load or store).

Prefetch:
> Indicates whether the data (Data / Instruction = Data) access was initiated by one of the SPARC-V9 prefetch instructions.

Privileged:
> Indicates whether this access is privileged.

Read / Write:
> Indicates whether this access is a read (instruction fetch or data load) or a write (data store) operation.

Atomic:
> Indicates whether this is an atomic load-store operation. Whenever atomic is asserted, the value of "Read/Write" is treated by the MMU as "don't care."

ASI:
> An 8-bit address space identifier. See 6.3.1.3, "Address Space Identifiers (ASIs)," for the list of ASIs that the MMU must support.

F.3.2 Attributes the MMU Associates with Each Mapping

In addition to translating virtual addresses to physical addresses, a SPARC-V9 MMU also stores associated attributes, either with each mapping or with each page, depending upon the implementation. Some of these attributes may be associated implicitly, as opposed to explicitly, with the mapping. This information includes

Restricted:
> Only privileged accesses are allowed (see F.3.1, "Information the MMU Expects from the Processor"); nonprivileged accesses are disallowed.

Read, Write, and Execute Permissions:
> An MMU may allow zero or more of read, write, and execute permissions, on a per-mapping basis. Read permission is necessary for data read accesses and atomic accesses. Write permission is necessary for data write accesses and atomic

accesses. Execute permission is necessary for instruction accesses. At a minimum, an MMU must allow for "all permissions," "no permissions," and "no write permission"; optionally, it can provide "execute only" and "write only," or any combination of "read/write/execute" permissions.

Prefetchable:

The presence of this attribute indicates that accesses made with the prefetch indication from the processor are allowed; otherwise, they are disallowed. See F.3.1, "Information the MMU Expects from the Processor."

Non-faultable:

The presence of this attribute indicates that accesses made with ASI_PRIMARY_NO-FAULT{_LITTLE} and ASI_SECONDARY_NOFAULT{_LITTLE} are allowed; otherwise, they are disallowed. An implementation may choose to combine the prefetchable and non-faultable attributes into a single "No Side Effects" attribute; that is, "reads from this address do not cause side effects, such as clear on read."

F.3.3 Information the MMU Sends to the Processor

The processor can expect one and only one of the following signals coming from any SPARC-V9 MMU for each translation requested:

Translation_error:

The MMU has detected an error (for example, parity error) in the translation process. Can cause a *data_access_error* or *instruction_access_error* exception.

No_translation:

The MMU is unable to translate the virtual address, since no translation exists for it. Some implementations may not provide this information and provide only Translation_not_valid. Can cause either a *data_access_exception* or an *instruction_-access_exception* exception.

Translation_not_valid:

The MMU is unable to translate the virtual address, since it cannot find a valid translation. Some implementations may not provide this information and provide only No_translation. Can cause either a *data_access_MMU_miss* or an *instruction_-access_MMU_miss* exception.

Privilege_violation:

The MMU has detected a privilege violation, i.e., an access to a restricted page when the access does not have the required privilege (see F.3.1, "Information the MMU Expects from the Processor"). Can cause either a *data_access_protection* or an *instruction_access_protection* exception.

Protection_violation:

The MMU has detected a protection violation, which is defined to be a read, write, or instruction fetch attempt to a page that does not have read, write, or execute permission, respectively. Can cause either a *data_access_protection* or an *instruction_-access_protection* exception.

Prefetch_violation:

The MMU has detected an attempt to prefetch from a page for which prefetching is disabled.

NF-Load_violation:

The MMU has detected an attempt to perform a non-faulting load from a page for which non-faulting loads are disabled.

Translation_successful:

The MMU has successfully translated the virtual address to a physical address; none of the conditions described above has been detected.

F.4 Components of the SPARC-V9 MMU Architecture

A SPARC-V9 MMU should contain the following:

— Logic that implements virtual-to-physical address translation

— Logic that provides memory protection

— Logic that supports prefetching as noted in A.41, "Prefetch Data"

— Logic that supports non-faulting loading, as noted in 8.3, "Addressing and Alternate Address Spaces"

— A method for specifying the primary, secondary and, optionally, nucleus address spaces

— A method for supplying information related to failed translations

— A method for collecting "referenced" and "modified" statistics

F.4.1 Virtual-to-Physical Address Translation

A SPARC-V9 MMU tries to translate every virtual address it receives into a physical address as long as:

— The MMU is enabled.

— The processor indicates that this is a non-RED_state instruction fetch (see the Data/Instruction description in F.3.1, "Information the MMU Expects from the Processor") or a data access with an ASI that indicates a translatable address space.

Although the MMU will attempt to translate every virtual address that meets the above two conditions, it need not guarantee that it can provide a translation every time. When the MMU encounters a virtual address that it cannot translate, it asserts either Translation_error, No_translation, or Translation_not_valid, as discussed in F.3.3, "Information the MMU Sends to the Processor."

F.4.2 Memory Protection

For each virtual address for which a SPARC-V9 MMU can provide a translation, the MMU checks whether memory protection would be violated. More specifically, the MMU

— Indicates Privilege_violation (see F.3.3) if the translation information indicates a restricted page but the access was not privileged (see F.3.1)

— Indicates Protection_violation (see F.3.3) if a read, write, or instruction fetch uses a translation that does not grant read, write, or execute permission, respectively

— Indicates Protection_violation (see F.3.3) if an atomic load-store uses a translation that does not grant both read and write permission

F.4.3 Prefetch and Non-Faulting Load Violation

For each virtual address, the MMU checks for prefetch or non-faulting load violation as long as

— The MMU can provide a translation, and

— The MMU does not detect any memory protection violation, as discussed in F.4.2, "Memory Protection."

More specifically, the MMU performs the following before sending the physical address to the rest of the memory system:

— Asserts Prefetch_violation (see F.3.3) if an access with the prefetch indication (see F.3.1) uses a translation that lacks the prefetchable attribute (see F.3.2)

— Asserts NF-Load_violation (see F.3.3) if the ASI (see F.3.1) indicates this access is a non-faulting load, but the translation it uses lacks the non-faultable attribute (see F.3.2)

F.4.4 Contexts

The MMU must support two contexts:

(1) Primary Context

(2) Secondary Context

In addition, it is also recommended that the MMU support a third context:

(3) Nucleus Context

On data accesss, the MMU decides which of these three contexts to use based on the ASI field, as illustrated in table 41. Because the SPARC-V9 MMU cannot determine the instruction opcode, it treats all data accesses with ASI_PRIMARY{_LITTLE} as normal loads or stores, even though the processor may issue them with load/store alternate instructions.

Table 41—Context Used for Data Access

MMU Inputs		Output Context
ASI	Mode	
ASI_PRIMARY	Either	Primary
ASI_PRIMARY_LITTLE	Either	Primary
ASI_PRIMARY_NOFAULT	Either	Primary
ASI_PRIMARY_NOFAULT_LITTLE	Either	Primary
ASI_AS_IF_USER_PRIMARY	Privileged	Primary
ASI_AS_IF_USER_PRIMARY_LITTLE	Privileged	Primary
ASI_SECONDARY	Either	Secondary
ASI_SECONDARY_LITTLE	Either	Secondary
ASI_SECONDARY_NOFAULT	Either	Secondary
ASI_SECONDARY_NOFAULT_LITTLE	Either	Secondary
ASI_AS_IF_USER_SECONDARY	Privileged	Secondary
ASI_AS_IF_USER_SECONDARY_LITTLE	Privileged	Secondary
ASI_NUCLEUS [†]	Privileged	Nucleus
ASI_NUCLEUS_LITTLE [†]	Privileged	Nucleus

[†] Support for the nucleus context is only a recommendation; if an implementation does not support the nucleus context it may ignore this row.

On instruction fetch, the MMU decides which context to use based on the ASI field, as illustrated in table 42. Note that the secondary context is never used for instruction fetch.

Table 42—Context Used for Instruction Access

ASI	Mode	Context
ASI_PRIMARY	Either	Primary
ASI_NUCLEUS [†]	Privileged [‡]	Nucleus

[†] Support for the Nucleus Context is only a recommendation; if an implementation does not support the Nucleus Context it may ignore this row.

[‡] It is implementation-dependent whether instruction fetch using ASI_NUCLEUS in nonprivileged mode is allowed.

F.4.5 Fault Status and Fault Address

A SPARC-V9 MMU must provide the following:

— Fault status information that specifies which condition listed in F.3.3, "Information the MMU Sends to the Processor," has resulted in a translation-related processor trap, and any other information necessary for privileged software to determine the cause of the trap; for example, ASI, Read/Write, Data/Instruction, etc.

— The Fault address associated with the failed translation. Since the address from an instruction translation failure is available in the processor as the trap PC, the MMU is not required to save the address of an instruction translation failure.

F.4.6   Referenced and Modified Statistics

A SPARC-V9 MMU shall allow, either through hardware, software, or some combination thereof, for the collection of "referenced" and "modified" statistics associated with translations and/or physical pages. That is, there must be a method to determine if a page has been referenced, a method to determine if a page has been modified, and a method for clearing the indications that a page has been referenced and/or modified. These statistics may be kept on either a per-translation basis or a per-physical-page basis.

It is implementation-dependent whether the referenced and/or modified statistics are updated when an access is performed or when the translation for that access is performed.

F.5   RED_state Processing

It is recommended that the MMU perform as follows when the processor is in RED_state:

— Instruction address translation is a straight-through physical map; that is, the MMU is always suppressed for instruction access in RED_state.

— Data address translation is handled normally; that is, the MMU is used if it is enabled. Note that any event which causes the processor to enter RED_state also disables the MMU, however, the handler executing in RED_state may reenable the MMU.

F.6   Virtual Address Aliasing

Hardware and privileged software must cooperate so that multiple virtual addresses aliased to the same physical address appear to be consistent as defined by the memory models described in Chapter 8, "Memory Models." Depending upon the implementation, this may require allowing multiple translations to coexist only if they meet some implementation-dependent alignment constraint, or it may require that software ensure that only one translation is in effect at any given time.

F.7   MMU Demap Operation

The SPARC-V9 MMU must provide a mechanism for privileged software to invalidate some or all of the virtual-to-physical address translations.

F.8   SPARC-V9 Systems without an MMU

It is possible to build a SPARC-V9 system that does not have an MMU. Such a system should behave as if contains an MMU that is disabled.

G Suggested Assembly Language Syntax

This appendix supports Appendix A, "Instruction Definitions." Each instruction description in Appendix A includes a table that describes the suggested assembly language format for that instruction. This appendix describes the notation used in those assembly language syntax descriptions and lists some synthetic instructions that may be provided by a SPARC-V9 assembler for the convenience of assembly language programmers.

G.1 Notation Used

The notations defined here are also used in the syntax descriptions in Appendix A.

Items in `typewriter font` are literals to be written exactly as they appear. Items in *italic font* are metasymbols that are to be replaced by numeric or symbolic values in actual SPARC-V9 assembly language code. For example, "*imm_asi*" would be replaced by a number in the range 0 to 255 (the value of the *imm_asi* bits in the binary instruction), or by a symbol bound to such a number.

Subscripts on metasymbols further identify the placement of the operand in the generated binary instruction. For example, reg_{rs2} is a *reg* (register name) whose binary value will be placed in the *rs2* field of the resulting instruction.

G.1.1 Register Names

reg:
> A *reg* is an integer register name. It may have any of the following values:[1]

`%r0..%r31`	
`%g0..%g7`	(*global* registers; same as `%r0..%r7`)
`%o0..%o7`	(*out* registers; same as `%r8..%r15`)
`%l0..%l7`	(*local* registers; same as `%r16..%r23`)
`%i0..%i7`	(*in* registers; same as `%r24..%r31`)
`%fp`	(frame pointer; conventionally same as `%i6`)
`%sp`	(stack pointer; conventionally same as `%o6`)

---

1. In actual usage, the `%sp`, `%fp`, `%gn`, `%on`, `%ln`, and `%in` forms are preferred over `%rn`.

Subscripts identify the placement of the operand in the binary instruction as one of the following:

reg_{rs1}	(*rs1* field)
reg_{rs2}	(*rs2* field)
reg_{rd}	(*rd* field)

freg:

An *freg* is a floating-point register name. It may have the following values:

```
%f0, %f1, %f2 .. %f63
```
        See 5.1.4, "Floating-Point Registers"

Subscripts further identify the placement of the operand in the binary instruction as one of the following:

$freg_{rs1}$	(*rs1* field)
$freg_{rs2}$	(*rs2* field)
$freg_{rd}$	(*rd* field)

asr_reg:

An *asr_reg* is an Ancillary State Register name. It may have one of the following values:

```
%asr16 .. %asr31
```

Subscripts further identify the placement of the operand in the binary instruction as one of the following:

asr_reg_{rs1}	(*rs1* field)
asr_reg_{rd}	(*rd* field)

i_or_x_cc:

An *i_or_x_cc* specifies a set of integer condition codes, those based on either the 32-bit result of an operation (`icc`) or on the full 64-bit result (`xcc`). It may have either of the following values:

```
%icc
%xcc
```

fccn:

An *fccn* specifies a set of floating-point condition codes. It may have any of the following values:

```
%fcc0
%fcc1
%fcc2
%fcc3
```

G.1.2 Special Symbol Names

Certain special symbols appear in the syntax table in `typewriter font`. They must be written exactly as they are shown, including the leading percent sign (`%`).

The symbol names and the registers or operators to which they refer are as follows:

```
%asi
```
        Address Space Identifier register

%canrestore	Restorable Windows register
%cansave	Savable Windows register
%cleanwin	Clean Windows register
%cwp	Current Window Pointer register
%fq	Floating-Point Queue
%fsr	Floating-Point State Register
%otherwin	Other Windows register
%pc	Program Counter register
%pil	Processor Interrupt Level register
%pstate	Processor State register
%tba	Trap Base Address register
%tick	Tick (cycle count) register
%tl	Trap Level register
%tnpc	Trap Next Program Counter register
%tpc	Trap Program Counter register
%tstate	Trap State register
%tt	Trap Type register
%ccr	Condition Codes Register
%fprs	Floating-Point Registers State register
%ver	Version register
%wstate	Window State register
%y	Y register

The following special symbol names are unary operators that perform the functions described:

%uhi	Extracts bits 63..42 (high 22 bits of upper word) of its operand
%ulo	Extracts bits 41..32 (low-order 10 bits of upper word) of its operand
%hi	Extracts bits 31..10 (high-order 22 bits of low-order word) of its operand
%lo	Extracts bits 9..0 (low-order 10 bits) of its operand

Certain predefined value names appear in the syntax table in `typewriter font`. They must be written exactly as they are shown, including the leading sharp sign (#).

The value names and the values to which they refer are as follows:

#n_reads	0	(for PREFETCH instruction)
#one_read	1	(for PREFETCH instruction)
#n_writes	2	(for PREFETCH instruction)
#one_write	3	(for PREFETCH instruction)
#page	4	(for PREFETCH instruction)
#Sync	40_{16}	(for MEMBAR instruction *cmask* field)
#MemIssue	20_{16}	(for MEMBAR instruction *cmask* field)
#Lookaside	10_{16}	(for MEMBAR instruction *cmask* field)

#StoreStore	08_{16}	(for MEMBAR instruction *mmask* field)
#LoadStore	04_{16}	(for MEMBAR instruction *mmask* field)
#StoreLoad	02_{16}	(for MEMBAR instruction *mmask* field)
#LoadLoad	01_{16}	(for MEMBAR instruction *mmask* field)
#ASI_AIUP	10_{16}	ASI_AS_IF_USER_PRIMARY
#ASI_AIUS	11_{16}	ASI_AS_IF_USER_SECONDARY
#ASI_AIUP_L	18_{16}	ASI_AS_IF_USER_PRIMARY_LITTLE
#ASI_AIUS_L	19_{16}	ASI_AS_IF_USER_SECONDARY_LITTLE
#ASI_P	80_{16}	ASI_PRIMARY
#ASI_S	81_{16}	ASI_SECONDARY
#ASI_PNF	82_{16}	ASI_PRIMARY_NOFAULT
#ASI_SNF	83_{16}	ASI_SECONDARY_NOFAULT
#ASI_P_L	88_{16}	ASI_PRIMARY_LITTLE
#ASI_S_L	89_{16}	ASI_SECONDARY_LITTLE
#ASI_PNF_L	$8A_{16}$	ASI_PRIMARY_NOFAULT_LITTLE
#ASI_SNF_L	$8B_{16}$	ASI_SECONDARY_NOFAULT_LITTLE

The full names of the ASIs may also be defined:

#ASI_AS_IF_USER_PRIMARY	10_{16}
#ASI_AS_IF_USER_SECONDARY	11_{16}
#ASI_AS_IF_USER_PRIMARY_LITTLE	18_{16}
#ASI_AS_IF_USER_SECONDARY_LITTLE	19_{16}
#ASI_PRIMARY	80_{16}
#ASI_SECONDARY	81_{16}
#ASI_PRIMARY_NOFAULT	82_{16}
#ASI_SECONDARY_NOFAULT	83_{16}
#ASI_PRIMARY_LITTLE	88_{16}
#ASI_SECONDARY_LITTLE	89_{16}
#ASI_PRIMARY_NOFAULT_LITTLE	$8A_{16}$
#ASI_SECONDARY_NOFAULT_LITTLE	$8B_{16}$

G.1.3 Values

Some instructions use operand values as follows:

const4	A constant that can be represented in 4 bits
const22	A constant that can be represented in 22 bits
imm_asi	An alternate address space identifier (0..255)
simm7	A signed immediate constant that can be represented in 7 bits
simm10	A signed immediate constant that can be represented in 10 bits
simm11	A signed immediate constant that can be represented in 11 bits
simm13	A signed immediate constant that can be represented in 13 bits
value	Any 64-bit value
shcnt32	A shift count from 0..31
shcnt64	A shift count from 0..63

G.1.4 Labels

A label is a sequence of characters that comprises alphabetic letters (a–z, A–Z [with upper and lower case distinct]), underscores (_), dollar signs ($), periods (.), and decimal digits (0-9). A label may contain decimal digits, but may not begin with one. A local label contains digits only.

G.1.5 Other Operand Syntax

Some instructions allow several operand syntaxes, as follows:

reg_plus_imm may be any of the following:

reg_{rs1}	(equivalent to reg_{rs1} + %g0)
reg_{rs1} + $simm13$	
reg_{rs1} − $simm13$	
$simm13$	(equivalent to %g0 + $simm13$)
$simm13$ + reg_{rs1}	(equivalent to reg_{rs1} + $simm13$)

address may be any of the following:

reg_{rs1}	(equivalent to reg_{rs1} + %g0)
reg_{rs1} + $simm13$	
reg_{rs1} − $simm13$	
$simm13$	(equivalent to %g0 + $simm13$)
$simm13$ + reg_{rs1}	(equivalent to reg_{rs1} + $simm13$)
reg_{rs1} + reg_{rs2}	

membar_mask is the following:

const7	A constant that can be represented in 7 bits. Typically, this is an expression involving the logical **or** of some combination of #Lookaside, #MemIssue, #Sync, #StoreStore, #LoadStore, #StoreLoad, and #LoadLoad.

prefetch_fcn (prefetch function) may be any of the following:

```
#n_reads
#one_read
#n_writes
#one_write
#page
0..31
```

regaddr (register-only address) may be any of the following:

reg_{rs1}	(equivalent to reg_{rs1} + %g0)
reg_{rs1} + reg_{rs2}	

reg_or_imm (register or immediate value) may be either of:

reg_{rs2}
$simm13$

reg_or_imm10 (register or immediate value) may be either of:

reg_{rs2}
simm10

reg_or_imm11 (register or immediate value) may be either of:

reg_{rs2}
simm11

reg_or_shcnt (register or shift count value) may be any of:

reg_{rs2}
shcnt32
shcnt64

software_trap_number may be any of the following:

reg_{rs1} (equivalent to reg_{rs1} + %g0)
reg_{rs1} + *simm7*
reg_{rs1} − *simm7*
simm7   (equivalent to %g0 + *simm7*)
simm7 + reg_{rs1} (equivalent to reg_{rs1} + *simm7*)
reg_{rs1} + reg_{rs2}

The resulting operand value (software trap number) must be in the range 0..127, inclusive.

G.1.6 Comments

It is suggested that two types of comments be accepted by SPARC-V9 assemblers: C-style "/*...*/" comments, which may span multiple lines, and "!..." comments, which extend from the "!" to the end of the line.

G.2 Syntax Design

The suggested SPARC-V9 assembly language syntax is designed so that

— The destination operand (if any) is consistently specified as the last (rightmost) operand in an assembly language instruction.

— A reference to the **contents** of a memory location (in a Load, Store, CASA, CASXA, LDSTUB(A), or SWAP(A) instruction) is always indicated by square brackets ([ ]); a reference to the **address** of a memory location (such as in a JMPL, CALL, or SETHI) is specified directly, without square brackets.

G.3 Synthetic Instructions

Table 43 describes the mapping of a set of synthetic (or "pseudo") instructions to actual instructions. These and other synthetic instructions may be provided in a SPARC-V9 assembler for the convenience of assembly language programmers.

Note that synthetic instructions should not be confused with "pseudo-ops," which typically provide information to the assembler but do not generate instructions. Synthetic instructions always generate instructions; they provide more mnemonic syntax for standard SPARC-V9 instructions.

Table 43—Mapping Synthetic to SPARC-V9 Instructions

Synthetic instruction		SPARC-V9 instruction(s)		Comment
cmp	reg_{rs1}, reg_or_imm	subcc	reg_{rs1}, reg_or_imm, %g0	*compare*
jmp	*address*	jmpl	*address*, %g0	
call	*address*	jmpl	*address*, %o7	
iprefetch	*label*	bn,a,pt	%xcc, *label*	*instruction prefetch*
tst	reg_{rs1}	orcc	%g0, reg_{rs1}, %g0	*test*
ret		jmpl	%i7+8, %g0	*return from subroutine*
retl		jmpl	%o7+8, %g0	*return from leaf subroutine*
restore		restore	%g0, %g0, %g0	*trivial* restore
save		save	%g0, %g0, %g0	*trivial* save (*Warning: trivial* save *should only be used in kernel code!*)
setuw	*value*, reg_{rd}	sethi	%hi(*value*), reg_{rd}	*(when ((value&$3FF_{16}$) = = 0))*
			— or —	
		or	%g0, *value*, reg_{rd}	*(when $0 \leq value \leq 4095$)*
			— or —	
		sethi	%hi(*value*), reg_{rd};	*(otherwise)*
		or	reg_{rd}, %lo(*value*), reg_{rd}	*Warning: do not use* setuw *in the delay slot of a DCTI.*
set	*value*, reg_{rd}			*synonym for* setuw
setsw	*value*, reg_{rd}	sethi	%hi(*value*), reg_{rd}	*(when (value > = 0) and ((value & $3FF_{16}$) = = 0))*
			— or —	
		or	%g0, *value*, reg_{rd}	*(when $-4096 \leq value \leq 4095$)*
			— or —	
		sethi	%hi(*value*), reg_{rd}	*(otherwise, if (value < 0) and ((value & $3FF_{16}$) = = 0))*
		sra	reg_{rd}, %g0, reg_{rd}	
			— or —	
		sethi	%hi(*value*), reg_{rd};	*(otherwise, if value > = 0)*
		or	reg_{rd}, %lo(*value*), reg_{rd}	
			— or —	
		sethi	%hi(*value*), reg_{rd};	*(otherwise, if value < 0)*
		or	reg_{rd}, %lo(*value*), reg_{rd}	
		sra	reg_{rd}, %g0, reg_{rd}	*Warning: do not use* setsw *in the delay slot of a CTI.*
setx	*value*, *reg*, reg_{rd}	sethi	%uhi(*value*), *reg*	*create 64-bit constant*
		or	*reg*, %ulo(*value*), *reg*	*("reg" is used as a temporary register)*
		sllx	*reg*, 32, *reg*	
		sethi	%hi(*value*), reg_{rd}	*Note that* setx *optimizations are possible, but not enumerated here. The worst-case is shown. Warning: do not use* setx *in the delay slot of a CTI.*
		or	reg_{rd}, *reg*, reg_{rd}	
		or	reg_{rd}, %lo(*value*), reg_{rd}	

Table 43—Mapping Synthetic to SPARC-V9 Instructions (*Continued*)

Synthetic instruction		SPARC-V9 instruction(s)		Comment
signx	reg_{rs1}, reg_{rd}	sra	reg_{rs1}, %g0, reg_{rd}	sign-extend 32-bit value to 64
signx	reg_{rd}	sra	reg_{rd}, %g0, reg_{rd}	bits
not	reg_{rs1}, reg_{rd}	xnor	reg_{rs1}, %g0, reg_{rd}	one's complement
not	reg_{rd}	xnor	reg_{rd}, %g0, reg_{rd}	one's complement
neg	reg_{rs2}, reg_{rd}	sub	%g0, reg_{rs2}, reg_{rd}	two's complement
neg	reg_{rd}	sub	%g0, reg_{rd}, reg_{rd}	two's complement
cas	[reg_{rs1}], reg_{rs2}, reg_{rd}	casa	[reg_{rs1}]ASI_P, reg_{rs2}, reg_{rd}	compare and swap
casl	[reg_{rs1}], reg_{rs2}, reg_{rd}	casa	[reg_{rs1}]ASI_P_L, reg_{rs2}, reg_{rd}	compare and swap, little-endian
casx	[reg_{rs1}], reg_{rs2}, reg_{rd}	casxa	[reg_{rs1}]ASI_P, reg_{rs2}, reg_{rd}	compare and swap extended
casxl	[reg_{rs1}], reg_{rs2}, reg_{rd}	casxa	[reg_{rs1}]ASI_P_L, reg_{rs2}, reg_{rd}	compare and swap extended, little-endian
inc	reg_{rd}	add	reg_{rd}, 1, reg_{rd}	increment by 1
inc	const13, reg_{rd}	add	reg_{rd}, const13, reg_{rd}	increment by const13
inccc	reg_{rd}	addcc	reg_{rd}, 1, reg_{rd}	incr by 1 and set icc & xcc
inccc	const13, reg_{rd}	addcc	reg_{rd}, const13, reg_{rd}	incr by const13 and set icc & xcc
dec	reg_{rd}	sub	reg_{rd}, 1, reg_{rd}	decrement by 1
dec	const13, reg_{rd}	sub	reg_{rd}, const13, reg_{rd}	decrement by const13
deccc	reg_{rd}	subcc	reg_{rd}, 1, reg_{rd}	decr by 1 and set icc & xcc
deccc	const13, reg_{rd}	subcc	reg_{rd}, const13, reg_{rd}	decr by const13 and set icc & xcc
btst	reg_or_imm, reg_{rs1}	andcc	reg_{rs1}, reg_or_imm, %g0	bit test
bset	reg_or_imm, reg_{rd}	or	reg_{rd}, reg_or_imm, reg_{rd}	bit set
bclr	reg_or_imm, reg_{rd}	andn	reg_{rd}, reg_or_imm, reg_{rd}	bit clear
btog	reg_or_imm, reg_{rd}	xor	reg_{rd}, reg_or_imm, reg_{rd}	bit toggle
clr	reg_{rd}	or	%g0, %g0, reg_{rd}	clear (zero) register
clrb	[address]	stb	%g0, [address]	clear byte
clrh	[address]	sth	%g0, [address]	clear halfword
clr	[address]	stw	%g0, [address]	clear word
clrx	[address]	stx	%g0, [address]	clear extended word
clruw	reg_{rs1}, reg_{rd}	srl	reg_{rs1}, %g0, reg_{rd}	copy and clear upper word
clruw	reg_{rd}	srl	reg_{rd}, %g0, reg_{rd}	clear upper word
mov	reg_or_imm, reg_{rd}	or	%g0, reg_or_imm, reg_{rd}	
mov	%y, reg_{rd}	rd	%y, reg_{rd}	
mov	%asr$n$, reg_{rd}	rd	%asr$n$, reg_{rd}	
mov	reg_or_imm, %y	wr	%g0, reg_or_imm, %y	
mov	reg_or_imm, %asr$n$	wr	%g0, reg_or_imm, %asr$n$	

H Software Considerations

This appendix describes how software can use the SPARC-V9 architecture effectively. Examples do not necessarily conform to any specific Application Binary Interface (ABI).

H.1 Nonprivileged Software

This subsection describes software conventions that have proven or may prove useful, assumptions that compilers may make about the resources available, and how compilers can use those resources. It does not discuss how supervisor software (an operating system) may use the architecture. Although a set of software conventions is described, software is free to use other conventions more appropriate for specific applications.

The following are the primary goals for many of the software conventions described in this subsection:

— Minimizing average procedure-call overhead

— Minimizing latency due to branches

— Minimizing latency due to memory access

H.1.1 Registers

Register usage is a critical resource allocation issue for compilers. The SPARC-V9 architecture provides windowed integer registers (*in*, *out*, *local*), global integer registers, and floating-point registers.

H.1.1.1 *In* and *Out* Registers

The *in* and *out* registers are used primarily for passing parameters to and receiving results from subroutines, and for keeping track of the memory stack. When a procedure is called and executes a SAVE instruction, the caller's *out*s become the callee's *in*s.

One of a procedure's *out* registers (%o6) is used as its stack pointer, %sp. It points to an area in which the system can store %r16..%r31 (%l0..%l7 and %i0..%i7) when the register file overflows (spill trap), and is used to address most values located on the stack.

A trap can occur at any time[1], which may precipitate a subsequent spill trap. During this spill trap, the contents of the user's register window at the time of the original trap are spilled to the memory to which its %sp points.

A procedure may store temporary values in its *out* registers (except %sp) with the understanding that those values are volatile across procedure calls. %sp cannot be used for temporary values for the reasons described in H.1.1.3, "Register Windows and %sp."

Up to six parameters[2] may be passed by placing them in *out* registers %o0..%o5; additional parameters are passed in the memory stack. The stack pointer is implicitly passed in %o6, and a CALL instruction places its own address in %o7.[3] Floating-point parameters may also be passed in floating-point registers.

After a callee is entered and its SAVE instruction has been executed, the caller's *out* registers are accessible as the callee's *in* registers.

The caller's stack pointer %sp (%o6) automatically becomes the current procedure's frame pointer %fp (%i6) when the SAVE instruction is executed.

The callee finds its first six integer parameters in %i0..%i5, and the remainder (if any) on the stack.

A function returns a scalar integer value by writing it into its *in*s (which are the caller's *out*s), starting with %i0. A scalar floating-point value is returned in the floating-point registers, starting with %f0.

A procedure's return address, normally the address of the instruction just after the CALL's delay-slot instruction, is as %i7+8.[4]

H.1.1.2 *Local* Registers

The *local*s are used for automatic[5] variables and for most temporary values. For access efficiency, a compiler may also copy parameters (that is, those past the sixth) from the memory stack into the *local*s and use them from there.

See H.1.4, "Register Allocation within a Window," for methods of allocating more or fewer than eight registers for local values.

---

1. For example, due to an error in executing an instruction (for example, a *mem_address_not_aligned* trap), or due to any type of external interrupt.

2. Six is more than adequate, since the overwhelming majority of procedures in system code take fewer than six parameters. According to studies cited by Weicker (Weicker, R. P., "Dhrystone: A Synthetic Systems Programming Benchmark," *CACM* 27:10, October 1984), at least 97% (measured statically) take fewer than six parameters. The average number of parameters did not exceed 2.1, measured either statically or dynamically, in any of these studies.

3. If a JMPL instruction is used in place of a CALL, it should place its address in %o7 for consistency.

4. For convenience, SPARC-V9 assemblers may provide a "ret" (return) synthetic instruction that generates a "jmpl %i7+8, %g0" hardware instruction. See G.3, "Synthetic Instructions."

5. In the C language, an automatic variable is a local variable whose lifetime is no longer than that of its containing procedure.

H.1.1.3 Register Windows and %sp

Some caveats about the use of %sp and the SAVE and RESTORE instructions are appropriate. If the operating system and user code use register windows, it is essential that

— %sp *always* contains a correct value, so that when (and if) a register window spill/ fill trap occurs, the register window can be correctly stored to or reloaded from memory.[6]

— Nonprivileged code uses SAVE and RESTORE instructions carefully. In particular, "walking" the call chain through the register windows using RESTOREs, expecting to be able to return to where one started using SAVEs, does not work as one might suppose. Since user code cannot disable traps, a trap (e.g., an interrupt) could write over the contents of a user register window that has "temporarily" been RESTOREd[7]. The safe method is to flush the register windows to user memory (the stack) by using the FLUSHW instruction. Then, user code can safely "walk" the call chain through user memory, instead of through the register windows.

To avoid such problems, consider all data memory at addresses just less than %sp to be volatile, and the contents of all register windows "below" the current one to be volatile.

H.1.1.4 *Global* Registers

Unlike the *ins*, *locals*, and *outs*, the *globals* are not part of any register window. The *globals* are a set of eight registers with global scope, like the register sets of more traditional processor architectures. An ABI may define conventions that the *globals* (except %g0) must obey. For example, if the convention assumes that *globals* are volatile across procedure calls, either the caller or the callee must take responsibility for saving and restoring their contents.

Global register %g0 has a hardwired value of zero; it always reads as zero, and writes to it have no program-visible effect.

Typically, the *global* registers other than %g0 are used for temporaries, global variables, or global pointers — either user variables, or values maintained as part of the program's execution environment. For example, one could use *globals* in the execution environment by establishing a convention that global scalars are addressed via offsets from a global base

---

6. Typically, the SAVE instruction is used to generate a new %sp value while shifting to a new register window, all in one atomic operation. When SAVE is used this way, synchronization of the two operations should not be a problem.

7. Another reason this might fail is that user code has no way to determine how many register windows are implemented by the hardware.

register. In the most general case, memory accessed at an arbitrary address requires six instructions; for example,

```
sethi    %uhi(address),tmp
or       tmp, %ulo(address), tmp
sllx     tmp, 32, tmp
sethi    %hi(address), reg
or       reg, %lo(address), reg
ld       [reg+tmp], reg
```

Use of a global base register for frequently accessed global values would provide faster (single-instruction) access to 2^{13} bytes of those values; for example,

```
ld       [%gn+offset], reg
```

Additional global registers could be used to provide single-instruction access to correspondingly more global values.

H.1.1.5 Floating-Point Registers

There are sixteen quad-precision floating-point registers. The registers can also be accessed as thirty-two double-precision registers. In addition, the first eight quad registers can also be accessed as thirty-two single-precision registers. Floating-point registers are accessed with different instructions than the integer registers; their contents can be moved among themselves, and to or from memory. See 5.1.4, "Floating-Point Registers," for more information about floating-point register aliasing.

Like the global registers, the floating-point registers must be managed by software. Compilers use the floating-point registers for user variables and compiler temporaries, pass floating-point parameters, and return floating-point results in them.

H.1.1.6 The Memory Stack

A stack is maintained to hold automatic variables, temporary variables, and return information for each invocation of a procedure. When a procedure is called, a **stack frame** is allocated; it is released when the procedure returns. The use of a stack for this purpose allows simple and efficient implementation of recursive procedures.

Under certain conditions, optimization can allow a leaf procedure to use its caller's stack frame instead of one of its own. In that case, the procedure allocates no space of its own for a stack frame. See H.1.2, "Leaf-Procedure Optimization," for more information.

The stack pointer %sp must always maintain the alignment required by the operating system's ABI. This is at least doubleword alignment, possibly with a constant offset to increase stack addressability using constant offset addressing.

H.1.2 Leaf-Procedure Optimization

A **leaf procedure** is one that is a "leaf" in the program's call graph; that is, one that does not call (e.g., via CALL or JMPL) any other procedures.

Each procedure, including leaf procedures, normally uses a SAVE instruction to allocate a stack frame and obtain a register window for itself, and a corresponding RESTORE instruction to deallocate it. The time costs associated with this are

— Possible generation of register-window spill/fill traps at runtime. This only happens occasionally,[8] but when either a spill or fill trap does occur, it costs several machine cycles to process.

— The cycles expended by the SAVE and RESTORE instructions themselves.

There are also space costs associated with this convention, the cumulative cache effects of which may be nonnegligible. The space costs include

— The space occupied on the stack by the procedure's stack frame

— The two words occupied by the SAVE and RESTORE instructions

Of the above costs, the trap-processing cycles typically are the most significant.

Some leaf procedures can be made to operate **without** their own register window or stack frame, using their caller's instead. This can be done when the candidate leaf procedure meets all of the following conditions:[9]

— It contains no references to %sp, except in its SAVE instruction.

— It contains no references to %fp.

It refers to (or can be made to refer to) no more than eight of the thirty-two integer registers, including %o7 (the return address).

If a procedure conforms to the above conditions, it can be made to operate using its caller's stack frame and registers, an optimization that saves both time and space. This optimization is called **leaf procedure optimization**. The optimized procedure may safely use only registers that its caller already assumes to be volatile across a procedure call.

The optimization can be performed at the assembly language level using the following steps:

(1) Change all references to registers in the procedure to registers that the caller assumes volatile across the call.

(a) Leave references to %o7 unchanged.

(b) Leave any references to %g0 .. %g7 unchanged.

(c) Change %i0 .. %i5 to %o0 .. %o5, respectively. If an *in* register is changed to an *out* register that was already referenced in the original unoptimized version of the procedure, all original references to that *out* register must be changed to refer to an unused *out* or *global* register.

---

8. The frequency of overflow and underflow traps depends on the application and on the number of register windows (NWINDOWS) implemented in hardware.

9. Although slightly less restrictive conditions could be used, the optimization would become more complex to perform and the incremental gain would usually be small.

(d) Change references to each *local* register into references to any unused register that is assumed to be volatile across a procedure call.

(2) Delete the SAVE instruction. If it was in a delay slot, replace it with a NOP instruction. If its destination register was not %g0 or %sp, convert the SAVE into the corresponding ADD instruction instead of deleting it.

(3) If the RESTORE's implicit addition operation is used for a productive purpose (such as setting the procedure's return value), convert the RESTORE to the corresponding ADD instruction. Otherwise, the RESTORE is only used for stack and register-window deallocation; replace it with a NOP instruction (it is probably in the delay slot of the RET, and so cannot be deleted).

(4) Change the RET (return) synthetic instruction to RETL (return-from-leaf-procedure synthetic instruction).

(5) Perform any optimizations newly made possible, such as combining instructions or filling the delay slot of the RETL (or the delay slot occupied by the SAVE) with a productive instruction.

After the above changes, there should be no SAVE or RESTORE instructions, and no references to *in* or *local* registers in the procedure body. All original references to *in*s are now to *out*s. All other register references are to registers that are assumed to be volatile across a procedure call.

Costs of optimizing leaf procedures in this way include

— Additional intelligence in a peephole optimizer to recognize and optimize candidate leaf procedures

— Additional intelligence in debuggers to properly report the call chain and the stack traceback for optimized leaf procedures[10]

H.1.3 Example Code for a Procedure Call

This subsection illustrates common parameter-passing conventions and gives a simple example of leaf-procedure optimization.

The code fragment in example 1 shows a simple procedure call with a value returned, and the procedure itself.

Since sum3 does not call any other procedures (i.e., it is a leaf procedure), it can be optimized to become:

```
sum3:
        add       %o0, %o1, %o0
        retl                          ! (must use RETL, not RET,
        add       %o0, %o2, %o0       !  to return from leaf procedure)
```

---

10. A debugger can recognize an optimized leaf procedure by scanning it, noting the absence of a SAVE instruction. Compilers often constrain the SAVE, if present, to appear within the first few instructions of a procedure; in such a case, only those instruction positions need be examined.

```
! CALLER:
!    int i;                              /* compiler assigns "i" to register %l7 */
!    i = sum3( 1, 2, 3 );
     ...
     mov        1, %o0                   ! first arg to sum3 is 1
     mov        2, %o1                   ! second arg to sum3 is 2
     call       sum3                     ! the call to sum3
     mov        3, %o2                   ! last parameter to sum3 in delay slot
     mov        %o0, %l7                 ! copy return value to %l7 (variable "i")
     ...
#define SA(x)    (((x)+15)&(~0x1F))      /* rounds "x" up to extended word boundary
*/
#define MINFRAME ((16+1+6)*8)            /* minimum size stack frame, in bytes;
                                          *    16 extended words for saving the
current
                                          *        register window,
                                          *    1 extended word for "hidden parameter",
                                          *    and 6 extended words in which a callee
                                          *        can store its arguments.
                                          */

! CALLEE:
!    int sum3( a, b, c )
!        int a, b, c;                    /* args received in %i0, %i1, and %i2 */
!    {
!        return  a+b+c;
!    }
sum3:
     save       %sp,-SA(MINFRAME),%sp ! set up new %sp; alloc min. stack frame
     add        %i0, %i1, %l7         ! compute sum in local %l7
     add        %l7, %i2, %l7         !   (or %i0 could have been used directly)
     ret                              ! return from sum3, and...
     restore    %l7, 0, %o0           ! move result into output reg & restore
```

Example 1—Simple Procedure Call with Value Returned

H.1.4 Register Allocation within a Window

The usual SPARC-V9 software convention is to allocate eight registers (%l0 .. %l7) for local values. A compiler could allocate more registers for local values at the expense of having fewer *out*s and *in*s available for argument passing. For example, if instead of assuming that the boundary between local values and input arguments is between r[23] and r[24] (%l7 and %i0), software could, by convention, assume that the boundary is between r[25] and r[26] (%i1 and %i2). This would provide ten registers for local values and six *in* and *out* registers. This is shown in table 44.

Table 44—Register Allocation within a Window

	Standard register model	10 local register model	Arbitrary register model
Registers for local values	8	10	n
In / out registers			
Reserved for `%sp` / `%fp`	1	1	1
Reserved for return address	1	1	1
Available for argument passing	6	4	$14 - n$
Total *ins / outs*	8	6	$16 - n$

H.1.5 Other Register-Window-Usage Models

So far, this appendix has described SPARC-V9 software conventions that are appropriate for use in a general-purpose multitasking computer system. However, SPARC-V9 is used in many other applications, notably embedded and/or real-time systems. In such applications, other schemes for allocation of SPARC-V9's register windows might be more nearly optimal than the one described above.

One possibility is to avoid using the normal register-window mechanism by not using SAVE and RESTORE instructions. Software would see 32 general-purpose registers instead of SPARC-V9's usual windowed register file. In this mode, SPARC-V9 would operate like processors with more traditional (flat) register architectures. Procedure call times would be more determinate (due to lack of spill/fill traps), but for most types of software, average procedure call time would significantly increase, due to increased memory traffic for parameter passing and saving/restoring local variables.

Effective use of this software convention would require compilers to generate different code (direct register spills/fills to memory and no SAVE/RESTORE instructions) than for the software conventions described above.

It would be awkward, at best, to attempt to mix (link) code that uses the SAVE/RESTORE convention with code that does not use it. If both conventions **were** used in the same system, two versions of each library would be required.

It would be possible to run user code with one register-usage convention and supervisor code with another. With sufficient intelligence in supervisor software, user processes with different register conventions could be run simultaneously.[11]

H.1.6 Self-Modifying Code

If a program includes self-modifying code, it must issue a FLUSH instruction for each modified doubleword of instructions (or a call to supervisor software having an equivalent effect).

---

11. Although technically possible, this is not to suggest that there would be significant utility in mixing user processes with differing register-usage conventions.

Note that self-modifying code intended to be portable **must** use FLUSH instruction(s) (or a call to supervisor software having equivalent effect) after storing into the instruction stream.

All SPARC-V9 instruction accesses are big-endian. If a program is running in little-endian mode and wishes to modify instructions, it must do one of the following:

— Use an explicit big-endian ASI to write the modified instruction to memory, or

— Reverse the byte ordering shown in the instruction formats in Appendix A, "Instruction Definitions," before doing a little-endian store, since the stored data will be reordered before the bytes are written to memory.

H.1.7 Thread Management

SPARC-V9 provides support for the efficient management of user-level threads. The cost of thread switching can be reduced by using the following features:

User Management of FPU:
> The FEF bit in the FPRS register allows nonprivileged code to manage the FPU. This is in addition to the management done by the supervisor code via the PEF bit in the PSTATE register. A thread-management library can implement efficient switching of the FPU among threads by manipulating the FEF bit in the FPRS register and by providing a user trap handler (with support from the supervisor software) for the *fp_disabled* exception. See the description of User Traps in H.2.4, "User Trap Handlers."

FLUSHW Instruction:
> The FLUSHW instruction is an efficient way for a thread library to flush the register windows during a thread switch. The instruction executes as a NOP if there are no windows to flush.

H.1.8 Minimizing Branch Latency

The SPARC-V9 architecture contains several instructions that can be used to minimize branch latency. These are described below.

Conditional Moves:
> The conditional move instructions for both integer and floating-point registers can be used to eliminate branches from the code generated for simple expressions and/or assignments. The following example illustrates this.

> The C code segment

```
double     x,y;
int        i;
...
i  = (x > y) ? 1 : 2;
```

can be compiled to use a conditional move as follows:

```
fcmp     %fcc1, x, y    ! x and y are double regs
mov      1, i           ! i is int; assume x > y
movfle   %fcc1, 2, i    ! fix i if wrong
```

Branch or Move Based on Register Contents:

The use of register contents as conditions for branch and move instructions allows any integer register (other than *r0*) to hold a boolean value or the results of a comparison. This allows conditions to be used more efficiently in nested cases. It allows the generation of a condition to be moved further from its use, thereby minimizing latency. In addition, it can eliminate the need for additional arithmetic instructions to set the condition codes. This is illustrated in the following example.

The test for finding the maximum of an array of integers,

```
if (A[i] > max)
max  = A[i];
```

can be compiled as follows, allowing the condition for the loop to be set before the sequence and checked after it:

```
ldx      [addr_of_Ai], Ai
sub      Ai, max, tmp
movrgz   tmp, Ai, max
```

H.1.9 Prefetch

The SPARC-V9 architecture includes a prefetch instruction intended to help hide the latency of accessing memory.[12]

As a general rule, given a loop of the following form (using C for assembly language, and assuming a cache line size of 64 bytes and that A and B are arrays of 8-byte values)

```
for (i  = 0; i < N; i++) {
    load A[i]
    load B[i]
    ...
}
```

which takes C cycles per iteration (assuming all loads hit in cache) and given L cycles of latency to memory, prefetch instructions may be inserted for data that will be needed **ceiling**(L/C') iterations in the future, where C' is number of cycles per iteration of the modified loop. Thus, the loop would be transformed into

12. Two papers describing the use of prefetch instructions are Callahan, D., K. Kennedy, A. Porterfield, "Software Prefetching," *Proceedings of the Fourth International Conference on Architectural Support for Programming Languages and Operating Systems*, April 1991, pp. 40-52, and Mowry, T., M. Lam, and A. Gupta, "Design and Evaluation of a Compiler Algorithm for Prefetching," *Proceedings of the Fifth International Conference on Architectural Support for Programming Languages and Operating Systems*, October 1992, pp. 62-73.

```
K  = ceiling(L/C');
for (i  = 0; i < N; i++) {

     load A[i]

     load B[i]

     prefetch A[i+K]

     prefetch B[i+K]

     ...

}
```

This ensures that the loads will find their data in the cache, and will thus complete more quickly. The first K iterations will not get any benefit from prefetching, so if the number of iterations is small (see below), then prefetching will not help.

Note that in cases of contiguous access (like this one), many of the prefetch instructions will in fact be unnecessary and may slow the program down. To avoid this, note that the prefetch instruction always obtains at least 64 (cache-line-aligned) bytes.

```
/* Round up access to next cache line. */
K'  = (ceiling(L/C') + 7) & ~7;

for (i  = 0; i < N; i++) {

     load A[i]

     load B[i]

     if ( ((int)(A+i) & 63)  = = 0) {

          prefetch A[i+K']

          prefetch B[i+K']

     }

     ...

}
```

or (unrolled eight times, assuming A and B are arrays of 8-byte values)

```
/* Be sure that we access the next cache line. */
K''  = ceiling(L/C') + 7;

for (i  = 0; i < N; i++) {

     load A[i]

     load B[i]

     prefetch A[i+K'']

     prefetch B[i+K'']

     ...

     load A[i+1]

     load B[i+2]

     ... (no prefetching)

     ...

     load A[i+7]

     load B[i+7]

     ...

}
```

In the first case, the prefetching is performed exactly when needed, and thus the distance need not be adjusted. However, the prefetching may not start on the first iteration, resulting in as many as $K' + 7$ iterations without prefetching.

In the second case, the prefetching occurs somewhere within a cache line, and thus, it is not known exactly how long it will be until the next cache line is needed. However, by prefetching seven further ahead, we ensure that the next cache line will be prefetched soon enough. In the worst case, as many as $K'' (\le K' + 7)$ iterations will execute without any benefit from prefetching.

Table 45 illustrates the cost tradeoffs between no prefetching, naive prefetching, and smart prefetching (the second choice) for a small loop (two cycles) with varying uncovered latencies to memory. Some of the latency may be overlapped with execution of surrounding instructions; that which is not is uncovered.

Table 45—Prefetch Cost Tradeoffs

					Limit cycles/iteration			Smart startup costs	
					No pf	Naive	Smart	Worst	Worst
C	C'	L	K	K"	C+L/8	C'	(7C+C')/8	Misses	Breakeven
2	4	8	4	11	3	4	2.25	2	N = 21
2	4	16	8	15	4	4	2.25	2	N = 18
2	4	32	16	23	6	4	2.25	3	N = 26

Here, we treat the arrays accessed as if one were not in the cache. Thus, every eight iterations, a cache line must be fetched from memory in the no-prefetch case; and thus, the amortized cost of an iteration is $C + L/8$. The cost estimate for the smart case ignores any benefits from unrolling, since it is reasonable to expect that the loop would be unrolled or pipelined in this fashion, even if prefetching were not used. The startup costs assume an alignment within the cache that maximizes the initial misses. The break-even cost was chosen by solving the following equation for N.

$$N * (C + L/8) = WM * L + N * (7C + C')/8 \ \{e.g., 3N = 16 + 2.25N \Rightarrow N = 21\}$$

Of course, this is a simplified model.

Another possibility to consider is the worst-case cost of prefetching. If, in the example provided, everything accessed is always cached, then the smart-prefetching loop takes 12.5% longer. For each memory latency, there is a break-even point (in terms of how often one of the array operands is cached) at which the prefetching loop begins to run faster. Table 46 illustrates this.

Table 46—Cache Break-Even Points

L	C-cached	C-missed	C-smart	Break-even % cached operands	Break-even loop cache miss rate
8	2	3	2.25	75%	1.56%
16	2	4	2.25	88%	0.75%
32	2	6	2.25	94%	0.375%
64	2	10	2.25	97%	0.188%

Note that one uncached operand corresponds to one load out of sixteen missing the cache; the operand miss rate is sixteen times higher than the load miss rate. Note that this is the miss rate for this loop alone; extrapolation from whole-program miss rates is not advised.

Binaries that run efficiently across different SPARC-V9 implementations can be created for cases like this (where memory accesses are regular, though not necessarily contiguous) by parameterizing the prefetch distance by machine type. In privileged code the machine type is available in the VER register; nonprivileged code should be able to obtain this from the operating system or ABI. Based on information about known machines and estimated loop execution times, a compiler could precalculate values for K" (assuming smart prefetching) and store them in a table. At execution time, the proper value for K" would be fetched from the table before entering the loop.

For regular but noncontiguous accesses, a prefetch would be issued for every load. If cache blocking is used, the prefetching strategy must be adjusted accordingly, since there is no point in prefetching data that is expected to be in the cache already.

The prefetch variant should be chosen based on what is known about the local and global use of the data prefetched. If the data is not being written locally, then variant 0 (several reads) should be used. If it is being written (and possibly also read), then variant 2 (several writes) should be used. If, in addition, it is known that this is likely to be the last use of the data for some time (for example, if the loop iteration count is one million and dependence analysis reveals no reuse of data), then it is appropriate to use either variant 1 (one read) or 3 (one write). If reuse of data is expected to occur soon, then use of variants 1 or 3 is not appropriate, because of the risk of increased bus and memory traffic on a multiprocessor.

If the hardware does not implement all variants, it is expected to provide a sensible overloading of the unimplemented variants. Thus, correct use of a specific variant need not be tied to a particular SPARC-V9 implementation or multi/uniprocessor configuration.

H.1.10 Nonfaulting Load

The SPARC-V9 architecture includes a way to specify load instructions that do not generate visible faults, so that compilers can have more freedom in scheduling instructions. Note that these are not speculative loads, which may fault if their results are later used; these are normal load instructions, but tagged to indicate to the kernel and/or hardware that a fault should not be delivered to the code executing the instruction.

Five important rules govern the use of nonfaulting loads:

(1) Volatile memory references in the source language should not use nonfaulting load instructions.

(2) Code compiled for debugging should not use nonfaulting loads, because they remove the ability to detect common errors.

(3) If nonfaulting loads are used, page zero should be a page of zero values, mapped read-only. Compilers that routinely use negative offsets to register pointers should map page "−1" similarly, if the operating software permits it.

(4) Any use of nonfaulting loads in privileged code must be aware of how they are treated by the host SPARC-V9 implementation.

(5) Nonfaulting loads from unaligned addresses may be substantially more expensive than nonfaulting loads from other addresses.

Nonfaulting loads can be used to solve three scheduling problems.

— On super-scalar machines, it is often desirable to obtain the right mix of instructions to avoid conflicts for any given execution unit. A nonfaulting load can be moved (backwards) past a basic block boundary to even out the instruction mix.

— On pipelined machines, there may be latency between loads and uses. A nonfaulting load can be moved past a block boundary to place more instructions between a load into a register and the next use of that register.

— Software pipelining improves the scheduling of loops, but if a loop iteration begins with a load instruction and contains an early exit, it may not be eligible for pipelining. If the load is replaced with a nonfaulting load, then the loop can be pipelined.

In the branch-laden code shown in example 2, nonfaulting loads could be used to separate loads from uses. The result also has a somewhat better mix of instructions and is somewhat pipelined. The basic blocks are separated.

Source Code:
```
    while ( x ! = 0 && x -> key ! = goal) x  = x -> next;
```

With Normal Loads:
```
    entry:
            brnz,a      x,loop      !
            ldx         [x],t1      ! (pre)load1 (key)
    loop:
            cmp         t1,goal     ! use1
            bpe         %xcc,out
            nop                     ! no filling from loop.
            ldx         [x+8],x     ! load2 (next)
            brnz,a      x,loop      ! use2
            ldx         [x],t1      ! load1
    out: ...
```

With Nonfaulting Loads:
```
    entry:
            mov         x,t2
            mov         #ASI_PNF, %asi
            ldxa        [t2]%asi,t1     ! (pre)load1 (nf-load for key)
    loop:
            mov         t2,x            ! begin loop body
            brz,pn      t2,out
            ldxa        [t2+8]%asi,t2   ! load2 (nf-load for next)

            cmp         t1,goal         ! use1
            bpne        %xcc,loop
            ldxa        [t2],%asi,t1    ! use2, load1 ! nf-load for x
    out: ...
```

Example 2—Branch-Laden Code with Nonfaulting Loads

In the loop shown in example 3, nonfaulting loads allow pipelining. This loop might be

Source Code:
```
d_ne_index (double * d1, double * d2) {
    int i = 0;
    while(d1[i]  =  = d2[i]) i++;
    return i;
}
```

With Normal Loads:
```
        mov         0,t
        mov         0,i
loop:
        lddf        [d1+t],a1
        lddf        [d2+t],a2       ! load
        add         t,8,t
        fcmpd       a1,a2           ! use
        fbe,a       loop            ! fcc use
        add         i,1,i
```

With Nonfaulting Loads:
```
        lddf        [d1],a1
        lddf        [d2],a2
        mov         8,t
        mov         0,i
loop:
        fcmpd       a1,a2           ! use, fcc def
        lddfa       [d1+t],%asi,a1
        lddfa       [d2+t],%asi,a2  ! load
        add         t,8,t
        fbe,a       loop            ! fcc use
        add         i,1,i
```

Example 3—Loop with Nonfaulting Loads

improved further using unrolling, prefetching, and multiple FCCs, but that is beyond the scope of this discussion.

H.2 Supervisor Software

This subsection discusses how supervisor software can use the SPARC-V9 privileged architecture. It is intended to illustrate how the architecture can be used in an efficient manner. An implementation may choose to utilize different strategies based on its requirements and implementation-specific aspects of the architecture.

H.2.1 Trap Handling

The SPARC-V9 privileged architecture provides support for efficient trap handling, especially for window traps. The following features of the SPARC-V9 privileged architecture can be used to write efficient trap handlers:

Multiple Trap Levels:
The trap handlers for trap levels less than MAXTL – 1 can be written to ignore exceptional conditions and execute the common case efficiently (without checks and branches). For example, the fill/spill handlers can access pageable memory

without first checking if it is resident. If the memory is not resident, the access will cause a trap that will be handled at the next trap level.

Vectoring of Fill/Spill Traps:

Supervisor software can set up the vectoring of fill/spill traps prior to executing code that uses register windows and may cause spill/fill traps. This feature can be used to support SPARC-V8 and SPARC-V7 binaries. These binaries create stack frames with save areas for 32-bit registers. SPARC-V9 binaries create stack frames with save areas for 64-bit registers. By setting up the spill/fill trap vector based on the type of binary being executed, the trap handlers can avoid checking and branching to use the appropriate load/store instructions.

Saved Trap State:

Trap handlers need not save (restore) processor state that is automatically saved (restored) on a trap (return from trap). For example, the fill/spill trap handlers can load ASI_AS_IF_USER_PRIMARY{_LITTLE} into the ASI register in order to access the user's address space without the overhead of having to save and restore the ASI register.

SAVED and RESTORED Instructions:

The SAVED (RESTORED) instruction provides an efficient way to update the state of the register windows after successfully spilling (filling) a register window. They implement a default policy of spilling (filling) one register window at a time. If desired, the supervisor software can implement a different policy by directly updating the state registers.

Alternate Globals:

The alternate global registers can be used to avoid saving and restoring the normal global registers. They can be used like the local registers of the trap window in SPARC-V8.

Large Trap Vectors for Spill/Fill:

The definition of the spill and fill trap vectors with reserved space between each pair of vectors allows spill and fill trap handlers to be up to thirty-two instructions long, thus avoiding a branch in the handler.

H.2.2 Example Code for Spill Handler

The code in example 4 shows a spill handler for a SPARC-V9 user binary. The handler is located at the vector for trap type *spill_0_normal* (080_{16}). It is assumed that supervisor software has set the WSTATE register to 0 before executing the user binary. The handler is invoked when user code executes a SAVE instruction that results in a window overflow.

H.2.3 Client-Server Model

SPARC-V9 provides mechanisms to support client-server computing efficiently. A call from a client to a server (where the client and server have separate address spaces) can be implemented efficiently using a software trap that switches the address space. This is often referred to as a **cross-domain call**. A system call in most operating systems can be viewed

```
T_NORMAL_SPILL_0:
    !Set ASI to access user addr space
    wr          #ASI_AIUP, %asi
    stxa        %l0, [%sp+(8* 0)]%asi      !Store window in memory stack
    stxa        %l1, [%sp+(8* 1)]%asi
    stxa        %l2, [%sp+(8* 2)]%asi
    stxa        %l3, [%sp+(8* 3)]%asi
    stxa        %l4, [%sp+(8* 4)]%asi
    stxa        %l5, [%sp+(8* 5)]%asi
    stxa        %l6, [%sp+(8* 6)]%asi
    stxa        %l7, [%sp+(8* 7)]%asi
    stxa        %i0, [%sp+(8* 8)]%asi
    stxa        %i1, [%sp+(8* 9)]%asi
    stxa        %i2, [%sp+(8*10)]%asi
    stxa        %i3, [%sp+(8*11)]%asi
    stxa        %i4, [%sp+(8*12)]%asi
    stxa        %i5, [%sp+(8*13)]%asi
    stxa        %i6, [%sp+(8*14)]%asi
    stxa        %i7, [%sp+(8*15)]%asi
    saved                                  ! Update state
    retry                                  ! Retry trapped instruction
                                           ! Restores old %asi
```

Example 4—Spill Handler

as a special case of a cross-domain call. The following features are useful in implementing a cross-domain call:

Splitting the Register Windows

The register windows can be shared efficiently between multiple address spaces by using the OTHERWIN register and providing additional trap handlers to handle spill/fill traps for the other (not the current) address spaces. On a cross-domain call (a software trap), the supervisor can set the OTHERWIN register to the number of register windows used by the client (equal to CANRESTORE) and CANRESTORE to zero. At the same time the WSTATE bit vectors can be set to vector the spill/fill traps appropriately for each address space.

The sequence in example 5 shows a crossp-domain call and return. The example assumes the simple case, where only a single client-server pair can occupy the register windows. More general schemes can be developed along the same lines.

ASI_SECONDARY{_LITTLE}

Supervisor software can use these unrestricted ASIs to support cross-address-space access between clients and nonprivileged servers. For example, some services that are currently provided as part of a large monolithic supervisor can be separated out as nonprivileged servers (potentially occupying a separate address space). This is often referred to as the **microkernel** approach.

H.2.4 User Trap Handlers

Supervisor software can provide efficient support for user (nonprivileged) trap handlers on SPARC-V9. The RETURN instruction allows nonprivileged code to retry an instruction

```
cross_domain_call:
        save         ! create a new register window for the server
        ..           ! Switch to the execution environment for the server;
        ..           ! Save trap state as necessary.

        ! Set CWP for caller in TSTATE
        rdpr         %tstate, %g1
        rdpr         %cwp, %g2
        bclr         TSTATE_CWP, %g1
        wrpr         %g1, %g2, %tstate
        rdpr         %canrestore, %g1
        wrpr         %g0, 0, %canrestore
        wrpr         %g0, %g1, %otherwin
        rdpr         %wstate, %g1
        sll          %g1, 3, %g1               ! Move WSTATE_NORMAL (client's
                                               ! vector)to WSTATE_OTHER
        or           %g1, WSTATE_SERVER, %g1   ! Set WSTATE_NORMAL to the
                                               !     vector for the server
        wrpr         %g0, %g1, %wstate
        ..                                     ! Load trap state for server
        done                                   ! Execute server code

cross_domain_return:
        rdpr         %otherwin, %g1
        wrpr         %g0, %g1, %canrestore
        wrpr         %g0, 0, %otherwin
        rdpr         %wstate, %g1
        srl          %g1, 3, %g1
        wrpr         %g0, %g1, %wstate         ! Reset WSTATE_NORMAL to
                                               ! client's vector
        ..           ! Restore saved trap state as necessary; this includes
                     ! the return PC for the caller.
        restore      ! Go back to the caller's register window.

        ! Set CWP for caller in TSTATE
        rdpr         %tstate, %g1
        rdpr         %cwp, %g2
        bclr         TSTATE_CWP, %g1
        wrpr         %g1, %g2, %tstate

        done         ! return to the caller
```

Example 5—Cross-Domain Call and Return

pointed to by the previous stack frame. This provides the semantics required for returning from a user trap handler without any change in processor state. Supervisor software can invoke the user trap handler by first creating a new register window (and stack frame) on its behalf and passing the necessary arguments (including the PC and nPC for the trapped instruction) in the local registers. The code in example 6 shows how a user trap handler may be invoked and how it returns:

```
T_EXAMPLE_TRAP:          ! Supervisor trap handler for T_EXAMPLE_TRAP trap
    save                 ! Create a window for the user trap handler

    !Set CWP for new window in TSTATE
    rdpr        %tstate, %16
    rdpr        %cwp, %15
    bclr        TSTATE_CWP, %16
    wrpr        %16, %15, %tstate

    rdpr        %tpc,%16    !Put PC for trapped instruction in local register
    rdpr        %tnpc,%17   !Put nPC for trapped instruction in local register
    ..                      !Get the address of the user trap handler in %15;
                            ! for example, from a supervisor data structure.

    wrpr        %15, %tnpc    ! Put PC for user trap handler in %tnpc.
    done                      ! Execute user trap handler.

USER_EXAMPLE_TRAP:          !User trap handler for T_EXAMPLE_TRAP trap

    ..                      !Execute trap handler logic. Local registers
                            ! can be used as scratch.

    jmpl        %16         !Return to retry the trapped instruction.
    return      %17
```

Example 6—User Trap Handler

I Extending the SPARC-V9 Architecture

This appendix describes how extensions can be effectively added to the SPARC-V9 architecture. It describes how new instructions can be added through the use of read and write ancillary state register (ASR) and implementation-dependent (IMPDEP1/IMPDEP2) instructions.

> **— WARNING —**
> *Programs that make use of SPARC-V9 architectural extensions may not be portable and likely will not conform to any current or future SPARC-V9 binary standards.*

I.1 Addition of SPARC-V9 Extensions

There are two approved methods of adding extensions to an implementation of the SPARC-V9 architecture. An implementor who wishes to define and implement a new SPARC-V9 instruction should, if possible, use one of the following methods.

I.1.1 Read/Write Ancillary State Registers (ASRs)

The first method of adding instructions to SPARC-V9 is through the use of the implementation-dependent Write Ancillary State Register (WRASR) and Read Ancillary State Register (RDASR) instructions operating on ASRs 16..31. Through a read/write instruction pair, any instruction that requires an *rs1, reg_or_imm*, and *rd* field can be implemented. A WRASR instruction can also perform an arbitrary operation on two register sources, or on one register source and a signed immediate value, and place the result in an ASR. A subsequent RDASR instruction can read the result ASR and place its value in an integer destination register.

I.1.2 Implementation-Dependent and Reserved Opcodes

The meaning of "reserved" for SPARC-V9 opcodes differs from its meaning in SPARC-V8. The SPARC-V9 definition of "reserved" allows implementations to use reserved opcodes for implementation-specific purposes. While a hardware implementation that

uses reserved opcodes will be SPARC-V9-compliant, SPARC-V9 ABI-compliant programs cannot use these reserved opcodes and remain compliant. A SPARC-V9 platform
that implements instructions using reserved opcodes must provide software libraries that
provide the interface between SPARC-V9 ABI-compliant programs and these instructions.
Graphics libraries provide a good example of this. Hardware platforms have many diverse
implementations of graphics acceleration hardware, but graphics application programs are
insulated from this diversity through libraries.

There is no guarantee that a reserved opcode will not be used for additional instructions in
a future version of the SPARC architecture. Implementors who use reserved opcodes
should keep this in mind.

In some cases forward compatibility may not be an issue; for example, in an embedded
application, binary compatibility may not be an issue. These implementations can use any
reserved opcodes for extensions.

Even when forward compatibility is an issue, future SPARC revisions are likely to contain
few changes to opcode assignments, given that backward compatibility with previous versions must be maintained. It is recommended that implementations wishing to remain for-
ward-compatible use the new IMPDEP1 and IMPDEP2 reserved opcodes with
$op3[5:0] = 11\ 0110_2$ and $11\ 0111_2$.

Compatibility Note:

> IMPDEP1 and IMPDEP2 replace the SPARC-V8 CPop1 and CPop2 opcodes. SPARC-V9 includes
> neither the SPARC-V8 coprocessor opcodes nor any other SPARC-V8 architectural support for
> coprocessors. The coprocessor opcodes were eliminated because they have been used in SPARC-
> V7 and SPARC-V8, as witnessed by the lack of coprocessor implementations.

It is further recommended that SPARC International be notified of any use of IMPDEP1,
IMPDEP2, or other reserved opcodes. When and if future revisions to SPARC are contem-
plated, and if any SPARC-V9 implementations have made use of reserved opcodes,
SPARC International will make every effort not to use those opcodes. By going through
SPARC International, there can be feedback and coordination in the choice of opcodes
that maximizes the probability of forward compatibility. Given the historically small number of implementation-specific changes, coordinating through SPARC International
should be sufficient to ensure future compatibility.

J Programming With the Memory Models

This appendix describes how to program with the SPARC-V9 memory models. An intuitive description of the models is provided in Chapter 8, "Memory Models." A complete formal specification appears in Appendix D, "Formal Specification of the Memory Models." In this subsection, general programming guidelines are given first, followed by specific examples showing how low-level synchronization can be implemented in TSO, PSO, and RMO.

Note that code written for a weaker memory model will execute correctly in any of the stronger memory models. Furthermore, the only possible difference between code written for a weaker memory model and the corresponding code for a stronger memory model is the presence of memory ordering instructions (MEMBARs) that are not needed for the stronger memory model. Hence, transforming code from/to a stronger memory model to/from a weaker memory model means adding/removing certain memory ordering instructions.[1] The required memory ordering directives are monotonically ordered with respect to the strength of the memory model, with the weakest memory model requiring the strongest memory ordering instructions.

The code examples given below are written to run correctly using the RMO memory model. The comments on the MEMBAR instructions indicate which ordering constraints (if any) are required for the PSO and TSO memory models.

J.1 Memory Operations

Programs access memory via five types of operations, namely, load, store, LDSTUB, SWAP, and compare-and-swap. Load copies a value from memory or an I/O location to a register. Store copies a value from a register into memory or an I/O location. LDSTUB, SWAP, and compare-and-swap are atomic load-store instructions that store a value into memory or an I/O location and return the old value in a register. The value written by the atomic instructions depends on the instruction. LDSTUB stores all ones in the accessed

---

1. MEMBAR instructions specify seven independent ordering constraints; thus, there are cases where the transition to a stronger memory model allows the use of a less restrictive MEMBAR instruction, but still requires a MEMBAR instruction. To demonstrate this property, the code examples given in this subsection use multiple MEMBAR instructions if some of the ordering constraints are needed in some but not all memory models. Multiple, adjacent MEMBAR instructions can always be replaced with a single MEMBAR instruction by *OR*ing the arguments.

byte, SWAP stores the supplied value, and compare-and-swap stores the supplied value only if the old value equals the second supplied value.

Memory order and consistency are controlled by MEMBAR instructions. For example, a MEMBAR #StoreStore (equivalent to a STBAR in SPARC-V8) ensures that all previous stores have been performed before subsequent stores and atomic load-stores are executed by memory. This particular memory order is guaranteed implicitly in TSO, but PSO and RMO require this instruction if the correctness of a program depends on the order in which two store instructions can be observed by another processor.[2]

FLUSH is not a memory operation, but it is relevant here in the context of synchronizing stores with instruction execution. When a processor modifies an instruction at address A, it does a store to A followed by a FLUSH A. The FLUSH ensures that the change made by the store will become visible to the instruction fetch units of all processors in the system.

J.2 Memory Model Selection

Given that all SPARC-V9 systems are required to support TSO, programs written for any memory model will be able to run on any SPARC-V9 system. However, a system running with the TSO model generally will offer lower performance than PSO or RMO, because less concurrency is exposed to the CPU and the memory system. The motivation for weakening the memory model is to allow the CPU to issue multiple, concurrent memory references in order to hide memory latency and increase access bandwidth. For example, PSO and RMO allow the CPU to initiate new store operations before an outstanding store has completed.

Using a weaker memory model for an MP (multiprocessor) application that exhibits a high degree of read-write memory sharing with fine granularity and a high frequency of synchronization operations may result in frequent MEMBAR instructions.

In general, it is expected that the weaker memory models offer a performance advantage for multiprocessor SPARC-V9 implementations.

J.3 Processors and Processes

In the SPARC-V9 memory models, the term "processor" may be replaced systematically by the term "process" or "thread," as long as the code for switching processes or threads is written properly. The correct process-switch sequence is given in J.8, "Process Switch Sequence." If an operating system implements this process-switch sequence, application programmers may completely ignore the difference between a process/thread and a processor.

---

2. Memory order is of concern only to programs containing multiple threads that share writable memory and that may run on multiple processors, and to those programs which reference I/O locations. Note that from the processor's point of view, I/O devices behave like other processors.

J.4 Higher-Level Programming Languages and Memory Models

The SPARC-V9 memory models are defined at the machine instruction level. Special attention is required to write the critical parts of MP/MT (multi-threaded) applications in a higher-level language. Current higher-level languages do not support memory ordering instructions and atomic operations. As a result, MP/MT applications that are written in a higher-level language generally will rely on a library of MP/MT support functions, for example, the *parmacs* library from Argonne National Laboratory.[3] The details of constructing and using such libraries are beyond the scope of this document.

Compiler optimizations such as code motion and instruction scheduling generally do not preserve the order in which memory is accessed but they do preserve the data dependencies of a single thread. Compilers do not, in general, deal with the additional dependency requirements to support sharing read-write data among multiple concurrent threads. Hence, the memory semantics of a SPARC-V9 system in general are not preserved by optimizing compilers. For this reason, and because memory ordering directives are not available from higher-level languages, the examples presented in this subsection use assembly language.

Future compilers may have the ability to present the programmer with a sequentially consistent memory model despite the underlying hardware's providing a weaker memory model.[4]

J.5 Portability And Recommended Programming Style

Whether a program is portable across various memory models depends on how it synchronizes access to shared read-write data. Two aspects of a program's style are relevant to portability:

— **Good semantics** refers to whether the synchronization primitives chosen and the way in which they are used are such that changing the memory model does not involve making any changes to the code that uses the primitives.

— **Good structure** refers to whether the code for synchronization is encapsulated through the use of primitives such that when the memory model is changed, required changes to the code are confined to the primitives.

Good semantics are a prerequisite for portability, while good structure makes porting easier.

Programs that use single-writer/multiple-reader locks to protect all access to shared read-write data are portable across all memory models. The code that implements the lock primitives themselves is portable across all models only if it is written to run correctly on RMO. If the lock primitives are collected into a library, then, at worst, only the library rou-

---

3. Lusk, E. L., R.A. Overbeek, "Use of Monitors in Fortran: A Tutorial on the Barrier, Self-scheduling Do-Loop, and Askfor Monitors," TR# ANL-84-51, Argonne National Laboratory, June 1987.

4. See Gharachorloo, K., S.V. Adve, A. Gupta, J.L. Hennessy, and M.D. Hill, "Programming for Different Memory Consistency Models," *Journal of Parallel and Distributed Systems*, 15:4, August 1992.

tines must be changed. Note that mutual exclusion (mutex) locks are a degenerate type of single-writer/multiple-readers lock.

Programs that use write locks to protect write accesses but read without locking are portable across all memory models only if writes to shared data are separated by MEMBAR #StoreStore instructions, and if reading the lock is followed by a MEMBAR #Load-Load instruction. If the MEMBAR instructions are omitted, the code is portable only across TSO and Strong Consistency,[5] but generally it will not work with PSO and RMO. The code that implements the lock primitives is portable across all models only if it is written to run correctly on RMO. If the lock routines are collected into a library, the only possible changes not confined to the library routines are the MEMBAR instructions.

Programs that do synchronization without using single-writer/multiple-reader locks, write locks, or their equivalent are, in general, not portable across different memory models. More precisely, the memory models are ordered from RMO (which is the weakest, least constrained, and most concurrent), PSO, TSO, to sequentially consistent (which is the strongest, most constrained, and least concurrent). A program written to run correctly for any particular memory model will also run correctly in any of the stronger memory models, but not vice versa. Thus, programs written for RMO are the most portable, those written for TSO are less so, and those written for strong consistency are the least portable. This general relationship between the memory models is shown graphically in figure 49.

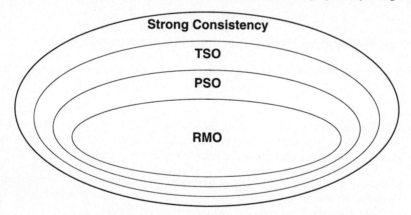

Figure 49—Portability Relations among Memory Models

The style recommendations may be summarized as follows: Programs should use single-writer/multiple-reader locks, or their equivalent, when possible. Other lower-level forms of synchronization (such as Dekker's algorithm for locking) should be avoided when possible. When use of such low-level primitives is unavoidable, it is recommended that the

---

5. Programs that assume a sequentially consistent memory are not guaranteed to run correctly on any SPARC-V9-compliant system, since TSO is the strongest memory model required to be supported. However, sequential consistency is the most natural and intuitive programming model. This motivates the development of compiler techniques that allow programs written for sequential consistency to be translated into code that runs correctly (and efficiently) on systems with weaker memory models.

code be written to work on the RMO model to ensure portability. Additionally, lock primitives should be collected together into a library and written for RMO to ensure portability.

Appendix D, "Formal Specification of the Memory Models," describes a tool and method that allows short code sequences to be formally verified for correctness.

J.6 Spin Locks

A spin lock is a lock for which the "lock held" condition is handled by busy waiting. The code in example 7 shows how spin locks can be implemented using LDSTUB. A nonzero value for the lock represents the locked condition, while a zero value means that the lock is free. Note that the code busy waits by doing loads to avoid generating expensive stores to a potentially shared location. The MEMBAR #StoreStore in UnLockWithLD-STUB ensures that pending stores are completed before the store that frees the lock.

```
LockWithLDSTUB(lock)

retry:
     ldstub    [lock],%l0
     tst       %l0
     be        out
     nop
loop:
     ldub      [lock],%l0
     tst       %l0
     bnc       loop
     nop
     ba,a      retry
out:
     membar    #LoadLoad | #LoadStore

UnLockWithLDSTUB(lock)
     membar    #StoreStore        !RMO and PSO only
     membar    #LoadStore         !RMO only
     stub      %g0,[lock]
```

Example 7—Lock and Unlock Using LDSTUB

The code in example 8 shows how spin locks can be implemented using CASA. Again, a nonzero value for the lock represents the locked condition, while a zero value means the lock is free. The nonzero lock value (ID) is supplied by the caller and may be used to identify the current owner of the lock. This value is available while spinning and could be used to maintain a time-out or to verify that the thread holding the lock is still running. As in the previous case, the code busy-waits by doing loads, not stores.

J.7 Producer-Consumer Relationship

In a producer-consumer relationship,the producer process generates data and puts it into a buffer, while the consumer process takes data from the buffer and uses it. If the buffer is full, the producer process stalls when trying to put data into the buffer. If the buffer is empty, the consumer process stalls when trying to remove data.

```
LockWithCAS(lock, ID)
retry:
      mov      [ID],%l0
      cas      [lock],%g0,%l0
      tst      %l0
      be       out
      nop
loop:
      ld       [lock],%l0
      tst      %l0
      bne      loop
      nop
      ba,a     retry
out:
      membar   #LoadLoad | #LoadStore      !See example 7
UnLockWithCAS(lock)
      membar   #StoreStore     !RMO and PSO only
      membar   #LoadStore      !RMO only
      st       %g0,[lock]
```

Example 8—Lock and Unlock Using CAS

Figure 50 shows the buffer data structure and register usage. Example 9 shows the producer and consumer code. The code assumes the existence of two procedures, IncrHead and IncrTail, which increment the head and tail pointers of the buffer in a wraparound manner and return the incremented value, but do not modify the pointers in the buffer.

Buffer Data Structure:

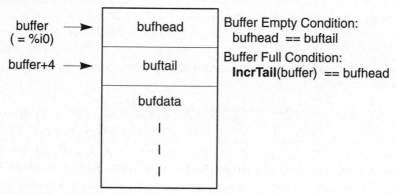

Register Usage:

%i0 and %i1	parameters
%l0 and %l1	local values
%o0	result

Figure 50—Data Structures for Producer-Consumer Code

```
Produce(buffer, data)
    call      IncrTail
full:
    ld        [%i0],%l0
    cmp       %l0,%o0
    be        full
    ld        [%i0+4],%l0
    st        %i1,[%l0]
    membar    #StoreStore        !RMO and PSO only
    st        %o0,[%i0+4]


Consume(buffer)
    ld        [%i0],%l0
empty:
    ld        [%i0+4],%l1
    cmp       %l0,%l1
    be        empty
    call      IncrHead
    ld        [%l0],%l0
    membar    #LoadStore         !RMO only
    st        %o0,[%i0]
    mov       %l0,%o0
```

Example 9—Producer and Consumer Code

J.8 Process Switch Sequence

This subsection provides code that must be used during process or thread switching to ensure that the memory model seen by a process or thread is the one seen by a processor. The `HeadSequence` must be inserted at the beginning of a process or thread when it starts executing on a processor. The `TailSequence` must be inserted at the end of a process or thread when it relinquishes a processor.

Example 10 shows the head and tail sequences. The two sequences refer to a per-process variable *tailDone*. The value 0 for *tailDone* means that the process is running, while the value −1 (all ones) means that the process has completed its tail sequence and may be migrated to another processor if the process is runnable. When a new process is created, *tailDone* is initialized to −1.

The MEMBAR in `HeadSequence` is required to be able to provide a switching sequence that ensures that the state observed by a process in its source processor will also be seen by the process in its destination processor. Since FLUSHes and stores are totally ordered, the head sequence need not do anything special to ensure that FLUSHes performed prior to the switch are visible by the new processor.

Programming Note:

A conservative implementation may simply use a MEMBAR with all barriers set.

```
HeadSequence(tailDone)
nrdy:
    ld          [tailDone],%10
    cmp         %10,-1
    bne         nrdy
    st          %g0, [tailDone]
    membar      #StoreLoad
TailSequence(tailDone)
    mov         -1,%10
    membar      #StoreStore        !RMO and PSO only
    membar      #LoadStore         !RMO only (combine with above)
    st          %10,[tailDone]
```

Example 10—Process or Thread Switch Sequence

J.9 Dekker's Algorithm

Dekker's algorithm is the classical sequence for synchronizing entry into a critical section using loads and stores only. The reason for showing this example here is to illustrate how one may ensure that a store followed by a load in issuing order will be executed by the memory system in that order. Dekker's algorithm is **not** a valid synchronization primitive for SPARC-V9, because it requires a sequentially consistent (SC) memory model in order to work. Dekker's algorithm (and similar synchronization sequences) can be coded on RMO, PSO, and TSO by adding appropriate MEMBAR instructions. This example also illustrates how future compilers can provide the equivalent of sequential consistency on systems with weaker memory models.

Example 11 shows the entry and exit sequences for Dekker's algorithm. The locations A and B are used for synchronization; $A = 0$ means that process P1 is outside its critical section, while any other value means that P1 is inside it; similarly, $B = 0$ means that P2 is outside its critical section, and any other value means that P2 is inside it.

Dekker's algorithm guarantees mutual exclusion, but it does not guarantee freedom from deadlock. In this case, it is possible that both processors end up trying to enter the critical region without success. The code above tries to address this problem by briefly releasing the lock in each retry loop. However, both stores are likely to be combined in a store buffer, so the release has no chance of success. A more realistic implementation would use a probabilistic back-off strategy that increases the released period exponentially while waiting. If any randomization is used, such an algorithm will avoid deadlock with arbitrarily high probability.

J.10 Code Patching

The code patching example illustrates how to modify code that is potentially being executed at the time of modification. Two common uses of code patching are in debuggers and dynamic linking.

Code patching involves a modifying process, *Pm*, and one or more target processes *Pt*. For simplicity, assume that the sequence to be modified is four instructions long: the old sequence is (*Old*1, *Old*2, *Old*3, *Old*4), and the new sequence is (*New*1, *New*2, *New*3,

```
P1Entry( )
        mov         -1,%l0
busy:
        st          %l0,[A]
        membar      #StoreLoad
        ld          [B],%l1
        tst         %l1
        bne,a       busy
        st          %g0,[A]

P1Exit( )
        membar      #StoreStore      !RMO and PSO only
        membar      #LoadStore       !RMO only
        st          %g0,[A]

P2Entry( )
        mov         -1,%l0
busy:
        st          %l0,[B]
        membar      #StoreLoad
        ld          [A],%l1
        tst         %l1
        bne,a       busy
        st          %g0,[B]

P2Exit( )
        membar      #StoreStore      !RMO and PSO only
        membar      #LoadStore       !RMO only
        st          %g0,[B]
```

Example 11—Dekker's Algorithm

*New*4). There are two examples: **noncooperative** modification, in which the changes are made without cooperation from *Pt*; and **cooperative** modification, in which the changes require explicit cooperation from *Pt*.

In noncooperative modification, illustrated in example 12, changes are made in reverse execution order. The three partially modified sequences (*Old*1, *Old*2, *Old*3, *New*4), (*Old*1, *Old*2, *New*3, *New*4), and (*Old*1, *New*2, *New*3, *New*4) must be legal sequences for *Pt*, in that *Pt* must do the right thing if it executes any of them. Additionally, none of the locations to be modified, except the first, may be the target of a branch. The code assumes that %i0 contains the starting address of the area to be patched and %i1, %i2, %i3, and %i4 contain *New*1, *New*2, *New*3, and *New*4.

The constraint that all partially modified sequences must be legal is quite restrictive. When this constraint cannot be satisfied, noncooperative code patching may require the target processor to execute FLUSH instructions. One method of triggering such a non-local FLUSH would be to send an interrupt to the target processor.

In cooperative code patching, illustrated in example 13, changes to instructions can be made in any order. When *Pm* is finished with the changes, it writes into the shared variable *done* to notify *Pt*. *Pt* waits for *done* to change from 0 to some other value as a signal that the changes have been completed. The code assumes that %i0 contains the starting

```
NonCoopPatch(addr, instructions...)
    st        %i4,[%i0+12]
    flush     %i0+12
    membar    #StoreStore              !RMO and PSO only
    st        %i3,[%i0+8]
    flush     %i0+8
    membar    #StoreStore              !RMO and PSO only
    st        %i2,[%i0+4]
    flush     %i0+4
    membar    #StoreStore              !RMO and PSO only
    st        %i1,[%i0]
    flush     %i0
```

Example 12—Nonxooperative Code Patching

address of the area to be patched, %i1, %i2, %i3, and %i4 contain *New*1, *New*2, *New*3, and *New*4, and %g1 contains the address of *done*. The FLUSH instructions in *Pt* ensure that the instruction buffer of *Pt*'s processor is flushed so that the old instructions are not executed.

```
CoopPatch(addr,instructions...)       !%i0 = addr, %i1..%i4 = instructions
    st        %i1,[%i0]
    st        %i2,[%i0+4]
    st        %i3,[%i0+8]
    st        %i4,[%i0+12]
    mov       -1,%10
    membar    #StoreStore              !RMO and PSO only
    st        %10,[%g1]

TargetCode( )
wait:
    ld        [%g1],%10
    cmp       %10,0
    be        wait
    flush     A
    flush     A+4
    flush     A+8
    flush     A+12
A:
    Old1
    Old2
    Old3
    Old4
```

Example 13—Cooperative Code Patching

J.11 Fetch_and_Add

Fetch_and_Add performs the sequence $a = a + b$ atomically with respect to other *Fetch_and_Add*s to location *a*. Two versions of *Fetch_and_Add* are shown. The first (example 14) uses the routine *LockWithLDSTUB* described above. This approach uses a lock to guard the value. Since the memory model dependency is embodied in the lock access routines, the code does not depend on the memory model.[6]

```
/*Fetch and Add using LDSTUB*/
int Fetch_And_Add( Index, Increment, Lock)
    int *Index;
    int Increment;
    int *Lock;
    {
        int old_value;
        LockWithLDSTUB(Lock);
        old_value  = *Index;
        *Index  = old_value + Increment;
        UnlockWithLDSTUB(Lock);
        return(old_value);
    }
```

Example 14—Fetch and Add Using LDSTUB

Fetch_and_Add originally was invented to avoid lock contention and to provide an efficient means to maintain queues and buffers without cumbersome locks. Hence, using a lock is inefficient and contrary to the intentions of the *Fetch_and_Add*. The CAS synthetic instruction allows a more efficient version, as shown in example 15.

```
FetchAndAddCAS(address, increment)  !%i0 = address, %i1 = increment
retry:
    ld      [%i0],%l0
    add     %l0,%i1,%l1
    cas     [%i0],%l0,%l1
    cmp     %l0,%l1
    bne     retry
    mov     %l1,%o0                  !return old value
```

Example 15—Fetch and Add Using CAS

J.12 Barrier Synchronization

Barrier synchronization ensures that each of N processes is blocked until all of them reach a given state. The point in the flow of control at which this state is reached is called the barrier; hence the name. The code uses the variable *Count* initialized to N. As each process reaches its desired state, it decrements *Count* and waits for *Count* to reach zero before proceeding further.

Similar to the fetch and add operation, barrier synchronization is easily implemented using a lock to guard the counter variable, as shown in example 16.

The CAS implementation of barrier synchronization, shown in example 17, avoids the extra lock access.

---

6. Inlining of the lock-access functions with subsequent optimization may break this code.

```
/*Barrier Synchronization using LDSTUB*/
Barrier(Count,Lock)
int *Count;
int *Lock;
{
    LockWithLdstUB(Lock);
    *Count   = *Count - 1;
    UnlockWithLdstUB(Lock);
    while(*Count > 0) { ; /*busy-wait*/ }
}
```

Example 16—Barrier Synchronization Using LDSTUB

```
BarrierCAS(Count)       !%i0 = address of counter variable
retry:
    ld       [%i0],%l0
    add      %l0,-1,%l1
    cas      [%i0],%l0,%l1
    cmp      %l0,%l1
    bne      retry
    nop
wait:
    ld       [%i0],%l0
    tst      %l0
    bne      wait
    nop
```

Example 17—Barrier Synchronization Using CAS

A practical barrier synchronization must be reusable because it is typically used once per iteration in applications that require many iterations. Barriers that are based on counters must have means to reset the counter. One solution to this problem is to alternate between two complementary versions of the barrier: one that counts down to 0 and the other that counts up to N. In this case, passing one barrier also initializes the counter for the next barrier.

Passing a barrier can also signal that the results of one iteration are ready for processing by the next iteration. In this case, RMO and PSO require a MEMBAR #StoreStore instruction prior to the barrier code to ensure that all local results become globally visible prior to passing the barrier.

Barrier synchronization among a large number of processors will lead to access contention on the counter variable, which may degrade performance. This problem can be solved by using multiple counters. The butterfly barrier uses a divide-and-conquer technique to avoid any contention and can be implemented without atomic operations.[7]

---

7. Brooks, E. D., "The Butterfly Barrier," *International Journal of Parallel Programming* 15(4), pp. 295-307, 1986.

J.13 Linked List Insertion and Deletion

Linked lists are dynamic data structures that might be used by a multi-threaded application. As in the previous examples, a lock can be used to guard access to the entire data structure. However, single locks guarding large and frequently shared data structures can be inefficient.

In example 18, the CAS synthetic instruction is used to operate on a linked list without explicit locking. Each list element starts with an address field that contains either the address of the next list element or zero. The head of the list is the address of a variable that holds the address of the first list element. The head is zero for empty lists.

```
ListInsert(Head,Element)   !%i0 = Head addr, %i1 = Element addr
retry:
      ld      [%i0],%l0
      st      %l0, [%i1]
      mov     %i1, %l1
      cas     [%i0],%l0,%l1
      cmp     %l0,%l1
      bne     retry
      nop


ListRemove(Head)            !%i0   = Head addr
retry:
      ld      [%i0],%o0
      tst     %o0
      be      empty
      nop
      ld      [%o0],%l0
      cas     [%i0],%o0,%l0
      cmp     %o0,%l0
      bne     retry

empty:
      nop
```

Example 18—List Insertion and Removal

In the example, there is little difference in performance between the CAS and lock approaches, however, more complex data structures can allow more concurrency. For example, a binary tree allows the concurrent insertion and removal of nodes in different branches.

J.14 Communicating With I/O Devices

I/O accesses may be reordered just as other memory reference are reordered. Because of this, the programmer must take special care to meet the constraint requirements of physical devices, in both the uniprocessor and multiprocessor cases.

Accesses to I/O locations require sequencing MEMBARs under certain circumstances to properly manage the order of accesses arriving at the device, and the order of device accesses with respect to memory accesses. The following rules describe the use of MEM-

BARs in these situations. Maintaining the order of accesses to multiple devices will require higher-level software constructs, which are beyond the scope of this discussion.

(1) Accesses to the same I/O location address:

— A store followed by a store is ordered in all memory models.

— A load followed by a load requires a MEMBAR #LoadLoad in RMO only..

Compatibility Note:
This MEMBAR is not needed in implementations that provide SPARC-V8 compatibility for I/O accesses in RMO.

— A load followed by a store is ordered in all memory models.

— A store followed by a load requires MEMBAR #Lookaside between the accesses for all memory models; however, implementations that provide SPARC-V8 compatiblity for I/O accesses in any of TSO, PSO, and RMO do not need the MEMBAR in any model that provides this compatibility.

(2) Accesses to different I/O location addresses:

— The appropriate ordering MEMBAR is required to guarantee order within a range of addresses assigned to a device.

— Device-specific synchronization of completion, such as reading back from an address after a store, may be required to coordinate accesses to multiple devices. This is beyond the scope of this discussion.

(3) Accesses to an I/O location address and a memory address.

— A MEMBAR #MemIssue is required between an I/O access and a memory access if it is required that the I/O access reaches global visibility before the memory access reaches global visibility. For example, if the memory location is a lock that controls access to an I/O address, then MEMBAR #MemIssue is required between the last access to the I/O location and the store that clears the lock.

(4) Accesses to different I/O location addresses within an implementation-dependent range of addresses are strongly ordered once they reach global visiblity. Beyond the point of global visibility there is no guarantee of global order of accesses arriving at different devices having disjoint implementation-dependent address ranges defining the device. Programmers can rely on this behavior from implementations.

(5) Accesses to I/O locations protected by a lock in shared memory that is subsequently released, with attention to the above barrier rules, are strongly ordered with respect to any subsequent accesses to those locations that respect the lock.

J.14.1 I/O Registers With Side Effects

I/O registers with side effects are commonly used in hardware devices such as UARTs. One register is used to address an internal register of the I/O device, and a second register is used to transfer data to or from the selected internal register.

In examples 19 and 20, let X be the address of a device with two such registers; X.P is a port register, and X.D is a data register. The address of an internal register is stored into X.P; that internal register can then be read or written by loading into or storing from X.D.

```
st       %i1, [X+P]
membar   #StoreStore              ! PSO and RMO only
st       %i2, [X+D]
```

Example 19—I/O Registers With Side-Effects: Store Followed by Store

```
st       %i1, [X+P]
membar   #StoreLoad |#MemIssue    ! RMO only
ld       [X+D], %i2
```

Example 20—I/O Registers With Side-Effects: Store Followed by Load

Access to these registers, of course, must be protected by a mutual-exclusion lock to ensure that multiple threads accessing the registers do not interfere. The sequencing MEMBAR is required to ensure that the store actually completes before the load is issued.

J.14.2   The Control and Status Register (CSR)

A control and status register is an I/O location which is updated by an I/O device independent of access by the processor. For example, such a register might contain the current sector under the head of a disk drive.

In example 21, let Y be the address of a control and status register that is read to obtain status and written to assert control. Bits read differ from the last data that was stored to them.

```
ld       [Y], %i1         ! obtain status
st       %i2, [Y]         ! write a command
membar   #Lookaside       ! make sure we really read the register
ld       [Y], %i3         ! obtain new status
```

Example 21—Accessing a Control/Status Register

Access to these registers, of course, must be protected by a mutual-exclusion lock to ensure that multiple threads accessing the registers do not interfere. The sequencing MEMBAR is needed to ensure the value produced by the load comes from the register and not from the write buffer since the write has side-effects. No MEMBAR is needed between the load and the store, because of the anti-dependency on the memory address.

J.14.3   The Descriptor

In example 22, let A be the address of a descriptor in memory. After initializing the descriptor with information, the address of the descriptor is stored into device register D or made available to some other portion of the program that will make decisions based upon the value(s) in the descriptor. It is important to ensure that the stores of the data have completed before making the address (and hence the data in the descriptor) visible to the device or program component.

```
st       %i1, [A]
st       %i2, [A+4]
...                          ! more stores
membar   #StoreStore         ! PSO and RMO only
st       A, [D]
```

Example 22—Accessing a Memory Descriptor

Access must be protected by a mutual-exclusion lock to ensure that multiple threads accessing the registers do not interfere. In addition, the agent reading the descriptor must use a load-barrier MEMBAR after reading D to ensure that the most recent values are read.

J.14.4 Lock-Controlled Access to a Device Register

Let A be a lock in memory that is used to control access to a device register D. The code that accesses the device might look like that show in example 23.

```
set A, %l1        ! address of lock
set D, %l2        ! address of device register
call lock         ! lock(A);
mov %l1, %o0
ld [%l2], %i1     ! read the register

...               ! do some computation

st %i2, [%l2]     ! write the register
membar #MemIssue  ! all memory models
call unlock       ! unlock(A);
mov %l1, %o0
```

Example 23—Accessing a Device Register

The sequencing MEMBAR is needed to ensure that another CPU which grabs the lock and loads from the device register will actually see any changes in the device induced by the store. The ordering MEMBARs in the lock and unlock code (see J.6, "Spin Locks"), while ensuring correctness when protecting ordinary memory, are insufficient for this purpose when accessing device registers. Compare with J.14.1, "I/O Registers With Side Effects."

K Changes From SPARC-V8 to SPARC-V9

SPARC-V9 is complimentary to the SPARC-V8 architecture; it does not replace it. SPARC-V9 was designed to be a higher-performance peer to SPARC-V8.

Application software for the 32-bit SPARC-V8 (Version 8) microprocessor architecture can execute, unchanged, on SPARC-V9 systems. SPARC-V8 software executes natively on SPARC-V9-conformant processors; no special compatibility mode is required.

Changes to the SPARC-V9 architecture since SPARC-V8 are in six main areas: the trap model, data formats, the registers, alternate address space access, the instruction set, and the memory model.

K.1 Trap Model

The trap model, visible only to privileged software, has changed substantially.

— Instead of one level of traps, four or more levels are now supported. This allows first-level trap handlers, notably register window spill and fill (formerly called overflow and underflow) traps, to execute much faster. This is because such trap handlers can now execute without costly run-time checks for lower-level trap conditions, such as page faults or a misaligned stack pointer. Also, multiple trap levels support more robust fault-tolerance mechanisms.

— Most traps no longer change the CWP. Instead, the trap state (including the CWP register) is saved in register stacks called TSTATE, TT, TPC, and TNPC.

— New instructions (DONE and RETRY) are used to return from a trap handler, instead of RETT.

— A new instruction (RETURN) is provided for returning from a trap handler running in nonprivileged mode, providing support for user trap handlers.

— Terminology about privileged-mode execution has changed, from "supervisor/user" to "privileged/nonprivileged."

— A new processor state, RED_state, has been added to facilitate processing resets and nested traps that would exceed MAXTL.

K.2 Data Formats

Data formats for extended (64-bit) integers have been added.

K.3 Little-Endian Support

Data accesses can be either big-endian or little-endian. Bits in the PSTATE register control the implicit endianness of data accesses. Special ASI values are provided to allow specific data accesses to be in a specific endianness.

K.4 Registers

These privileged SPARC-V8 registers have been deleted:

— PSR: Processor State Register

— TBR: Trap Base Register

— WIM: Window Invalid Mask

These registers have been widened from 32 to 64 bits:

— All integer registers

— All state registers: FSR, PC, nPC, Y

The contents of the following register has changed:

— FSR: Floating-Point State Register: *fcc1*, *fcc2*, and *fcc3* (additional floating-point condition code) bits have been added and the register widened to 64-bits..

These SPARC-V9 registers are fields within a register in SPARC-V8:

— PIL: Processor Interrupt Level register

— CWP: Current Window Pointer register

— TT[MAXTL]: Trap Type register

— TBA: Trap Base Address register

— VER: Version register

— CCR: Condition Codes Register

These registers have been added:

— Sixteen additional double-precision floating-point registers, $f[32]..f[62]$, which are aliased with and overlap eight additional quad-precision floating-point registers, $f[32]..f[60]$

— FPRS: Floating-Point Register State register

— ASI: ASI register

— PSTATE: Processor State register

— TL: Trap Level register

— TPC[MAXTL]: Trap Program Counter register

— TNPC[MAXTL]: Trap Next Program Counter register

— TSTATE[MAXTL]: Trap State register

— TICK: Hardware clock-tick counter

— CANSAVE: Savable windows register

— CANRESTORE: Restorable windows register

— OTHERWIN: Other windows register

— CLEANWIN: Clean windows register

— WSTATE: Window State register

The SPARC-V9 CWP register is incremented during a SAVE instruction and decremented during a RESTORE instruction. Although this is the opposite of PSR.CWP's behavior in SPARC-V8, the only software it should affect is a few trap handlers that operate in privileged mode, and that must be rewritten for SPARC-V9 anyway. This change will have no effect on nonprivileged software.

K.5 Alternate Space Access

In SPARC-V8, access to all alternate address spaces is privileged. In SPARC-V9, loads and stores to ASIs $00_{16}..7f_{16}$ are privileged; those to ASIs $80_{16}..FF_{16}$ are nonprivileged. That is, load- and store-alternate instructions to one-half of the alternate spaces can now be used in user code.

K.6 Little-Endian Byte Order

In SPARC-V8, all instruction and data accesses were performed in big-endian byte order. SPARC-V9 supports both big- and little-endian byte orders for data accesses only; instruction accesses in SPARC-V9 are always performed using big-endian order.

K.7 Instruction Set

All changes to the instruction set were made such that application software written for SPARC-V8 can run unchanged on a SPARC-V9 processor. Application software written for SPARC-V8 should not even be able to detect that its instructions now process 64 bit values.

The definitions of the following instructions were extended or modified to work with the 64-bit model:

— FCMP, FCMPE: Floating-Point Compare—can set any of the four floating-point condition codes

— LDUW, LDUWA(same as "LD, LDA" in SPARC-V8)

— LDFSR, STFSR: Load/Store FSR: only affect low-order 32 bits of FSR

— RDASR/WRASR: Read/Write State Registers: access additional registers

— SAVE/RESTORE

— SETHI

— SRA, SRL, SLL: Shifts: split into 32-bit and 64-bit versions

— Tcc: (was Ticc) operates with either the 32-bit integer condition codes (*icc*), or the 64-bit integer condition codes (*xcc*)

— All other arithmetic operations now operate on 64-bit operands and produce 64-bit results. Application software written for SPARC-V8 cannot detect that arithmetic operations are now 64 bits wide. This is due to retention of the 32-bit integer condition codes (*icc*), addition of 64-bit integer condition codes (*xcc*), and the carry-propagation rules of 2's-complement arithmetic.

The following instructions have been added to provide support for 64-bit operations and/or addressing:

— F[sdq]TOx: Convert floating point to 64-bit word

— FxTO[sdq]: Convert 64-bit word to floating point

— FMOV[dq]: Floating-point Move, double and quad

— FNEG[dq]: Floating-point Negate, double and quad

— FABS[dq]: Floating-point Absolute Value, double and quad

— LDDFA, STDFA, LDFA, STFA: Alternate address space forms of LDDF, STDF, LDF, and STF

— LDSW: Load a signed word

— LDSWA: Load a signed word from an alternate space

— LDX: Load an extended word

— LDXA: Load an extended word from an alternate space

— LDXFSR: Load all 64 bits of the FSR register

— STX: Store an extended word

— STXA: Store an extended word into an alternate space

— STXFSR: Store all 64 bits of the FSR register

The following instructions have been added to support the new trap model:

— DONE: Return from trap and skip instruction that trapped

— RDPR and WRPR: Read and Write privileged registers

— RESTORED: Adjust state of register windows after RESTORE

— RETRY: Return from trap and reexecute instruction that trapped

— RETURN: Return

— SAVED: Adjust state of register windows after SAVE

— SIR: Signal Monitor (generate Software Initiated Reset)

The following instructions have been added to support implementation of higher-performance systems:

— BPcc: Branch on integer condition code with prediction

— BPr: Branch on integer register contents with prediction

— CASA, CASXA: Compare and Swap from an alternate space

— FBPfcc: Branch on floating-point condition code with prediction

— FLUSHW: Flush windows

— FMOVcc: Move floating-point register if condition code is satisfied

— FMOVr: Move floating-point register if integer register contents satisfy condition

— LDQF(A), STQF(A): Load/Store Quad Floating-point (in an alternate space)

— MOVcc: Move integer register if condition code is satisfied

— MOVr: Move integer register if register contents satisfy condition

— MULX: Generic 64-bit multiply

— POPC: Population Count

— PREFETCH, PREFETCHA: Prefetch Data

— SDIVX, UDIVX: Signed and Unsigned 64-bit divide

The definitions of the following instructions have changed:

— IMPDEP*n*: Implementation-Dependent instructions (replace SPARC-V8 CPop instructions)

The following instruction was added to support memory synchronization:

— MEMBAR: Memory barrier

The following instructions have been deleted:

— Coprocessor loads and stores

— RDTBR and WRTBR: TBR no longer exists. It has been replaced by TBA, which can be read/written with RDPR/WRPR instructions.

— RDWIM and WRWIM: WIM no longer exists. WIM has been subsumed by several register-window state registers.

— RDPSR and WRPSR: PSR no longer exists. It has been replaced by several separate registers which are read/written with other instructions.

— RETT: Return from trap (replaced by DONE/RETRY).

— STDFQ: Store Double from Floating-point Queue (replaced by the RDPR FQ instruction).

K.8 Memory Model

SPARC-V9 defines a new memory model called Relaxed Memory Order (RMO). This very weak model allows the CPU hardware to schedule memory accesses such as loads and stores in nearly any order, as long as the program computes the correct answer. Hence, the hardware can instantaneously adjust to resource contentions and schedule accesses in the most efficient order, leading to much faster memory operations and better performance.

Bibliography

General References

For general information, see the following:

-----. *The SPARC Architecture Manual, Version 8*, Prentice-Hall, Inc., 1992.

Boney, Joel [1992]. "SPARC Version 9 Points the Way to the Next Generation RISC," *SunWorld*, October 1992, pp. 100-105.

Catanzaro, Ben, ed. *The SPARC Technical Papers*, Springer-Verlag, 1991.

Cmelik, R. F., S. I. Kong, D. R. Ditzel, and E. J. Kelly, "An Analysis of MIPS and SPARC Instruction Set Utilization on the SPEC Benchmarks," *Proceedings of the Fourth International Symposium on Architectural Support for Programming Languages and Operating Systems*, April 8-11, 1991.

Dewar, R. B. K. and M. Smosna. *Microprocessors: A Programmer's View*, McGraw-Hill, Inc., 1990.

Ditzel, David R. [1993]. "SPARC Version 9: Adding 64-Bit Addressing and Robustness to an Existing RISC Architecture." Videotape available from University Video Communications, P. O. Box 5129, Stanford, CA, 94309.

Garner, R. B. [1988]. "SPARC: The Scalable Processor Architecture," *SunTechnology*, vol. 1, no. 3, Summer, 1988; also appeared in M. Hall and J. Barry (eds.), *The SunTechnology Papers*, Springer-Verlag, 1990, pp. 75-99.

Garner, R. B., A. Agrawal, F. Briggs, E. W. Brown, D. Hough, W. N. Joy, S. Kleiman, S. Muchnick, M. Namjoo, D. Patterson, J. Pendleton, K. G. Tan, and R. Tuck [1988]. "The Scalable Processor Architecture (SPARC)," *33rd Annual IEEE Computer Conference (COMPCON)*, February, 1988, San Francisco, CA.

Hennessy, J. and D. Patterson. *Computer Architecture: A Quantitative Approach*, Morgan Kaufman Publishers, Inc., San Mateo, CA. 1990.

IEEE Standard for Binary Floating-Point Arithmetic, IEEE Std 754-1985, IEEE, New York, NY, 1985.

Katevenis, M. [1983]. Reduced Instruction Set Computer Architectures for VLSI, Ph.D. dissertation, Computer Science Div., Univ. of California, Berkeley, 1983; also published by M.I.T. Press, Cambridge, MA, 1985.

Kleiman, S. and D. Williams [1988]. "SunOS on SPARC," *33rd Annual IEEE Comp. Conf. (COMPCON)*, February, 1988, San Francisco, CA; also appeared in M. Hall and J. Barry (eds.), *The SunTechnology Papers*, Springer-Verlag, 1990, pp. 13-27.

Muchnick, S. [1988]. "Optimizing Compilers for SPARC," *SunTechnology*, Summer 1988, pp. 64-71; also appeared in W. Stallings (ed.), *Reduced Instruction Set Computers* (2nd edition), IEEE Computer Society Press, 1990, pp. 160-173, and in M. Hall and J. Barry (eds.), *The SunTechnology Papers*, Springer-Verlag, 1990, pp. 41-68.

Patterson, D. [1985]. "Reduced Instruction Set Computers," *Communications of the ACM*, vol. 28, no. 1, January, 1985.

Patterson, D., and D. R. Ditzel, "The Case for the Reduced Instruction Set Computer," *Computer Architecture News*, vol 8, no. 7, 1980.

Memory Model References

The concept of a memory model has become a significant one as shared memory multiprocessors are more widely used. The issues are complex and interesting, and have created an active and extensive literature. A partial annotated list of references is as follows:

Collier, W. W. *Reasoning About Parallel Architectures*, Prentice Hall, 1992.

> Provides a mathematical framework for the study of parallel processors and their interaction with memory.

Dill, David, Seungjoon Park, and Andreas G. Nowatzyk, "Formal Specification of Abstract Memory Models" in *Research on Integrated Systems: Proceedings of the 1993 Symposium*, Ed. Gaetano Borriello and Carl Ebeling, MIT Press, 1993.

> Describes an application of software tools to the verification of the TSO and PSO memory models.

Gharachorloo, K., D. Lenoski, J. Laudon, P. Gibbon, A. Gupta, and J. Hennessy. "Memory Consistency and Event Ordering in Scalable Shared-Memory Multiprocessors," *Proceedings of the 17th Annual International Symposium on Computer Architecture*, May 1990, pp. 15-29.

> Provides an overview of contemporary research in memory models.

Gharachorloo, K., S. Adve, A. Gupta, J. Hennessy, and M. Hill. "Programming for Different Memory Consistency Models," *Journal of Parallel and Distributed Processing*, 15:4, August 1992.

> This paper proposes a new programming model which allows programmers to reason about programs that have not been reduced to sequential consistency.

Gharachorloo, K., A. Gupta, and J. Hennessy, "Performance Evaluation of Memory Consistency Models for Shared Memory Multiprocessors," *Proceedings of the 4th International Conference on Architectural Support for Programming Languages and Operating Systems*, pp. 245-257, ACM, New York, 1991.

This paper discusses the performance benefits that can be obtained when a relaxed memory model is used in a shared-memory model processor.

Lamport, Leslie. "How to Make a Multiprocessor Computer That Correctly Executes Multiprocess Programs," *IEEE Transactions on Computers*, C-28, 9, September 1979, pp. 690-691.

Defines sequential consistency and shows how it can be used in simple shared-memory systems.

Reynal, M. *Algorithms for Mutual Exclusion*, MIT Press, 1986.

Provides an overview of the mutual exclusion problem and the extensive literature associated with it.

Scheurich, C., and M. Dubois. "Dependency and Hazard Resolution in Multiprocessors," *Proceedings of the 14th International Symposium on Computer Architecture*, pp. 234-243, IEEE CS Press, Los Alamitos, CA, 1987.

Sindhu, Predeep, Jean-Marc Frailong, and Michel Ceklov. "Formal Specification of Memory Models," Xerox Palo Alto Research Center Report CSL-91-11, December 1991.

Introduces the formal framework used to define the SPARC-V8 TSO and PSO memory models.

Treiber, R. Kent. "Systems Programming: Coping with Parallelism," IBM Research Report RJ5118 (53162), 1986.

Provides an overview of the operational issues for systems programming in a multiprocessing environment.

Prefetching

Callahan, D., K. Kennedy, A. Porterfield. "Software Prefetching," *Proceedings of the Fourth International Conference on Architectural Support for Programming Languages and Operating Systems*, April 1991, pp. 40-52.

Mowry, T., M. Lam, and A. Gupta. "Design and Evaluation of a Compiler Algorithm for Prefetching." *Proceedings of the Fifth International Conference on Architectural Support for Programming Languages and Operating Systems*, October 1992, pp. 62-73.

Index

A

a field of instructions, **64**, 136, 139, 142, 145, 146, 150

ABI, see *SPARC-V9 Application Binary Interface (ABI)*

accrued exception (*aexc*) field of FSR register, 46, **48**, 98, 243, 250

activation record, see *stack frame*

ADD instruction, **135**, 290

ADDC instruction, **135**

ADDcc instruction, **135**, 219, 290

ADDCcc instruction, **135**

address, **118**

    aliased, 118

    physical, 118, 275

    virtual, 118, 275

address, **287**

address aliases, 275

address mask (AM) field of PSTATE register, **53**, 149, 170, 212

address space, 4, **275**, 276

address space identifier (ASI), **9**, 16, 17, 50, 61, 65, 67, 71, **118**, 119, 172, 176, 204, 224, 250, 277, 307, 331

    architecturally specified, **120**

    restricted, 71, 120, 250

    unrestricted, 71, **120**, 250

address space identifier (ASI) register, 16, 21, **50**, 56, 71, 87, 120, 155, 173, 178, 180, 204, 224, 229, 232, 242, 306

addressing conventions, 17, 68

addressing modes, 4

ADDX instruction (SPARC-V8), 135

ADDXcc instruction (SPARC-V8), 135

aexc, see *accrued exception (aexc) field of FSR register*

AG, see *alternate globals enable (AG) field of PSTATE register*

aggregate data values, see *data aggregates*

alias

    address, 118

    floating-point registers, 36

alignment, 294

    data (load/store), 17, **67**, 119

    doubleword, 17, **67**, 119

    extended-word, **67**

    halfword, 17, **67**, 119

    instructions, 17, **67**, 119

    integer registers, 176, 178

    memory, 119

    quadword, 17, **67**, 119

    stack pointer, **294**

word, 17, **67**, 119

alternate address space, 204

alternate global registers, 15, 30, **30**, 306

alternate globals enable (AG) field of PSTATE register, 30, 31, **54**

alternate space instructions, 18, 50, 331

AM, see *address mask (AM) field of PSTATE register*

ancillary state registers (ASRs), 18, 35, 36, **59**, 211, 212, 241, 242, 248, 249, 284, 311

AND instruction, **181**

ANDcc instruction, **181**, 290

ANDN instruction, **181**, 290

ANDNcc instruction, **181**

annul bit, 35, 136

    in conditional branches, 139

annulled branches, 136

application program, **9**, **14**, 16, 30, 46, 47, 50, 60, 102, 331

architectural extensions, 7, 311

arguments to a subroutine, 292

arithmetic overflow, 41

ASI register, see *address space identifier (ASI) register*

ASI, see *address space identifier (ASI)*

ASI_AS_IF_USER_PRIMARY, **72**, 121, 250, 281, 306

ASI_AS_IF_USER_PRIMARY_LITTLE, **72**, 121, 250, 281, 306

ASI_AS_IF_USER_SECONDARY, **72**, 121, 250, 281

ASI_AS_IF_USER_SECONDARY_LITTLE, **72**, 121, 250, 281

ASI_NUCLEUS, 72, **72**, 120, 250, 281

ASI_NUCLEUS_LITTLE, **72**, 120, 250, 281

ASI_PRIMARY, 71, 72, **72**, 120, 121, 250, 280, 281

ASI_PRIMARY_LITTLE, 52, **72**, 120, 250, 281

ASI_PRIMARY_NOFAULT, 72, **72**, 121, 250, 278, 281

ASI_PRIMARY_NOFAULT_LITTLE, **72**, 250

ASI_SECONDARY, 72, **72**, 121, 250, 281, 307

ASI_SECONDARY_LITTLE, **72**, 250, 281, 307

ASI_SECONDARY_NOFAULT, 72, **72**, 121, 250, 278, 281

ASI_SECONDARY_NOFAULT_LITTLE, **72**, 250, 281

asr_reg, **284**

assembler

    synthetic instructions, 288–289

assigned value

    implementation-dependent, **248**

E

F

G

N

O

T

SPARC ARCHITECTURE COMMITTEE
READER RESPONSE CARD

What part of the V9 SPARC Architecture Manual did you find most useful?

_____

Were there any sections that were confusing or that needed clarification?

_____

What would you like to see in future versions of the SPARC architecture?

_____

Do you have any other comments (e.g., technical errors, typos, etc.)?

_____

❏ *Please notify me when support materials for the SPARC V9 architecture are available. Such materials may include software and/or hardware development tools, verification tools, sample implementations, application notes, white papers, etc.*

Name, Title: _____

Company: _____

Address: _____

City/State/Zip (Country): _____

Phone: _____ Fax: _____

SPARC INTERNATIONAL
REQUEST FOR INFORMATION

Please send me information on the following:

_____ Other SPARC International Publications _____ SPARC Trademark Licensing

_____ SPARC International Membership _____ Other SPARC International Programs

Send to:

Name, Title: _____

Company: _____

Address: _____

City/State/Zip (Country): _____

Phone: _____ Fax: _____

My company is a(n):

_____ System Supplier _____ Independent Software Vendor   Other (_____)

Product(s) _____

SPARC International
535 Middlefield Road, Suite 210
Menlo Park, CA 94025

Attn: SPARC Architecture Committee

SPARC International
535 Middlefield Road, Suite 210
Menlo Park, CA 94025

Attn: Marketing/Fulfillment